THE CHAIN OF QUALITY

THE CHAIN
OF QUALITY

Market Dominance
Through Product Superiority

J. M. GROOCOCK

JOHN WILEY & SONS

New York   Chichester   Brisbane   Toronto   Singapore

Library of Congress Cataloging-in-Publication Data:

Groocock, J. M.
    The chain of quality.

    Bibliography: p.
    Includes index.
    1. Quality of products.   I. Title.

HF5415.157.G76   1986   658.5'62   85-32291
ISBN 0-471-82847-5

Printed in the United States of America

10 9 8 7 6 5 4 3 2 1

PREFACE

This book gives managers and engineers an account of modern quality improvement. It should also be useful to MBA and engineering students. The book attempts to describe key concepts logically and clearly. It then addresses the problems of practical implementation in real business situations. Several case studies are presented and analyzed. Some subjects, such as quality costs, which are not covered adequately in existing books, are dealt with here in detail. For other subjects, such as metrology, statistical process control and reliability, on which there is already much written, only brief, nonmathematical descriptions of the concepts are given.

Most books on business management are written by consultants or academics. Practicing managers have very little time for writing, and published books are of virtually no career advantage to them. For these reasons relatively few books on management are written by managers. This is a pity, not only because first-hand experience is obviously an advantage in really understanding a subject, but also, as I discovered when I was a research chemist, actually working on a subject gives one the interest and incentive to think long and deeply about its theoretical principles.

A book written by a manager is necessarily personal. The manager is much less well placed than either an academic or a consultant to carry out a comprehensive survey of the work of others though, hopefully, he or she will be familiar with the most important work. The manager must mainly describe direct experiences and perceptions. My own work in quality management spans 25 years, first as the line quality manager of an operating division and then as the senior staff quality professional of three major companies, based in the United Kingdom, continental Europe, and the United States respectively.

The book starts with a summary of the evidence for the importance of product quality to business success, and it is shown that only market share is of equal importance. This section leads into a discussion of quality improvement. Only by a continual high rate of improvement can a business achieve and maintain the superiority in the quality of its products compared to competing products that is a requirement for success. For product quality, good is not enough. Quality improvement must be addressed energetically so that the product quality becomes even better. The major benefits come only to those businesses whose products are best in quality compared with competing products—and the managers of such businesses must still strive for quality improvement to maintain that superiority. The book then discusses four necessary conditions that a business must satisfy in order to achieve a high rate of quality improvement: it must have a top-management *policy* requiring quality improvement; it must have a business philosophy emphasizing *honesty*; it must elevate the *priority* accorded to quality improvement; and it must have *capability* in many areas.

The following chapters deal with the meaning of product quality and how quality improvement is measured in terms of quality to the customer and quality costs. The quality definition derived in the book suggests the concept of "the chain of conformance," which indicates that product quality is the result of a series of marketing, design-development, purchasing, and manufacturing processes that link a customer's need to the product purchased to satisfy that need. This concept which is expressed in the title, The Chain of Quality, defines the structure of the book. The next part of the book deals in turn with the marketing, design-development, purchasing, and manufacturing aspects of quality improvement. The multifunctional nature of quality improvement is emphasized throughout, and in the succeeding chapters, the methods of achieving cooperation between these functions are described explicitly—and the important contribution to quality improvement of people-oriented programs, such as quality circles, is also described.

All three of the companies I have worked for are very large, but they are also decentralized, and their operating divisions are in many ways similar to small or medium-sized companies. Most of the book is therefore relevant to managers of such companies. However, one chapter is devoted to the role of staffs in large companies, and particularly to the activities of a staff which is responsible for providing functional leadership for quality to the company's operating divisions. Another chapter discusses the purposes and methods of system quality audit. It includes a description of an audit procedure which readers can use to assess the status of their own organization's application of the quality systems outlined in the rest of the book.

I have limited the scope of the book to product quality. My reasons for this are that I have had much more experience with products than services, and that application of the methods of quality improvement are more advanced for the former than the latter. Work on quality improvement of products may be considered to have started more than 50 years ago with the ideas of Shewhart, whereas service quality improvement is a new field. As a consequence, one of the ways in which service quality improvement may advance is by seeking analogues to the methods which have worked for products, and for this reason the book should be useful to managers in service industry. The extension of quality improvement into services and areas of a business remote from the product is explicitly discussed in the last chapter.

Quality improvement is a subject of enormous importance to all business managers, but it is not one that it is easy to make interesting. I have tried my best throughout and have used personal experiences whenever relevant. Another device used is an attempt at a lighter touch. "Quality complaints" and "The Toledo Syndrome" are examples of this.

Cleveland, Ohio   JOHN M. GROOCOCK
April 1986

ACKNOWLEDGMENTS

My views on quality have been shaped during my years with the companies, STC, ITT, and TRW, and I give grateful acknowledgment to my colleagues in these three companies. Specific acknowledgment is given to the members of TRW's Quality Steering Committee, Jack Christman, Tom George, Jack Isken, Dick Jones, Mike Ryan, Heine Shaw, and particularly to TRW's Director Quality, Tom Hughes. Many of the ideas in the book were first discussed with them. Four people, Ray Wachniak of Firestone Tire and Rubber Company, Ernie Karlin of Karlin Associates, and Professors Atkin of Carnegie Mellon and Hancock of the University of Michigan, read the first 12 chapters in draft and made many helpful comments and suggestions. My particular thanks go to my secretary Ann Landfield who typed the manuscript and bore my continual changes with unfailing patience. Finally, my thanks are expressed to the management of TRW and particularly to John S. Foster, Jr., Vice President Science and Technology, for support of this project.

J. M. G.

CONTENTS

THE CHAIN OF QUALITY

CHAPTER 1

THE STRATEGIC IMPORTANCE OF PRODUCT QUALITY

In 1980 NBC transmitted a two-hour, prime-time television program for its *News White Paper* series entitled, "If Japan Can ... Why Can't We?" The program compared Japanese and American business practices and described the current successes of the former and the failures of the latter. Although the principal emphasis was on productivity, a major aspect of the program was quality. The superior quality of many Japanese products was contrasted with the static or even declining quality of competing U.S. products. Dr. W. Edwards Deming, one of the United States' leading consultants in quality control, described how he had introduced the concepts of statistical quality control to the Japanese in visits made in the early 1950s, and how they had energetically adopted these methods throughout a major part of their industry—while American management, although familiar with the methods in principle, had largely ignored them in practice.

The NBC program epitomized a change in the communication media's attitude to product quality. Heretofore, they had viewed it as a worthy subject, but too dull to merit serious attention. Now, by presenting product quality as the focus of a conflict between the United States and Japan, they had found a way of making it exciting to Americans, both management and the general public. Earlier examples of this change could be found in *Business Week's* issue of March 12, 1979, in which a whole series of articles had been devoted to quality under the title, "American manufacturers strive for quality—Japanese style," and the unprecedented success of a book on quality—P. B. Crosby's *Quality is Free,* published early in 1979 (1).

THE JAPANESE EXPERIENCE

Briefly summarized, the Japanese quality success had been characterized by their supremacy in a number of world markets. It is, of course, in export markets that a company or a nation proves its commercial superiority. Success at home may, at least partly, be the result of special advantages. However, to take on the rest of the world in their own home markets and achieve dominance gives a convincing demonstration of superiority. The Japanese had performed this feat for a variety of products. They had wrested leadership of the watch and camera markets from the Swiss and West Germans. They had established a primary position for consumer television and audio products in the United States, and only artificial restrictions had prevented a similar takeover of Western Europe.

Many opinions have been expressed about the reasons for the Japanese success, and it is likely that there were several contributing factors. However, there seems little doubt that the quality of their products was a key element. Those of us old enough to remember the 1930s know that at that time Japanese products had a well-deserved reputation for poor quality. I myself remember shoddy-looking Japanese clockwork toys. Their crude design and inferior workmanship were echoed by their poor reliability. Such examples that worked initially rarely continued to do so for more than a few minutes or, at most, an hour or so. These products sold only because they were very cheap. The Japanese success in the 1960s and 1970s could not have been achieved with the quality standard of 1930s. Quality improvement then was clearly a vital (if not sufficient) condition for it.

Equally clear, by the 1960s and 1970s the Japanese had achieved extraordinary quality improvement. Their products were superior, had pleasing visual designs, and good workmanship. They had prices that addressed some major segment of a chosen market—neither the cheap nor the small, luxury end—and at these prices the products had high quality in measurable ways. For prices of about $100, the Japanese quartz watches had an accuracy and stability that before had been realized only by very expensive, certified Swiss chronometers. Their cameras, at prices in the same mid-range, had lens quality that equalled West German luxury products—and added new, reliable, electronic controls. Compared with American and European competitors, the Japanese color televisions were an order of magnitude better in both initial "dead-on-arrival" failure proportion and long-term reliability. The achieved reliability (a mean time between failures of about 10 years) was such that the repair and maintenance of a television set was no longer a factor of concern to customers. When an owner finally discarded a set in 10 or 15 years because of its obsolete design and the effect of wear and tear on its appearance, there was a good chance that it would still be functioning satisfactorily and would never have needed repair.

Although some of the products discussed were commercially important, they were relatively insignificant compared with the passenger car, and it was the ever-increasing success of the Japanese in the car market, that finally triggered the media interest in the Japanese quality challenge to American industry. Table 1.1 shows the total sales of passenger cars in the United States over a 10 year period, and the proportion of those sales that were of U.S. and Canadian manufacture, and imported from West Germany, Japan, and other countries.

Over a period from 1974 to 1980 the proportion of the U.S. passenger car market captured by the Japanese rose from 6.7 percent to over 20 percent, and was prevented from rising still further by the "voluntary" agreement of the Japanese manufacturers to restrict their sales artificially. The problem caused to the U.S. car manufacturers by this growth of Japanese sales was aggravated because its effect reached a maximum during 1980 to 1983 when the total market was depressed.

As for consumer electronics, watches and cameras, no doubt many things contributed to the passenger-car success of the Japanese. However, again one key factor was product quality. In an important segment of the

TABLE 1.1   U.S. Passenger Car Sales by Country of Manufacture

Year	Total Sales 000s	%	Country of Manufacture % U.S./Canada	West Germany	Japan	Other
1974	8,857	100	84.1	6.7	6.7	2.4
1975	8,633	100	81.7	5.7	9.5	3.1
1976	10,106	100	85.2	3.5	9.3	2.0
1977	11,179	100	81.4	4.1	12.4	2.0
1978	11,310	100	82.2	3.9	12.0	1.8
1979	10,660	100	78.1	3.3	16.6	2.0
1980	8,979	100	73.3	3.4	21.2	2.1
1981	8,533	100	72.7	2.9	21.8	2.6
1982	7,980	100	72.1	3.1	22.6	1.1
1983	9,181	100	74.0	3.0	20.9	2.1

market—small cars of good performance and fuel economy—the Japanese became clear quality leaders. The Consumers Union, an independent nonprofit organization (one of whose main purposes is "to provide consumers with information and counsel on consumer goods and services,") has regularly reported the results of its tests on passenger cars in its publication, *Consumer Reports*. It has invariably found that in particular sizes and price ranges, Japanese cars have been best in quality for the characteristics of number of defects at the time of sale, and reliability and cost of maintenance in long-term use. As recently as March 1984, *Consumer Reports* stated, "no domestic subcompact approaches the high quality and reliability of Japanese competition. . . . But that's not to say that all small cars made in America are poor cars." In January 1984, writing about compact cars, *Consumer Reports* (2) stated, "Even the staunchest advocates of the American automobile industry admit that the Japanese lead the way in product reliability. The respondents to our questionnaire—who reported on some 300,000 cars—bear that out with specific information on the cars they own." In addition, the Japanese have started to achieve superiority in engineering quality by providing design features in their moderately priced (but not cheap) cars, that previously were available only in high-priced imports from Europe.

For the series of products previously discussed the Japanese have become the commercial leaders of the world, proving their preeminence through export success. There seems no doubt that the inferior quality of the 1930s would have completely prevented this success, however, it had been offset by other advantages. In contradistinction, in the 1970s every one of these Japanese products had a clearly measurable quality advantage over the competing products, and it seems reasonable to conclude that this advantage was a direct and important contribution to their business success.

THE PIMS RESULTS

Although the Japanese experience gives the most dramatic illustration of the strategic importance of quality, the evidence is circumstantial. For particular products, the Japanese have had superior quality and have achieved business success. The cause and effect relationship is persuasive but not proved, and there is no quantitative assessment of how much of the success was due to quality and how much to other factors. A different source of data—the PIMS results—is not open to these objections.

The Strategic Planning Institute of Cambridge, Massachusetts (3) is a combination of a research institute and a management consulting firm. Its research is devoted to the study of the causes of business success and failure. It is best known for its PIMS analysis concerned with the Profit Impact of Market Strategy. The Institute has some 200 major companies who supply it with data. These companies comprise more than 2000 "businesses," which the Institute defines as, "operating components with a distinct set of products, customers and competitors." Most of these businesses are concerned with industrial products, capital equipment and components, and a small proportion with raw materials and services. Data comes to the Institute about each business rather than about total companies. The Institute's consulting staff use its models and unique data bases to prepare general analyses, and special studies of individual businesses. The results are supplied to member companies thereby helping them to make better business decisions.

The PIMS approach is relative. It compares one business with other businesses. Success or failure is judged in comparison with a relevant group of peer businesses, rather than against some absolute standard. Frequently, PIMS uses Return on Investment (ROI) as a measure of success; at other times it uses Return on Sales (ROS). PIMS then examines the effect of a wide range of business parameters on ROI and ROS. Two such parameters are productivity and relative quality.

SPI used to measure relative quality by asking each respondent to judge, for its business, what proportion of its sales are from products of a quality respectively superior to, about the same as, or inferior to the quality of the products with which they compete. A rough measure of quality was then calculated by subtracting the percentage judged inferior from the percentage judged superior. This gave a relative quality score which could be related to ROI, ROS, relative price, and change in market share. With this method, if 100 percent of the sales of a business are for products rated superior, a rating of +100 percent results. One hundred percent rated inferior gives a −100 percent rating, and 50 percent each of inferior and superior gives a zero percent rating. If all of the sales are for products rated "about the same" in quality, again a zero percent rating results (0 percent superior minus 0 percent inferior).

However, this measure of quality did not work very well for single-product businesses, and it did not indicate how to improve relative quality. In the early 1980s, SPI began to use a new measure of quality. Respondents now identify all of the key product and service attributes (except price), and weigh these for their importance to customers. They rate themselves and leading competitors on a scale from 1 to 10 for each attribute. A high quality score results from high ratings on attributes with high weightings. Use is made of whatever market researches, product comparisons, and competitor literature studies are available. SPI consultants may help, and add objectivity to the evaluations.

Figure 1.1 shows the effect of relative quality on return on investment and return on sales. It shows that businesses with superior quality (in the top quintile of the PIMS data base) get on average an ROI of 32 percent and an ROS of 13 percent. Businesses in the inferior quality quintile have on average an ROI of 12 percent and an ROS of 5 percent. Throughout the whole range of relative quality, Figure 1.1 shows a strong positive correlation between relative quality and business success. This is not a minor effect—ROI is increased by a factor of 2.7 times and ROS by 2.4 times. This one graph, based on the actual results—not the predictions or plans—of some 2700 businesses, is possibly the most powerful existing evidence for the strategic importance of quality. It expresses, factually and quantitatively, the same concept that was derived circumstantially from the Japanese experience—the concept that superior quality is a key parameter for business success and that inferior quality is associated with poor business performance.

The PIMS results for quality are so impressive that it is in some ways surprising that they have had so little effect on American management. For example, a similarly important conclusion derived from PIMS-type research—that market share is of paramount importance to a business—is accepted much more widely and has had a much greater effect on busi-

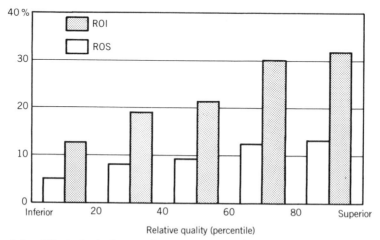

Figure 1.1. Effect of relative quality on return on investment and return on sale (Source: PIMs data base).

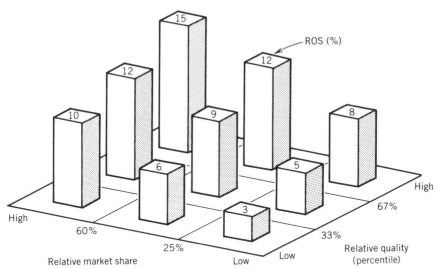

Figure 1.2. Effect of relative quality and relative market share on return on sales.

ness operations. The PIMS data base allows comparison of both of those key parameters simultaneously and Figure 1.2 shows the result: that relative quality has about the same weight as market share in determining profitability.

Some of the reasons for the lack of response to the PIMS quality results will be discussed later in the book, but one or two can be addressed now. The first is that there may be skepticism about the correctness of the results, and there *are* serious objections to the PIMS methodology. The most important is that the results come largely from assessments of businesses' quality status made by their own managers. Some of the latter may support their subjective judgments by objective data (e.g., from market research) but many do not. There is some evidence that such self-assessments tend to be overly optimistic. An earlier version of Figure 1.1 published by PIMS recorded an essentially similar result, but was arranged so that the data from the same number of businesses was given in each of the five columns—342 businesses in each column, 1712 businesses in all. This version showed that only about 342 businesses had a negative relative quality and about 1370 had positive values. If all of the businesses in a given population had been assessed, this result could not be correct. There would have had to be as many inferior as superior. However, most of the competitors of the businesses participating in PIMS might not themselves be PIMS participants, and if the PIMS businesses had on average a much better quality performance than nonPIMS businesses the result could be explained. Most likely, both effects are present: the self-assessments are too optimistic, and the performance of the PIMS participants, on average, is better than their nonparticipating competitors. Another objection to the PIMS methodology was that the early measure did not give a precise definition of quality and the methods to be used to measure it, so it was likely that their respondents were inconsistent in this regard. A general objection to the PIMS results, like all cross-sectional results, is that they show correlations between parameters, but a cause-and-effect relationship can only be inferred.

For these and other reasons it could be that the quantitative values given in the graphs of ROI and ROS against relative quality (Figure 1.1) may have serious errors. However, it strains credibility to assert that the overall qualitative conclusion is incorrect.

Again, the PIMS data base allows the effect of more than one business parameter to be assessed. Another such pair of parameters is relative quality and productivity, defined as added value per employee. PIMS took the results from 1712 businesses, ranked them for relative quality and productivity, and divided them into nine groups of roughly equal numbers. The group with both the best quality and the best productivity—comprised of businesses in the top third of the PIMS data base on each measure—had an average ROI of 23 percent. The group with the worst quality and productivity—in the bottom third on each measure—had an average ROI of zero, many of the businesses of this group making a loss.

PIMS draws other quality-related conclusions. One conclusion is that the only parameter that ameliorates the adverse effect of bad quality is keeping the manufacturing plant loaded. For businesses with bad quality, popular strategies such as spending more than competitors on marketing or research and development (R&D), or having a higher-than-average rate of new product introduction have an adverse effect on ROI. Another important result is that there is no correlation between relative quality and direct costs. However, there *is* a relationship between relative quality and price to customers. For the businesses of Figure 1.1, the group with the highest relative quality had a relative price that averaged about 8 percent more than that of the group with the lowest relative quality. Finally, PIMS found that low or falling relative quality markedly increased the probability of a business losing market share.

Overall, PIMS concluded that "quality comes close to being a panacea." Of all the many business parameters evaluated by PIMS, superior relative quality was the only one that always correlated with superior ROI and ROS. The result applied to both consumer and industrial products, in periods of low and high inflation, in declining and growing markets, and in North America and Europe.

Despite the PIMS results, the strategic importance of quality to businesses has received virtually no recognition or analysis from academic-based writers on business management. Recently while browsing around my local book shop I examined the indices and scanned the pages of five books written by representatives of leading business schools—*Renewing American Industry, Strategy in Action, Competitive Strategy, The Change Masters,* and *Managing for Excellence.* None contained any significant analysis of quality.

However, two books did discuss quality. The first, *High Output Management,* was written by A. S. Grove (4), the President of Intel, a leading maker of semiconductor devices, and the other was *In Search of Excellence* (5), the best selling account of how a group of superior companies actually conduct their businesses. Grove's book devoted several pages to a description of normal quality assurance activities, and mentioned quality a number of other times. *In Search of Excellence* identified eight attributes that characterize excellent, innovative companies. The second of these attributes is titled, "Close to the customer," and companies which have this attribute, "provide unparalleled quality, service and reliability—things that work and last," to their customers. The book also includes a ten page section entitled, "Quality Obsession," and frequently refers in other pages to the emphasis on product quality which characterizes these selected, excellent companies.

My small sample of books seems to indicate that the actual managers of superior companies recognize the strategic importance of product and service quality to their businesses, and devote much effort to addressing it, but they have not subjected the topic to any serious analysis. The academic-based writers and consultants do not yet seem to understand the subject and therefore have not addressed it so far.

MAJOR INDUSTRIAL PURCHASERS

Another factor that has further increased the strategic importance of quality to many businesses is the unprecedented emphasis that major industrial companies are giving to the quality of the things that they buy. Such companies, known in business jargon as original equipment manufacturers (OEMs), typically spend 30 to 40 percent of their sales value on purchased items for incorporation in their own products. Many of them have a purchased value that equals or exceeds the value they add by their own manufacturing. When OEMs are emphasizing quality, this has a profound effect on the strategic importance of quality to their suppliers.

Because of its vast purchasing power, the automobile industry is particularly important, and in the past few years the automobile OEMs have certainly been emphasizing to their suppliers the importance of quality. In 1982, Ford introduced a "Preferred Supplier Award" (6) and announced it with major presentations to the chief executives of its suppliers. They let it be known that they accepted one of the tenets of Dr. Edwards Deming whom they had hired as a consultant—that an OEM could deal effectively with only a limited number of suppliers—and that in North America it was their intention over a period of years to reduce the number of their suppliers from over 3000 to about 1500.

In the selection of the 1500 surviving suppliers product quality would be a major factor. All of the surviving suppliers might expect to be recipients of the Ford Preferred Supplier Award. Qualification for the latter would result from an assessment of several quality-related aspects of a supplier's business made by three of Ford's functional departments—purchasing, quality, and engineering—and, in addition, recipients of the award would have had to have implemented statistical process control in their manufacturing of the products offered for sale to Ford.

Both General Motors and Chrysler have given similar emphasis to their suppliers on product quality. F. James McDonald, President of GM, wrote in September 1982, "At GM, we have made it clear that quality is our number one operating priority—not just a top goal, but the top goal. The quest for better quality has assumed a fervor beyond anything I've seen in my 40 years at GM . . ." (7). McDonald wrote also of the power of statistical process control and stated that "the quality way is the low-cost way," a point that will be discussed in Chapter 3.

The Department of Defense (DoD), which is probably the largest single buyer of products in the United States, or indeed the world, has given close attention to product quality since World War II. Many of the best known quality assurance techniques were developed and formalized by the DoD and its contractors. Nonetheless, the results of the DoD's quality programs have not been fully satisfactory, and examples of hardware and system failure continue to receive publicity in the media. In the 1980s the DoD has been making increasing attempts to achieve quality improvement. "The Carlucci Initiative" was one such approach. On April 30, 1981 Frank C. Carlucci, then Deputy Secretary of Defense, issued a decision memorandum to the Secretaries of the Military Departments, the Chairman of the Joint Chiefs of Staff, the Under-Secretary of Defense, and so on, entitled "Improving the Acquisition Process." Many of the 34 *recommendations* (which became directives with Carlucci's signature) were specifically intended to improve various aspects of quality. In another initiative the Secretary of Defense himself issued on January 19, 1984 a directive concerned with quality in the "Transition from Development to Production." It stated that "Too often in the past, when faced with funding and schedule constraints, we have compromised the technical integrity of our programs by deleting or deferring vital program elements that contribute to system performance, producibility, and supportability." In other words, because of cost and schedule constraints quality had been sacrificed. Many of the actions required by the memo had the objective of redressing that balance.

With similar quality-related objectives, the DoD has sponsored in 1982, 1983, and 1984, high-level "Bottom Line Conferences," inviting the participation of top executives from its contractors. The importance that the DoD gives to this activity is indicated by the high level of the speakers. Table 1.2 lists those at the 1984 conference, and it is not surprising that the attendees at that meeting included a dozen chief executive officers, and hundreds of presidents, executive vice presidents, division presidents, and vice presidents.

With its "Bottom Line Academia Conferences" the DoD has also at-

TABLE 1.2.   Department of Defense's "Bottom Line III Conference"

"Quality—The Ultimate Achievement"

Honorable Clarence J. Brown, Deputy Secretary of Commerce
Honorable Richard D. DeLauer, Under Secretary of Defense (Research & Engineering)
Honorable Barry M. Goldwater, United States Senator
General John W. Vessey, Jr., USA, Chairman, Joint Chiefs of Staff
General J. A. Wickham, Jr., USA, Chief of Staff, United States Army
General P. X. Kelley, USMC, Commandant, United States Marine Corps
General Lawrence A. Skantze, USAF, Vice Chief of Staff, United States Air Force
Admiral Steven A. White, USN, Chief of Naval Material, United States Navy
Vice Admiral E. A. Grinstead, SC, USN, Director, Defense Logistics Agency
Lt. Gen. James A. Abrahamson, USAF, Director, Strategic Defense Initiatives, Office of
    the Secretary of Defense
David Lewis, Chairman of the Board and Chief Executive Officer, General Dynamics
    Corporation
Thomas Pownall, Chairman of the Board and Chief Executive Officer, Martin Marietta
    Corporation
Gerald G. Probst, Chairman of the Board and Chief Executive Officer, Sperry Corpora-
    tion
Donald B. Rassier, Chief Executive Officer, Fairchild Industries Inc.
Warde F. Wheaton, Executive Vice President, Honeywell Aerospace & Defense, Hon-
    eywell Inc.
Howard K. Smith, Commentator, Journalist and Author
Dr. Joseph Juran, Chairman, Juran Institute, Inc.
Dr. John W. Rosenblum, Dean of the Colgate Darden Graduate School of Business Ad-
    ministration, University of Virginia

tempted to stimulate an interest in quality improvement at the universities and business schools.

At one of its 1983 conferences the DoD announced a new "Defense Quality Excellence Award Program," which was "designed to recognize contractors who consistently produce high-quality material for the military services and to motivate other contractors to do so." The program is voluntary and contractors interested in being evaluated for the award have to make the first approach.

These few examples indicate the powerful influence that major purchasers such as the OEMs and the DoD can exert on the vast range of manufacturers who are their suppliers—and how they can therefore build up the strategic importance of quality.

That excellent companies are already responding to the strategic importance of quality is illustrated by the following quotation from *In Search of Excellence*:

> The excellent companies were, above all, brilliant on the basics. Tools didn't substitute for thinking. Intellect didn't overpower wisdom. Analysis didn't impede action. Rather, these companies worked hard to keep things simple in a complex world. They persisted. They insisted on top quality. They fawned on their customers. They listened to their employees and treated them like adults. They allowed their innovative product and service "champions" long tethers. They allowed some chaos in return for quick action and regular experimentation.

CONCLUSION

This chapter started with an account of the communication media's unprecedented interest in product quality in the years since 1979—possibly because they felt it was one focus of the exciting commercial conflict between the United States and Japan. Business managers are influenced by the media just as much as any other section of the community, so there has been a corresponding increase in their awareness of the importance of product quality, and also of their intention to respond to its challenge.

The chapter continued by presenting the evidence that product quality really is a primary determinant of business success. The Japanese world domination with particular groups of products has had superior product quality as one of its essential bases. The PIMS results show quantitatively that quality, relative to competing products, is comparable to market share in determining business profitability, and has more effect than any other business parameter. Finally, the new emphasis that major industrial companies and defense agencies are giving to the quality of the products they buy has brought to a new level the business importance of product quality to their suppliers.

There is some indication that media interest in quality is already waning. Although articles continue to appear in major journals, and the consultants continue to enjoy boom conditions, there has been nothing in 1983 or 1984 to equal the *Business Week* issue of March 12, 1979, or the NBC television program of 1980. There was a White House Conference in 1983, but this was primarily devoted to productivity, and quality was covered as just one subject among a dozen others. If it is true that media interest in quality is waning, it could well be that management interest will wane also, though possibly at a slower rate. If so, the next few years could be a period of special opportunity to make improvements in quality.

CHAPTER 2

PRINCIPLES OF QUALITY IMPROVEMENT

In Chapter 1, it was shown that quality was of great importance to virtually all product businesses. The PIMS analysis of about 2700 such businesses showed that those with high "relative product and service quality" had an average ROI of about 30 percent, 2.7 times the returns of businesses with low relative product quality. It was also shown that customers' expectations for product quality were rising—partially as a result of their experience with Japanese products—and that many businesses were working actively on quality improvement so that competitive pressures on quality were increasing.

All of these factors point to the importance to a business not only of quality improvement but also of a high rate of improvement. Without improvement action the absolute level of quality of a business will deteriorate because of the natural tendency of everything to decay from order to chaos (for the physical world this principle is defined in the Second Law of Thermodynamics). A significant rate of introduction of specific quality improvement projects is therefore necessary to counteract this general process. To retain a constant *relative* status of product quality against the rising expectations of customers and the improvement activities of competitors, requires a higher improvement rate—which for a business already having a superior level of product quality is the minimum necessary for it to retain its position. For a business with only an average level of quality to reap the major strategic advantages which arise from superiority requires yet another increment of improvement rate.

POLICY, HONESTY, PRIORITY, AND CAPABILITY

The current status of a business's product quality is never good enough. A business whose current status is poor must improve rapidly if it is to survive, one whose status is superior must improve to retain the major advantages of that position, and one which is average must improve to prevent its status from becoming poor, and to make it superior.

The major challenge to a business's treatment of quality is to master the art of quality improvement, and to make this a continuing part of the total business philosophy. Simply to maintain an existing quality level, even a good one, is not enough.

Products and services are sold by existing companies and their divisions. Such divisions have a large number of interlocking systems which enable them to buy materials, design new products, perform manufacturing operations, measure costs, pay wages, maintain inventories, take orders, deliver products, and so on. The actual way these systems operate, which may not be fully defined or may be different from the way they are supposed to operate, forms a complex equilibrium. Within this equilibrium different people and groups of people perform familiar activities in interaction with each other. The result of their efforts is that the products are made and delivered, and all of the other functions of the business are performed. However, no one person, or group of persons will comprehend the equilibrium in its total complexity.

Because the complex equilibrium has typically been built-up over many years by an evolution involving hundreds of people, and because each piece has a workable interaction with many others, it is very stable. Therefore, it is relatively easy to maintain the existing status, but difficult to improve it. Using product quality as an example, the maintenance of product quality at whatever level it is, good or bad, against the effects of natural deterioration, is relatively easy. What is difficult is to improve—and to do so at a rate sufficient to meet the rising expectations of customers, and to outpace the efforts of competitors. There is yet one more requirement: the pace must be such that the objective of dramatic improvement is achieved in a defined period of time, at most five years. A program with a longer time perspective has little hope of ever reaching its target.

There are four necessary conditions for a company to achieve a good rate of quality improvement. They can be described under the headings of policy, honesty, priority, and capability. First of all, to strive for quality improvement must be a top-level policy of the company. Unless the chief executive of the company states this clearly, quality improvement will not be achieved. It is often claimed that the unsatisfactory quality performance of companies could be corrected if only their chief executives would state and support such a policy. At quality control conferences it is frequently bewailed that the wrong audience is being addressed—that the actual audience of quality professionals is already converted, but that they do not have the power to make changes. If an audience of chief executives could be converted . . . it would *really* make the difference.

In fact, the chief executives of many great companies are already convinced of the importance of the quality of their products and services, and possibly a majority of companies already have quality policies issued by their chief executives. Few of these policies explicitly address quality *improvement,* but that is not the main reason why so many companies have good quality policies and so few have good quality performance. The reality is that the establishment of a quality policy is only the necessary starting point for a long, difficult, and complex task. In a fairy tale, as soon as the king *really* believed and signed the proclamation, the good fairy would wave her magic wand and the whole country would be changed instantaneously. Improving companies, unfortunately, is not that easy.

Honesty is one essential requirement for achieving quality superiority. If the managers of a company are not honest all of their quality related efforts will be wasted. Typical quality-related actions by such managers are the following: they commit to do certain tests on the product, record the results, and send the test sheets to the customer. They do not do the tests and put fictitious results on the sheets, or they do the tests, get results that show the product has failed, and put different results on the sheet to indicate that the tests were passed. Another example is they agree to do certain tests before they ship the product, the scheduled delivery date arrives and they have not had time to do the tests, but they ship the product anyway.

It is possible to imagine the real benefit that the actual owner of a small business might get from being dishonest. But it is hard to see which manager in a large, reputable corporation gets benefit from such dishonesty. Is it the chief executive, division manager, manufacturing manager, sales manager, or the quality manager? Nonetheless, there are pressures within major companies which encourage dishonesty and sometimes they are not resisted. In 1984, the semiconductor industry was involved in just this kind of behavior (8). The three examples I have known about personally in my career did not involve someone clearly deciding to be dishonest. They involved a group of people covering up a problem, and progressively getting into deeper difficulty. After-the-fact analysis showed the behavior was irrational. The number of people involved made it very likely that the wrong-doing would be exposed. The benefits to be realized were small compared with the personal exposures of those involved. In these examples, senior managers were dismissed and reputations built up over decades were shattered. I asked my legal contact in TRW about personal liability and the following was his answer (9).

> You raised the issue of various liabilities that may result from falsified test information. I have not spent a lot of time researching specific cases and jurisdictional rules, but let me give you some general guidance.
>
> 1. Both the company and the involved individuals could incur criminal and civil liabilities in a situation where test information is falsified.
>
> 2. Depending upon the exact nature of the falsification, in most states and under federal law, making a false quality entry in our records constitutes a criminal fraud. The authorities can prosecute both the company and individuals for such conduct under any number of criminal fraud statutes such as mail fraud, wire fraud, conspiracy, etc. If the products involved are eventually sold to the U.S. Government, there are specific federal statutes that will be violated if false quality entries are made. In every instance, criminal fraud is a felony punishable by a jail term of up to five years or a fine of up to ten thousand dollars *for each false entry.* Obviously, the company cannot indemnify its employees for criminal acts.
>
> 3. In some circumstances and in some states other criminal statutes may also be violated. Examples might include: chemical exposure and/or pollution under EPA rules, vehicular homicide with respect to automotive parts, and wrongful death actions related to aircraft or electronic components.
>
> 4. On the civil side:
>   a. the company could be liable under a variety of theories including civil fraud, negligence, breach of contract, false advertising, product liability, etc.;
>   b. the individual (quality manager) may be sued and be found personally liable in a civil action. While the company indemnifies its employees for their actions taken in good faith in the course of business, such indemnification would not apply in this case. Thus, the individual would be on his own as to his defense.

5. In any case, there is a high likelihood that the individuals involved would be fired. Note that the first of the four CEO "Objectives for the 80s" relates to high standards of legal and ethical conduct.

The bottom line, John, is that quality managers or others are taking on significant personal risks in addition to subjecting the company to liability when they falsify quality records.

The knee-jerk reactions to such events are to deal heavily with the guilty, to hush-up comment as much as possible hoping this will limit damage to the company's reputation, and to add new inspection or audit activities to detect such occurrences in the future. The latter is not very effective. It is unnecessary in the division concerned—they will never do it again anyway—and has virtually no long-term effect on the other divisions. The use of quality departments to police for dishonesty is a waste of money. (Real police departments have great difficulty and they are professionals. Crime rates go up and down for demographic and social reasons, relatively unaffected by police efficiency. No one would argue that England's murder rate is a fraction of the United States' because English police are several times as efficient as American.) It is a good idea to examine the activities of quality departments from time to time and delete any that have no other purpose than the detection of dishonesty.

Source inspection is a case in point. Many companies, particularly in defense industry, will not let their suppliers ship product until their own inspectors, who are resident in the suppliers' plants or who have traveled there, have inspected the product and certified it as acceptable. Why is this procedure followed? It would seem to be much simpler and cheaper for the customer to specify whatever tests and inspections the source inspector would do, and contract for the supplier's own people to do them. Occasionally the supplier may not have the ability to do the tests, but that is the minority of cases. Apart from this minority, it does not seem an efficient system. It clouds the issue of who is responsible for the quality of the product reaching the customer. It should, unequivocably, be the supplier. But now the source inspector can be a convenient whipping boy for bad quality, even though, with limited time and facilities, he or she does not have the means to meet the quality responsibility. Why is the procedure followed? Because it is custom and practice to follow this procedure. A long time ago someone wanted to be "sure" about the quality, and without thinking the thing through, told someone to go off to the supplier and inspect the product. Now, the source inspection system, except for the minority situation mentioned above, carries an often unintended and undeserved implication that the supplier is dishonest. It would be better if this were made explicit. The customer should ask, "Do I believe that Supplier X is dishonest?" If the answer is yes, the next question is, should the customer continue to do business with Supplier X? If, as is usually the case, the answer is no, the necessity or usefulness of the source inspection should be seriously questioned.

A national trade association asked eight major companies the question: What role does the vice president/director quality play in your company? Two of them included among those responsibilities, "to be the conscience of the organization," showing that this ancient fallacy still persists. The conscience of an adult person is theirs alone: no one else can take that responsibility. Guidance can come from a clergyman, not a quality manager.

A company that is serious about quality and quality improvement must ensure that all of its efforts are not nullified by dishonesty. This can only be done by effectively communicating that such behavior is not acceptable to the company. A general climate of opinion must be created making dishonesty unthinkable. Dishonesty must be excluded from the list of subjects which managers consider in making trade-offs or establishing priorities. Despite pressures for performance and profit, they must know that there are some responses that are not permitted. This should be enough, because most managers of major companies do not have criminal tendencies and it is obvious that the objectives of such companies are not realized by dishonesty. If the climate of opinion is right quality department audits for dishonesty are unnecessary. If it is wrong the quality manager's own exhortations will be ineffective, and reporting to the general manager, who will be part of the problem, will be unacceptably difficult. In a divisionalized company quality auditors reporting to senior management have their special problems (see Chapter 14). Such dishonesty is not a quality problem but rather a problem with the total ethics of the company.

The third necessary condition for effective quality improvement in a company is for product quality and its improvement to be given sufficient priority. Priority is different from policy: priority means making trade-off decisions between different policies. It is relatively easy to establish a policy. It is much more difficult to implement the policy—to give it such priority that scarce resources in people, money, and time are withdrawn from other activities to ensure its achievement.

In making and selling products, companies often provide inadequate resources to do the job properly. They spread their resources too thinly, and plan to do more in a certain time than is feasible ("If we don't launch the product this year we shall lose the market."). Products have to meet a price set by the market—this defines a required cost. However, a company may use obsolete manufacturing equipment ("This year we have to restrict our capital budget.") and achieve neither low cost nor high quality. They may not provide enough technically competent people to do the task well ("Control of indirect manpower is a key part of our business strategy.").

There seems little doubt that lack of priority is a principal reason for selling bad quality products. Of course, it is a matter of great judgment to determine what are the necessary resources to perform a task properly. How much time and money must be provided to make a product that is better than the competing products, but costs less? Management often worries that if the correct level of resources are provided they will be dissipated in uncompetitive pricing, unnecessary design frills, fancy manufacturing methods, and under-employed indirect staff.

In one of the sessions I conduct in a training program for TRW's division general managers, I ask them to list the names of the important projects which their divisions will be giving high priority in the next few years. Everyone of these projects is a major drain on the limited effort that the division has left over after it has carried out the essential requirements of its current business. Table 2.1 lists some of the answers they have given. In the real world, quality improvement has to compete for priority with such projects as these.

The fourth reason for inadequate product quality and a too slow rate of quality improvement is a lack of capability. If a company lacks necessary abilities—managerial, technical, personal, and so on—it will not be able to achieve its quality objectives. Of course, if it has sufficient financial resources a company can build up necessary capabilities, but this may take a long time.

The important reasons for an unsatisfactory quality performance by a company are insufficient priority and insufficient capability. The quality

TABLE 2.1. Planned Business-Improvement Projects

Pricing strategy and tactics	Plant closures
RD&E and new product introduction	Inventory or receivables reduction
Acquisitions	Develop new, for example, export, markets
Reorganization	
Management recruitment & training	Improve customer selling/advertising activities
Management compensation	
Union relationship improvement	Reduce product costs
Employee involvement	Product rationalization
Purchase of new machines	Capital structure and borrowing

policy and the achievement of honesty are necessary ground-clearing before the real effort starts.

WHAT IS QUALITY?

In Chapter 1, evidence was presented showing that the quality of the products sold to its customers is vital to a company's success. In this chapter it has been argued that to achieve and maintain a position of superiority in product quality a company needs to have a high rate of quality improvement. Such a high rate of quality improvement requires satisfaction of four necessary conditions discussed under the titles: policy, honesty, priority, and capability. As one part of their quality capability, business managers need to know precisely what they mean when they talk about "improving product quality," they need to know how to divide overall product quality into manageable improvement projects, and how to measure product quality. The rest of this chapter will address these issues.

At the 1980 Technical Conference of the European Organization for Quality Control held in Budapest, Hungary, I had a conversation with Dr. J. M. Juran, the doyen of quality control consultants and author and editor of many books including the *Quality Control Handbook* (10). One point in the discussion concerned the definition of quality developed by my ex-colleague, P. B. Crosby, and used for many years in the large multinational corporation, ITT. During the conversation Juran suggested that ITT had developed a private language for quality control. He accepted that this might be internally self-consistent and useful for the company, but that it was different from common usage and different from the language used by most quality managers.

Crosby's book, *Quality is Free* (1), has sold thousands of copies, with probably the majority going to managers who are not quality professionals. It is likely that for many of these it will be the only book on quality management they will ever read. There could be a serious problem of communication if this group of managers received an understanding of the meaning of quality which was different from that of most quality managers—possibly including those in their own companies. It seemed, therefore, that it might be useful to analyze the definitions of quality given by Juran and Crosby to see if there were real differences and, if so, to clarify them. In addition, the definition of quality given in the European Organization for Quality Control's *Glossary of Terms used in Quality Control* (11) and in the American National Standard *Quality Systems Terminol-*

ogy (12), were also considered, because they are the most official quality glossaries. Finally, an English and an American dictionary were consulted.

Crosby defines quality as, "conformance to requirements," and the following quotation from his book gives his reasons:

> The first erroneous assumption is that quality means goodness, or luxury, or shininess, or weight. The word 'quality' is used to signify the relative worth of things in such phrases as 'good quality,' 'bad quality,' and that brave new statement 'quality of life.' 'Quality of life' is a cliché because each listener assumes that the speaker means exactly what he or she, the listener, means by the phrase. It is a situation in which individuals talk dreamily about something without ever bothering to define it.

> That is precisely the reason we must define quality as 'conformance to requirements' if we are to manage it. Thus, those who want to talk about quality of life must define that life in specific terms, such as desirable income, health, pollution control, political programs, and other items that can each be measured. When all criteria are defined and explained then the measurement of quality of life is possible and practical. In business the same is true. Requirements must be clearly stated so that they cannot be misunderstood. Measurements are then taken continually to determine conformance to those requirements. The nonconformance detected is the absence of quality. Quality problems become nonconformance problems, and quality becomes definable. All through this book, whenever you see the word 'quality' read 'conformance to requirement.'

> If a Cadillac conforms to all the requirements of a Cadillac, then it is a quality car. If a Pinto conforms to all the requirements of a Pinto, then it is a quality car. Luxury or its absence is spelled out in specific requirements, such as carpeting or rubber mats. The next time someone says someone or something has 'lousy quality' interrogate that person until you can determine just exactly what he or she means. Quality means conformance to the requirements, and that is all it means. If you start confusing quality with elegance, brightness, dignity, love, or something else, you will find that everyone has different ideas. Don't talk about poor quality or high quality. Talk about conformance and nonconformance.

Juran has a similarly terse definition, "fitness for use." (Juran and Crosby are both great salesmen and they appreciate that it is much easier to sell a 3-word definition than a 30-word one.) Both Juran and Crosby assert that their two definitions are not just different words expressing essentially the same idea: they state that their definitions of quality are fundamentally different. The following quotation from Juran's handbook (10) summarizes his ideas:

Of all concepts in the quality function (and in this Handbook) none is so far-reaching or vital as 'fitness for use . . .' Among these overall needs, the extent to which the product successfully serves the purpose of the user during usage is called 'fitness for use.' This concept of fitness for use popularly called by such names as 'quality' is a universal concept applicable to all goods and services. Fitness for use is determined by those features of the product which the user can recognize as beneficial to him, e.g., fresh baked taste of bread, clear reception of radio programs. . . .

To the user, quality is fitness for use, not conformance to specification. The ultimate user seldom knows what is in the specifications. His evaluation of quality is based on whether the product is fit for use on delivery to him and on whether it continues to be fit for use.

The European Organizations for Quality Control (EOQC) and the American Society for Quality Control (ASQC) have the same definition of quality, "the totality of features and characteristics of a product or service that bear on its ability to satisfy a given need." It would have been very surprising if the EOQC and the ASQC had independently decided on exactly the same wording for their definitions. But, of course, this is not the case—the definition is the result of a cooperative effort.

Dictionaries list all usages of a word, unlike glossaries which give one specific definition of a term. The *Concise Oxford Dictionary* and *Webster's New Collegiate Dictionary* give many usages of the word, "quality" but the most relevant are, "degree of excellence," and "a distinguishing attribute."

For the 10 years during which Crosby had been vice president and director, quality of ITT and I had had the same position for the European half of ITT, I had used his definition, "conformance to requirements" and found it practical and useful. However, my discussion with Juran lead me to believe it might be useful to analyze and compare Crosby's definition with its alternatives.

The exercise led me to some general conclusions about the best ways to define technical terms, which I describe at the beginning of the glossary, but two of them are important to the present discussion. In English, and I expect in most languages, the sentence is the fundamental unit for communicating information. Parts of sentences—clauses, phrases, words, and letters—are unsatisfactory media for conveying information. Brief phases like "fitness for use" and "conformance to requirements," and indeed pseudo sentences like the ASQC/EOQC definition convey information only if readers can successfully determine the extra words needed to make them sentences. But, of course, this leads to error and ambiguity.

One reader may add different words from another, and neither may use the words the author had in mind. So, it is easier to understand a definition if it is written as a complete sentence. It is also clearer if all ideas in a definition are made explicit and not just implied.

Applying these conclusions to the definitions of quality, we first ask: Quality of what? Quality is a word of very wide applicability, but it is clear that Juran and the EOQC/ASQC are restricting its usage to the quality of products or services sold by vendors to customers. Crosby implies a wider usage, but this book is not concerned with the "quality of the environment," and so on, so we will concentrate on products.

Examining Crosby's definition, the word "conformance," which has a long and honorable history of usage by the quality profession, implies conformance of something to something. What are these two somethings and how can their conformance be checked? Having restricted attention to products, one something is the product and the other is "the requirement." What is the requirement? Well, in dealings between commercial organizations, for example, a company selling a product to the DoD, the requirement will be defined in a product requirement specification, which will be agreed by the vendor and the customer, and will define the required features and characteristics (to use the ASQC/EOQC's phrase) of the product. In assessing conformance, the actual features and characteristics of the product will be compared with the specified features and characteristics. Finally, does the definition apply only when the product is perfectly conformant to the requirement? If it did the usage would be extremely restricted, so it seems more useful to introduce the "degree" idea (as in the dictionaries' "degree of excellence"). Making explicit all of these ideas implicit in Crosby's "conformance to requirements" gives:

> The quality of a product is the degree of conformance of all of its features and characteristics to the product requirement specification.

Applying the same sort of reasoning to Juran's definition "fitness for use," we still have the product with its actual features and characteristics, and the degree idea. We have to ask: whose "use?" Well, it could be anyone's but clearly the most important use is the customer's. So, Juran's definition becomes explicitly:

> The quality of a product is the degree of fitness of all of its features and characteristics for the customer's use.

There is no implication in Juran's definition that the customer's use is recorded in a product requirement specification, and, as he points out, this is realistic for the vast majority of products bought by individual customers as opposed to commercial organizations. Food, clothing, and many other products are all bought without any explicit specification. Capital goods, such as cars, dishwashers, and television sets may appear to have product requirement specifications but most of them contain relatively little information and are unsuitable for assessing conformance. In practice, there is no easy way of measuring the degree to which a product conforms to the customer's use, and this is why Juran's definition includes the less precise word "fitness" rather than conformance.

So, on the one hand we have Crosby's definition which is practical to use, but applies only to products and services bought and sold by commercial organizations, and on the other hand Juran's definition, which is generally applicable, but hard to use.

The EOQC/ASQC definition introduces the good idea of "the totality of features and characteristics of a product or service." However, it is badly structured because the main clause of the definition is concerned only with the product or service, the conformance or fitness idea is barely implied, and the degree idea ("ability") and the customer's requirement idea ("given need") are buried in the subclause.

One further point merits discussion: the relationship of the price and quality of a product. The three sets of definitions by Juran, Crosby, and the EOQC/ASQC have different positions with regard to this issue. Juran introduces (10) a grade concept related to increasing price, "a private Volkswagen, a private Rolls Royce, a private jet airplane. . . ." Crosby says a high-price Cadillac and a low-price Pinto have the same quality provided they conform similarly to their own requirements. The EOQC and ASQC include the statement that "the phrase 'given needs' includes defining a price as well as stating what must be achieved since it is usually possible to improve use characteristics if the price is not a limitation. . . ."

Crosby and Juran select examples in which the "use" or "requirement" is not really the same—the small Pinto and the large Cadillac satisfy different needs, as do the Volkswagen and the jet airplane. Another example is to compare two similar cars made by General Motors—the Cadillac Seville and the Chevrolet Malibu. These can both be four-door sedans with V-6 or V-8 engines of about the same size (100 cubic feet interior space). The Seville does satisfy virtually the same need as the Malibu and there are few people who, offered either as a gift, would not select the Cadillac because the "features and characteristics" of a Seville are better than those of a Malibu. To buy the Cadillac is another question. The price of a Malibu is well below $10,000 and of a Seville is well above $20,000. In fact, of course, the price difference is so great that separate classes of customers buy Sevilles and Malibus and any comparison of the quality of the two cars is of no practical usefulness to either group. This is the point that resolves the problem.

There is no practical relationship between the quality of the Volkswagen and the jet airplane because they satisfy such different needs. Equally, there is no practical relationship between the quality of the Seville and the Malibu because, although they satisfy the same need, they have such different prices.

Useful quality comparisons are restricted to those between products satisfying the same customer's need, at about the same price.

Traditionally, three factors have been taken to influence a customer's purchase of a product and his or her satisfaction with it: price, quality, and delivery. The previous discussion covers the relationship between price and quality. Similar arguments can be applied to delivery and quality. One could extend the EOQC/ASQC idea—"The phrase 'given needs' indicates defining a 'delivery need' as well as stating what must be achieved." However, common-usage separates quality from delivery just as it separates quality from price, and there is a great deal to be said for retaining as clearly separated factors the old trio of price, quality, and delivery.

When I started this analysis I had no intention of proposing a new definition of quality and my first account of it in the EOQC's journal, *Quality* (13), did not make such a proposal. However, that paper led to some correspondence, and in a second paper (14) a year later I felt pushed by the logic of the analysis to propose the following definition:

The quality of a product is the degree of conformance of all of the relevant features and characteristics of the product to all of the aspects of a customer's need, limited by the price and delivery he or she will accept.

The definition replaces the EOQC's "totality of" and "bear-on" with "all" and "relevant." It emphasizes the important point that a product does not inherently have quality—it has quality only in relationship to a customer's need*—by giving "all of the aspects of a customer's need" a

---

* Being pedantic, the need goes beyond the customer's in such things as the government's need for compliance with regulations and the safety needs of third parties.

weight equal to that of "all of the relevant features and characteristics of the product." The last clause deals with the price and delivery issue by utilizing the conclusion reached previously: useful quality comparisons are restricted to those between products satisfying the same customer's need at about the same price. Of course, in practice a customer will be prepared to make some price trade-off but, as shown by the PIMS results, this will usually be less than 10 percent. (This point is returned to in Chapter 9 in a discussion of the economics of quality.)

The meaning of "all of the aspects of a customer's need" can be clarified by considering an example—my own need as a customer which I satisfied by buying a new car. Various aspects of that need are as follows:

To go frequently from Beachwood to Euclid, Ohio

To support my self-image as a middle-aged business executive

To satisfy my regard for well-engineered machines

To meet my requirement for comfort and convenience in traveling

To please my aesthetic sensibilities

To satisfy various aspects of my wife's need, and so on

When I bought my new car I first decided on price and delivery limitations. Then I evaluated the features and characteristics of a dozen or so cars within those limitations to determine which gave the best satisfaction of the various aspects of my need. Of course, in practice my need was undefined and changing.

The definition makes clear that there is no practical usefulness in a customer having a need (in its totality of aspects) which he or she wishes to satisfy by buying a product, if no product to satisfy that totality can be bought for the price he or she is willing to pay, or can be delivered in the time period the customer is willing to wait. The totality of aspects of a need, in practice, must be limited by price and delivery. For example, some of the group of customers in the United States willing to pay $8000 for a four-door, 100 cubic foot interior space car, might like to define a totality of aspects that could be met only by a Cadillac Seville—which could not be bought for $8000. The definition prevents this by placing a restriction on the need—"limited by the price and delivery he or she is willing to accept." In practice, the problem is overcome by comparing actually competing products, which necessarily have a similar price, for example, the Malibu and Granada. The customer decides to buy one or the other and this automatically limits the totality of aspects of their need to that which the alternatives can satisfy. The definition also follows common usage in that price and delivery are *not* included as features and characteristics of a product.

Throughout this discussion, in one respect, a narrow view of quality has been taken. Attention has been concentrated on the quality of products sold by vendors to customers. We have not been concerned with such things as the quality of the environment, the quality of work life, or the quality of performance of various business activities. However, we have defined product quality itself to be completely comprehensive: it embraces "*all* of the features and characteristics" of the product. The phrase "performance, quality, and reliability" is often used, but to make performance and reliability separate from quality leads to serious logical difficulties. In principle, it requires three separate analyses—one each for performance, quality and reliability—rather than a single one for quality. It necessitates compatible definition of performance, quality, and reliability, and rules for assigning particular features and characteristics to each. (What is left for quality? In this context, is reliability restricted to its technical meaning, or does it include maintainability, safety, environmental resistance, etc?) For these reasons product quality is made comprehensive in this book. Where it is useful to make separate references to performance and reliability, the phrase, "quality, including performance and reliability" can be employed. In this analysis, the things that are kept separate from product quality, as discussed later in this chapter, are support quality, delivery quality, and price, not performance or reliability.

It could be commented that the suggested definition and the associated discussion are complicated—too complicated to be practically useful. But the truth of the matter is that quality is complicated. In the proposed definition nine ideas have been included—quality, product, degree, conformance, all features and characteristics, relevant, all aspects of a customer's need; limited by the price he or she is willing to accept, and limited by the delivery they will accept—and it would be difficult to assert that any of them has no place in a comprehensive definition of quality. Also, it is difficult to express 10 ideas in less than 40 words.

As we saw, the short definitions of quality achieve their apparent simplicity by implying much more than they state. In a similar way the suggested definition can also be shortened by implying rather than stating its complexities as follows:

Product Quality: conformance to a customer's price-limited need. However, even in its shortened version the definition still includes the word customer. It is perhaps surprising that none of the other definitions of quality discussed above explicitly mentions the customer.

"THE CHAIN OF CONFORMANCE"

In the last section we have defined product quality in a usable way. This book is about quality improvement, and, following the definition, we can now say that one purpose of quality improvement is to increase the degree of conformance of the product to the customer's need. That is easier said than done. In fact, the gap between the product and the customer's need is usually so wide that it is impracticable to attempt to cross it in one step. The gap can be bridged by a "chain of conformance" (Figure 2.1) in which marketing, design, purchasing, and manufacturing links are short enough to be the subjects of practical improvement projects.

The chain starts with the actual need of a single customer. For a mass-produced product marketing processes are then used to define a target group of customers of which the customer is a member. These customers have a distribution of all of the aspects of their needs which embraces the need of the one customer but which is narrower than the distribution of the needs of the whole population. For example, when I bought my new car I was a member of a group of middle-aged men who did not require to transport small children and their necessary paraphernalia. By another marketing process, a specification is defined summarizing all of the relevant features and characteristics of a product which it is judged will best satisfy the distribution of needs of the target group of customers. For a car this will cover all of the relevant features, size, styling, power-steering, and so on, and the required values of relevant characteristics, maximum speed, acceleration, fuel consumption, braking rate, and so on. (Simultaneously, the marketing people will define a suggested price and a required availability time, there being a close, practical relationship between the marketing specification and the target price and delivery.)

For a custom-made product the single customer is considered individually and often participates actively in the process of defining the features and characteristics of the product to be purchased.

The next stage is for the design-development department to add further detail to the marketing specification converting such things as "highly reliable" to a required mean time between failures, "excellent durability" to an ability to pass specified environmental tests, "very safe" to conformance to internal and legally required safety standards, and so on. The result of this activity is a product requirement specification which defines in technical detail all of the required features and characteristics of the product. It is the key document that tells marketing what they will have to sell and tells design-development what they have to design. All too often in real life the product requirement specification (which goes

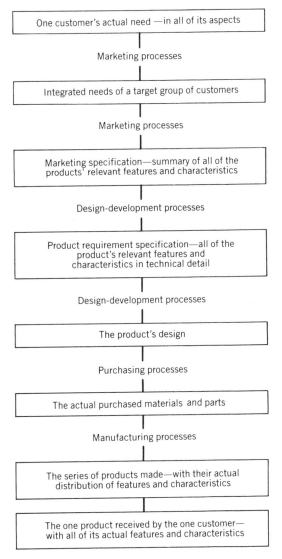

One customer's actual need —in all of its aspects

Marketing processes

Integrated needs of a target group of customers

Marketing processes

Marketing specification—summary of all of the products' relevant features and characteristics

Design-development processes

Product requirement specification—all of the product's relevant features and characteristics in technical detail

Design-development processes

The product's design

Purchasing processes

The actual purchased materials and parts

Manufacturing processes

The series of products made—with their actual distribution of features and characteristics

The one product received by the one customer— with all of its actual features and characteristics

Figure 2.1. Chain of conformance.

under many names) is not properly defined at this stage. The excuse is that until the development has progressed, insufficient information is available—market research is incomplete, the customer will not make up his or her mind, technical possibilities have not been evaluated, and so on. However, the suspicion is that the concerned people do not want to be tied down, or want to get on with the exciting work of original design rather than the dull task of specification writing and negotiation. Of course, the product requirement specification, in fact, does not tie anyone down: if there is good reason it can always be changed. However, it ensures that changes are made in an orderly manner and everyone has the same clear, up-to-date information.

The marketing and design-development processes that link the customer's need and the product requirement specification are largely judgmental. The customer's need is undefined (and in some respects undefinable). The determination of the best combination of features and characteristics, within the constraints of marketing estimates of price and delivery, is a major exercise of judgment. Trade-offs have to be made. Shall the car have automatic transmission and carburetion or manual transmission and fuel injection? Shall the suit be made of 100 percent wool or a polyester mixture? With so much imprecision how can the "degree of conformance" of the product requirement specification to the customer's need be measured? Well, market research and other ways of asking the customer may give a partial answer, but the customer does not know what are "all of the aspects" of their need. Some customers will not understand the technicalities of the product requirement specification. For this length of the chain, therefore, the degree of conformance cannot be measured with precision and the idea of aiming for exact conformance has no meaning.

For the links in the chain from the product requirement specification onwards there is no such fundamental uncertainty. The degree of conformance between adjacent links is readily measurable, the concept of complete conformance is understandable, and is a possible objective.

The customer's expectation can now be discussed. His or her expectation of what he or she can get places bounds on what is established as a need. Expectations are influenced by previous experience, advertisements, magazine articles, conversations with friends, and so on. They will change with time. When I acquired my first television I rented it, as did most people in England at that time. My expectation was that it would break down a couple of times a year and the excellent repair organization operated as a no-charge service by my rental company was one important reason why I selected it. When the set did break down I suffered inconvenience but was not particularly upset. Twenty years later I bought my current set from a Japanese company and repair service was not a factor. My expectation was that it would operate without failure for perhaps 10 years. If it had broken down two or three times a year I should have felt cheated and angry. Progress in the reliability of consumer electronics had changed my expectation.

Once the product requirement specification, or some summary of its implications, is communicated to the customer, whether it is in a contract or an advertising brochure, their expectation is changed. Before it was ill-defined and fuzzy. Now it is precise: the customer expects the product to conform to their idea of the specification and they will be upset if it does not. If it conforms to the specification but is not a good match to important aspects of their need, they will not like the product and may think they made a poor choice, but will not feel cheated.

With the issue of the product requirement specification, which defines what the product must *do* (including the way it looks and the space it occupies) the design/development process can proceed leading to the design of the product. This defines what the product shall *be*. With the design defined, purchasing processes are used to buy the materials and parts for the product, and manufacturing processes are used to manufacture the product. Unlike the marketing, design-development, and purchasing processes, the manufacturing processes themselves are often specified (how the product shall be made) and the degree of conformance between the actual and specified manufacturing processes can be determined.

Finally, the customer receives one item of the product and judges the quality of that item by its "degree of conformance" to his or her need. It is apparent that the degree of conformance can be less than perfect between each pair of links in the chain. Inevitably, the marketing specification and the product requirement specification will not correspond exactly to the customer's need. By policy or, more likely, by inefficiency, the product design may not conform to the product requirement specification, or the manufactured product may not conform to the design. Conceptually, there could be perfect conformance between the two ends of the chain—between the customer's need and the product received to satisfy that need—and the product would have perfect quality. In practice, there can be a loss of quality, due to a degree of conformance less than unity, between any of the links of the chain of conformance.

The use of the word "degree" in the quality definition implies that the quality of a product can be expressed as a number. It is probably simplest conceptually to call perfect conformance to all of the aspects of the customer's need 100 percent. Then one product might have a 98 percent degree of conformance and another a 95 percent. The former would clearly have better quality than the latter. Because of the difficulty of defining the customer's need, and because of the requirement to limit that need by price and delivery considerations, it might be more practical to assign the 100 percent rating to the product with the best quality available at the price and delivery limit. For our example, the first product would have a 100 percent quality and the second a $95/98 = 97$ percent quality.

Because people find percentages easy to visualize, we have used them for this discussion. However, more often than not percentages are a poor unit for measuring quality. The human tendency to feel that one percent defective separates good quality from bad, irrespective of the product, has been a principal reason for lack of progress in quality improvement. On the one hand, where the whole length of the chain of conformance is considered, it is usually not practicable to assign a quality number to a product in this way. However, it is possible to place a group of competing products in a ranking order. In Chapter 4, the results of making such quality rankings for some hundreds of groups of products will be discussed. On the other hand, measurement of quality in terms of conformance to the product requirement specification (the bottom half of the chain of conformance) is often best measured in parts per million (ppm). In one example, discussed in Chapter 8, the effect on a whole industry of reducing the proportion of defective electronic components from 500 ppm to 15 ppm (i.e., improving the quality from 99.95 percent to 99.9985 percent) will be examined.

An important advantage of this book's definition of quality, which is a consequence of its inclusion of the word degree, is that it can be used directly to express improvements (and deteriorations) in the quality of successive items of products coming from manufacturing lines, or successive newly designed models.

The concept of the chain of conformance leads to three very important conclusions. The first, which has been discussed, is that the chain itself is divided into two distinct parts. In establishing the first half, which goes from the customer's need to the product requirement specification, judgments and trade-offs have to be made, and the application of the concept of conformance is limited by the imprecision and uncertainty of these links at the start of the chain. The second half of the chain is not limited in this way. There is no fundamental difficulty in measuring the degree of conformance of the actual product to the product requirement specification, practical methods of achieving a very high, or perfect, degree of conformance are available, and increasingly customers' expectations are that products should conform to their requirement specifications. However, the difficulty of managing the first half of the chain does not reduce its importance. Fundamentally, a customer wants a product that satisfies their need. Offered two products at the same price, both of which conform to their product requirement specifications, a customer will choose the one that best satisfies that need. This applies both to an institutional customer buying to a contractually agreed product requirement specification and to an individual buying without any formal agreement. However well the notorious Edsel car conformed to its own requirement specification it proved to be a bad product; the customers did not buy it because it did not meet their needs. The product requirement specification is only a means, albeit a vital one, for linking the product to the customer's need. It is not an end in itself. A wise vendor not only works obsessively on conformance to the product requirement specification, but also systematically evaluates the need of the customer to find new achievable aspects of that need. Taguchi has discussed design tolerances in this context. He points out that a fabricated part having its dimensions at the nominal values may have (in my terminology) a better degree of conformance to the customer's need, and therefore lose less quality, than one that utilizes all of the dimensional tolerances even though it conforms exactly to the design specification (e.g., the drawing) and the product requirement specification (e.g., for performance).

The second important conclusion is that, because the chain of conformance is built-up by marketing, design-development, purchasing, and manufacturing processes, the departments responsible for performing those processes determine the quality of the product. It will be shown later that the quality department has a direct input into some or all of these processes, so it also must be included in the list of responsible departments. These five departments—marketing,* design-development, purchasing, manufacturing, and quality—all control the quality. Failure by any one puts a degree of nonconformance into the chain and reduces the quality of the product. This conclusion is different from two conflicting pieces of conventional wisdom: the old-fashioned, "quality can be left to the quality department," and the contemporary, "quality is everybody's business." The former needs no discussion. The latter is true if one is talking about quality in general, but not if one is confining attention to the quality of the products a company sells. Of course, the accounting department has responsibility for the quality of the financial data it publishes, the human relations department has responsibility for the "quality of work-life" provided by the company, and so on. But for *product* quality the indirect and support responsibilities of such departments is different from the direct role of the five designated departments. Finally, the general manager, to whom all of these functions report, has a special responsibility for product quality.

The third important conclusion is that, although the achievement of product quality has been likened to a chain, it would be wrong to infer

---

* The definition of quality and the concept of the chain of conformance can be used in preparing logically consistent definitions of marketing quality, design quality, purchasing quality and manufacturing quality, and these are given in the glossary.

that the processes go in one direction only, from marketing to design-development and then to purchasing and manufacturing. In fact, the main flow *is* in that direction, but the processes are optimized by feedback loops, for example, the product engineers strongly influencing the marketing specification, and the cost and capability of manufacturing processes and the cost and availability of purchased items constraining the design. Achievement of superior quality requires all of the five functions to cooperate together as equals. The all-too-common perception that there is a pecking order in which marketing determines the product requirement specification (and often agrees it with a customer), and design-development has to come up with a design to meet that specification, and then purchasing and manufacturing have to make the design irrespective of its manufacturability or cost, is not conducive to the achievement of superior quality.

"QUALITY TO THE CUSTOMER, THE FIRST MEASURE OF QUALITY IMPROVEMENT"

At the start of this chapter it was argued that the "major challenge to a business's treatment of quality is to master the art of quality improvement." Having now defined product quality and shown how it can be divided into pieces small enough to be the subject of practical improvement projects, we can discuss how a business can measure the current status of its product quality, and how it can go about improving it. However, before doing so it is useful to place product quality in the context of a business's overall interaction with its customers—in a way that emphasizes improvement opportunities.

As noted, such interactions have been traditionally categorized as price, quality, and delivery. This is a good starting point for the discussion. Table 2.2 shows how the total performance of a division as perceived by a customer can be categorized into areas of product quality, support quality, and delivery quality and then shows how the categories can be divided into subcategories highlighting improvement responsibilities. Invariably a vendor of products will provide support services to its customers and these are an important part of its total performance. However, the quality of these services is different from product quality and the people responsible for improving support quality are different from those responsible for improving product quality. It is useful, therefore, to have a separate category for support quality. (The name support quality is used

TABLE 2.2. Customer Perceptions and Improvement Responsibilities

Main Categories	Sub-Categories	Improvement Responsibility
Product quality	Product requirement specification and design quality	Marketing/design-development
	Conformance to design at time of delivery	Purchasing/manufacturing
	Performance after delivery (reliability, maintainability, durability, safety, etc.)	Design-development
Support quality	Customer design support	Design-development
	Customer (sales) service	Marketing
	After-sales service	Marketing
	Assurance documentation	Quality
Delivery quality	Promised delivery (short or long times)	Manufacturing/marketing
	Conformance to promised delivery	Manufacturing/purchasing

rather than service quality. Service quality is reserved for application to businesses selling services not products.) Similarly, delivery quality is separated from product quality and support quality. The price that a vendor gets from a customer is justified by the product quality, support quality, and delivery quality provided.

Because this is a book about product quality the other two categories and their subcategories are only illustrative, and will not be discussed except to say that each one is open to improvement and different groups of people within a business are responsible for leading such improvement.* Product quality and its three subcategories can be described in more detail. The first covers the initial five links of the chain of conformance: how well the product requirement specification expresses the customer's need, and how well the design conforms to the product requirement specification. Leadership for improvement is clearly the responsibility of the marketing and design-development departments. The second subcategory covers how well the manufactured product (or series of products) conforms to the design at the time it is dispatched to the customer. Improvement is the responsibility of the purchasing and manufacturing departments. The third subcategory is concerned with the performance of the product as the customer continues to use it. How good is its reliability, safety, maintainability, durability, and so on? Does it continue to conform to its actual product requirement specification (or to an ideal-

---

* The responsibilities for most improvement activities are multifunctional, but unless a particular function takes the lead and accepts the main task little will happen.

ized specification that includes mean time between failures, resistance to environmental conditions, etc.)? Experience indicates that product failures in this third category are sometimes caused by purchasing or manufacturing deficiencies, but the more serious failures are caused by design defects, so design-development is given the primary improvement responsibility.

It might be asked: Why use only three subcategories when the chain of conformance indicates a larger number, and why does the last subcategory not relate directly to the chain? The reason is that the three selected subcategories can be measured relatively easily and the responsibilities for improvement can be assigned clearly. Of course, for any particular product the three main subcategories of product quality might usefully be broken down further. For example, the first subcategory might be divided into functional performance and styling parts, the conformance-at-delivery into dimensional defects and appearance defects, and the post-delivery performance into reliability and corrosion resistance, and so on.

An effective program of quality improvement should include a method of measuring the current product quality status and of targeting improvements in a quantitative way. Comparison with competing products—by performing a "competitors' quality evaluation"—is a way of doing these two tasks. Such comparisons can be made product by product, or in some businesses it may be practicable to evaluate products combined in groups. Table 2.3 gives a form on which the results of such assessments of product quality can be summarized. For each group of products the principal competitive products sold to the same customers are identified. The form suggests that up to three competitive products should be considered, the rest being grouped together. The approximate sales of each of the com-

TABLE 2.3. Competitor's Quality Evaluation

Competing Products	Division	1	2	3	Others
Annual Sales ($M)	20	25	15	8	12
Product requirement specification and design	Average	Best	Average	Worse	Worse
Delivered conformance	Joint Best	Joint Best	Average	Average	Worse
Post-delivery performance	Average	Best	Average	Worse	Average
Overall product quality	Average	Best	Average	Worse	Worse
Customer's opinion	Average	Best	Average	Average	Worse
Price premium	Medium	High	Medium	Low	Medium

peting products is listed. The products are then ranked for the three product quality subcategories previously discussed. The ranking is made according to the following definitions:

Best. No competitor's product has as good quality

Joint Best. No competitor's product has better quality

Average. The product quality is average

Worse. The product quality is worse than average

In Table 2.3 some hypothetical rankings have been inserted. The relationship between the overall ranking and those for the subcategories implies that the latter have been weighted in some way. Often, as in the example, the overall ranking will be obvious. On other occasions, one subcategory may clearly be most important in determining the overall ranking. When there is doubt about which of two adjacent rankings to apply the less extreme should be chosen—joint best instead of best, and average rather than joint best or worse.

It is possible for the customers to have a subjective opinion of the quality status that is different from the objective evaluations, for example, because a product was better (or worse) in the past than it is now and the customers have not yet fully recognized the change. The "customer's opinion" line enables such differences to be expressed.

All of the competing products will have similar prices, otherwise they cannot be competitive. Nonetheless, they may have limited price differences (e.g., as a result of the quality leader exacting a price premium) and it is useful to record these too.

The completed form can be used to identify areas for improvement. Actions can then be defined in projects, responsible persons can be assigned, and time scales can be established for completion of the projects. In the example given, the design-development department might agree with marketing to improve the features and characteristics of the product to make it as good as or better than the market leader. In the absence of this, improved conformance might have little market effect.

Special actions are required when the customers' subjective opinion differs from the objective evaluation. If the customers' opinion of the product quality is worse than the reality, marketing has a task in image building and communication. If this opinion is better than the reality it is important to improve the actual product quality very quickly; otherwise, there is a great danger of a disastrous effect in the market when the customers eventually recognize the reality.

This book has not suggested that once certain specific quality programs are completed the company's energies can be diverted into other priorities. On the contrary it has emphasized the vital importance to a company of having a quality philosophy that gives primacy to quality improvement—as a permanent, continuing way of doing business. Nonetheless, modern businesses work in annual cycles and it is very important that annual targets and forecasts for quality improvement be formally established. The long-term achievements of the company will result from actions that have to start this year. Table 2.3 can be used to give a powerful method for targeting annual improvement in the quality of a group of products. The form is filled in for the actual status at the end of the current year. It is then duplicated for the target status at the end of the planned year. Reassessment a year later shows whether the forecast has been achieved.

A division with a complex product range needs a method of adding up its current quality status and its annual quality improvement plans. Table 2.4 summarizes the overall product quality in terms of sales value of a hypothetical division. It shows that the percentage of the division's sales having worse than average product quality is planned to be reduced from 20 to 10 percent and the percentage that is joint best is planned to increase from 10 to 20 percent. An improvement of this magnitude—10 percent of the sales going up two classes—might represent a reasonable target for a division. Such a target is harder than it appears because the competing products are likely also to have improving quality, and unless the division's products are improved as fast, the table will show a deterioration and not an improvement. A division having a quality improvement program which met a target of this kind for five years would inevitably become the product quality leader in the market it served. Such leadership always yields sharply increased profitability and market share.

This chapter has dealt primarily with product quality, but it is clear that the form given in Table 2.3 could be extended with additional lines

TABLE 2.4. Competitor's Quality Evaluation—Annual Summary

Overall Product Quality	Current Year's Actual		Next Year's Forecast	
	Sales ($000s)	Sales (%)	Sales ($000s)	Sales (%)
Best	0	0	0	0
Joint best	4,000	10	8,800	20
Average	28,000	70	30,800	70
Worse	8,000	20	4,400	10
Not rated	0	0	0	0
Total	40,000	100	44,000	100

to cover some or all of the support quality and delivery quality subcategories defined in Table 2.2. Similarly, overall ratings could be determined for these three main categories though it would probably be impracticable in most cases to get a meaningful overall rating covering everything.

The competitors' quality evaluation, as summarized in Table 2.3, enables "quality to the customer—the first measure of quality improvement" to be determined. It provides a practical way of measuring the current quality status, of allowing the effect of planned improvement actions to be assessed, and of enabling actual progress to be compared with the plan. The results of actual measurements will be discussed in Chapter 4.

QUALITY AND VALUE

The previous discussion about the definition of quality can be logically extended to cover the meanings of "value" and "value for money." Product value is most conveniently measured in money. It is dependent on the product quality, the support quality (the quality of the various services—sales, maintenance, application engineering, etc.—that the supplier of a product usually provides to customers), and the delivery quality. Each of these three parts can be expressed in money value according to the following equation:

$$\text{Product Value (in dollars)} = (A \times \text{Product Quality}) + (B \times \text{Support Quality}) - (C \times \text{Delivery Quality}).$$

Here, dollar weighting factors (A, B, and C) have been introduced to convert product quality, support quality, and delivery quality, which are ratios (*degree* of conformance . . .), to monetary units. When we defined product quality we assumed there was a particular delivery time the customer was "willing to accept," and we ignored support quality. Here, it is indicated that support quality adds dollar value to product quality and that delivery quality slower than immediate takes away dollar value.

The value for money of a product depends on its value and its price, and can be expressed by the following equation:

$$\text{Product Value for Money} = \text{Product Value/Price}.$$

In the quality definition we assumed there was a particular price the customer was willing to pay for a product, and their objective was to get as much quality (i.e., as high a degree of conformance to their need) as possible for that price. Here, it is allowed that a customer may trade price and value; the customer may be prepared to pay a higher price for more value or may accept less value if offered a lower price. They will only buy a product with a value perceived higher than its price. If two or more competing products meet that criterion, the customer will select the one with the highest product value/price ratio.

Product value, like product quality, has no clear meaning except in terms of the needs of particular customers. As one extreme, when we say an item has only sentimental value, we mean that it has value to only one or two people. At the other extreme, when we talk about the intrinsic value of an item, we mean that it has at least that minimum value to a very large number of people; we do not mean that it has some value entirely divorced from people. Consider the car I bought some time ago. I expected to pay about $12,000. There were several cars at about that price that I considered but none of them was the car I really liked. For a Rolls Royce Silver Sprite I would have paid $20,000, for a Mercedes 280S $16,000, and for a Jaguar JTS about the same. This was their value to me. Unfortunately, their prices were much more than this. In the opposite direction there were cars in the $6000 to $8000 bracket that I might have bought if they had cost half as much. Figure 2.2 gives a graph of my value-for-money against price. The graph shows that only near to a price of $12,000 is the value-for-money ratio near unity. Away from this region the ratio drops away steeply. Of course, different customers will put different values on these cars. A few will put such a high value on a Rolls Royce that they will be prepared to pay the actual price for it. In most cases an individual customer's graph of value-for-money against price has a fairly sharp peak, and in such cases, we can assume the required price has been preestablished, in my case $12,000, and delivery, and think in terms of product quality rather than in terms of the more complicated concept of value for money.

Product quality can be expressed as a narrow vertical band on the value-for-money against price graph. The value-for-money idea gives another way of quantifying the overall product quality of a series of products offered at the same price, by asking how much a customer would pay for each one. For example, a customer offered several different cars priced $12,000 selects one. This one has a value of $12,000 and a quality of unity. How much would the price of the others need to be discounted to be the preferred purchase? For one, it might be $1000, for another $6000, and so on. The quality would then be 0.92 and 0.50 respectively.

The word "value" also occurs in the term "value engineering." Value engineering has the purpose of increasing the value of a product or de-

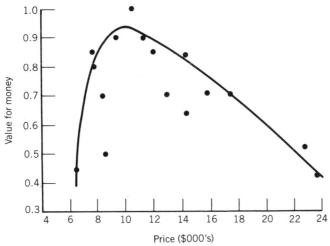

Type	Price ($)
Chevrolet Chevette	6,400
Volkswagen Golf	7,800
Chevrolet Cavalier CS	7,900
Renault Alliance LX	8,420
Ford Escort LX	8,480
Chrysler E-Type Turbo	10,600
Oldsmobile Cutlass Sierra Brougham	11,280
Oldsmobile Delta 88 Royal Brougham	11,960
Cadillac Cimarron	12,960
Ford Thunderbird Turbo Coupe	14,100
Chrysler New Yorker Turbo	14,290
Pontiac 6000 STE	15,870
Peugeot 505 STI	17,500
Mercedes Benz 190E	22,850
Cadillac Seville	23,730

Figure 2.2. Graph of value-for-money to the author against maker's price cars.

creasing its cost. In either case it can give increased value-for-money to the customer, increased profit to the supplier, or both. In practice, value engineering is not usually concerned with support quality or delivery quality, and concentrates on product quality and cost. Value engineering differs from manufacturing cost reduction, which assumes the product's design is fixed, by allowing progression up the chain of conformance. Usually, both design and manufacturing changes will be considered, but the existing product requirement specification is taken as fixed. Sometimes even further changes may be considered—by going another link up the chain of conformance and relating product changes directly to a judgment about "all of the aspects of the customer's need." If it is proposed to change a previously agreed product requirement specification, marketing must be involved and usually customers also.

Marketing people talk about "market differentiation." This term can be related to either quality or value-for-money. In terms of quality, a potential customer may have a particular need which he or she wants to satisfy by buying a product at a particular price. If the market is highly differentiated, there will be products with very different product requirement specifications to choose from, and only products with the same product requirement specification if the market is not differentiated. For example, a customer with a transportation need and a price of about $12,000 in mind will have widely different cars to choose from in the highly differentiated mid-price car market. On the other hand, the customer will find little differentiation between the various gasolines available at a particular price.

A supplier can differentiate his or her product from competing products by adding, deleting, or changing features or characteristics (while keeping the price constant so as to stay in the same market). For a $12,000 car, such changes are easy, but for gasoline they are very difficult (e.g., increasing the miles per gallon by 20 percent might affront the laws of thermodynamics and be impossible).

If the price is not constrained, a similar analysis can be made in terms of value for money instead of quality, but it is more complicated and does not add any new insights. Similarly, the discussion could be extended to cover the contribution of support quality and delivery quality to market differentiation.

CONCLUSION

In this chapter the vital necessity for a business to work on quality improvement as the only means of achieving the superiority in product quality that is essential for success has been discussed. It has been argued that an effective rate of quality improvement depends on satisfaction of four necessary conditions defined by the titles policy, honesty, priority, and capability.

One important capability is for the managers of a business to understand fundamental quality concepts—to know precisely what they mean by product quality, to know how to divide it into manageable improvement projects, and how to measure its current status and rate of improvement. The meaning of product quality was therefore defined. The definition then suggested the idea of the chain of conformance, which enables product quality to be divided into pieces each of which can be the subject of improvement projects. The definition and the chain also suggested the means by which quality to the customer can be measured—by comparing the quality of a product with the quality of competing products through a competitors' quality evaluation. The chapter concluded with a brief discussion of the logical relationship of product quality to value and value for money.

Effective measures of product quality are a vital tool for quality improvement. Quality to the customer, which is outward looking at the customers and competitors, is the first of "the two measures of quality improvement." The second—quality costs, which is mainly used to measure a unit's internal activities—will be described in Chapter 3.

CHAPTER 3

QUALITY COSTS, THE SECOND MEASURE OF QUALITY IMPROVEMENT

Americans love to coin new business jargon. Perhaps it's because they find it easier than sorting out the correct English. Perhaps it is because fame, and even immortality, can be the reward of the creator of a particularly colorful piece of jargon.

Two current pieces of American business jargon are "high-leverage" and "institutionalize." A high-leverage project or activity is one which, when compared with other projects or activities, requires relatively little effort to produce a large effect. It is analogous to the old 80-20 (20 percent of the problems cause 80 percent of the damage) or Pareto rule. To institutionalize some activity is to repeat it over and over again in a standardized way so that everyone knows how to do it. The activity soon becomes an ingrained habit, and (hopefully) no longer is any special effort required to make it happen.

American business is currently involved in both searching for high-leverage situations and trying to institutionalize good activities. The logical difficulty of institutionalizing high-leverage activities is causing some concern.

In the United States quality cost improvement has preoccupied quality professionals since Feigenbaum discussed it in his classic book, *Total Quality Control*, published in 1961 (15). In 1984 the American Society

47

for Quality Control issued a booklet (16), compiling 91 papers on quality costs which had been published in the ASQC's various journals between 1970 and 1982. Interest did not end in 1982. Since then the ASQC has published several more papers on the subject. Unfortunately, few if any of these papers describe successful systems in action or give actual statistics of real achievement. The April 1983 issue of *Quality Progress* (17), of which 35,000 copies were mailed, contained a one-page survey designed to gather information about the implementation of quality cost systems. There were only 40 replies from the United States and Canada, and five more from overseas, giving further evidence of a lack of real achievement.

One reason for this lack of success in implementation of quality cost systems is because a "high-leverage" approach has usually been used. The quality people have identified some special situation in which quality cost improvement might be particularly advantageous. The situation might concern a particular division of a multidivision company, or a certain product line or plant. With backing from senior management, the quality people persuade the accountants, as a special exercise, to measure the quality costs over a prescribed period of time. Presuming the special situation has been selected with good judgment, the quality cost to sales ratio will be high and some good quality cost improvement projects will be identified and addressed energetically. However, after some months—or at most a year—the special situation has ended, the project teams have completed their main actions, prime members send deputies to meetings which become infrequent, and the accountants stop measuring the quality costs. The hope that other divisions or plants will pick up the system by example is not realized, and soon the whole exercise is over.

In principle, a much more effective approach is to "institutionalize" the quality cost improvement system. This, however, is a task of daunting difficulty. It is hard enough to get quality cost improvement into one or two model divisions for a temporary period, but to install it as a permanent activity in every division of a company seems to verge on the impossible. However, having suceeded in institutionalizing quality cost improvement in a major company not once but twice, I affirm that it really is possible, and I think I can describe the way of doing it.

INSTITUTIONALIZING QUALITY COST IMPROVEMENT

The first example of an institutionalized quality cost improvement system concerns Standard Telephones and Cables (STC), which at one time was a subsidiary of the American multinational corporation, ITT. STC is one of the United Kingdom's principal designers and manufacturers of telecommunication and other electronic equipment. Quality cost reporting on a monthly basis commenced in all of STC's divisions in 1967. A sister ITT company, Standard Electric Lorenz, in West Germany, started at the same time, and over the next year or two the system was introduced into all of the companies of ITT Europe, which was then a $10 billion a year company manufacturing in every country of Western Europe. For the next 10 years some hundreds of ITT Europe divisions reported quality costs every month. In the later years these costs exceeded $400 million and quality cost improvement projects saved $30 to $40 million a year.

The second example concerns TRW, another multinational company, with sales of about $6 billion per annum. Quality cost reporting was started in all of TRW's 80 divisions in 1981, totaling about $400 million a year. Quality cost improvements of $30 to $40 million per year were achieved during 1982 to 1984.

How was this done? There were only four essential requirements:

A brave champion

A special event

Some simple know-how

A reasonable level of top-management support

I will now describe how it happened in STC and TRW. I was appointed company quality manager of STC in October 1966. The start of the UK's first Quality and Reliability Year was imminent and STC had no plans for it. Apart from being a missed opportunity, lack of any action was likely to cause the company embarrassment with its major customers. That was the special event. My new boss said to me, "What do you suggest we do for Q&R Year?"

I replied, "Introduce quality cost reporting and start Crosby's 14 Step Quality Improvement Program."

Crosby had just given me a copy of a first draft of his now-famous program, and the recently constituted ITT Europe Quality Council had defined a quality cost reporting procedure, but no one had actually used it.

I knew this answer would cause me great trouble. The suggestion was likely to be accepted, and then I would have to become the champion of the two programs—I did not feel at all brave. (The actual word champion was not in my mind. I met its use in such a context only many years later in the book, *In Search of Excellence* (5).)

The suggestion was accepted by my boss and the managing director of the company, and, inevitably, I was made responsible for implementation of the program. By now we had the special event, Q&R Year, the champion, me, the necessary level of top management support, and the know-how provided by the Quality Council's procedure. It was agreed that I would present the ideas at the forthcoming annual company management conference. I was young and scared, and not a practiced public speaker, but nothing terrible happened.

Then I sought out the right accountant. He was responsible for accounting systems throughout the company, and reported to the controller. He showed me how to write a controller's procedure and together we did so. He suggested we should make quality costs a quarterly report instead of a monthly report. That seemed rational. Quality costs do not change all that rapidly, and he said that it would save the divisional controllers, who were already greatly overworked, a substantial amount of effort. I had never asked a senior accountant for anything before in my life and was surprised that he was taking my request so seriously. However, I felt intuitively that, as most of the financial system was on monthly reporting, a quarterly measure would always be a low-prestige bother (it would never become institutionalized, in the term I heard for the first time many years later). So, I kept my nerve, dug my heels in, and got away with monthly reporting.

I used the Q&R Year and the annual accounting cycle to create an aura of urgency. We circulated the draft controller's procedure to the division quality managers and controllers and quickly incorporated their comments. Most of them felt it was not serious and that it would not really happen.

Early in December the controller's procedure was signed-off. People had been surprised to find that they could not think of any good reason for disapproving it. No one had stood up and shouted "nonsense!" during my presentation at the conference. The division people had their chance to table rational objections, and these were taken into account. My colleague in accounting devoted so much personal effort that he was becoming a champion himself.

Suddenly, it was no longer an academic exercise, and amazingly at the end of February most of the required reports for January 1967 came in (January is a quiet month for accountants). The delinquents were a minority and were exposed to the pressures that minorities suffer, and soon came into line.

I nursed the fledgling system for three years, and after I went to Brussels as director quality ITT Europe (ITTE) in 1969, I championed the system throughout Europe for the next 11 years. The quality cost reporting procedure that we had developed and used in Europe from 1965 to 1967 was issued as an ITT Comptroller's Procedure of worldwide application in October 1967.

At the end of 1980 I joined TRW in the newly established position of vice president, quality. TRW has a strong tradition of decentralization, and the decision to give a new thrust of centralized leadership in the quality area was one expression of a major policy decision to make quality one of "four priority projects" for the company in the 1980s. For a foreigner to immigrate into the United States is a complicated business of long duration, so I had to spend my first few months working with TRW's European operations, and I did not reach the company headquarters in Cleveland until March 1981.

The already existing company quality steering committee had started an investigation of quality costs, and there was a certain level of interest. The combination of this, the four priority projects, and my own appointment created the special event, and once again I became the champion. Contact had already been established with the appropriate accountant. His name is Bill Hamilton. I immediately felt comfortable with him, and later his successor, Tom Connell. I suggested we should draft a "standard practice instruction" for the accountants, and in a few days, we did.

I tabled the draft at the quality steering committee and immediately there were strong objections. The representatives of the sectors did not want a centralized procedure—every division should be free to have its own system. Some of them were already doing quality cost reporting in their own way. Why should they change? For a company whose product range extends from spacecraft (in 1983 TRW's Pioneer 10 passed Neptune and left the solar system still transmitting data 11 years after its launch) to car engine valves and electronic resistors, this seemed very reasonable. However, I was no longer a young man. I expected to retire in 10 or 15 years, and I felt it would take at least that long for 80 divisions each to develop and implement their own system. Through many battles I persisted with the centralized system.

We circulated the draft to the divisional quality and accounting people, and instantaneously incorporated their comments (11 drafts in two months). As with STC, I think that most of them felt it was not serious and that it would not really happen.

Then I had a stroke of luck. Bill Hamilton told me he would be conducting a series of training programs for divisional controllers on inflation-adjusted accounting. Would I like to tack on a session on quality cost reporting? I jumped at the chance. In the next couple of months I taught some 300 accountants the principles of quality cost reporting in sessions in Cleveland, Los Angeles, Chicago, London, and Frankfurt. I exploited the "priority-project" theme without shame, and once again built up an aura of urgency. If we could install the system in the fourth quarter of 1981, then 1981 would be the shake-down year and we would get a good lead-in to 1982. If we delayed, a year would be lost.

By July the standard practice instruction was ready for approval. I signed it and asked the controller to do so also. Once again, by now there was no rational reason not to. All of the divisional comments had been taken into account. The accountants had been trained and no one had said the system was not practical. The controller suggested the president's opinion should be determined. Of course, he gave full support. If he had felt the approach was wrong he would have reined me in long before. In fact, TRW made available far more top management support than the necessary minimum provided by STC in 1966.

The instruction went out. To the surprise of many people it was really happening, and in the middle of November 1981—with credit due the professionalism of TRW accountants—the quality cost results for October came in from 68 TRW divisions.

Since then my director quality, Tom Hughes, and I have nursed the system, and together with the controllers and quality steering committee, have progressively strengthened it. It is essential to continue this. In 1981 the reporting started. In 1982 every division had to forecast its quality costs for the year and total its quality cost improvement projects. Then in 1983 we refined the forecast to include reporting of actual 1982 results. Also in 1983 every group vice president presented the quality costs of each of his divisions to the company's large management meetings. In 1984 most divisions identified and described their quality cost improvement projects as part of the forecast package, and the internal auditors are auditing the system.

From the beginning in 1967 through 1984 the three companies where I was the principal quality professional, STC, ITT, and TRW, measured quality costs, month by month and division by division. Over that 18 year period, the total came to about $15 billion (1985 dollars). Throughout that period it was essential that I be the champion of the system—continually motivating general managers, quality managers, accountants, and other people by a variety of methods—if the whole quality cost improvement program was to succeed. Although I have indicated the importance of a champion, it must be emphasized that the quality cost improvements, which are the real product of the whole system, are achieved by the operating people at the plant and division level, and the majority of credit for a successful system is due them.

WHAT ARE QUALITY COSTS?

In his book, *Total Quality Control*, Feigenbaum (15) listed a number of categories of costs incurred while manufacturing products—quality planning, scrap, rework, inspection, test, and so on—and called them quality costs. He divided them into four distinct groups: prevention, appraisal, and internal and external failure. The ASQC published a booklet in 1967 entitled *Quality Costs—What and How* (18), which followed the same pattern and extended the list of subcategories to 37. Neither Feigenbaum nor the ASQC gave a general definition for quality costs—they simply listed various cost categories and arbitrarily defined them as quality costs. Examination of these categories reveals that they are all costs associated either directly or indirectly with making defective products. A general definition of quality costs is "costs resulting from making defective products" (19). Quality cost is an unsatisfactory name for this definition and the commonly used "cost of quality" is even worse. The costs included in the definition are not the positive costs of achieving superior quality but rather the negative costs of doing things incorrectly. They are "unquality" costs. However, the name "quality cost" is so ubiquitous that it is not practicable to change it, but it is important to remember what it really means and not be misled by the apparent meaning.

In order to make the definition of quality costs more precise it is useful to consider products manufactured and sold by a particular division. Because the products might be defective they must be inspected and tested. This results in appraisal costs for the division. Products may also fail a test or inspection, or may fail in the hands of customers. Failure costs are then incurred by the division which must rework or replace the failed product during manufacturing, or replace or repair the product for customers, for example, under warranty. The division will also incur prevention costs which are supposed to reduce the failure and appraisal costs of current products and those under development.

The division's actual costs for manufacturing and selling products are higher than if its products did not fail inspections or tests during manufacture and did not fail during customer use. The costs would be even lower if there was no possibility that the products would fail so that no inspection or test was needed, and no preventive activities were required. These concepts may be expressed as:

Actual cost = No failure cost + appraisal cost + failure cost + prevention cost.

The "no failure cost" is the cost of manufacturing and selling products if there is no possibility of failure. Quality cost is then given by the relation:

$$\text{Quality cost} = \text{Actual cost} - \text{no failure cost}.$$

(By combining the two equations we obtain the familiar relation: Quality cost = Appraisal cost + failure cost + prevention cost.) Quality cost is defined specifically as follows:

> The quality cost of a division is the difference between the actual cost to the division of manufacturing and selling products and the cost to the division if there was no failure of the products during manufacturing or use, and no possibility of failure.

The definition provides a general rule for deciding whether or not any particular cost should be categorized as a quality cost. However, the main use of the definition is during the establishment of a quality cost reporting procedure. The latter defines detailed quality cost categories and these become the controlling rule rather than the general definition (though the general definition may be useful later in deciding marginal cases or if new categories are to be added to the procedure). The three main categories of quality costs can be defined as follows:

> The appraisal costs of a division are the costs of inspecting and testing purchased items and products during manufacturing because of the possibility of their failure.

> The failure costs of a division are the costs resulting from the actual failure of products during manufacture or use.

> The prevention costs of a division are the costs incurred in trying to reduce appraisal and failure costs.

Table 3.1 shows a tabulation of TRW's quality costs for 1983. It is the sum of the reported quality costs, year-to-date, for December 1983, of 80 TRW divisions. (The actual reports also included the results for the month of December, and were the last of a series of 12 reports for each of the months of the year.) The quality costs are divided between the three conventional categories of prevention, appraisal, and failure. Appraisal has three subcategories covering the inspection and test of purchased items and during manufacturing. (The discussion is clearer by starting with the appraisal category rather than the prevention category.) The first two of these cover the costs of the inspectors and testers—their wages, salaries, and extra compensation costs (holidays, taxes, pensions, etc.),

TABLE 3.1. TRW's Quality Costs for 1983

	Quality Costs ($000's)	As a Percent of Sales	MAC[a]
Test and inspection planning costs	32,040		
Quality department prevention costs	26,479		
Qualification test costs	18,626		
Total Prevention Costs	77,145	1.37	3.33
Incoming and source inspection and test costs	21,681		
In process and final inspection and test costs	127,740		
Test and inspection equipment costs	29,730		
Total Appraisal Costs	179,151	3.19	7.73
Rework costs	55,272		
Scrap costs: gross	93,118		
salvage value	(9,288)		
External failure costs	13,577		
Total Failure Costs	152,679	2.71	6.58
Total quality costs	408,975	7.27	17.64

[a] Manufacturing added cost.

and other personally related costs. The costs are the same irrespective of whether the inspectors and testers are categorized as direct or indirect for standard cost purposes. This is an important practical point which prevents double booking of costs, and wide variation in the recorded cost of an inspector or tester from one division to another. The cost is usually compensation cost plus about 50 percent. The cost of any person whose main job is inspection or test of purchased or manufactured items is included. It makes no difference whether he or she works for the quality, manufacturing, purchasing, or any other department. Also included are the costs of supervisors and support personnel, for example, clerks. This measures the total cost of inspection and test better than putting these costs in some other category. A point of difficulty occurs when the costs of inspections or tests are done as a part-time activity by people engaged mainly in another activity, for example, gauging done by a machine operator for process control purposes. The accurate measurement of such costs is very expensive, and to estimate instead of accurately measuring them yields no benefit for quality cost improvement purposes. In practice, it is probably best to exclude such costs from the quality cost reporting.

The third subcategory in appraisal deals with the cost of the test and inspection equipment used by the people whose costs are reported in the first two categories (plus any part-time appraisal activities discussed previously). The depreciation costs of capitalized equipment are used and the actual costs of noncapitalized equipment. Also included is the cost of the calibration and maintenance of this equipment. Despite the increasing use of expensive automatic test equipment, hardware costs remain relatively low compared with people costs. Appraisal costs are always a major part of the total quality costs and their measurement is mainly a matter of keeping track of the costs of inspectors and testers.

Failure costs include two categories of internal failure costs: rework and scrap. Full manufacturing burden is included for both of these. This might be inconsistent with the position for appraisal costs, but in practice it is the simplest way, and it does not create those problems discussed previously for appraisal costs. Good internal recording procedures are needed for these two categories. For appraisal costs some estimations may be acceptable provided the inspection and test manpower is tracked carefully. This is not true for failure costs, with rework, in particular, often seriously underreported. Scrap costs are divided into two parts: the gross scrap and the salvage value of scrap that is sold. The latter is a negative item reducing the quality cost total and is included because it is logical to do so, and to prevent the allegation (which is sometimes made) that the quality costs are being overstated for political reasons. For both scrap and rework the actual cost must be measured, not the variance from some standard. Companies that supply to government agencies are usually tightly controlled by the customer and often utilize a "material review board" (MRB) to document decisions about the disposition of products which have failed tests or inspections—can they be used as is, be reworked, or must they be scrapped? Clearly MRB costs result from defective products and are therefore quality costs, but they are not usually large enough to justify a special category of their own. They are best included in the rework costs.

The last failure subcategory covers the costs to the division resulting from failure of the product after it has been handed over to customers. This category is especially important because such failures not only cost the division money, but also directly impact the customer's perception of the division's product quality in a way that internal failures do not. External failure costs should be recorded at the time when they are borne by the division even if this is long after the failed product was manufactured. Again, actual costs are reported, not costs of reserves, insurance, and so on.

The discussion of prevention costs has been held until the end because they are the most difficult costs to deal with. How are appraisal and failure costs prevented? How do we prevent defective products from being made? Using the chain of conformance, the simple answer is with marketing, design-development, purchasing, and manufacturing people doing their jobs properly. It seems a false idea that these departments have "normal" activities which lead to the production of defective products, and they, or the quality department, have some additional special "prevention" activities, whose performance results in nondefective products. Accepting this idea as false, what proportion of the total costs of these departments should go into prevention? In practice, there is no answer to this question. What actually happens is that an arbitrary set of activities are called prevention activities and their costs are included in the quality costs. Typical activities include quality management, quality assurance, quality engineering, training, motivation programs, statistical quality control, and so on. Some of these activities have little direct effect on defect prevention, and in total may well have less effect on quality than the work of the design-development, purchasing, and manufacturing departments. Again, it is important to remember the cost items that are actually put in the prevention category rather than being misled by the name. Table 3.1 shows that TRW only includes the costs of three very specific activities. The first is the planning of inspection and test (as will be discussed in Chapter 8) whoever it is done by. The second covers the quality engineering and assurance activities of people in the *quality department.* (This is the only place that organization affects the quality costs: in all other categories a particular type of activity either does or does not incur a quality cost, irrespective of which department the person performing the activity belongs.) The third covers the costs of the formal qualification of new products. This is an extremely important quality assurance activity that is omitted all too often and its inclusion in the prevention costs is one way of emphasizing it.

It is often argued (e.g., by Feigenbaum (15)) that the balance of quality costs in many companies is wrong—too much being spent on appraisal and failure and not enough spent on prevention. Analyses of reported quality costs are made to support this argument. The general proposition that there is too much emphasis put on appraisal and failure *activities,* and not enough on prevention is usually correct. However, because of the difficulty of defining and measuring the costs of prevention, quantitative analyses of quality costs are usually unproductive for this purpose.

In retrospect, it would probably have been better if the name prevention had not been used by TRW in the quality cost context. Of the three subcategories in the prevention category, inspection and test planning could have been transferred to the appraisal category, and the other two subcategories could have been placed in a new category called "quality assurance," which more accurately defines them.

THE IMPORTANCE OF QUALITY COSTS

For a company that is divided into a number of separate divisions for management control, the purposes of quality cost measurement can be listed as follows:

1. To enable the division's managers to know the size of their quality cost opportunity so that they can apply appropriate resources for its realization
2. To show broadly where the opportunity is, for example, in inspection or in warranty, so that the division's managers can concentrate effort effectively
3. To enable the division's managers to set targets for quality cost reduction and plan actions that meet the targets
4. To enable progress towards meeting the targets to be measured
5. To enable company management to help division management set ambitious targets and assist in their achievement

Four of the five purposes exclusively concern the operating divisions. Only the fifth involves the superstructure of the company, and then in terms of helping the operating divisions. It cannot be overemphasized that the purpose of quality cost reporting is to be a tool of quality cost improvement—and this can take place only in the operating divisions. Quality costs are not needed to satisfy legal accounting requirements, pay taxes, or declare dividends (though some astute financial analysts are starting to take an interest in them). It is therefore a complete waste of effort for a division to measure its quality costs in order to comply with a company policy—with the thought that someone on company staff is doing something very important with them—while ignoring their improvement use. Unfortunately, I have known cases where the divisional accountants regularly submitted quality cost reports to headquarters, but none of the division's operating managers, including the quality manager, took any interest in them.

Quality costs are measured in $000's (thousands of dollars), but to understand their importance it is necessary to express them in the form of an index, and the most commonly used index is the ratio of quality cost to sales. Reported values of this ratio vary from 2 to 20 percent. Very low ratios are usually a result of inefficient gathering of the quality costs or low added value so a typical number might be 10 percent. Any cost that is as much as 10 percent of the total sales merits careful control—quality costs merit control more than other costs of similar size.

Figure 3.1 shows how the sales value of a typical manufactured product is used. Thirty-five percent pays for purchased materials, components, subassemblies, and so on; 35 percent is added manufacturing cost (labor and overhead); and 30 percent is gross margin for research and development costs, marketing costs, administrative and general costs, interest costs, profit, and so on. The quality cost categories defined in Table 3.1 were mainly applicable to the 35 percent of the sales value added in manufacturing. (The extension of quality cost reporting outside of manufacturing will be discussed in a later section.) In Table 3.1 only three of the quality cost subcategories—qualification test, incoming and source inspection, and external failure—cover activities outside of manufacturing, and comprise only 13 percent of the total. Because the quality costs as defined are concentrated in manufacturing it is very useful to use the manufacturing added cost (MAC) as another base, like sales, to which

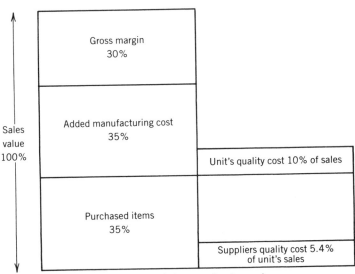

Figure 3.1. Breakdown of sales value.

quality costs can be related. In our example, the *total* quality costs are 29 percent of MAC (10 percent divided by 35 percent). The *manufacturing-related* quality costs are about 25 percent of MAC. A "normal" quality cost to sales ratio of 10 percent can indicate that a quarter of the value added in manufacturing is spent on quality costs. The largeness of this proportion is the first reason why quality costs are more important than might initially seem apparent.

The second reason is a consequence of the fact that the suppliers of the division's purchased items have quality costs, even though these are not measurable by the division, and are not therefore included in the division's quality cost to sales ratio. However, the division inevitably pays for these quality costs, like all of the costs of its suppliers, in the prices it pays for its purchases. By making the reasonable assumption that the suppliers' quality cost performance is the same as the division's the magnitude of these quality costs can be estimated as follows:

> Assume the division's suppliers have the same breakdown between purchased items, MAC, and gross margin as the division, and the same quality cost to sales ratio of 10 percent. Assume the same principles apply to the suppliers' suppliers, and so on. Then the suppliers' sales are 35 percent of the division's sales and its quality costs are 35 percent of the division's quality costs, that is, 3.5 percent of the division's sales. The suppliers' suppliers have 35 percent of that, that is, 1.2 percent. The next three terms in the series are 0.43, 0.15, and 0.05 percent, and the sum of the whole series is 5.4 percent.

By adding in the estimate of its suppliers' quality costs, the division's 10 percent quality cost to sales ratio is increased to 15.4 percent.

It must be emphasized that the quality cost ratios of 25 percent of manufacturing added cost and 15 percent of sales are "hard" numbers. They are derived from an arbitrary, round number base of 10 percent of sales, but the measured average of TRW's 80 divisions over several years has been about 8 percent of sales, and ITT Europe measured a similar average for its 100 or more divisions. TRW's accounting rules are conservative, preventing any over-statement of the numbers, for example, inspection and test costs do not include full manufacturing overhead, and net scrap cost (allowing salvage value) is used not gross scrap cost. No cost estimates are included for the cost of carrying extra inventory because of scrap and rework, and the costs of the disruption and delay caused by quality-cost-causing activities are similarly excluded. Also, no attempt has been made to include the quality costs of activities remote from manufacturing—accounting, sales, design-development, and so on.

What about the last part of the sales value (see Figure 3.1), the gross margin (and the suppliers' gross margin)? Well, in the limited way that we have defined quality costs—concentrating on manufacturing activities—there are no quality costs, other than warranty, in the gross margin. The suppliers have quality costs, according to our definition, because they perform manufacturing operations. However, one could extend the definition of quality costs to cover the costs of activities within the gross margin that were not done right the first time. If their density was say half of that in manufacturing—12 percent not 25 percent—this would add another 3.6 percent to the quality cost to sales ratio, bringing it up to 19 percent. However, it is emphasized that this number requires a change in the definition of quality costs.

Any set of activities whose cost is 15 percent of sales or 25 percent of added manufacturing cost is obviously of great importance to a business. However, the importance of quality costs is even greater than the magnitude of the numbers indicates. This is because virtually all of the activities whose costs are measured as quality costs are unnecessary. Quality costs are *defined* as the costs of a set of activities associated with doing things incorrectly. This is obvious for scrap and rework. If products are made right the first time there is no scrap and rework. It requires only a small extension of thinking to apply the same ideas to external failure costs (remembering that we are including only hard costs to the supplying division, like warranty, not intangible costs or costs to the customer). What about inspection and test? Aren't these necessary to prove that the product is right? In a later chapter it will be shown that most inspection and testing is done to identify defective items and pinpoint the actual defects for determining whether the product must be scrapped, or how it can be reworked. If the product is not defective this inspection and test is not needed: if there is high confidence that the product has been made correctly then further inspection and testing is unnecessary. These ideas, though apparently good in principle, might not be so in practice. However, I have seen the reality in tramping around hundreds of manufacturing plants. Often, I have examined a machine and process that is fully capable of meeting the design tolerances and that is held under statistical control (see Chapters 5 and 9). It produces no defective product and there is no scrap or rework. The only inspection or test is the small amount needed for process control purposes. More often, I have seen machines and processes that are incapable, uncontrolled, or both. The resultant product of such processes has a defective level that customers would not tolerate. So, it has to be tested or inspected 100 percent every item, with the defective pieces being scrapped or reworked. Sometimes, just by walking a few yards, I have gone from a process having a high quality cost level to another with virtually none. Every time a machine is made capable and brought under control, and the now unnecessary screening and defect identification inspection and test is eliminated, the quality cost is virtually wiped out. It is not reduced by 10 or 20 percent but in fact is reduced by 80, 90, or an even higher percent.

All that is left for consideration are prevention costs. In this book a very restricted position has been taken on these costs. As we have defined and measured them, the inspection and test planning and quality assurance activities could be eliminated also by making products defect-free the first time, and knowing this was being done. In total, a small quality cost remains if products are confidently manufactured correctly the first time.

Because of the way they are defined, quality costs are different from other costs. Consider, for example, the costs of purchased supplies. In Figure 3.1 they are shown as 35 percent of the sales value, which is more than twice as much as the quality costs. The opportunity for cost reduction in purchased supplies is extremely important, but in magnitude it is not twice that available from quality costs, because, even in theory, the cost of purchased supplies cannot be reduced to zero.* In purchasing, cost reductions come two ways. The first is to pay less for the same items. In this way expert purchasing can pay a few percent less than the market price. Unfortunately, the negotiation for every new contract starts at the market price and the same expertise is needed to save the same few percent. The second way is for purchasing to work with engineering to substitute lower cost materials. These cost savings, like quality cost savings, continue while the particular product is being manufactured. However, the net effect of both methods is likely to be 10 percent of the purchasing cost. Purchased items *have* to be bought: there is no possible way of making cost savings of 80 or 90 percent. The same considerations apply to many other major costs. To sell products salespeople have to be employed; to develop new products requires product engineers; to manufacture products requires machines and operators. Important improvements in productivity can be made in all of these areas, but they are all essential activities and their costs cannot approach zero. Quality costs are different: because of the way they are defined they *can* approach zero. For this reason quality costs measure activities which are particularly fruitful for cost improvement.

---

* Manufacturing all the currently purchased items would be a cost transfer and not a real cost saving.

Because the largest category of quality costs in many divisions is appraisal it is sometimes suggested that quality costs may be reduced by arbitrarily cutting inspection and test. In this way an improvement in quality cost is exchanged for a deterioration in quality-to-the-customer. However, the art of quality improvement is to improve quality-to-the-customer with no deterioration in quality cost, or to improve quality cost with no deterioration in quality-to-the-customer. In fact, the most useful quality improvement projects—those that involve defect prevention, making products right the first time, and improving the efficiency and effectiveness of inspection and test—improve both measures of quality. Intuitively, it seems likely that the quality of products made right the first time will be better than that of products some of which were initially made defectively and then most of the bad ones were identified by a screening inspection or test, and most of those were then put right. In a later chapter it will be shown that this is a correct intuition. Another reason then for the importance of quality cost improvement is that it does correlate loosely with improvement in quality-to-the-customer. As an operation is improved and brought under control, the quality costs give an immediate internal measure of success. The same improvements will show up later in the customers' recognition of improved product quality.

A point of controversy concerns the costs of inspections and tests which are contractually specified by a customer and paid for by the customer (and which are presumably a source of profit to the division). Should the cost of these inspections and tests be included in the quality costs? My answer is, yes, for the following reasons. The cost of these inspections and tests can be reduced in two ways. First, the efficiency of the methods of doing them can be improved, for example, by replacing a manual test with an automatic test. Second, by using defect prevention activities making the product right the first time, the need for some of the tests and inspections may be eliminated. Customer approval for the first group of cost reductions should be obtained fairly easily. Approval for the second is likely to present greater difficulty. Nonetheless, with persistence it should be possible to get agreement for elimination of tests that really are unnecessary—but this is of no advantage to the vendor some people believe. The test is removed, but the price of the product is immediately reduced and the vendor gets the same, or even less, profit. However, in this regard, eliminating customer mandated tests is no different than eliminating any other unnecessary test. Who profits from a cost reduction always depends on competitive position. If a vendor achieves a cost reduction, the competitive position may push the price down. Then, a competitor who has not achieved the cost reduction must take a loss of profit from the reduced price. Cost reduction is not used to increase profits—if this was true, all profits would steadily increase—but rather is used to maintain and improve competitive position. A vendor who shows a customer that their product quality has improved in a way that makes a mandatory test unnecessary has improved their competitive position. For those reasons, therefore, the costs of customer mandated tests and inspections should not be excluded from the quality costs. They differ from other inspections and tests only in that the customer's agreement is needed before proposed improvements are implemented.

QUALITY COST BUDGETING AND IMPROVEMENT

In this chapter it has been repeatedly emphasized that measuring and reporting quality costs is a useful tool only for quality cost improvement. However, reported quality costs deal with events that have already happened. They describe past events which cannot be changed (rewriting history does not change what actually happened). The measured quality costs of the past are useful only in so far as they influence actions of the present and into the future which can lead to improved product quality or reduced costs. A division will realize its full potential for quality cost improvement only if it has a formal program with this purpose. Quality improvement never just happens; it must be planned and managed.

A key planning method is to prepare a financial budget or forecast that states what the quality costs should be for the coming year. At the same time, specific quality cost improvement projects are listed. The achievement of the budget depends upon implementation of these projects.

The simplest way to prepare such a budget is to address the quality costs directly. If the measured quality costs for a particular division were $1 million in 1983, management might require an aggressive improvement of 10 percent, giving a budget of $900,000 for 1984. When I first budgeted quality costs at the start of 1968, it was immediately apparent that this was not a good method. My company was in a period of rapid expansion, and it was clear that for many of its divisions quality cost increases resulting from planned production volume increases would more than offset the effects of quality improvement projects. A division with quality costs of $1 million in 1967 and planning a volume increase of 15 percent for 1968 (if it had no quality cost improvement program) might expect quality costs of $1.10 to $1.15 million. As most quality costs—inspection, test, scrap, rework, and so on—are variable costs, not fixed, the quality cost would most likely be near the upper end of the range, say $1.14 million. An aggressive improvement program saving $114,000 would bring the quality costs down to $1.026 million, giving a large adverse variance against the $900,000 budget. It did not seem sensible to set up a system which would doom most divisions into missing their quality cost budgets, and would make the company's quality cost improvement program appear to fail.

The solution was to place the requirement, not on reducing the absolute value of the quality costs, but on reducing the quality cost to sales ratio. If a division's quality cost to sales ratio decreased compared with the previous (base) year, this would be deemed to indicate an improvement even if the absolute value of the quality cost increased. I developed a formula (20), expressing the improvement in money terms as follows:

$$\text{Quality cost savings in budgeted year (\$)} =$$

$$\left[\left(\frac{\text{quality cost}}{\text{sales}} \right)_{\substack{\text{base} \\ \text{year}}} - \left(\frac{\text{quality cost}}{\text{sales}} \right)_{\substack{\text{budgeted} \\ \text{year}}} \right] \times \left[\text{sales} \right]_{\substack{\text{budgeted} \\ \text{year}}}$$

Table 3.2 shows how this works for my example. The sales volume increases from $10 to $11.5 million. The base year quality cost of $1 million yields a quality cost to sales ratio of 10 percent. If there were no improvements, but only the effect of fixed and variable costs, the quality costs would be $1.14 million in the budgeted year. The implementation of improvement projects to save 10 percent of this saves a total of $114,-000. The quality cost is therefore $1.026 million or $8.9 percent of sales. Applying the formula for calculating the cost saving in money indicates a savings of $126,000. With the new method of budgeting the $114,000 of improvement projects (which would be a good achievement) enables the 9 percent quality cost to sales budget to be exceeded by 0.1 percent and, at the end of the year, management can be told $126,000 has been saved

TABLE 3.2. Quality Cost to Sales Method of Budgeting Improvement

	Base Year (1967)	Budgeted Year (1968)
Sales volume	$10 million	$11.5 million
Quality cost	$1 million	
Quality cost/sales	10%	
Quality cost (no improvement)		$1.14 million
Improvement projects		$114,000
Quality cost		$1.026 million
Quality cost/sales		8.9%
Quality cost savings in 1968 = (10% − 8.9%) × $11.5 million = $126,500		

(taking advantage of the fixed to variable cost ratio). That seemed to be a much better system—good performance would be rewarded by exceeding budget rather than be punished by missing it horribly. I have introduced the idea of quality cost improvement projects to clarify the theoretical basis of the system, but the definition and tracking of such projects was not, in practice, well developed in 1968. Another refinement that could have been applied with advantage at that time, but was not, is the use of the quality cost to MAC ratio in preference to the quality cost to sales ratio.

The quality cost to sales method of budgeting quality costs was used successfully by STC and ITT Europe for six years from 1968 to 1973. However, there was the Organization of Petroleum Exporting Countries oil crisis and by 1974 the companies of ITT in Europe were no longer in a period of expansion—some of them actually had decreasing sales. The "fixed" part of the quality costs was deteriorating the quality cost to sales ratio, partially, or even totally, offsetting the effect of real improvements. The apparent advantage enjoyed in the days of expansion changed to a serious disadvantage, with the whole system breaking down. Consequently, in early 1974 a new methodology was developed and incorporated into the business planning requirements that ITTE placed on the companies for which it was responsible.

The new method of quality cost budgeting has been refined in detail in the years since 1974. Its current state of evolution as used by TRW is indicated in Table 3.3. This table was prepared in early 1984 by summing the figures from similar tables for each of 80 TRW divisions. Each division was required to analyze its actual quality costs for 1983 and to forecast its quality costs for 1984. The method examines the *changes* in the

TABLE 3.3. TRW'S 1984 Quality Cost Forecast

	1983 Actual $ Millions	1984 Forecast $ Millions
Initial quality cost	427	409
Effect of changes in reporting	2.1	26.4
Effect of production volume or mix changes	11.7	36.5
Effect of compensation rate changes	10	11.5
Effect of other similar changes	(4.4)	3.7
Expected quality cost without improvement or deterioration	436	487
Effect of quality cost improvement projects	(30)	(38)
Effect of quality deteriorations	3.0	0
1983 Actual and 1984 Forecast Quality Cost	409	449

quality costs from one year to the next. These changes are in two categories. The most important changes are reductions in quality costs due to
quality cost improvement projects (mainly specific projects, but also general improvements). The second category covers changes due to other
reasons. Five such reasons are separately identified:

1. Measurement changes—changes in the reported numbers which
    do not indicate real increases or decreases; examples are extension
    of the reporting system to a new area (which had quality costs in
    the previous year but which were not reported) and rectification of
    incorrect accounting in the previous year.
2. Increases or decreases in manufacturing volume or changes of
    product mix.
3. Increases in compensation (wages, salaries, and fringe benefits).
4. All other similar changes, such as those due to material price in-
    creases (which increase scrap costs) or resulting from deliberate
    changes to improve quality-to-the-customer (e.g., extra testing).
5. Quality cost increases due to real quality deteriorations (e.g., costs
    due to letting an existing process go out of control). Such changes
    are applicable mainly to the actual results, not the forecast.

When keeping track of quality cost improvement projects it is very
useful for each project to be defined on a standardized form. There are
many different ways of doing this. Table 3.4 shows a method that was introduced by M. Ryan when he was director quality of the automotive
worldwide sector of TRW.

The starting date for a quality cost improvement project affects the
quality cost forecast. A project which will save, for example, $10,000 in a
full year, will produce only a $5000 change in the quality costs for the
forecasted year compared to the previous year if it is not implemented
until July 1 of the forecasted year. However, a year later the same project
can go into the next forecast as a "carry-over" project worth another
$5000.

In this brief section, the various methods of budgeting quality costs
have been discussed. Most of the companies that measure and report
quality costs do not budget their quality costs. They thereby miss a vital
part of the whole quality cost system. It may not be overstating the position to say that a quality cost system that lacks formal budgeting—and a
consequential strong emphasis on planned quality cost improvement
projects—may be of little value. It is budgeting and project planning that

TABLE 3.4. Quality Cost Improvement Project Form

Plant XYZ   Forecast 84-2   New × Carryover Project
Problem/opportunity High scrap and rework costs. Scrap is 3.2 percent of cost of goods manufactured and sort and rework cost is 0.4 percent.
Cause Machines are not controlled to limits of process capability. They are adjusted only after they have produced parts outside of drawing tolerances.
Interim action Establish statistical process control on all processes. Correct unstable processes. Then control to process capability limits.
   Planned result—cost of sort, scrap and rework reduced by $1020 per month.
   Effective date—January 1984
Long-range action Continue interim action.
   Planned result—Cost of sort, scrap and rework reduced by $8040 per month.
   Effective date—July 1984
Verification of cause Nonconformant items are produced, inspected, sorted, scrapped and reworked.
Verification of success of actions Processes controlled with SPC produced 50 percent less scrap.
Interim outlook 70 percent probability of reducing scrap and rework costs by 10 percent.
Long-range outlook 90 percent probability of reducing scrap and rework costs by 20 percent.

	Cost of Planned Action $	Quality Cost Improvement Annualized $	First Year $
Interim	8,000	12,240	12,240
Long range	1,275	96,480	48,240
Total	9,275	108,720	60,480

changes the quality cost system from one directed at the past (which cannot be changed) to one directed to the future (with the objective of making it more profitable than the present).

QUALITY COSTS OUTSIDE OF MANUFACTURING

In the 1960s quality costs were defined intuitively for product manufacturing. They were divided into failure costs (typically scrap and rework), appraisal costs (typically incoming, in-process, and final inspection and test), and prevention costs (typically inspection and test planning, quality engineering, and quality assurance). Quality costs were measured for a defined manufacturing unit, for example, a plant or division. In the 1970s quality costs were redefined as costs resultant from defective products.

The scope was still limited to the manufacturing activities of a defined unit, plus some activities peripheral to manufacturing. It was argued that if products were manufactured right the first time, and moreover that this was known, some costs could be eliminated. The difference between the actual cost and this idealized right the first time cost is the quality cost.

Expanding on this idea, if products were correctly manufactured the first time using components and materials that were not defective, most scrap and rework would be eliminated. If the product design was right, the rest of the scrap and rework would not occur and the product would conform to its specified requirements in the customers' hands so that customer originated failure costs would also be eliminated. The elimination of scrap and rework would eliminate the need for much inspection and test. If, in addition, *it was known* that the product was made right the first time the rest of the inspection and test and other quality assurance activities would be unnecessary. Also, elimination of inspection and testing removes the need for inspection and test planning.

An important question to ask at this point is: How do we know that a product has not been manufactured right the first time? The answer: We do not know until it fails. There will be a moment in time when an item fails (i.e., when someone knows that it does not conform to its requirements). The failure can be in the customer's hands and he or she can be the person who observes the failure. Alternatively, the failure can occur at any one of the inspections, and tests from incoming, through in-process to final. Most quality cost reduction concerns "defect prevention"—preventing defects that cause failures. (These concepts are discussed more thoroughly in Chapter 8.)

It is apparent that this concept of quality cost—the difference between actual cost and idealized right the first time cost—embraces virtually all of the types of costs that were intuitively defined as quality costs for product manufacturing in the 1960s. However, the generalized definition allows the scope of quality cost measurement to be extended into areas of business other than manufacturing. Quality cost measurement and reporting is a tool for cost reduction and quality improvement. When extending the scope beyond product manufacturing, cost reduction and quality improvement must always be emphasized.

It is not useful to extend the scope of quality cost measurement to all of the activities of a defined unit. Rather, one or more areas should be identified, which may have a high concentration of costs caused by not doing things right the first time. Ideally, there should be clear cut failures, or it should be possible to introduce cost-effective inspections or tests to identify the result of doing things wrongly. Practical and useful quality cost improvement systems can be realized most easily for areas of the business which are subjected to inspection or test (even if they are called something different). The costs should also be measurable without too much difficulty, and should be open to improvement (hopefully to approach zero). Examples of such areas are computer software development, engineering projects, and accounting (a surprisingly high proportion of the total financial accounting effort is spent on various kinds of formal and informal audits—which is another name for inspection).

Having identified a likely area, the costs in the area resulting from not performing right the first time should be identified and placed in a small number of categories, which are then clearly defined. The sum of the costs in these defined categories then becomes the practical definition of the quality costs of the area. The categories should be selected in a way that helps the identification, assignment of responsibility, planning, and progressing of quality cost improvement projects.

Quality costs are usually expressed as one or two indices. The TRW standard practice instruction uses the quality cost to sales ratio, and, because of its concentration on manufacturing, the quality cost to MAC ratio. For another business area, the quality cost to sales ratio should be retained (expressing the importance of quality costs to the total business) but the MAC base should be replaced by another more appropriate base, for example, if the quality costs were being measured during development of computer software an appropriate base might be the software development cost.

In principle, as well as extending quality cost reporting beyond manufacturing into other areas of the business, the reporting could be extended outside of the business altogether (e.g., by including suppliers' and customers' quality costs). (Many of the costs in "total life costs" are quality costs.) In practice, however, no useful way of doing this has been devised, so it will not be discussed further.

QUALITY, PRODUCTIVITY, AND PROFITABILITY

In Chapter 1 it was pointed out that management and media attention to quality has been especially high in the past few years. Equal or more attention has been given in the same period to productivity, and often "quality and productivity" have been discussed together. Sometimes it has been suggested that they are different names for essentially the same thing, and those with a passion for coining new words have put forward the name "qualitivity" for this joint concept. In Chapter 2 we devoted considerable effort to defining quality and the result bore little resemblance to the definition of productivity (which roughly is output divided by input). Also in Chapter 2, we concentrated attention on *product quality* and the specific marketing, design-development, purchasing, and manufacturing activities that primarily contribute to it. Productivity, on the other hand, is not restricted to particular parts of the business, and a productivity improvement program, in principle, can extend to every area of a business. Figure 3.2 expresses this all embracing aspect of productivity (21). Suppose a division in one year makes a million units of product output and in all of its divisional activities—manufacturing, marketing, human relations, accounting, and so on—expends a million units of input. The next year it makes 1.036 million units of output and expends only 959,000 units of input. Its productivity ratio is 1.079 in the second year compared to the first. If the product was sold for a price of $1 in the first year and $1.019 in the second year, the output price per unit ratio is 1.019. If the cost of input went up from $1 to $1.034, the input unit cost

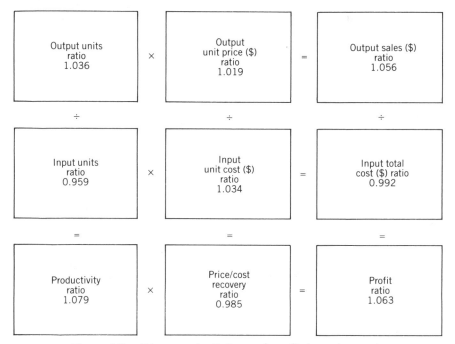

Figure 3.2. Price, productivity, and profit (year-to-year).

ratio is 1.034 and the price/cost recovery ratio is 0.985. The third column gives the product of the first two, showing that the sales ratio is 1.056, the cost ratio is 0.992, and the profit ratio is 1.063. This chart clearly shows that everything affecting the division, except the cost of a unit of input and the selling price of a unit of output, is part of productivity.

Despite this demonstration of the clear and substantial differences between product quality and productivity, the two do have important relationships. The first is a consequence of the relative nature of product quality—the fact that it is measured by comparing the quality of competing products sold at about the *same price*. Figure 3.2 shows that a product sold at the same price as another will yield the same profit if the productivity of the division making it and its cost of a unit of input is the same (or products of the two are the same). Price is fixed by the market and if either productivity is lower than that of competitors or the cost of input is higher, there will be great pressure arbitrarily to reduce the amount of input. Without a corresponding increase in productivity, reducing input will only reduce quality. Inferior productivity (unless offset by a lower cost of a unit of input) is likely to give either inferior quality or profit, or both. The basis of superior quality must be superior productivity.

Conversely, defect prevention is perhaps the most effective way of improving productivity. Defect prevention activities simultaneously increase the output (quality to the customer) and reduce the input (quality costs).

The importance of quality cost improvement to profitability is illustrated in Table 3.5. In 1980, RPU Inc.* started to measure quality costs and developed a program to improve them. By 1984, the program was mature. The measured quality costs were $479 million and quality cost improvement projects had contributed $46 million, approaching the company's 10 percent target. Page 1 of the RPU's annual report showed that pretax profits were $427 million. Without the $46 million of quality cost improvement, the profits would have been only $381 million: quality cost improvement contributed 12 percent of RPU's pretax profits. It made the same contribution to the aftertax, net earnings. However, the real contribution was even greater. Careful reading of RPU's annual report revealed that, when allowance was made for the effects of inflation, their real, before-tax profits were not $427 million but rather only $280 million, and their after-tax net earnings were as small as $92 million. Quality costs are virtually all current costs, so inflation adjustment makes little difference to them. Without the effect of quality cost improvement, RPU's real pretax profits would have been only $234 million,

---

* RPU is not a real company but the numbers are realistic. Readers can test this by reproducing Table 3.5 using the relevant data from the annual report of their company.

**TABLE 3.5.   Effect of Quality Cost Improvement on RPU's
1984 Profits ($ millions)**

	Historical Accounting	Current-Cost Accounting
Quality costs	479	479
Quality cost improvement	46	46
Improvement percentage	9.6%	9.6%
Pretax profits	427	280
Income taxes (44%)	188	188
Net earnings	239	92
Without quality cost improvement:		
Pretax profits	381	234
Income taxes (44%)	168	168
Net earnings	213	66
Contribution of quality cost improvement:		
To pretax profits	12%	20%
To net earnings	12%	40%

and its after-tax net earnings would have been only $66 million. Quality cost improvement contributed 20 percent of the before tax profits and 40 percent of the after tax net earnings.

In 1983 RPU established the ambitious target of reducing its quality costs by 50 percent in six years. The achievement of this program would give, in the sixth year, quality cost savings of $250 million, far more than the profit or earnings. Of course, the reason for any kind of productivity improvement, and its consequent cost reduction, is to enhance competitiveness. How much of the savings ever goes to increased profits depends on what the competitors do. If RPU's quality cost improvement program is more aggressive than its competitors, it may be able to keep a major part of its saving. On the other hand, if RPU's program fails and a competitor's succeeds, RPU might well experience a serious profit erosion.

THE ITT EUROPE QUALITY COST IMPROVEMENT CASE

I conclude this chapter by describing an actual quality cost improvement program—that of ITT Europe in 1975 (22). It is of interest because with that program, for the first time, all of the elements of a modern quality cost improvement activity came together. Subsequent innovations have been refinements rather than fundamental changes. It also shows how functional staff members can exercise leadership, even though the actual improvement projects are the achievement of the operating units.

During the weekend of November 2 and 3, 1974, I met with ITT Europe's three quality engineering managers, the Welshman John Jones; the American from Georgia, Lance Arrington; and the Spaniard from Madrid, Cris Serra, to hold the annual quality department strategy meeting.

The place was the rambling La Verniaz Hotel in Evian, the small French spa famous for its bottled water and its magnificent position on the south bank of Lake Geneva. During the previous week we had conducted one of the ITT quality colleges—on quality management—for 16 quality managers drawn from companies in Spain, France, Scandinavia, Switzerland, Italy, and West Germany. The hotel had been selected for its central position in Europe, good facilities, and superb food. When not leading quality college sessions we took time off and visited units in Frankfurt, Zurich, and Milan.

In the first strategy meeting session it was agreed that in 1975 first emphasis should be given to quality cost improvement. In previous years the ITTE quality department had thrown its weight behind other important programs. Such programs had included Crosby's 14 step quality improvement program, the product qualification program which now ensured that hundreds of new products each year were subjected to formal qualification testing (e.g., 650 in 1975), the development of a detailed and carefully documented model quality system for use in all of the many factories making printed board assemblies which are the key subassemblies of virtually all modern electronics, and many other programs.

Quality cost control had always been a key objective of the ITT quality improvement program, second only to conformance of products to their requirements. However, we decided to give extra urgency to quality cost improvement in 1975 because of the anticipated, and extremely adverse, economic climate of that year. The newly appointed president of ITT Europe, M. R. Valente, had recently been visiting the various companies in Europe, reviewing their programs, and emphasizing that 1975, in contrast to earlier years, would not be a year of expansion but, because of the economic environment, would be a year in which profitability and company health would depend on extraordinary efforts by everyone to improve efficiency. I had participated in this series of onsite reviews and it was one of the main reasons that led to the decision to start emphasizing quality cost improvement.

At the time of the meeting in Evian in early November 1974 ITTE's business planning for 1975 was complete. We had included in the planning guidelines a very ambitious target, stating: "The total cost reduction should be targeted as at least 10 percent of the forecasted quality cost without improvement for the planned year." All of the plans had been reviewed in detail by the office of the president of ITT and by the president of ITT Europe and their respective staffs in a concentrated series of meetings held in Brussels during September and the first weeks of October.

For quality, the plans showed among other items that the various groups and companies of ITT in Europe having sales of $5840 million in 1974 expected their quality costs to total $342 million in 1975. The plans, as submitted, had included quality cost improvement projects worth $17 million for 1975 and during the review period the ITTE quality department asked for changes that increased the commitment to $22 million. This was still well below the 10 percent target and, as I wrote to the president of ITTE on November 7, 1974, "there is low probability of achieving this target." After having decided that quality cost improvement was the principal program for 1975, the discussion was now concentrated on how to achieve it successfully. One other input was the obvious success of the president's face-to-face reviews with his units in their own headquarters.

The decision was made that the main means of improving and consolidating programs would be a series of detailed reviews with the quality directors of the operating units and their plant quality managers; these reviews to be held, not in Brussels, but in the various company locations.

The aim was to make a big profit improvement during the actual fiscal year 1975. Two decisions followed from this: the reviews must be conducted quickly or part of 1975 would be lost; and the limited staff resources must be concentrated in selected units where experienced and competent quality directors worked and effective quality organizations functioned. With the correct help and motivation, these units could be expected to respond rapidly and make significant savings. Smaller and less developed units whose money savings in 1975 would probably be less were treated as a second priority. Their contribution might not come until late in 1975 or even 1976. Applying these principles, 19 units were selected for these on-site reviews.

While at Evian, the program of visits was established. It was decided that, if the meetings were started early in the day, each review could be completed in one day. This presupposed that the visited unit had made careful and detailed preparations for the meeting. The first day of the strategy meeting ended at this point.

The introductory telex is reproduced in Table 3.6. It was sent to the first of the selected quality directors and copied to their managing directors or group executives as well as the president of ITT Europe and his key department heads. The last sentence of the telex stated that the cost savings must be made while maintaining quality. This was the principal theme of our introduction to each review meeting. The cost savings must be made by improving efficiency: there could be no compromise with the primary task of ensuring that products conformed to their requirements.

TABLE 3.6. Telex Introducing ITT Europe's 1975 Quality Cost Improvement Program, Dated November 6, 1974

During the business plan period the ITTE units have committed to quality cost improvement projects that should give a cost saving in 1975 totalling US $22 million. Achievement of these targets will be an extremely important contribution to each unit's net income performance in 1975. In order to assist you in the analysis of these projects and to help you to get them started as quickly as possible, which will be essential if they are to give the planned results in 1975, I intend to visit your units in the near future, together with the concerned quality engineering manager.

My proposed schedule is as follows:

Components Group, Germany, 20th November
Consumer Products Group, Germany, 22nd November
SEL, Stuttgart, 11th and/or 12th December
SESA, Madrid, 16th and/or 17th December
STC, London, 18th or 19th December
BTM, Antwerp, 20th December
CGCT, Paris, 8th January
LMT, Paris, 9th January
FACE, Milan, 16th and/or 15th January
Scandinavia, 28th, 29th, 30th January

The quality engineering managers will be in contact with you to see if these dates are agreeable to you and to define the details. I suggest the unit cost improvement coordinators should be involved, and sub-unit quality managers should also attend. It may also be necessary for some plant managers to participate if they control a major part of the quality cost improvement program. We want the managers who are really responsible for the major projects to be present. Please take responsibility for arranging the people to attend from your unit.

The agenda is as follows:

1. ITT Europe quality, ¾ hour—Introduction
2. Group or company quality director, 1¼ hours—Summary of changes in quality costs 1974 to 1975.
3. Sub-unit quality managers, 3 hours—Review of individual quality improvement projects and required key actions.
4. Unit cost improvement coordinator and manpower controller, ¾ hour—comments on practicality and realism of program.
5. Actions and plan for future reviews.

The second day of the strategy meeting was devoted to other programs and activities. At the meeting's end the three quality engineering managers set out for their return journey to their homes in Brussels. I moved on to Strasbourg, France to join the president at another of his own on-site reviews.

During the following weeks the review meetings were conducted as planned. The progress of these meetings can be summarized by quoting from my monthly reports for November and December 1974.

Projects identified by the two units (Components Group and Consumer Products Group, Germany) total $4.8 millions. The projects covered key improvement areas, but many were inadequately defined to give confidence in their achievement. Specific recommendations for clarification were given. Also, some plants had inadequate programs and these will be improved. All projects will now be redefined and will be formally entered into the cost improvement program of the units. The work will be reviewed again on-site in 6 weeks.

Serra conducted a similar review with Citesa. As a consequence, the quality cost improvement program given in the Citesa business plan will be revised by December 6th.

Projects identified by SEL Group 9 total $2.5 million. Specific recommendations for project clarification were given. SEL central quality department will send a report on the results of the actions by end January.

At SESA, when projects were deleted which involved only accounting changes but not real improvement, the total cost improvements were only $1,322,000 against a target of $1,980,000, the major shortfalls being in the Switching and Transmission Divisions. These divisions agreed to examine additional projects; defect reduction in the Metaconta PBA activity; inspection efficiency and defect reduction at Villaverde; defect reduction in the transmission PBA activity, etc.

At STC the program totalled $2.8 millions, compared with $1.5 millions in the business plan, and now meets the target. A relatively small part was deleted as not affecting net income, but additional projects were identified.

BTM had a very well documented program giving great credibility for achievement, but with some shortfalls against the target, and possible additional projects were identified.

For the Components Group German region, the program was substantially improved over the first review. Planned cost saving has increased to $3.5 million and is supported by adequately defined projects to give confidence in achievement. Twenty action assignments were given to clear up remaining deficiencies.

For each review covering a company or unit employing 15 or 20 thousand people in many plants and divisions, the unit quality director prepared detailed premeeting documentation (e.g., at CGCT in France of 96 pages, for Components Group in West Germany of 105 pages, at SESA in Spain of 71 pages) analyzing the quality cost changes and defining the individual projects planned to save anything from a few thousand dollars to more than $100 thousand. By the end of January 1975 the 14 covered units had identified a total of 549 such projects. The total value was $5.3 million more than the business plan submission and now met the overall target.

After each meeting the quality engineering manager issued an action report to the managing director. Follow-up meetings were arranged. Close examination was made of the efficiency of the cost improvement system for tracking progress and recording savings.

The program that started in Evian high above Lake Geneva ended with a memorandum sent early in 1976 to the managing directors, group executives, and general managers of the 21 units finally involved. It included the following quotation:

> The Table [Table 3.7] shows that the ambitious targets were achieved and that the program saved $18.4 million, reducing quality costs by more than 10 percent. These reported results have been subjected to independent checking by your cost improvement coordinators.

CONCLUSION

In this chapter the long-established system of quality cost measuring and reporting has been described from both conceptual and practical viewpoints. Reasons have been given which indicate the key importance of quality cost improvement to businesses, but, despite this, it was pointed out that effective programs have been implemented by comparatively few companies (though enough to affirm the practicability of such programs). This chapter illustrated the major contribution that quality cost improvement can make to profitability, and, when based on defect prevention, to improvement in quality to the customer.

Quality costs and quality to the customer are the two measures of qual-

TABLE 3.7. ITT Europe's 1975 Quality Cost Improvements (000's)

Unit	Target	Actual
SEL	1,575	1,670
STC	2,000	3,006
BTM (Groups 2 and 9)	1,992	1,728
SESA	1,754	2,302
LMT	917	734
CGCT	1,325	1,348
FACE	980	980
NSEM	294	269
ITT Austria	162	166
Citesa	153	132
Consumer Products Group		
SEL	1,707	1,755
Steiner	97	80
Components Group		
Germany	2,100	1,913
UK	1,600	1,301
France	107	77
Italy	42	76
Spain	62	56
Cannon	112	131
Scandinavia Group		
STK	816	516
SRT	19	40
SEA	74	142
Total	17,888	18,422

ity improvement. They enable the overall status of a quality improvement program to be determined, the planned effect of improvement projects to be established, and the actual progress to be compared to the plans. They provide essential tools for quality improvement.

CHAPTER 4

MARKETING ASPECTS OF QUALITY

In the first three chapters I have presented evidence for the strategic importance of product quality to businesses. It was shown that businesses with superior product quality are more successful and profitable than those with average or even joint best quality. It was argued that the achievement and maintenance of superior product quality requires businesses to have rapid and sustained rates of quality improvement. Necessary conditions for such a rate of quality improvement can be described under the headings: policy, honesty, priority, and capability. An important extension of "capability" is that one understands precisely what is meant by product quality, knows how this can be divided into pieces that can be the subject of manageable improvement projects, and has methods of measuring product quality. In these three chapters the two measures of product quality, quality to the customer and quality costs were defined, and the chain of conformance was used to show how quality improvement could be divided between marketing, design-development, purchasing, and manufacturing links. Chapters 4 through 10 take each of these links in the chain of conformance and show how quality improvement may be applied to each in turn.

Quality management had its origin in inspection and testing, and the statistical control of processes—as applied in manufacturing. It has slowly progressed up the chain of conformance into purchasing and product design, but its ultimate extension into marketing has not started.

Most marketing managers have little appreciation of their key responsibilities for quality. Typically, they believe it is the responsibility of the company's quality people to maintain a "market" level of quality (i.e., more or less as good as the competitors') and that sales growth and profit will then result from the practice of marketing skills—pricing, negotiation with customers, advertising, and so on. Many marketing managers are unfamiliar with the PIMS results discussed in Chapter 1, which indicate that pricing changes are usually rapidly matched by competitors, but *superiority* in quality cannot be quickly matched and gives a much better basis for growth of market share. Although marketing people will frequently speak of the importance of quality, all too often they will press for the release of an incompletely tested product to meet a scheduled delivery. More seriously, in order to make a sale, they will agree with customers' product features or delivery schedules that are not practically realizable by the design engineers, purchasing managers, and manufacturing people. The corner cutting and rushing that follows amplifies the problem. Some of the most serious of all product quality problems are results of this scenario—but rarely does marketing take the blame.

These are some of the negative effects marketing has on quality. Attention is now turned to a key, positive responsibility. The first part of the chain of conformance (Figure 2.1) is reproduced in Figure 4.1. A vital

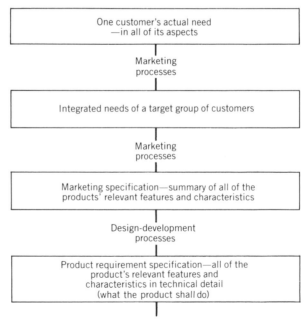

Figure 4.1.   Chain of conformance—marketing links.

part of the total quality process is the conversion of an ill-defined customer's need into a fully defined marketing specification, and then into a product requirement specification. An equally important marketing responsibility is the determination of the price category for a given product—is it a $10,000 or $20,000 car?—and, for a new design, the delivery date. All of these are fundamental marketing activities which depend on knowledge special to each product.

COMPETITORS' QUALITY EVALUATION

A different approach, touched on in Chapter 2, is to examine the quality status of existing products in their own markets. Are they better or worse than competing products? During the first half of 1984, 47 TRW divisions asked this question of 148 of their products representing annual sales of more than $2.5 billion. The comparison was made with 560 competing products. The methodology used was described in Chapter 2. The divisions were asked to evaluate their product quality compared to the quality of competing products offered at about the same price. They were asked to consider three aspects of product quality:

1. The product requirement specification and the design of the product.
2. The proportion of product nonconformant to the design at the time of delivery to the customer ("manufacturing" quality).
3. The continuing performance of the product in the customers' hands (reliability, safety, etc.)

They were asked to identify the competing products and their market share, and to rate them and the TRW product as "best" in quality, "joint-best" (i.e., two or more products that are equally good), "average" in quality, and "worse" than average.

After having rated the three aspects of product quality, the units were asked to rate for overall product quality, and also to consider whether they thought their customers would give a different rating. Finally, they were asked to indicate whether the price charged was high, medium, or low (within the limited range of price differential applicable to products which really compete).

The results, which are summarized in Table 4.1, show that 54 products were judged best in quality, 52 joint-best, 40 average, and 2 worse than average. Trying to take account of the likely customers' opinion

TABLE 4.1. Quality to the Customer—Self-Evaluations by 47 TRW Divisions of 148 Product Lines Against 560 Competing Product Lines

	Product Design	Delivered Conformance	Postdelivery Performance	Overall Product Quality	Customer's Opinion	Relative Price	Overall Product Quality	Customer's Opinion	% TRW Sale
Best	41	36	51	54	47		44	45	
Joint-best	57	54	68	52	54	58 High	34	29	$2564 million sales
Average	34	50	26	40	44	80 Medium	22	26	
Worse	6	5	2	2	2	9 Low	<1	<1	

made the numbers slightly worse. The results can also be expressed as volume of sales rather than number of product lines: 44 percent of the sales of $2564 million were for products rated best, 34 percent for products rated joint-best, and 23 percent for those rated average or worse.

The PIMS results (3) show that to be rated best in quality gives an important financial advantage, measured as return on sales and return on assets employed. Do the TRW results show the same correlation? TRW has ROS and return on assets employed (ROAE) information by divisions, not product lines, so to make the evaluation it is necessary to calculate a quality to the customer rating by division. This was done by assigning points as follows: best, 5; joint-best, 3; average, 1; and worse than average, −1. A division that sold $60 million worth of products best in quality and $30 million of joint-best would get an index of $(60 \times 5 + 30 \times 3)/90 = 4.3$.

The 47 divisions were ranked according to this quality index. Seven divisions had a rating of 5, all of their sales being in the "best" quality category. Five divisions had a rating of 1, all of their sales being for products rated "average" in quality. No division had a rating less than one. The ranking was divided into three groups containing 16, 15, and 16 divisions. The divisions of the top group had quality indices from 5 to 4.36, those of the middle group from 3.91 to 3.00, and those of the bottom group from 2.93 to 1.00. The average indices for the three groups were 4.8, 3.3,

TABLE 4.2. Relationship Between Quality to the Customer and Return on Sales and Return on Assets Employed for 47 TRW Divisions

Group Average	Overall Product Quality			Customers' Opinion		
	Quality Index	ROS %	ROAE %	Quality Index	ROS %	ROAE %
Top 16	4.8	5.5	17.9	4.6	7.7	26.6
Middle 15	3.3	3.1	12.8	3.1	1.4	5.1
Bottom 16	2.0	3.9	12.0	1.9	2.9	8.9

and 2.0 respectively. In Table 4.2 these average indices are compared with the average ROS and ROAE for the divisions in the three groups. (The averages were not weighted for sales volume because each division provides a separate piece of information of equal value to that of every other division.) Table 4.2 gives the results of this analysis for both "overall product quality" and the divisions' estimates of the "customers opinion" of product quality.

The TRW results repeat the PIMS conclusion: the group with the highest quality index—4.36 or greater (i.e., at least 68 percent of the sales in the "best" category)—has much higher ROS and ROAE than the other two groups. The correlations between the best quality rating and ROS and ROAE is even more pronounced for customers' opinion. This is primarily because three divisions with poor ROSs and ROAEs gave themselves best product quality ratings, but only average or joint-best ratings when expressly trying to consider the customers' opinion. Figure 4.2 shows the relationship in graphical form.

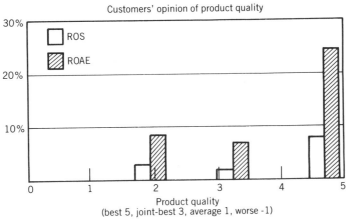

Figure 4.2. Product quality and profitability—148 product lines from 47 TRW divisions, compared with 560 competing product lines.

It is noteworthy that improved ROS and ROAE are earned only by a "best" quality rating. Joint-best will not do. The divisions of the middle group, whose sales came mainly from products with a joint-best rating, had no better financial performance than the divisions of the bottom group, half of whose sales were from products only "average" in quality.

Table 4.3 shows the correlations between the price charged to customers—high, medium, or low—and the overall product quality and the customers' opinion of the product quality. For over 100 product lines the pricing seems normal: either a medium price is charged, or a high price for best quality, or a low price for average quality. For a handful of product lines the pricing seems peculiar: a low price for best or joint-best quality. The most important conclusion concerns 36 product lines for which a high price is charged without justification by a best quality rating. This number increases to 40 if customers' opinion is considered. The explanation of these apparent anomalies is that the people who established the prices had no explicit opinion about the quality status of the products they were dealing with. It is not, therefore, surprising that there is a partially random relationship between price and quality. It is also likely that for some of the product lines, prices were mainly determined by applying some factor to costs, rather than by attention to the market.

The ideal combination of the parameters—cost, price, and quality— would seem to be lowest cost, best quality, and medium price. (To achieve the first two simultaneously requires best productivity.) Lowest cost and medium price gives good profitability and best quality and medium price gives market share growth. If the latter is not desired, for example, to avoid achieving a monopoly, high prices can be charged for best quality.

Performance of the competitors' quality evaluation obviously gives in-

TABLE 4.3. Correlation of Price and Overall Product Quality and Customers' Opinion of Product Quality ( )—147 TRW Product Lines

Price	Product Quality			
	Worse	Average	Joint-Best	Best
High	2	10	24	23
	(2)	(13)	(25)	(19)
Medium	0	26	24	29
	(0)	(29)	(26)	(24)
Low	0	5	5	2
	(0)	(3)	(3)	(3)

formation useful for rational pricing. But even more importantly, it sets the framework for quality improvement—and for the establishment of specific projects having the objective of improving quality to the customer. For this purpose the overall product quality rating is not much help (it does not suggest any improvement actions). However, the need to improve the design quality, or the manufacturing conformance, or the reliability raises issues that do lead to improvement plans and actions. Table 4.1 shows that 55 TRW product lines had average or worse than average delivered conformance, but only 40 and 28 product lines respectively had these low ratings for product requirement specification/product design and postdelivery performance. Therefore, at least 15 product lines could be improved to the joint-best category if manufacturing improved the level of delivered conformance to the design. For each product line, the data on the subdivisions of quality gives the basis for specific quality to the customer improvement projects—just as the data on the subdivisions of quality cost—in-process inspection, scrap, rework, and so on—is the basis for quality cost improvement projects.

MEASURING QUALITY TO THE CUSTOMER

How was the data given in Table 4.1 (148 different product lines compared with 560 competing product lines) obtained? Basically, small working groups of marketing, design engineering, and quality people from the division sat down together and pooled their information. Obviously, one consequence of such an exercise is the realization that the information available is inadequate—that the resulting opinions have a significant chance of being wrong. The question then is, how may better information be obtained? The answers to this question differ for each of the three subdivisions of product quality and will be dealt with in turn.

For the product requirement specification the most fruitful method of obtaining information is to gather copies of the competitors' published data sheets and other descriptions of their products and to compare these with the data sheets and product requirement specifications of the division's own product. To perform a competitors' quality evaluation directed at the product design, the straightforward approach is to buy examples of the competing products and for the division's own design engineers to examine and test them in the laboratory. In addition to the primary assessment of the superiority or inferiority of the design quality judged from the viewpoint of the customer, such an examination will often indicate the method of manufacture and enable an estimate to be made of the cost of the product.

Examining one or two samples of a competitors' product is not likely to yield much information about manufacturing conformance. Sampling will be discussed in Chapter 6; here it is sufficient to note that if 1 out of a 100 of the items of a particular competitive product, as sold, is functionally defective, the division would have to buy and test several hundred samples of the product to measure such a proportion with reasonable accuracy. Also, the competitors' design drawings and workmanship standards are really needed for correct evaluation of manufacturing defects (though some comparison could be made using the division's own documentation).

A simpler approach is to concentrate on the proportion defective of the division's own product. For some products there are published industry standards of proportion defective (often called acceptable quality levels (AQLs)). The manufacturing conformance quality of a division meeting such an AQL is likely to be average. When there are no such standards it can be assumed that the proportion defective will also be average (i.e., much the same as that of competing products), unless the division has had some specific and effective program with the objective of reducing the proportion defective, or there have been serious complaints from customers. If neither of those conditions apply, the quality is unlikely to be either much better or much worse than average. Having determined the current quality and established this as average compared with competing products, the task is now to improve it. An order of magnitude improvement (e.g., from an average 0.5 percent defective to 0.05 percent) may, in the absence of information to the contrary, justify the claim to "best" quality for manufacturing conformance.

Whenever I visit one of the divisions of my company, I always ask the division or plant quality manager, "What proportion defective did you ship last month?" When I first started to ask that question, they seemed to be surprised and discomfited, and the sort of answers I received were:

"Oh, pretty low. The customers don't reject too many . . ."

"Well, I guess between one and two percent . . ."

"Well none, we do a 100 percent inspection at the end of the line . . ."

(My follow-up question to the last answer was, "Well, why did the customers reject 183 lots last year?")

It would seem obvious that a division that is serious about the quality of its products and that is working energetically for quality improvement would want to know, on a running basis, its quality to the customer status. In Chapter 2 it was shown that product quality is a fairly complicated concept, but one key aspect—the proportion nonconformant to the product requirement specification or the product design—is simple and straightforward. It is this aspect that my question addressed. Why then were the quality managers, who were by no means incompetent, unable to answer the question? Many of them argued that it was the difficulty of getting the data, but this, as will be shown, is not really true. I believe that the information is psychologically unpleasant and that obtaining it is therefore avoided. This is not usually an explicit decision; rather there is an inhibition against initiating the actions which would provide the information. What is the basis of this inhibition? Well, the quality status of such divisions is often fairly quiet. Operations are proceeding in a routine manner, customers are rejecting some products but no more than usual—and no one is getting excited. To start measuring the proportion defective sent to customers cannot improve this pleasant situation and could destroy it. One result might be that the outgoing quality is found to be excellent, but this is unlikely in the absence of prior knowledge and specific improvement actions. A much more likely result is that the measured proportion defective seems "normal." Human beings tend to think that about 1 percent defective is normal. Ten percent defective is usually intolerable and causes a lot of excitement and action. 0.1 percent defective seems much more trouble than it is worth. Because such numbers may be applied to virtually any product, it is apparent that they have little to do with the real benefit of high quality for a particular product or the "economics of quality" (which will be discussed in Chapter 9). They simply reflect the way people feel. If the result of measuring the proportion defective turns out to be normal, strong arguments can be made for stopping the measurements (e.g., "The method doesn't in any way *improve* the quality, it just measures what it is, and is therefore a waste of limited resources"). If this is the likely outcome, why bother to start? Conversely, there is always the danger that the division manager or some other authoritative person might be impressed by the results and press hard for improvement. This unpleasant consequence can also result if the quality turns out to be not "normal" but obviously bad—more than 3 percent defective. In teaching quality improvement, I sometimes make reference to an imaginary character, "the quality manager who wants a quiet life." Although imaginary, there is a little of him or her in all of us, and he or she is never more obvious than when systematic measurement of quality to the customer is the issue. Many companies depend entirely on their customers to tell them about their product quality. If they are not complaining, why turn over stones? On the other hand, if they are complaining, why not address their complaints directly, and not confuse the issue with in-house measurements? Of course, all of these arguments are just rationalizations to support the psychological inhibitions described previously. The reality is that it is very important to know about a deteriorating quality situation before the customers do, that one's own data give a much better basis for action than the customers' because the latter is necessarily late and incomplete—and is often not believed at first—and, finally, one's own data is a vital tool for reaching the superior, not just average, quality that alone gives major financial reward.

How can the proportion defective that is shipped to customers be measured each month? The primary means is by an outgoing quality audit. In Chapter 6 the difficulty of doing an outgoing *acceptance* test will be discussed. This is a test to determine whether or not the product meets some predetermined standard of quality before it goes to the customer. An outgoing audit builds up information over a period of time (usually a month) and by the time the data is complete the product whose quality was measured will have already gone to the customers. The purpose of the audit is not to stop bad products from going to the customer (which is another reason why many quality—and other—managers have difficulty with it) but rather to give information to help future improvement actions.

I had relatively little success in getting operating divisions to perform outgoing quality audits until I devised the two examples given in Table 4.4, and asked two simple questions about them: How much effort would it take to perform such an audit each month? and How many defectives would it find?

The first example concerns mechanical parts, the sort of things that are sold to manufacturers of mechanical machines, such as cars, aircraft,

TABLE 4.4. Monthly Outgoing Quality Audits for Mechanical Parts and Electronic Components

	Number of Tests or Inspections	
Type of Test or Inspection	Mechanical Parts	Electronic Components
Visual inspection	10×100	10×100
Measurement of dimensions	$10 \times 10 \times 10$	—
Tests for complete failure	—	10×1000
Tests for specified characteristics	—	$10 \times 10 \times 100$

agricultural and construction machines, and so on. For the audit, it is suggested that each month a division manufacturing and selling such products should select 10 different part types. For each of these part types 100 items should be visually inspected for workmanship and similar visual defects, 1000 inspections in total. Then the same 10 part types should be gauged for dimensions against the drawings and their specified tolerance—10 items for each part type for 10 selected dimensions, 1000 tests in all.

In answer to the question, How long would such an audit take?, quality managers were initially reluctant to answer, but finally gave times depending on the complexity of their particular parts and the sophistication of the gauging methods available to them. Each visual inspection would take a few seconds, say 5 to 10 inspections per minute. The visual audit would therefore take a few hours work a month. Generally, the gauging was estimated to take longer, though with modern gauging systems, only a little, giving a time of say 10 hours per month. In answer to the question about the number of defects observed, most replies were in the range 2 or 3 to 20 or 30, for visual defects, that is, from 0.2 percent to 3 percent. Sampling theory indicates that the measurements at the upper end of the range would be accurate and those at the lower end only approximate. For the dimensional audit the numbers of defects were estimated to be somewhat higher, in the range 5 to 50 defects for the sample of 1000 measurements.

Answering these questions forced these quality managers to face up to the fact that with the expenditure of very little effort—considerably less than the full-time work of one inspector—an adequately accurate measure of the defective level of many mechanical products could be made.

Table 4.4 also deals with electronic components—which are sold to the manufacturers of electronic equipment, such as televisions, computers, telephone exchanges, and so on. The visual inspection is the same as that for the mechanical parts. In addition, the audit requires the components to be electrically tested. First, 1000 items of each of 10 different components of one category (e.g., 10 types of capacitor) are tested for complete defectiveness—open circuit, short circuit, or drastically outside-of-specification for major characteristics. Then 100 each of the same 10 types are tested for 10 specified characteristics, 10,000 measurements in all. Once again, such an audit is easily performed at very little cost.

The answer to the question about the number of defects may be more complex for electronic components than for mechanical parts. Many electronic components have traditionally been the subject of specifications in which defective proportions are defined in standardized AQLs.

Often these AQLs are near to 1 percent—0.65 percent is particularly popular—and such defective levels, in the range 0.1 to 1.0 percent, can be accurately measured by an outgoing quality audit like that defined in Table 4.4. However, 10 years or more ago Japanese electronic component and electronic equipment manufacturers cooperated together effectively to reduce drastically the defective proportion of commercial electronic components. The quality of such components could not conveniently be described in terms of percentages, and a new measure, parts per million (ppm), was coined. Chapter 10 will discuss ppm components. Here it is sufficient to note that sample sizes 100 times greater than those given in Table 4.4 would be needed for an accurate measure of ppm quality levels, and this markedly increases the difficulty and cost of performing such an audit. For this reason, ppm defective levels are better measured by the electronic equipment maker (e.g., by careful analysis of failures during the ubiquitous test of printed board assemblies) and communicated to the electronic component makers. Alternatively, the component maker can estimate the ppm defective rate by multiplying the failure rate at the final 100 percent test by the inspection effectiveness of the test (see Chapter 8).

Table 4.4 gives examples of outgoing quality audits for only two types of product, and both of these components. For other types of product the outgoing audit has to be tailored to the product. For consumer electronics, such an audit might include measurements of functional performance, inspections for appearance and damage, and also internal inspections of attributes related to reliability (e.g., conformance of soldered joints to workmanship standards). For mechanical products functional performance might also be tested and visual appearance inspected. Samples of the product might be dismantled and conformance of their components to drawings and tolerances be measured. In all cases, the aim of the audit is to give statistically significant measures of key quality variables and attributes at regular intervals of time so that the progress of improvement activities can be assisted and monitored.

The third subdivision of product quality covers the performance of the product after it has been accepted by the customer. It includes such characteristics as the reliability of the product, measured as failure rate (proportion failing per unit of time) or mean time between failures, the safety of the product, its durability, maintainability, and so on. These characteristics can be estimated from the results of life tests, environmental tests, and so on, and information can also be obtained from "field-failure reporting systems." However, as will be discussed in Chapter 10, the determination of the reliability parameters of products is usually difficult and expensive. This third subcategory of product quality is therefore the one for which the performance of a satisfactory competitors' quality evaluation is the most difficult.

All too often, the main source of a unit's information about the quality of its products comes directly from its customers—in the form of product rejections and complaints. This is obviously vital information for quality improvement but should be a supplement to the unit's own-generated data. Comparisons of the two types of data can give clarification about the problems of main importance to the customer and help prioritization of improvement actions.

MARKET RESEARCH

A different approach to a competitors' quality evaluation is to use market research to ask customer representatives about their perceptions of the quality of the unit's products and competing products.

One such market research was carried out by a consultant on behalf of a TRW division selling machine tools through distributors. Telephone interviews were carried out with 250 end-user respondents and 70 distributor respondents selected from lists supplied by the TRW division. Table 4.5 gives information about the respondents and Table 4.6 summarizes the questions they were asked.

The main purposes of this study as defined by the consultant were to

TABLE 4.5. Respondents to a Market Research about the Quality of Machine Tools

Involvement in Decision Making about the Specification or Purchase of Machine Tools	End Users (250)	Distributors (70)
Deeply involved	60%	56%
Somewhat involved	26%	29%
Not involved	14%	15%
Position		
Purchasing manager/agent/buyer	27%	29%
Manufacturing or machine shop manager	14%	0%
General/plant manager	33%	37%
Engineer	13%	0%
Salesperson or sales manager	1%	14%
Other	12%	20%

TABLE 4.6. Market Research Questions—Quality of Machine Tools

Rate on a scale of 1 to 10 how well your overall expectation is met by all producers of the tools, and what makes you feel that way.

Name three brands of the tools which come to mind for each of seven named factors about the way the producers offer service. Rate the three as a group for their performance.

Which of these factors means the most, next, and least in dealing with a tool producer? Which of these factors have you paid a premium for?

Which three specific problems (excluding price) have you found most troublesome?

Name the three producers who have been most successful in avoiding such problems.

Name the three producers who you think are most likely to have such problems.

What is your level of familiarity with six (named) producers and what are the causes of this familiarity? (three questions).

measure the effectiveness of the producers for seven key factors and to determine which producers were doing the best job. Other purposes were to determine the expectations of respondents and how well they were met. Secondary objectives included: determination of the respondents' familiarity with and favorability to six producers, the likelihood of their doing business with them, their degree of involvement in purchasing decisions, and the brands purchased by them in the past year.

Four-fifths of the end users and more than nine-tenths of TRW's distributors recorded satisfaction of their expectations (scores of 7 through 10). However, the results summarized in Table 4.7 show that the

TABLE 4.7. Seven Factors Influencing Tool-Users' Satisfaction

	Ranking			
	Importance		Satisfaction	
Factor	End Users	Distributors	End Users	Distributors
Availability and delivery of standard items	1	1	2	4
Combination of tool-life and cutting ability	2	4	4	2
Tool-to-tool consistency	3	3	1	1
Ability to meet dimensional specifications	4	7	3	3
Cooperative and timely customer service	5	6	5	5
Skilled applications and technical assistance	7	2	6	6
Quoted lead time and delivery of special items	6	5	7	7

two factors they considered most important—"availability and delivery of standard items," and "combination of tool-life and cutting ability"— both had scope for improvement. Only a minority of end users and distributors had paid a premium for any of these factors, and most of this minority had paid for the two delivery factors.

The most troublesome problems of end users were "availability of standard and special items," "late or slow deliveries," and "short tool life." Those of distributors were "late or slow deliveries," "availability problems," and "unresponsive customer service personnel." Two-fifths of both types of respondent had no problems at all with the producers they bought from. The producers who were most and least successful in avoiding problems were identified.

Three-fifths of end users were well or somewhat acquainted with the TRW division but three other producers were better known. End users gave the same rankings for "generally favorable opinion," but TRW's distributors gave TRW first ranking. The most frequently cited reason for a favorable opinion of the TRW division was, "high quality, durable, reliable products." The most frequently cited reason for respondents claiming a "good" likelihood of doing business with a producer in the future was, "deal with them now."

The consultants recommended that the TRW division conduct a professional program to reach the two-fifths of respondents who were not acquainted with it and its products. It also recommended that the program should emphasize the factors of Table 4.7 rated of most importance to customers. The survey indicated that the TRW division had a good reputation for these factors, but nonetheless the management of the division decided to give them increased emphasis in their improvement programs.

Another quality-related market research conducted by TRW was reported by A. Randall Evans (23). In early 1982 a group of second year MBA students from Harvard Business School, directed by Professor Michael Porter, conducted a pilot market research for TRW's Aircraft Components Group. The survey involved personal interviews with respondents from two leading customers—Pratt and Whitney Aircraft and General Electric. The pilot program was later expanded to cover all of the group's business units and a much larger number of customers and competitors. This second phase was conducted by McKinsey and Company. Table 4.8 shows some of the results for one of the group's divisions.

Evans listed some of the benefits of the survey:

Confronting firmly held beliefs about quality performance with actual quality performance.

TABLE 4.8. Customer Comparison of Product Attributes

| Customer Requirements | 1982 Rating[a] | | | | Anticipated Change by 1987 |
	ACG Div	Comp A	Comp B	Comp C	
Quality/reliability	1	0	2	2	Competitor A will improve but remain behind leaders
Performance/noise	2	1	2	2	Competitors A and B will improve but competitor B will still be average
Weight	1	0	2	1	All competitors will be at parity.
Price	2	2	0	0	Price differentials will narrow but ACG and competitor A will remain less expensive than Competitors B and C
Delivery	2	2	2	2	None
Product support	2	0	1	2	None
Technological competence	1	0	1	2	None
Total	11	5	10	11	
Total excluding price	9	3	10	11	

[a] 2 = Best, 1 = Average, 0 = Worst

Confirming or denying that the present quality performance is acceptable from the customer's viewpoint.

Maintaining high customer regard for quality and promoting a quality image.

Identifying and prescribing solutions to problems affecting quality image.

Developing an ongoing feedback system for quality business planning.

For a few types of products, quality-directed market research is well developed. For example, there are consultants who make a speciality of market research for passenger cars, selling their services to the car makers. *Consumer Reports* also covers passenger cars comprehensively. However, for most products quality-directed market research is rarely performed and market-research consultants are generally inexperienced in its special requirements. As can be noticed from the two examples discussed, they have a tendency to slant the research towards matters, such as brand recognition, with which they are more familiar. The general managers and marketing managers, who finally decide whether or not a division will conduct a competitors' quality evaluation using market research, have interests that extend well beyond product quality. Actual exercises are therefore unlikely to be restricted solely to product quality. The services provided to customers (support quality) by companies selling products are significant factors in determining their level of success, and delivery quality is also invariably of importance to customers. Quality-directed market research can therefore with advantage examine not only product quality but also support quality and delivery quality (see Table 2.2). It can be used to determine the specific features and characteristics, in all three of these main categories, which are of most importance to customers. It can then examine the superiority or inferiority of the unit in supplying these features and characteristics. A key requirement is that the market-research questions are well organized, precise, and clear, so that the resulting answers define the need for specific, practicable actions—and help to initiate such actions.

Despite the current emphasis by business on product and service quality and the apparent obviousness of the need for clear customer-related data on quality status for improvement purposes, there has generally been little activity on this subject. Why is this? I believe there are a number of deterrents to the activity, and no clear source of "champions" resolved to overcome them. Chapter 12 will discuss why managers do some things and do not do others. Here, we simply list possible deterrents in Table 4.9 and evaluate possible champions in Table 4.10.

In establishing any business it is usual to set up procedures that can be operated routinely. People become comfortable with such activities and go on performing them happily until some special problem occurs. Then the methods of problem solving comes into play—crisis meetings, special working parties, and so on—which is another effective way of engaging

TABLE 4.9. Deterrents to Quality-Directed Market Research

1. Quality-directed market research is neither an established routine, nor a response to a special problem.
2. It is not a commonly performed activity of competitors or consultants.
3. Results at best will confirm preconceptions and at worst will indicate serious problems.
4. Consequential actions may be required that are unfamiliar and a new load on an already burdened organization.
5. It has to compete for the small availability of discretionary time and money with more popular projects.

TABLE 4.10. Attitude of Potential "Champions" to Quality-Directed Market Research

Potential Champion	Attitude
Quality manager	Knows nothing about market research and is more comfortable inside the factory. Too low in the "pecking order" to overcome opposition from other managers.
Marketing manager	Believes that sales and profits are determined by pricing, customer relations, negotiations, campaigns, and so on, not quality. Fears adverse customer reaction to questions about quality.
Chief engineer	More interested in own new designs than competitors' products
Division manager	Not a specialist in quality or market research. Has less risk by pushing quality programs supported by peers (e.g., statistical process control or quality circles).
Market research consultant	Has a very unfocused view of product quality. Will react positively to initiatives of others, but will not be proactive.
Staff quality director	Best hope, but shares some of the aversions of the quality manager and division manager.

the attention of people. Quality-directed market research does not fit into either of these categories: it is neither an established routine nor a response to a special problem; nor does it benefit from the peer pressure of competitors' activity or the sales pressure of consultants. Quality-directed market research also has the psychological disadvantages that it is unlikely to give good news, that it has the possibility that it may reveal nothing new and therefore he perceived as a waste of effort, and that it may indicate the need for new, unpleasant actions. It normally takes an enthusiast, a "champion" the word used in *In Search of Excellence,* to overcome such difficulties. Unfortunately, Table 4.10 indicates that none of the involved managers are very likely to become champions for this project. It is not surprising therefore that quality-directed market research has been relatively unsuccessful in competing for the small amount of discretionary money and effort available to any business for such activities.

QUALITY COMPLAINTS

One apparently important source of marketing information about the quality of a company's products is customers' quality complaints. The old saying that "the customer is always right" and the modern recognition of their importance to the business suggest that prompt, effective action should always follow a customer's complaint. The reality is quite different. Most businesses have no satisfactory method of dealing with quality complaints. Logically, there should be two types of action: the specific complaint should be dealt with to the satisfaction of the customer, and general action should be taken to prevent such problems from occurring in the future. The first kind of action is inhibited by human psychology. Everyone hates complainers. The natural reaction to a complaint is therefore negative and defensive. It might be thought that the treatment of a complaining customer would somehow be different from the treatment of a complaining wife, husband, parent, or child. This might be so if the people dealing with complaints had been carefully trained and motivated. However, I have never known this to happen so the reaction to a quality complaint is usually natural (i.e., negative) rather than professional. An employee's reaction to a complaint is more likely to exacerbate the problem than to solve it. What about general action to prevent similar problems in the future? Well, this has a characteristic common to all quality improvement—it is very difficult. If a company or division is working hard and persistently on quality improvement, the analysis of its customers' quality complaints will be valuable in influencing and prioritizing its improvement actions. If, like most companies, it is not working hard on quality improvement, there is nothing it can do about the generality of quality complaints. If one raises the subject with a company in the latter category, it will usually turn out that there is not even a single repository of the complaints—sales will have some, product engineering will have others, and quality a third set—and no one will have analyzed them, because there is no point. The company has no effective mechanism for taking *improvement action* on the basis of such analysis.

Most quality improvement programs flounder on the rock of improvement action. There is often plenty of quality data. Sometimes it will have been analyzed to determine causes of failures. Rarely will action have been taken to eliminate the causes.

The vast majority of the quality complaints of the world are made about services rather than about products. This book is mainly about product quality, but I hope I will be excused a diversion into service quality. Service organizations, for example hotel chains and airlines, irritate their customers by asking them to fill-in quality surveys. Most service organizations have no defined method of getting quality improvement—and furthermore they already know about their major quality problems—so they have no need for further quality information. For example, every traveler (and hotel manager) knows what the quality problems of hotels are: long lines at the check-out counter in the morning; room service that usually does not answer and if it does, gets the order wrong; air-conditioning that is noisy, uncontrollable or not working; and television sets that have adequate signals on only two channels, poor color, or are not working. It is pointless for a hotel chain that is incapable of the improvement actions needed to solve those problems to seek further quality information from its customers. Similar examples could be given for airlines, hospitals, government departments, and most other service organizations.

The only good reason for accumulating and analyzing quality data is to assist improvement action—and usually the action is much more difficult than the accumulation and analysis.

Early in 1982 I started to distribute an internal journal called *TRW Quality Communication* to TRW's quality mangers (see Chapter 13). Most of the issues were serious studies of important quality topics or accounts of successful quality projects. However, in 1982 I thought it would be kind to the readers to make the last issue of the year light-hearted—though still with a quality message—and wrote a story entitled, "The Toledo Syndrome" (see Chapter 13). The following year I could not think of a story, but I hoped the readers might be amused by a set of letters about a quality complaint made to a bank, which I titled the Jones' Bank Quality Complaint. This correspondence actually took place though I have changed the names of the bank and its managers.

THE "JONES' BANK QUALITY COMPLAINT" CASE

Quality professionals should complain more about bad quality. We spend our working lives trying to improve the quality of the products and services sold by our companies. It could be argued that that is enough, that we have done our share. But because we are dedicated to quality, we should be in the vanguard when it comes to complaining about the bad quality we suffer in our private lives. I sometimes have a vision of, say, every member of the American Society for Quality Control making 10 quality complaints a year—and making them stick. Perhaps we could involve the European Organization for Quality Control. I expect that, privately, even the Japanese have quality problems, and we might bring in

JUSE to run another campaign with the dedication they applied to quality circles. It could be worldwide.

For quality complaints, I count myself an amateur, not a professional. I have never sued anyone, or even reaped significant monetary benefit. But sometimes I have felt—perhaps deluding myself—that some other customer might have fared better in the future as a result of one of my complaints.

As you all know, getting quality improvement is difficult, and any individual program alone may be ineffective. It is certainly true that to get effect from a quality complaint one has to be very aggressive and persistent. The low-key approach is no use at all. The sales department just gives you the standard, bland response and that is the end of it. Even worse is when your complaint is received with anger, contempt, and abuse. Unless you are in perfect health, quality complaints should be made in person only under the supervision of a physician. For such reasons, I recommend quality complaints be made in writing.

Another problem with complaints made face-to-face is that they can get out of hand. You need to be aggressive, but you do not want to go too far. For example, one time I wished to bring a complaint to the attention of an airline employee. A long series of quality-of-service problems had brought me within minutes of missing a vital connection. The employee was bent over her desk, fiddling with some forms. My polite inquiry was ignored, and my stentorian follow-up also. It was only when I rapped with my knuckles that I got attention—and perhaps to have knocked on her desk, rather than on the neat little cap she was wearing, would have been enough. . . . Another time the adversary was a Spanish stewardess who spoke perfect English, but was not giving an inch. One sentence spoken very slowly and clearly left her incoherent with a complex mixture of negative emotions, "Your English is not very good, and you are just not understanding what I am saying . . ."

With taxi drivers I remember one success and one failure. My French is extremely limited, but I managed to insult a Paris taxi driver (he was taking me on a grand tour of the city rather than to my destination a kilometer or so away) to such good effect that he threw me out of the cab. I count that as a victory, because at last we were nearing the destination, and there was $20 on the meter that he did not get. The defeat came when the same thing happened in Belgium: I refused to pay the excess and he reported me to the authorities. The local police came to my door, and I was summoned to the station. I count this as a failure because I broke the cardinal rule of quality complaints: *never cause yourself more trouble than it is worth.*

Another time my wife and I were on vacation in Portugal. We had a tiny room. The carefully angled photograph in the brochure, including one or two midgets, had made it seem much larger. I was promised a suite—at extra payment—"In two or three days, sir. . . ." As the days passed, I was put off again and again. I was complaining about it to a man by the swimming pool, who had arrived the previous day. He said he had had the same problem, but he had "come to an accommodation" with the head receptionist. . . . Something clicked in my mind—that was *my* suite. As an Englishman who finds even tipping embarrassing, I have always envied the Continental his facility with bribery. Per haps for $20, he had received what I, with several days of pressure, had failed to get. I stormed up to the hotel, was told my suite was still not available, and that the manager was out of the building. I went to his office, found him at his desk, and began shouting at him. I got my suite, but I still remember the quiet dignity with which the manager took my abuse, and the reproachful look in his eyes. Yes, again I went too far.

So, I really recommend making quality complaints in writing. Apart from allowing a greater measure of control, and being less harmful to the blood pressure, they are more likely to produce improvement. The initial reaction to any quality complaint is always negative and defensive, and it is rare with a face-to-face complaint for this first reaction to be reversed. With a written complaint there is always a chance that wise counsels may prevail from the start. More importantly, the written complaint allows the progressive build-up of a campaign. Each negative and defensive an-swer gives ammunition for the next attack, and the problem can legiti-mately be moved up the management hierarchy, involving more and more people. Of course, this requires a willingness to write more than one letter: it is rarely possible to make any impact with fewer than three letters.

A case from my files illustrates the principles involved. It concerns a bank. I have changed its name because the example was selected only be-cause of its suitability for illuminating concepts. The actual misdeeds of its managers were no worse than many others. You will see that I do not pull punches. To have any effect you have to get their attention. I partic-ularly ask you to note the reference to spanning "four generations" in the first letter. I almost had tears in my eyes when I wrote that.

By chance, the bank is British, and for it to be the subject of a quality-complaint case is really unfair because this bank is actually considerably better both in "design" quality—the range of services they provide—and conformance to design, than the Belgian and American banks I have used. American banks go into a tizzy at the mention of any international business, and are surprisingly primitive in computerization (e.g., a person with an excellent credit rating still fears bouncing a check, and in any case will get a neurotic-sounding notification if one of his or her accounts inadvertently goes into debit. This does not happen in Britain, except by special decision or by mistake—a point that should be kept in mind in reading the following correspondence).

In my third letter to the bank, I make reference to a book called *Gamesmanship* by Steven Potter. This, and its follow-up, *Lifemanship*, are perhaps less well known in the United States than in the United Kingdom. In the United Kingdom, these books are in a class with *Parkinson's Law* and *The Peter Principle*, and have strongly influenced two generations of Britons. That letter itself is written as a parody of Potter's style.

10th September, 1983

The Manager
Jones Bank
Central London Branch

Dear Sir,
I have been following with growing concern the recent interactions of you and your staff with my daughter, Nikki Groocock. You seem to have overlooked the key point that she is a customer of Jones Bank and that you are employees of the bank. The way you have treated her does not seem to have been appropriate to that relationship.
The facts, as I understand them, are as follows. For three years my daughter has been a customer of your branch. Every month during this period she has received a fixed amount of money from me by means of a standing order from my account with the North Kent branch of Jones. Occasionally, she has received additional sums of money. From time to time she has had an overdraft, but never disproportionate to her monthly income. Recently, while she has been staying with her mother and me in America, you refused payment of some of her checks. On her return, instead of apologizing to her you lectured her (a moment's thought will tell you that it is not usual for employees to lecture customers) and persisted in charging her for the rejected checks. Also, apparently to punish her further, you said that it would take a month to clear the check for $1000 I had given her, and that meanwhile you could not let her have any money. Later, you said she could have money in four days, but there would be overdraft charges. (The logic of that escapes me. If the check was cleared in four days, why the charges? And if you were granting credit, why did it take four days?)
The only legitimate causes of concern a bank has about a customer are his

honesty and his creditworthiness. For my daughter you had no rational reason to question either of these.

In 1947 my father introduced me to the Jones Bank and I opened an account; many years before, his father had done the same for him. Because of your actions, my daughter is closing her account, breaking a relationship that has spanned four generations. If I had been treated the same way when I was a student I would have closed my account and Jones would have lost 35 years or more of my business.

I suggest that you now withdraw the charges associated with the dishonored checks (I do not object to interest payments on the overdraft). You should also write a letter of apology to my daughter. I would like to receive a copy of that. I should also like to have from you a clear description of the system that takes four weeks to clear my dollar check. Sending letters both ways across the Atlantic would take only a couple of weeks, and surely Jones has a better system than that.

Your reaction to this letter may well be negative and defensive, but I remind you that we have a business not a personal relationship and you should try to respond in a way that is in Jones' best interest—and your own. If you do not feel able to accede to those requests I suggest that you discuss the matter with your supervisor. I shall certainly want to present the issue to him and he would undoubtedly prefer to hear about it from you first. Please send me his name and address.

Yours faithfully,

Dr. J. M. Groocock

Jones Bank
6th October 1983

Dear Dr. Groocock,

I have today received your letter dated the 10th September 1983 concerning the account of your daughter, Miss Nikki Groocock.

The various points which you raised have been carefully noted but I regret that I am unable to discuss details relating to your daughter's account with anyone other than your daughter herself.

I am aware that you are a long established and valued customer of our bank and it is deeply regretted that we should have had this difference, but I am sure you will understand that it would be unprofessional for me to comment on the operation of your daughter's account.

Yours sincerely,

M. G. Kaiser
Pro-Manager

12th October 1983

The Manager
Jones Bank
London, England

Dear Sir,

I have just received the answer to my letter of 10th September written by some deputy of yours. It uses the crude device of claiming professional confidentiality to avoid answering any of the issues I raised.

Will you now answer the following points:

Have you apologized in writing to my daughter, or do you intend to?

Does it take a month for Jones to clear a dollar check and if so what is the process?

What is the title, name, and address of your supervisor?

Yours faithfully,

Dr. J. M. Groocock

P.S. I think it would be courteous of you to answer this letter yourself.

Jones Bank
21st October 1983

Dear Dr. Groocock,

Thank you for your letter of 12th October concerning the operation of your daughter's account at this Branch.

I am now the manager dealing with your daughter's account since the amalgamation of two of our branches. Consequently, I have looked into this matter and have written to your daughter setting out the details as I see them and asking for her comments. At the same time, I must beg to differ about your claim that professional confidentiality is not at issue when discussing someone else's account without their permission.

However, in answer to your question relating to the clearance of U.S. dollar checks, I can say that the process can take up to four weeks due to the fact that the check has to be physically shipped back to the United States before the bank on which it is drawn will give an answer. Our only method of circumventing this problem is if we sell the check in the London market for our customer on the proviso that if the check is not cleared, the customer is still liable for the amount outstanding. This enables us to provide funds within four of five working days. I believe that you will find that your daughter can corroborate this information.

Yours sincerely,

M. Brown
Assistant Manager

November 1, 1983

Mr. M Brown
Assistant Manager
Jones Bank
London, England

Dear Mr. Brown:

No one likes a customer with a quality complaint. He may cause someone to have to accept that he is in the wrong, and even to have to apologize. Both of these actions are deeply repugnant to people. So, the *classical response* to the complaint, as I said in my first letter, is "negative." In addition, the disinclination to admit any fault makes the response "defensive." Various ploys (cf. *The Theory and Practice of Gamesmanship*, S. Potter, 1947) have been devised for implementing the classical response. A key one is the avoidance of answering the primary points of the complaint. (A subploy requires that no direct question shall be answered—though it is entirely proper, and even recommended, to simulate answering a question without actually doing so.) A second ploy is to fasten upon any inaccuracy or exaggeration in the complaint and build a lengthy and detailed rebuttal of that point. If careful examination of the complaint cannot identify such an inaccuracy, a third ploy is to misinterpret some statement (preferably a misinterpretation that only a child or half-wit would make, thereby indicating that one has not bothered to read the complaint, or that the misinterpretation is deliberate). Then the rebuttal can address the misinterpretation. In expert hands, these two ploys can be developed into full-blooded attacks on the complainer.

Many other ploys have been devised by experienced consumer affairs practitioners, and are recorded in the professional literature. The result of the application of the classical response is enraged customers, lost customers, and law suits. Here in America there have been cases of physical assault, arson, and murder.

As a connoisseur of the classical response, I judge Jones' two letters as superior. I admired the initial use of the professional confidentiality ploy to avoid answering all questions, whether confidential or not. Your own misinterpretation of my position on the same issue, which you developed into an attack, was clever as well. But it was Jones' master-class use of the "underling" ploy (first response from a pro-manager, second response from an *assistant manager*) that really earned the superior rating.

The *professional response* is different from the classical response. It is based on *pretending that the quality complaint is justified* and dealing with it as if it were. Usually, the complaint *is* justified, but even if it is not it is immaterial; the same good results flow from the professional response in either case. Questions are answered simply and honestly, graceful apologies are offered, and inexpensive corrective actions are taken. (Those who are not yet quite professional cannot resist putting in a few tiny twists to let the complainer know that they are only pretending that the complaint is justified. The real professional will rigorously exclude all such points—and get colleagues to inspect the response for any hint—so that, however cynical, the complainer can never be sure that the professional response is insincere.)

The result of the application of the professional response is happy customers, retained customers, and general human good will.

Having explained the principles to you, I suggest you now get your manager to give me a professional response. He will find it a very useful exercise, and really not as painful as it may seem.

First, he should take out my second letter and, simply and directly, answer the three questions. (Hints: In your letter for question 1, you avoided the key word "apology"; for question 2, you started from the no-fault premise and tried to justify it—with an implausible result; and question 3 you ignored.) Then the manager should explain (either honestly or imaginatively) why he has refused for so long to answer letters from a customer addressed to him. Finally, he should add any simple apologies to me he feels I might appreciate (remembering to pretend that I am in the right). You may ask: why do I bother to send three letters on such a subject? The short answer is because I want to. A second reason is in the hope that in the future your manager and his staff just might deal with Jones' customers in a better way.

Yours sincerely,

Dr. J. M. Groocock

P.S. I have asked three times for the names of the real manager and his supervisor. If I do not get them I shall send the whole correspondence to the managing director of Jones (who is a public figure) and ask *him* for the names. I shall also give him my permission to use this correspondence as the basis of a case for use in internal management training programs.

Jones Bank
8th November 1983

Dear Dr. Groocock,

Thank you for your letter, received on 7th November, expressing your feelings as to our treatment of your correspondence. I hope that by now you have received the letter sent to you by my colleague, Mr. Brown, on 4th November. As you will note, we have conveyed our apologies in writing to your daughter and are at present hoping she will continue to maintain her account at this branch.

Responding to the main questions raised in your letter of 12th October 1983, I believe the processing times required to clear a cheque drawn on the United States were explained in our letters of 21st October. However,

if you wish for further clarification, I shall be only too pleased to comply. As for the "supervisor" of this branch, I assume this to be myself, although I am in turn responsible to the regional general manager, Mr. D. Smith, Central London (West), who resides at 6 Crocker Street, London SW1. While I appreciate that your daughter has not received the standard of service I would normally expect from a branch of Jones Bank, I should hasten to add that I now feel the position is being correctly handled. Since our amalgamation, Mr. Brown, one of my managerial team has been delegated the duty of looking after your daughter's account, and I am satisfied that everything is being done to remedy the previous situation. Indeed, I would hope that the contents of our letters of 4th November will ensure that we do not become subject to "physical assault, arson, and murder." It goes without saying that both Douglas Brown and myself would welcome the chance of meeting you should you ever be in this country and no doubt we could then discuss in greater detail *The Theory and Practice of Gamesmanship* over a spot of lunch. I am sorry that all this correspondence has been necessary and I hope that you now feel satisfied that your daughter is being well looked after.
Yours sincerely,

J. D. Johnson
Manager

I am not sure that quality complaints do any real good. Even companies that apparently go out of their way to solicit complaints do not really want them. They are just going through the motions and hope they do not actually get any because when they do, they seldom deal with them any better than their less hypocritical competitors.

CONCLUSION

The marketing aspects of product quality are vitally important but they are rarely addressed explicitly. They start with the key task of specifying the features and characteristics of a product which it is planned will satisfy a perceived customer need in all of its aspects. They include determining the quality status of products in comparison with competing products by conducting competitors' quality evaluations. They should be a prime driver for quality improvement. They should conclude by taking full advantage of quality superiority in market-share growth or price premium.

CHAPTER 5

DESIGN ASPECTS OF QUALITY

Making superior quality products requires an integrated series of processes that goes from marketing to manufacturing. In Chapter 2 this concept was expressed as the chain of conformance (Figure 2.1) and the marketing section of the chain was discussed in Chapter 4. The next length of the chain is concerned with product design—with the group of activities that realize the features and characteristics of the product requirement specification in the design of the product.

It is not practicable in one book about product quality to discuss all of the aspects of product design that impact quality. It could well be that everything about design has some effect, greater or lesser, on the quality of products. In this chapter we shall examine only the applicability of three great quality methodologies to design, discuss the methods of specifying products (because specification is a design activity that is fundamental to the conformance aspects of quality), and then discuss process capability, and finally examine two classical design quality disciplines—design review and product qualification.

THE THREE METHODOLOGIES OF QUALITY IMPROVEMENT

Traditionally, there have been three methodologies of quality improvement. First, there was defect detection and removal. Second, there was defect prevention, and third quality assurance. These methodologies have been applied in manufacturing and purchasing, and in principle, they could also be applied in marketing and design. However, so little progress has been made in such application in marketing that it was thought best to delay introducing the topic until the chapter on design quality.

In Figure 2.1 the chain of conformance was given. It showed how a customer's need was transposed by marketing processes to a marketing and then a product requirement specification. Design-development processes resulted in a product design hopefully conforming to the product requirement specification, and then purchasing and manufacturing processes gave one unit, or a series of units, of manufactured product. The degree to which the unit of product received by an individual customer conformed to their need measured the overall quality of the product.

In Figure 5.1 the manufacturing part of the chain of conformance is expanded. It shows that manufacturing people plan a series of manufacturing processes to realize the product's design in units of output. These processes may already be available, or new processes may have to be developed to achieve the design requirements. In either case, the manufacturing processes really used may not conform exactly to the planned processes. The latter often do not produce products which conform to

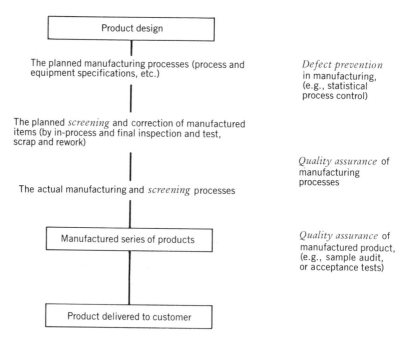

Figure 5.1.   Chain of conformance—manufacturing process.

the design, and manufacturing people adjust them without having the process specifications corrected. Often the manufacturing operatives do not have the skill, training, or motivation to follow the specifications exactly. Also, the process specifications are often incomplete. The conformance of the product to the design is then improved interactively—by inspecting and testing the product and scrapping or reworking units that do not conform. This screening inspection and test is a planned part of the total manufacturing process—and itself may be carried out with a greater or lesser degree of conformance to the plan.

Figure 5.1 also shows how the three quality improvement methodologies of screening, defect prevention, and quality assurance are applied in manufacturing. Screening—defect detection and removal—is the primary purpose of inspection and test. Products, or the items from which they are made, are inspected and tested. When an item fails, the defect causing the failure may be obvious or may be identified by further tests and inspections. The item is then scrapped or reworked. This process, which has been central to quality improvement in manufacturing since time immemorial, and is no less important today, will be discussed in detail in Chapter 8.

Defect prevention, as an explicit discipline, probably started when W. A. Shewhart published his classic book on statistical quality control, *Economic Control of Quality of Manufactured Products*, in 1931 (24). The fundamental idea is to prevent defects from being made rather than making them, detecting them, and removing them. In manufacturing, there are three general methods of defect prevention. The first is process capability and control. If products are manufactured by processes that are statistically capable of making almost defect-free product, and the processes are held under statistical control, few defects should be made. The second is a series of methods applicable to a running production line that is making defects of different kinds. Data on the frequency and types of defects is collected systematically, analyzed quantitatively, with the causes of the defects being determined and corrected. The third method is to work with the people performing the processes to ensure that they are competent and properly trained, that they are motivated to try to make defect-free products, and that they are given recognition of quality successes.

Quality assurance can be applied to both the manufacturing processes and the manufactured product. In the former, people independent of manufacturing (e.g., from a separate quality assurance department) check whether manufacturing processes are actually being performed in conformance to the way they were planned to be performed. Nonconformances are progressively eliminated by changing the processes or the specifications, leading to improvement and greater consistency. In practice, quality assurance is more often applied to the product than the processes because the customer is primarily interested in the quality of the product. However, in one way this is counter-productive. If a *product* fails a quality assurance procedure the normal consequences are for the failed product to be subjected to additional screening and scrap or rework, none of which improves the quality of subsequent products. Failure of a *process* quality assurance procedure could lead to process improvement—which is likely to improve the quality of subsequent product.

After having introduced the term quality assurance, it may be useful to comment on the words ensure, assure, and insure. These words are used randomly in business literature and the dictionary regards them as synonyms. This is a missed opportunity because there are three different meanings for these words. In most circumstances "ensure" can be used when referring to a primary activity, for example, "We ensure that our product is within its specified tolerances by using only capable and controlled processes in its manufacture." "Assure" can be used for secondary activities, especially those performed to check that a primary activity gave the desired result, for example, "We assure that at most one percent of the product is defective by inspecting a sample of 390 units from every lot and rejecting if we get more than one failure." "Insure" can be used for activities that limit the consequences of failure, for example, "We insure against being bankrupted by a failure by taking out product liability insurance." In this book, I try to stick to these meanings.

The quality improvement methodologies of screening, defect prevention, and quality assurance can be applied to design-development. Figure 5.2 shows an expansion of the design-development part of the chain of conformance including these methodologies. In practice, design-development is usually much less structured than manufacturing. Most managers expect manufacturing processes to be specified and the actual manufacturing methods to follow the specifications. They feel that companies that do not control their manufacturing in this way are working improperly and inefficiently. There is a lower expectation that the methods of product design are, or should be, controlled. To some extent, this is a consequence of the creative aspects of design which may be uncontrollable. However, it could be that people dislike being controlled, and that design engineers have been more successful in resisting control than assembly operators. Certainly, the implementation of computer-aided design (CAD) greatly increases the practicability of planning and

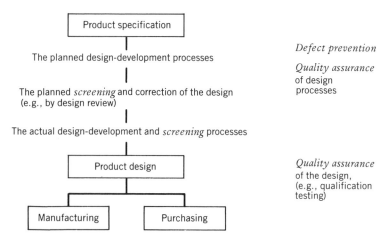

Figure 5.2. Chain of conformance—design-development processes.

controlling design processes. Complex semiconductor devices such as the microprocessors and memories used in computers give an example of the progress of design control. Such devices can only be designed by CAD methods, and the "design rules" controlling the design process are an integral part of the CAD software. Compared with conventional design methods, CAD greatly reduces the defect level of the design—which, together with time saving, is why conventional methods are no longer practical for semiconductor device design. The same advantages might be realized in the computer aided design of many other products.

Figure 5.2 indicates planned and actual screening activities among the design processes. Development testing is invariably used as a means of correcting initial designs. Although development testing may feel different from manufacturing testing, it applies the same principles: failures during testing lead to the identification and correction of (design) defects. Design review, which will be discussed in detail later in this chapter, is another well-established method of screening designs.

I do not know of many explicit applications of defect prevention in design, though, as mentioned previously, CAD gives great opportunities for the future. In the past, I have known of sporadic attempts to analyze and prevent drawing defects. In principle, the method is simple. As drawing changes are needed, their causes are categorized. There should really be only three main categories: changes initiated by the customer or by marketing; those initiated by manufacturing or purchasing (e.g., for cost reduction); and those to correct design defects. The last category may be analyzed to assist defect prevention. It may turn out that particular subsystems are especially prone to defects and can be the subject of special improvement programs. However, another obvious approach is to determine which design engineers or draftspeople make many defects and which make few, and then use the methods and experience of the latter to help the former. In practice, this does not work because no one wants to make it work. The design engineers are opposed to it, the chief engineer perceives that it will cause nothing but trouble, and the quality manager is too low in the pecking order to insist after the first rebuff—which is likely to be the chief engineer's claim that there is no design effort available to analyze the causes of drawing changes. Existing categorizations will be unsuitable for defect prevention purposes and will hide (behind such titles as "design improvements") the fact that 80 percent or more of the drawing changes are for correction of design defects. The chief engineer will claim that he or she already knows the engineers who make few defects, citing the most experienced personnel, and those making many defects (the newcomers) and state that only years of experience can improve the latter to the standard of the former. He or she concludes: "If you could only get me 20 engineers like (naming the best engineer) the whole problem would be solved. . . ."*

An essential aspect of quality assurance is an independent examination of how well an actuality conforms to a plan. As design processes are rarely formalized and specified, it is not surprising that quality assurance has had little application to design *processes*. However, there is an extremely important quality assurance procedure—product qualification—that is applied to the product design. As with most quality assurance procedures, it was the strong institutional customers, particularly military agencies, that first used product qualification. Subsequently, some companies have used it for their own protection even in the absence of customer insistence. Such companies are very wise because product qualification is perhaps the most cost effective of all quality assurance procedures.

Following this brief introduction to the application of the three methodologies of quality improvement to product design, the next section will discuss a key design quality topic—the ways of specifying quality—and the following sections will return to the three methodologies, describing important examples of their application to design: process capability for design defect prevention, design review for design defect identification and correction, and product qualification for design quality assurance.

---

* See *The Toledo Syndrome*, Chapter 13.

THE SIX WAYS OF SPECIFYING PRODUCT QUALITY

Conformance to specification is fundamental to much of quality improvement. This section will discuss the types of specifications to which conformance may be required. There are six ways a product may be specified, as follows:

1. The product's performance (what it shall do)
2. Tests of its conformance to the required performance
3. The product's design (what it shall be)
4. Inspections of its conformance to the required design
5. The processes for manufacturing the product (how it shall be made)
6. Tests and inspections of conformance to the required processes

In summary, one can specify what a product is required to do, what it is required to be, or how it is required to be made. Then, in each case, one can specify particular tests or inspections having the purpose of confirming that the product does what it should do, is what it should be, or is made the way it should be made.

The three primary types of specifications have complete redundancy going up the sequence (from five to three to one) but not going down. If a product is manufactured exactly the way it should be, it must have one defined design, and the defined design must have one defined performance. It may not be very easy to understand this point because our thinking normally goes from required performance to product design to manufacturing method, rather than the reverse. An example may make it easier to understand. Suppose a set of manufacturing specifications reads as follows:

Break one egg into a two-pint capacity bowl. Add three tablespoons of plain flour and one teaspoon of salt. Add a quarter of a pint of milk and mix to a thick, smooth cream with a fork. Add cold water and mix until the liquid is a thin, smooth cream. Pour into a preheated 10 inch × 7 inch baking dish, which contains beef dripping. Cook in a preheated oven at 375°F for 40 minutes.

With a certain amount of luck, the end result (after performing those specified manufacturing processes on the specified manufacturing parts and materials) will be a food that has the design of Yorkshire pudding. It will also have the performance of Yorkshire pudding in taste and the ability to sustain one through an English winter afternoon. (In practice, actual ingredients are not reproducible, so the partly cooked pudding is inspected, and is taken out of the oven when it is golden-brown in color, not excessively risen, and still soft in the center.)

It is apparent that performing these manufacturing processes correctly will always result in Yorkshire pudding which tastes like Yorkshire pudding. The opposite is not true. There may be many different product designs that give a required product performance (many other dishes, for example, blackberry and apple pie and cream, or golden pudding and custard, will sustain one through an English winter afternoon). Similarly, there are many different ways of manufacturing a product in conformance to its design. (Though I confess to a prejudice against the mass-production methods of manufacturing Yorkshire pudding.)

The three types of test and inspection specifications are also redundant, both with each other and with the primary specifications to which they refer. As an example, instead of specifying the fuel consumption of a car as less than 25 miles per gallon, one could specify a test such as, "When driven in both directions along a horizontal road five miles long at a speed of 55 ± 2 mph, no more than two-fifths of a gallon of gasoline shall be used."

The redundancy is both an advantage and a disadvantage. In principle, one could specify only the manufacturing methods—with great precision—and conform exactly to those specifications, knowing that the required design and performance would then result. However, taking advantage of the redundancy, it is much easier to specify—not over-tightly—the required performance thereby allowing slack in the manufacturing methods and, if necessary, using tests and inspections to confirm realization of the required performance. The disadvantage of the redundancy occurs if some of the six types of specifications are incompatible, for example, if a product that conforms to the design does not conform to the performance, and modificiation to improve the performance makes the product nonconformant to the specified design.

All six of these types of specifications are used by designers and manufacturers to define and control their products. The six types of specifications can also be contractually agreed between vendors and customers, and for this use they are very different from each other, as will now be explained.

An end-user customer buying a functional product will normally specify it as "black-box," covering only the "function, form, and fit" of the product. Essentially, only the performance of the product (Type 1 specification), its external appearance, and its ability to fit into an enclosure are contractually agreed. The form and fit are covered by Type 3 specifications (what the product shall be), but the main utility of Type 3 specifications—to define the complete design, internal as well as external—is not applied. Even when the performance specification is not contractually defined, it is legally implicit in the merchantability of the product. What I have called the "product requirement specification" (see the chain of conformance, Figure 2.1), is either a Type 1 specification or the black-box combination of Type 1 and Type 3 specifications.

Contractual agreement of black-box specifications does not require the vendor to have any particular internal design for the product, or to use any particular manufacturing, inspection or test methods. The vendor may change any of these at will, or leave them uncontrolled, without any contractual consequences—provided the product received by the customer meets its black-box specification.

Nonfunctional products and parts sold to other manufacturers for incorporation into their own products are often contractually required to conform to drawings—essentially a Type 3 specification. The design of the product is specified, not its performance. Contractual specification of products with either Type 1 or Type 3 specifications presents no special legal problem for vendors. In the United States, the contract often implicitly follows the Uniform Commerical Code (UCC). Under this, the customer has the right to test or inspect the products he or she has purchased, and to reject products found nonconforming to the specification. Even after the customer has accepted a product, he or she may revoke the acceptance if the product is subsequently found to be nonconforming, but the customer must do so before an unreasonable time has elapsed and before the product has been changed. The UCC does not contain any implication that all units of product will be conformant to the contractually agreed specification. There is often no penalty to the vendor for a "reasonable" level of nonconformance, and at higher levels the usual consequences are rejection of the product and loss of future business, rather than legal penalties.

Some institutional customers feel that Types 1 and 3 specifications give them inadequate confidence of receiving conforming products. Instead of working with their vendors to get progressively improved quality (see Chapter 10), they try a legal approach. They may contractually require the vendor to perform certain specified tests and inspections (Type 2 or 4 specifications) before the product is shipped. This may be on every unit of product or on a sample drawn from a lot. Only units (or lots) which pass the specified tests or inspections may be supplied. The contract often requires the results to be documented and to be authenticated by an approved signatory.

Nonconformant products can now reach the customer in three ways. First, even if performed on every unit of product, the tests and inspections will give incomplete coverage of the performance and design requirements. The car fuel consumption test discussed previously applied at a speed of 55 mph and another test might be specified at 80 mph. The customer is interested in the fuel consumption over a much wider range of speed, which can be inferred by interpolation and extrapolation, but which is not confirmed by test.

The second way the customer can receive nonconformant product is as a result of the test being wrongly done. (Actually, the customer gets a bad product only if the product is bad *and* the test is done wrongly. If the product is good, it does not harm the customer if the test is wrongly done.) The legal situation for nonconformant products received for these two reasons may be similar to those where only Type 1 or 3 specifications are applied.

The third way the customer can receive nonconformant product is a result of tests or inspections that are deliberately falsified. They may not be done at all, they may be done in a nonspecified way, or they may be failed—but recorded as passed. The people responsible for the tests and inspections are behaving illegally, and the delivery of nonconformant product in this way is clearly different from delivery for all of the other reasons discussed. It is therefore a serious matter for a vendor to make contractual agreements for Type 2 or 4 specifications. The vendor is imposing legal requirements on those responsible for the contractually agreed tests and specifications which differ from those generally applicable. The fact that from time to time accounts of illegalities of this kind are published in the press—in 1984 there were two different examples involving the semiconductor industry—may arise, at lease in part, because vendors do not fully realize the significance of contracts of this kind. The situation is further complicated because, if the product is actually good—and there may well be strong alternative evidence suggesting this—falsifying the tests does not make it bad. The people responsible for the falsifying can therefore tell themselves they are doing no real harm, because there is nothing wrong with the product going to the customer. Of course, that is no excuse; they contractually committed to do the tests and the customer paid the vendor for the tests.

Because falsification of tests or inspections is very clear-cut and obvious to those involved—much more obvious, for example, than their shipping a product that, without their knowing, is nonconformant to a Type 1 performance specification—contractual requirements to perform and pass such tests can be a powerful way of assuring product quality, and authenticated test and inspection reports can be much more valuable than vague "certificates of conformance" to Type 1 or 3 specifications.

Contractual specification can go one stage further. An institutional customer sometimes lacks confidence that he or she can adequately specify all of the performance requirements of a product being purchased, or get adequate conformation of their realization by specifying the design, tests, and inspections. The customer may have performed elaborate tests on early units of the product, for example, long-duration reliability tests, and may be unwilling to repeat them on subsequent units (and this would be impracticable for destructive tests). The customer believes that he or she can only have confidence that the desirable characteristics of the initial units will be repeated in subsequent units if there is no change, not only in the design, but also in the manufacturing methods. Therefore, the customer contractually specifies Type 5 and 6 specifications. For the vendor this is the most onerous of all types of contract. The vendor cannot change the design or the manufacturing methods to improve product performance or reduce costs. If, by some mistake, the product manufactured according to specification does not meet some requirement of the performance or design specifications the vendor is in a bind which can only be released by the customer.

Even more serious is the fact that manufacturing processes are rarely precisely specified and controlled. One of the reasons for using skilled rather than unskilled operators is that it reduces the need to define and specify manufacturing processes. However, even when it is not legitimate to rely on operator skill, processes are often unspecified or poorly specified. In addition, custom-and-practice often drifts away from conformance to process specifications, and different operators use different methods. Regular independent auditing is needed to define the actions needed to correct such problems, and then production supervision, manufacturing engineering, and design engineering need an exceptional level of discipline—and available effort—to keep the corrections up-to-date. Even in a well controlled situation it is very difficult to ensure day after day and week after week that every process is conducted exactly according to specification by every operator. To compensate for process inadequacies, products are tested, inspected, and reworked, and performance specifications are set lower than the ultimate achievable by exactly conforming to specified manufacturing processes. Such methods help to ensure that the product is good, but do not solve the problem of achieving exact conformance to contractually specified processes.

For all of these reasons, it is very serious for a vendor to make contractual agreements with its customers about manufacturing processes. Many different groups of design, manufacturing, purchasing, and quality people have their freedom of activity limited and have to work in a much more controlled way than is customary. Again, it is not uncommon for the media to carry reports of customers or vendor's upper management uncovering nonconformances to such contractually agreed manufacturing process specifications—with serious legal consequences.

PROCESS CAPABILITY

Most products fall into one of two categories. They are either made directly by processes or they are assembled from parts. Food, chemicals, and clothing may be typical "process" products, but many of these are also assembled. Mechanical and electronic products are typical assembled products. Even assembled products are made by assembly processes and the parts from which they are made are themselves manufactured by processes. Manufacturing processes are therefore important for assembled products as well as for process products.

Manufacturing processes are inherently variable. If a process is performed once and then repeated, the second performance will not be exactly the same as the first. Consequently, the product made the second time will not be exactly the same as the product made the first time. If the difference between the two units of product is greater than the tolerance allowed by the design, at least one of the units of product will be nonconformant to the design (i.e., it will be defective). This simple effect is the cause of much of the bad quality of the world's products. If a product's design requires achievement of tighter tolerances than the variability of the processes used to manufacture it allows, defective products will be made. A fundamental part of the art of designing superior quality products therefore is knowing the variabilities of the available manufacturing processes, and preparing designs that are compatible with those variabilities. It is also a fact of life that manufacturing processes capable of achieving tight tolerances usually cost more than processes capable of only loose tolerances. Superior product quality is defined by comparing competing products sold at about the same price. Superior design quality therefore requires designs that use the lowest cost (greatest variability) manufacturing processes that enable the product requirement specification to be achieved.

Many people believe that quality control is an esoteric subject based on mathematical statistics. I hope that readers of this book, having reached Chapter 5 without any mention of statistics, are disabused of this idea. In fact, there are only two statistical techniques—both relatively simple—that are widely used in practical quality control. The first is statistical process capability and control, which will be discussed in this chapter and Chapter 9, and the second is attribute sampling which will be discussed in Chapter 6. (Statistical design of experiments, a third classic statistical quality control technique of great value, is currently fashionable particularly in the version applied by the Japanese statistician, Taguchi. However, the actual level of its application, even though it is considerably more than it was even two years ago, is still very low.)

Imagine a simple manufacturing process such as turning pieces of metal or wood on a lathe to produce one-inch diameter cylinders. Successive cylinders, measured with a micrometer, will be found to have diameters that are different from each other and that are not exactly one inch. Several different process variations will cause the product variation. First there will be variations of the machine—the lathe—such as different positions of the mounting chuck, looseness in the bearings, resonances of vibrations in the frame, and so on. There will be variations in the tool, its sharpness, hardness, edge straightness, and so on. There will be variations in the initial status of the wooden or metal feed pieces, their original diameter, circularity, and so on. The operator will add further variability—how tightly the piece is clamped, how much pressure is applied to the tool, and so on. The environment provides variability—the temperature of the machine shop may be rising or falling causing the machine, tool, and workpiece to expand or contract. The inaccuracy of the micrometer will add further variation. Each process variation will produce consequential variations in the units of product—in this case in the diameters of the cylinders. Unfortunately, I do not know how much of an effect a 3°F increase in shop temperature, or a sixteenth of an inch increase in the diameter of the feed bar, or any of the other process variables would have on the final diameter of such cylinders, so I cannot describe the real example. However, it can be replaced by a simulation, as follows.

Imagine 10 different, simultaneously applied, process variables, one of which can produce up to twenty one-thousandths of an inch variation in the cylinder's diameter and the other nine of which can each produce up to one-thousandth of an inch variation. Imagine the first process variable can have 10 different values, giving diameter variations, measured in units of ten thousandths of an inch, of 0, 20, 40, 60, and so on, and imagine the other nine variables can also have 10 different values of 0, 1, 2, 3, and so on, of the same unit. To make the arithmetic easy all of the variations are considered increases in the diameter of the cylinder beyond the intended one inch. The manufacture of a series of cylinders can be simulated by adding together a random value of each one of the variables to get each cylinder. I have done this in Table 5.1 using a table of random numbers. Each line in the table corresponds to one cylinder, the whole table corresponding to the manufacture of 50 cylinders. The first 10 random numbers I read were 1, 0, 4, 8, 0, 1, 7, 7, 9, 2. I multiplied the first by 20 to correspond to the large variable, and wrote the other nine numbers down to correspond to the smaller variables. Adding the resulting 10 numbers together gave 58 (i.e., the first cylinder had a diameter of 1.0058 inches). Subsequent cylinders had diameters of 1.0118 inches, 1.0113 inches, and so on.

Examing all 50 values of the diameter, the smallest is 1.0024 inches and the largest 1.0235 inches. How are the rest distributed? Are they spaced evenly between the extremes, concentrated near the middle, or what? The question can be answered by plotting the measurements in a histogram. I have done this in Figure 5.3. For the 50 values, I used seven columns, so that on average a column contains about seven points. The answer to the question is that, except for the two extremes, each column seems to have about the same number of points with considerable, apparently random variation.

If this was a real process, the manufacturing engineer responsible for it might notice that the variation—over twenty-thousandths of an inch—was excessive. He or she might discover that there was a problem with the lathe (e.g., a worn bearing) which could be corrected. Let us assume that this eliminates the first of the process variables—the big one—in Table 5.1. The manufacturing engineer could then make 50 more cylinders. The last column in Table 5.1 shows the cylinder diameters without the variation due to process-variable-one, so it can represent the 50 new cylinders. The smallest diameter is 1.0013 inches and the largest 1.0061 inches. Eliminating one machine problem has reduced the variation to about one-quarter of what it was before. Again we can ask the question: How are the new values distributed? Figure 5.4 gives a new histogram, without process-variable-one. Again, I have used seven columns for the 50 values. Now the distribution has a special shape like a bell. Many of the cylinders have diameters of about 1.0040 inches, and progressively less have values greater or lesser than this. The bell shape is associated with a way of distributing such values called the *normal distri-*

TABLE 5.1. Simulation of Manufacturing Variation of Diameter

(unit = one ten thousandth of an inch)

Cylinder Number	Process variables										Sum	Sum, exvariable-one
	1	2	3	4	5	6	7	8	9	10		
1	20	0	4	8	0	1	7	7	9	2	58	38
2	100	0	1	1	0	1	0	6	9	0	118	18
3	100	3	6	0	2	0	1	1	0	0	113	13
4	20	1	8	1	6	4	4	2	7	5	58	58
5	140	9	1	6	4	6	2	7	7	5	187	47
6	120	9	1	7	9	1	5	3	4	9	168	48
7	80	1	9	4	6	2	1	8	6	0	117	37
8	100	9	0	3	6	2	7	0	6	5	138	38
9	0	7	2	0	9	6	9	0	6	5	44	44
10	180	9	9	5	7	0	1	5	0	5	221	41
11	180	1	2	9	1	9	2	1	9	1	215	35
12	0	7	0	0	2	2	8	1	8	2	30	30
13	60	6	8	4	6	5	4	4	3	9	109	49
14	140	3	2	5	5	9	4	2	8	8	186	46
15	100	8	5	3	9	3	9	9	5	6	157	57
16	60	0	9	9	5	8	7	2	9	0	109	49
17	180	1	9	8	2	7	5	6	4	2	224	44
18	180	8	2	5	3	4	6	9	9	9	235	55
19	0	2	9	3	9	6	9	8	8	7	61	61
20	120	5	3	4	0	9	3	1	0	1	146	26
21	100	5	2	6	6	6	7	1	1	9	143	43
22	20	9	1	7	4	3	1	8	7	3	63	43
23	180	6	1	5	9	9	4	4	0	1	219	39
24	100	0	5	2	4	1	4	8	8	4	136	36
25	60	0	4	8	3	6	6	3	2	1	93	33
26	0	2	2	5	2	7	2	1	0	6	27	27
27	180	7	2	6	5	7	1	0	6	3	217	37
28	120	3	9	3	6	4	1	2	9	5	162	42
29	160	0	9	1	5	1	9	6	3	0	194	34
30	140	9	2	4	8	3	9	1	9	7	192	52
31	0	4	9	3	4	0	0	5	4	6	35	35
32	60	2	0	8	1	3	0	7	9	7	97	37
33	0	6	8	0	1	9	1	8	8	7	48	48
34	120	5	5	6	3	3	2	0	9	2	155	35
35	80	8	5	8	0	2	9	4	5	9	130	50
36	40	4	2	1	6	7	5	6	8	6	85	45
37	180	3	0	9	3	0	6	9	0	1	211	31
38	120	2	4	3	6	1	6	0	0	4	146	26
39	120	8	0	0	7	8	1	8	4	2	158	38
40	100	6	1	6	3	7	8	4	9	0	144	44
41	120	3	9	4	4	0	4	2	5	0	151	31

TABLE 5.1. (Continued)

(unit = one ten thousandth of an inch)

Cylinder Number	Process variables										Sum	Sum, exvariable-one
	1	2	3	4	5	6	7	8	9	10		
42	100	3	5	3	7	7	3	2	3	0	133	33
43	20	3	4	1	5	7	8	9	5	7	69	49
44	0	0	4	0	0	8	1	4	3	4	24	24
45	80	9	7	4	9	1	6	3	6	6	131	51
46	140	9	7	7	5	8	1	0	2	8	187	47
47	20	6	3	7	8	3	1	7	4	5	64	44
48	140	5	7	0	3	9	1	8	1	0	174	34
49	180	7	5	8	1	8	5	7	7	4	232	52
50	60	7	1	6	6	5	8	4	3	7	107	47

bution. The actual normal distribution is a mathematical function that goes continuously from minus infinity to plus infinity (like the continuous line drawn on Figure 5.4) so any real distribution of actual values—such as our 50 diameters—is only an approximation to the normal distribution of greater or lesser closeness.

Our simulation leads to two very important conclusions. The first is that the sum of a number of separate variables of about the same magnitude results in an approximation to the normal distribution. In our case the nine small variables each having permitted values of 0, 1, 2, 3, and so on, times one ten-thousandth of an inch gave the approximately normal distribution of Figure 5.4. This conclusion applies irrespective of the shapes of the distributions of the constituent variables. Figure 5.5 shows the distribution of process-variable-two of Table 5.1, and the other eight small variables have similar distributions (as does process-variable-one,

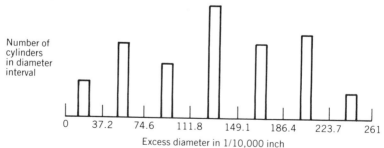

Figure 5.3. Histogram of the diameters (excess diameter beyond one inch).

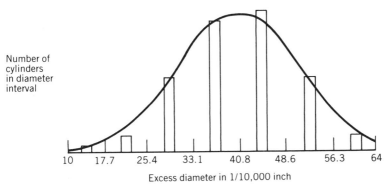

Figure 5.4. Histogram of the diameters (excess diameter beyond one inch).

except that the magnitude is 20 times as great). These variables lack a normal distribution. With only 50 cylinders, by chance the central columns for process-variable-two have less values than the outer columns—the opposite of a normal distribution. If a large number of cylinders was turned, each column would have about the same number of values in it. However, despite the fact that the nine distributions individually do not have anything like normal distributions, their random sum does.

The second important conclusion is that the resulting distribution will *not* be normal if one or two of the process variations are much bigger than the rest and the one or two are not themselves normally distributed. When all 10 process variations were present, including the large process-variable-one, the distribution was the one plotted in Figure 5.3. It is not normal but intermediate between the approximately normal distribution of Figure 5.4 and the flat distribution of Figure 5.5.

The method of plotting in Figure 5.4 gives the familiar bell-shaped curve. However, there is a different method of plotting that is more practically useful—cumulative plotting. In Table 5.1, the sum of the nine

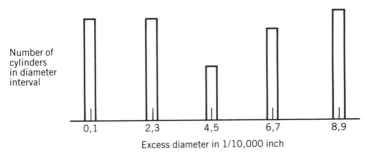

Figure 5.5. Histogram of one of the process variations of the diameters.

small variables 38, 18, 13, and so on, can be placed in rank order from the lowest to the highest, and can then be plotted as a distribution. This has been done in Figure 5.6. The sigmoid shape of this curve is typical of the cumulative normal distribution. The reason that this distribution is practically more useful than the bell shaped version is that special graph paper is available, called normal probability paper, which has one scale contracted in the middle and expanded at the ends. When a normal distribution in its cumulative form is plotted on this paper, a straight line appears. Figure 5.7 shows the ranked values of Figure 5.6 plotted on such paper. The 50 values have been converted to percentages, 2 percent for each value. One other adjustment has been made. If the 50 values had been plotted at 2 percent, 4 percent, 6 percent, and so on, the fiftieth value would be at 100 percent which is not on the paper (it is at infinity). This would make the highest value appear to be special, which it is not. It is no different from the lowest or any of the other values. This problem can be dealt with in several ways, which have different statistical accuracy depending on the sample size. However, the simplest is to move all of the points half an interval. For our example, this means that the points are plotted at 1 percent, 3 percent, 5 percent . . . 97 percent, and 99 percent.

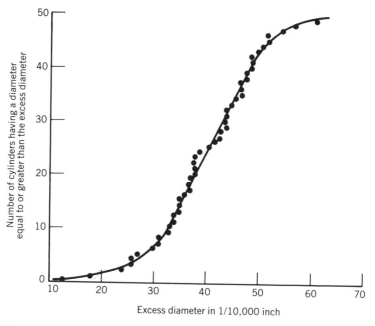

Figure 5.6. Ranked order and cumulative distribution plot of sum of nine small variables of Table 5.1.

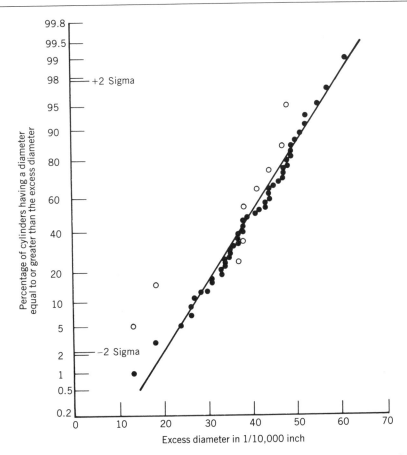

Figure 5.7. Cumulative distribution plot of the sum of the nine small variables of Table 5.1.

Actually, this problem applies equally to the sigmoid version of the graphs and I moved the points in Figure 5.6 half an interval too.

The ranking of Figure 5.6 (which came from the values of Table 5.1) gives quite a good overall straight line on the probability paper. This shows that adding nine variables (none of which was anything like normally distributed) gives a fairly close approximation to a normal distribution. With only four or five variables the line might well have had a distinct curve. Of course, the simulation can give only a limited approximation to a normal distribution. However many cylinders were manufactured, none of them could have a diameter less than 1.0000 inch or more than 1.0081 inch (the nine process variables all having their minimum or maximum values), whereas an actual normal distribution goes ever nearer to plus and minus infinity as more units are made.

Apart from its overall shape the line has small irregularities due to "sampling error." Such error is reduced if the sample size is made larger (e.g., if I had continued Table 5.1 to 100 or 200 values) and is increased if the sample size is made smaller. On Figure 5.7 the circles are the plot of the first 10 values of Table 5.1 (in ranked order, 13, 18, 37, 38, 38, 38, 41, 44, 47, and 48). This is a random sample from all 50 of the values and, apart from sampling error, should follow the same line. The deviation from the line shows how much sampling error can occur with as small a sample as 10.

Sampling error is least near the mean because for any given sample size the values are concentrated near the mean. In our simulation there are 22 values between the fifth and fiftieth percentiles, only three between the 0.5th and fifth percentiles and none between the 0.05th and 0.5th percentiles. Our conclusion that the simulation is a reasonable approximation to a normal distribution is well supported between the fifth and fiftieth percentiles, has little support between the 0.5th and fifth percentiles, and has no support below the 0.5th percentile. It could be that the distributions of real products are progressively less normal in their tails, because the process variables with relatively small standard deviations will not contribute to the product variation in the tails of the distribution. When only a few variables are contributing the distribution may become nonnormal. Fortunately, the practical usefulness of process capability does not depend on the normality of distributions' tails.

Any normal distribution can be defined by two parameters, the mean and the standard deviation. The probability paper plot of Figure 5.7 gives an easy way of getting these parameters for our distribution. The mean is read off from the fiftieth percentile line as 39 thousandths. The standard deviation is obtained by subtracting the -2 sigma point (22 thousandths) from the $+2$ sigma point (58 thousandths) and dividing the result by 4 to give sigma (i.e., 9 thousandths). The mean gives the central position of the whole distribution. The standard deviation is a measure of how widely the distribution is dispersed from the mean. A small standard deviation indicates that most of the values are near to the mean, and a large standard deviation indicates the values are spread out. Table 5.2 shows the percentage of the total values which are within specific numbers of standard deviations from the mean of a normal distribution. As mentioned, the normal distribution is a continuous distribution that goes from minus infinity to plus infinity, so however many standard deviations are taken there is still some proportion of values outside. Of course, any

TABLE 5.2. Percentages of Total Values Which Are Outside Specific Numbers of Standard Deviations of the Mean of a Normal Distribution

Standard Deviations	Total Values (%)
±1	±15.9
±2	± 2.3
±3	± 0.135
±4	± 0.003

real distribution is only an approximation to a normal distribution, and many real distributions, even if they look normal, have finite upper and lower values. In our simulation, only 50 cylinders were turned after the lathe was corrected, and the actual smallest and largest diameters were 1.0013 and 1.0061 inches. Even if the manufacture of a large number of cylinders had been simulated, none could have a diameter less than 1.000 inch or more than 1.0081 inch.

We are now in a position to discuss the capability of our process for making one-inch-diameter cylinders. Initially, if the cylinder drawing had given the tolerance as one inch, −0, +25 thousandths, the process would have seemed capable because the diameters of all 50 cylinders were within this tolerance. However, such a process is not regarded as capable for two reasons. The first is conventional. Only processes whose product is approximately normally distributed are considered capable by quality control professionals. The second is practical. A nonnormal product distribution is usually controlled by one process variable and any change to that variable will cause a corresponding change to the product, for example, a 30 percent increase in that process variable will cause a similar large increase in the product variation. Most changes are deteriorations. (This is not just Murphy's Law; it also has a basis in the Second Law of Thermodynamics). In our example, the worn bearing is likely to get worse, and even the 25 thousandths tolerance is likely to become unachievable. Also, the behavior of nonnormal processes is very hard to predict.

In measuring the capability of a process, quality control professionals first make a consecutive number of units of output—30 or 50—under standardized conditions, and plot the measurements on probability paper to determine if the distribution is normal. If it is not, the process has to be investigated to determine the cause of the deviation from normality. Invariably, there will be just one cause or a small number of causes (if there were several causes of similar magnitude, the distribution would be approximately normal). Because there is only, for example, one cause of most of the variation, it is usually practicable to eliminate that cause (our

manufacturing engineer replaced the defective bearing of the lathe). Another 30 or 50 units are then made, measured, and the results plotted.
Usually, the distribution will now be approximately normal. If not, the
search for, and elimination of, a "special" cause is repeated. It is also useful to plot the results sequentially, because some special causes result in
progressive trends.

For our simulation, the probability plot of the distribution of cylinder
diameters after the elimination of process-variable-one has already been
given in Figure 5.7. It is interesting to see also the plot of the data including process-variable-one, and this is given in Figure 5.8. The wiggles
are similar to those shown in Figure 5.7, but the overall shape is sigmoid,
not straight. A capability study giving a probability curve of this kind
would lead to a search for the special cause of the nonnormality.

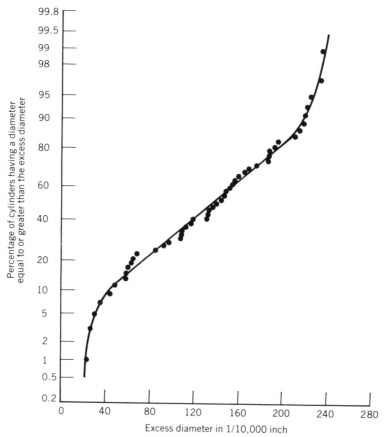

Figure 5.8. Cumulative distribution plot of the sum of the nine small variables
and one large variable of Table 5.1.

When the measurements of the units made by the process are apparently normally distributed the process may be stable. The variability of the product may be determined not by one special process variable but by many ordinary process variables each contributing a similar magnitude to the product variability. This makes the product variability inherently stable. In statistical jargon the process is "under control." Large percentage increases in one ordinary process variable give relatively small percentage increases in the product variation. Table 5.1 shows that, after correction of process-variable-one, the range of product variation was 61 10-thousandths of an inch. If one of the processes, say process-variable-two whose own range was from 0 to 9 10-thousandths, became more variable by say 30 percent, it would contribute only three extra units to the product variation (actually less for statistical reasons) increasing the range of variability not by 30 percent but by less than 5 percent. This result may be compared with the effect of a 30 percent increase in "special cause" process-variable-one. This would add a 20 or 25 percent increase to the product range. Of course, if the deterioration in process-variable-two continued to increase, it would eventually reach a level at which it had a big effect on the product variability. Process-variable-two would then cease to be an ordinary cause of variation and have become a special cause of variation requiring analysis and correction.

The stability of a process which is under control is an advantage if the process is capable of achieving the tolerances required by the product design, but a disadvantage if it is not. Improving one special cause has a major effect on the variability of the product. Improving one ordinary cause has very little effect on the variability of the product. In our corrected simulation, to get a further 30 percent reduction in the variability of the diameters of the cylinders would require a 30 percent improvement in every one of the nine ordinary process variables—process-variable-two, process-variable-three, and so on—and this might be virtually impossible. If a tighter tolerance were needed, it would probably be better to go to a completely different method of manufacture.

Having eliminated the special cause associated with process-variable-one, Figure 5.7 shows that the cylinders made by the improved process have diameters that are approximately normally distributed. The capability of the process can now be read off from Figure 5.7. Conventionally, process capability is usually defined as "plus or minus three sigma." If the design tolerance is made just equal to the capability so defined, then 0.135 percent of the pieces will be undersized and 0.135 percent oversize. However, for a measurement made at one time, as we did, the more conservative plus or minus four sigma is often used. This allows for the extra variability that may come from the ordinary causes over a prolonged period of time. As the mean and standard deviation of the process were 1.0039 and 0.0009 inches respectively the capability is 0.0072 inches, or from 1.003 inches to 1.0075 inches. So, if the design specification for the diameter of the cylinder was 1 inch, −0, +0.01 inches, the process would be well capable. Conversely, if the specification was 1 inch, −0, +0.005 inches, the process would be incapable. It is worth emphasizing that processes are not inherently capable or incapable. They are capable or incapable of meeting a particular, specified design-tolerance. A process capable of meeting one tolerance may be incapable of meeting a tighter tolerance.

For a general book on quality improvement like this, rather than a specialized book on statistical quality control, the above treatment of the theory of process capability is probably sufficient. In summary, the treatment pointed out that products are manufactured by processes and because processes are inherently variable successive units of a product are not exactly the same. If the product variability is greater than the tolerance of the design some of the manufactured units will be defective. Usually a number of process variables will contribute to the product variability. If there are, say, 10 or more of these process variables, each contributing a similar amount to the product variability, then the variability of successive units of product will have a distribution that approximates to a normal distribution (irrespective of the distributions of the individual process variables). Such a process is inherently stable. Conversely, if one or two of the process variables contributes much more to the product variability than the others, the process is inherently unstable. Getting the process under control requires elimination of such special causes of product variability. Whether or not a process is stable can be determined by plotting the results of measurements of successive units of product—30 or 50—on cumulative, normal, probability paper. If the process is stable the capability of the process is conventionally determined as ±4 sigma, allowing ±3 sigma to be achieved by a series of measurements made over a long period of time.

Obviously, real products having many different design parameters, not just one like the diameter of our cylinder, and made by many different processes in series and parallel, are more complicated than the above treatment suggests. Is this the reason that the vast majority of products are designed and manufactured without any explicit attention to process capability? Typically, design tolerances are applied arbitrarily by design engineers on the basis of more or less personal experience (possibly following some general scheme, such as "worse-case" or "statistical" tolerancing for functional or fitting dimensions). Very often design engineers will specify tolerances that they feel are tighter than necessary, because, cynically, they do not believe manufacturing will achieve the specified tolerances. These "safety-margins" help to ensure that products function, and prevent the criticisms of the design engineers that result from nonfunctional designs. An iterative process of manufacture is used rather than one of exact conformance to a correct design. Failures of the product on functional test lead to design changes or process improvements. After a few iterations the product will seem more or less satisfactory (though by no means in exact conformance to a correct design or of optimum manufacturing cost) and the design, manufacturing methods, and methods of inspection and test will stabilize. From then on, none of these will be deliberately changed unless there is a major quality problem or a good idea for cost reduction. My answer to the question I posed at the beginning of this paragraph is that the relatively rare application of formal process capability studies in design (and of the associated formal process control methods in manufacturing) is not because of inherent theoretical difficulties, nor because process capability and control do not work in practice (there are enough examples to prove that they do), but because their implementation is psychologically unattractive to people, and because such implementation takes exceptional managerial skill and persistence. I shall discuss these important points in more detail in Chapter 9, after discussing manufacturing process control.

DESIGN REVIEW

In Chapter 2 the concept of the chain of conformance was introduced, expressing the idea that a series of marketing, design-development, purchasing, and manufacturing processes converts a customer's need successively into a marketing specification of a product, a product requirement specification, a product design, a series of manufactured products, and finally the one unit of product received by the one customer. The product quality is an expression of how well that unit of product conforms to the customer's need. This concept suggests simplistically that in a new-product project, each phase—marketing, design-development, purchasing, and manufacturing—is separate from the others, and one phase should be completed before the next is started. However, it was emphasized in Chapter 2 that such separation is not the optimum way of making superior-quality products. It is much better for there to be continuous interaction between the people of the four involved functions (plus people of the quality function) and regular feedback of information from the later phases of the project, causing revision of earlier phases.

Unfortunately, the reality of new product introduction is often nearer to the simplistic representation of the chain of conformance than the more complex optimum. Marketing agrees to a product requirement specification with the customer without proper input from design-development, and the latter completes the design without taking proper account of the needs of purchasing and manufacturing. Often the problem is exacerbated by a pecking order of status (and salary levels). The marketing and design-development functions have the highest status, the one because of its direct relationship with customers and because only it can get the orders on which all else depends; and the other because of its perceived creative and intellectual superiority. Manufacturing and manufacturing engineering are intermediate in status, with purchasing and quality the lowest. Because of their low status manufacturing, purchasing and quality people are often unable effectively to represent their views to marketing and design-development people. Ideally, a whole range of informal contacts should take place between the key people of all five functions on terms of equality and in recognition that everyone makes essential contributions to the success of the overall new-product project. In practice, such informal contacts are never sufficient and often they are inadequate. Formal design review is therefore an essential part of the optimum method of making new products.

As an introduction to the subject it is useful to define a few terms as follows:

An *item* is a concrete or abstract object. For example, a material, a part, a subassembly, a product, a customer's need, a product specification, and a product design.

A *product* is an item that is sold by a vendor to a customer.

A *design project* has the objective of completing the design of a new or modified product.

A *project manager* is the manager of all aspects of a design project including marketing, design, scheduling, provision of personnel and other resources, and so on.

A *design manager* is the manager, reporting to the project manager, of the design-development activities of a design project. He or she heads the team of design-development engineers.

A *design review* is a series of formal meetings (and the activities which precede and follow such meetings) during which a group of design and/or functional experts, who are independent of the design team, review a design project to identify design defects and to recommend design improvements.

In any business there are a number of activities that happen virtually automatically. In this class are the primary activities of the major functions of the business. Once these functions are established their primary activities will be performed. Marketing will interact with customers and sell products, purchasing will buy things, and manufacturing will produce things. A group of design-development engineers will inevitably design new products, and manufacturing engineers will "fight fires" and set up new production lines. Another group of activities will be performed almost automatically because they are intrinsically interesting and people like doing them. Much computerization happens for this reason; quality people love to get and operate new test or inspection equipment; and so on. Other activities are performed because powerful customer's insist, either contractually or as a condition of doing business. However, there is another set of activities that happen only if management policies and implementation programs are established for them—and also if "champions" drive them. There is no simple correlation between the importance of a program and which of these categories it falls into. Some of the most important improvement programs—which are vital to the long-term health, and even survival, of a division—fall into the last category, and unfortunately, virtually all quality improvement programs, except those mandated by customers, are of this type. Included in this is design review. It is a rare division that performs design review in the absence of customer insistence. Occasionally, an especially competent design-development manager will institute the system; occasionally a division manager (usually as a result of a previous painful experience) will insist on its performance.

The first requirement therefore for design review is for the division manager to establish a policy whereby all of the division's design projects will be subjected to a design review, and to give enough personal regard to the process to ensure that it happens. This applies irrespective of the type of product to be sold to the customer—whether it is a hardware product, a design to which such a product could be manufactured, or a software product such as a computer program.

There are two different approaches to design review. For the first, the design review is conducted by independent experts who have similar skills to the members of the design team. The approach is practicable for large design-development organizations with several teams working simultaneously on different design projects. Members of one or more design teams can participate in the design review of another team's project. This approach is often applied to development projects for major computer-software products. For large companies, members of the company-level research and development staff may conduct design reviews of divisional projects. In smaller companies, external consultants may be used.

For the second, the design review is conducted by functional specialists representing marketing, purchasing, manufacturing engineering, test engineering, and quality. The controller may be represented to review cost issues. In large organizations, reliability, safety, and other experts may participate. In practice, design reviews following the second approach are of major value for virtually all significant design projects, while those following the first approach may have a less universal application. The design manager is not a formal member of the design review committee but it is important for him or her and other appropriate members of the design team to participate in the meetings.

Having established a policy requiring design review, the division manager must appoint one of the department heads to manage the program. For the "independent-expert" approach this may well be the design-development manager. For the functional approach, it should not be the design-development manager, but rather the quality, manufacturing, or purchasing manager.

Each design review is performed by a specific design review committee. In a large organization utilizing project managers, the design review committee chairperson is appointed by, and reports to, the project manager. (The chairperson is a part-time job and the chairperson may well report to someone else for other responsibilities.) In a smaller organization the chairperson reports to the division manager.

A design review plan must be prepared by the design team as part of its overall planning for the design project, and, for a long duration project, the plan should be extended periodically as the project proceeds. The plan is approved by the design manager, the project manager, and the design review committee chairperson. It includes the design review meeting schedule related to key project milestones, the budget allocation, the names of the chairperson, secretary, and other committee members, the data requirements for each meeting, and the extent, if any, of participation by customer representatives.

For a complex product the first meeting of the design review committee may be held during the proposal phase of a project. Preliminary design review meetings may then be held to evaluate the design of individual hardware and softwware items comprising the product, the definition of requirements, the development and qualification test plans, and so on. A final design review meeting (sometimes called a critical design review meeting) examines the results of qualification testing and evaluates the start of manufacturing. For simpler products only one or two meetings may be required.

The primary objective of the design review committee at each of its meetings is to identify defects present in the design at that time which might cause the design, or product manufactured according to the design, to fail to meet any of its quality, cost or schedule requirements. Secondary objectives are to recommend design changes to eliminate such defects or to improve quality, cost or schedule beyond the existing requirements, to evaluate alternative designs, and to resolve open issues by assigning actions. Table 5.3 lists some of the design aspects that should be evaluated by the design review committee.

TABLE 5.3. Design Aspects for Evaluation by a Design Review Committee

1. Conformance of the product requirement specification to all aspects of the customer's need.
2. Completeness of the product requirement specification with regard to requirements for reliability, maintainability, safety, environmental resistance, quality assurance, government regulations, and so on.
3. Conformance of the design to all requirements of the product requirement specification.
4. Conformance of the design to all relevant divisional engineering standards.
5. For a manufactured product, the expected cost of a product manufactured in conformance to the design.
6. The manufacturability, testability, and inspectability of the design.
7. Achievability of design tolerances by existing manufacturing processes of known capability.
8. The purchasability of items needed to manufacture the design.
9. The schedule for the design project.
10. The schedule for manufacture of a manufactured product.
11. The plans for and results of appropriate analyses (reliability, thermal stress, mechanical stress, safety, etc.).
12. The plans for and results of appropriate tests (design, qualification, field application, etc.).
13. The allocation of product requirement specification features and characteristics to subsystems, assemblies, and components.
14. Synthetic models of the design approach.
15. Engineering documentation (product requirement specification, design specifications, drawings, component specifications, process specifications, etc.).
16. Applicability of experience on previous designs.

In conducting a design review, the chairperson should issue the agenda at least two weeks before a meeting. The secretary should follow-up with necessary information supplied by the design team at least a week before the meeting. During a meeting the chairperson should use good judgment in allocating time for discussion of different points—including ones raised for the first time at the meeting. The committee should not just address major defects—in fact, a competent design team is unlikely to be plagued by major defects. The committee's objective should be to identify all defects, however small, and achievement of this objective takes time and close attention to detail. However, it is always cost effective to identify a defect by design review, rather than by allowing it to remain in the design to prejudice the future of the project.

The chairperson should define actions clearly and assign them to the design team or a committee member. An assignee must accept the action (possibly subject to his or her department head's approval) or give reasons for refusal. On completion of an action he or she must give the secretary a brief report which is checked by the committee member who raised the issue. When all issues raised at a particular meeting have been cleared, the secretary issues a close-out report. The secretary also issues minutes of each meeting, listing identified defects, requirements for analyses, unresolved issues, and agreed, refused, and uncompleted actions.

In dealing with the topic of design review at one of TRW's management training programs called "The TRW Quality College," participants are asked to discuss the six statements given in Table 5.4. Readers may wish to form their own opinions before reading the consensus views of some hundreds of TRW managers and engineers.

TABLE 5.4. Six Statements about Design Review

1. The purpose of design review is to enable design engineers to exchange ideas and philosophies, and the participants need to be technical experts.
2. Design reviews must be conducted in an organized manner with a planned agenda, and the participants must have evaluated relevant data before each meeting.
3. The design manager (the head of the design team) has final approval over the design review.
4. Design review can only be successful if the division manager is committed to the process.
5. A simple product, such as an automotive engine valve, does not justify imposition of design review.
6. Thinking small, thinking negatively, and playing devil's advocate works well in design review.

Statement 1: *False.* Design review is conducted during a series of formal meetings. Design engineers have many more suitable opportunities for informal discussions with each other and with technical consultants. Independent technical experts may be members of the design review committee, but it is essential for representatives of marketing, purchasing, manufacturing, quality, and other functions to be members also.

Statement 2: *True.* The design review meetings must be conducted in an organized manner with agendas, minutes, and committed actions. However, the chairperson must allow flexibility for discussion of any important points which emerge at a meeting even if they are not on the agenda. The time of the meeting should not be spent on informative presentations by the design manager and design team members. The design review committee members should receive significant design data well ahead of each meeting and should carefully evaluate this from their specialized viewpoints. At the meeting the consequences of those evaluations should be discussed.

Statement 3: *False.* The design review committee and its chairperson are independnet of the design manager. The chairperson reports separately to the project manager or division manager. Usually, the committee and the design team will reach a consensus view on the correct response to points raised at design review meetings. When, as happens occasionally, there is a serious disagreement between the committee and the design manager, the latter has the right to disregard the recommendation of the committee. The existence of design review does not dilute the clear responsibility of the design manager for his or her design, and the design review committee is not empowered to order the design manager to take particular actions. However, the design review committee chairperson has the right and responsibility to report such disagreements to the project manager or division manager who may exercise normal authority over the design manager.

Statement 4: *True.* Without the commitment of the division manager, design review is unlikely to survive even if lower-level managers support it. In the real world there are too many other pressures on these managers. Of course, many division managers give their commitment only in response to customer insistence.

Statement 5: *False.* The first version of these questions was written by a group of quality people from one of TRW's spacecraft divisions. From the viewpoint of their very complex product, they were trying to provoke their colleagues from divisions making simpler products. However, their serious answer, like those of all subsequent groups, was false. All new designs should be subject to design review. Chairpeople should exercise judgment about the time duration appropriate to each review, taking account of the complexity and degree of innovation of each design.

Statement 6:   True. In design review, the details are all-important. It is unlikely that a competent design team will have committed a major blunder (or if they have that they do not know). The difference between a superior product and an average one is the difference between 100 percent and 99 percent. To achieve superiority it is necessary to search diligently for the small things that are wrong. However, in playing devil's advocate and nit-picking, design review committee members should carefully avoid an adversarial attitude toward the design team. They should attack the design, but never attack the members of the design team.

PRODUCT QUALIFICATION

In the early years of the 1970s the telecommunications industry was making a major technological transition. The most complex and expensive part of the entire telephone system is the telephone exchange. Its function is to perform the switching operations necessary to connect one subscriber to another. The two subscriber's may be wired to the same exchange, or they may be in different towns, countries or even continents, so that switching operations in a whole series of exchanges may be involved. Before 1970 the technology of telephone exchanges was electromechanical. They consisted of vast numbers of relays, multiselectors and similar devices in which electrical currents flowing in coils caused metallic contacts to open or close—to switch. In the 1970s the first transition to an electronic technology was made. The final speech path was still electromechanical, made by tiny, sealed reed-relays, but all of the control operations were performed electronically by solid-state, semiconductor devices. Also, for the first time the operation was controlled by computers.

The companies of ITT in Europe, West Germany, France, Belgium, the United Kingdom, and so on, were very active in the design and development of these semielectronic, computer-controlled exchanges, because telephone exchanges accounted for more of ITT's sales than any other of its thousands of products. The design of the previous generation of electromechanical exchanges had been initiated more than 20 years before and had evolved in an informal way. Consequently, from time to time there had been major, expensive quality problems caused by design deficiencies. The president of ITT Europe, M. C. Bergerac (now CEO of Revlon) feared that the new product, which was much more complicated than the old one, would be even more prone to such problems, and was searching for ways of preventing this. A number of us, including P. B. Crosby, the late Carl Abissi, and myself, emphasized the importance of product qualification. Product qualification is essentially a very formal phase of testing to prove that the design of a new product meets its requirements. In the past, it had mainly been performed either by, or at the insistence of, major institutional customers, particularly defense agencies. However, we believed that its techniques were also applicable as a self control.

Many of ITT Europe's design-development community were opposed to the idea. Product qualification was not traditional in telecommunications. They saw it as an additional burden on their already stretched resources, and a potentially serious cause of schedule delays. No doubt they also had the normal human aversion to being subjected to test or examination.

Nonetheless, the president insisted. It was decided that the first subject of the methodology would be the special-purpose computer which was to be the "brain" of the new exchange. The technical people continued to insist that the qualification tests were unnecessary, that the design was complete, that the computer was working perfectly, and that they could not release a unit from its essential use as a tool for the development of the rest of the system. However, in the end the tests were carried out. It is a long time ago and I no longer have available my ITT records, but my recollection is that out of 24 tests, more than half were failed, and it took a year or more of further development to make a unit able to pass the tests. Fortunately, the computer was only a subsystem, not a complete product, and the additional development went on in parallel to the design of the other parts of the system, and did not seriously impact the overall schedule. When launched, the new product had an almost unbelievable lack of problems.

The initial failure on test of this computer firmly launched ITT Europe's product qualification program. Even the technical people had to admit its value. The adverse consequences of unknowingly continuing with the computer in its original state would have been incalculable. At the request of the president, I wrote a policy for his signature stating that all new products must be qualification tested and none should be released to a customer until the tests had been passed. Working with the ITT Europe Electronic Switching Quality Council, under its Chairman Jean Stievenart of Belgium, a standard practice was developed on how to do the testing (those two documents later became ITT worldwide policies). The methods, which will be described next, turned out to be very practical. In the years that followed, they were applied to many hundreds of new products not just in telecommunications. I remember applications to lipsticks and frozen meals, car brake systems, submersible pumps—and the multimegawatt under-sea power cable connecting Sweden and Denmark.

Of all quality assurance systems, product qualification is the most cost effective. The most expensive quality problems are usually caused by design deficiencies. If the design of a product is right, blunders or ill luck in purchasing or manufacturing can cause serious problems but they can usually be resolved by a single-stage correction process. However, if a new product is launched with serious design defects the consequences are horrendous. The customers are complaining bitterly and the product is being returned. The design-development people are frantically searching for a solution. They launch an inadequately tested correction into production. As often as not it does not work and a further correction is introduced. Now production has three different versions to cope with—retrofit of the original design and two different corrections. The majority of the world's biggest quality problems—those that are headlined in the newspapers and discussed in courts and parliaments—have this kind of genesis. Product qualification is a key means of preventing such problems.

All new products are subjected to tests and inspections during the design-development phase. In the early stages of design, tests are part of an iterative process for achieving the product's requirements. In later stages the purpose of the tests is increasingly to confirm that features of the product work and that characteristics have their required quantitative values. Testing and inspection is also carried out in manufacturing as a means of identifying and correcting defects (see Chapter 8). It is possible for the informal testing of the development phase to merge into the routine testing of the manufacturing phase with no particular test event separating the two. Engineering, on the basis of its own information, "releases the product" to manufacturing, production starts, and a little while later product is delivered to customers. Unfortunately, because development testing is informal it is not possible for its adequacy to be appraised as a whole. Because of time and money pressures on the design engineers and their confidence in the quality of their design, it is unlikely to be complete. Because manufacturing testing's objective is to check conformance to the design and, because it has cost and schedule constraints, it is also inadequate for proving a newly designed product.

As mentioned previously, major institutional customers may require that a development is not declared complete until they have "qualified" the product. Such customers usually base their decision to qualify or not on the results of formal tests performed by themselves, or the producer, or an independent laboratory. The tests are called "qualification tests" and their definition and performance are part of the contract between the vendor and the customer.

For products where there is no customer requirement to perform qualification tests, it is still extremely useful for the development of a new product to conclude with formal qualification testing. In the absence of contractual requirements, as with design review, for a division to impose on itself the discipline of product qualification requires strong leadership from the division general manager (or, as in ITT Europe, a higher-level line manager).

In essence, qualification testing is a particularly thorough phase of testing carried out on the product when development is complete to give assurance that the design is correct. One approach is to have an "open-ended" investigation of the product. This is possible only when a group of experts are available (e.g., from an external laboratory). Because it is not generally applicable, this method will not be discussed any further. A different approach, applicable to virtually any new product, is to examine conformance of the product to its product requirement specification.

The purpose of product qualification is to give assurance by the formal performance of a series of specified qualification tests that the product (manufactured in conformance to its design) conforms to all of the requirements defined in its product requirement specification.

The product requirement specification, which defines exactly what the product must be able to do—its performance, appearance, external dimensions, environmental resistance, reliability, safety, and so on—should be issued before the start of design, and revised and made more precise as the development proceeds. It is the primary document that defines the product to be sold. The product requirement specification should be mature before the start of qualification testing, but it can be revised even to take account of the results of the qualification testing. Of course, any reduction in specified requirements may have an adverse marketing effect.

Each requirement of the product requirement specification should then be reflected in a qualification test specification. The tests and inspections that yield the best technical and economical methods of determining whether or not a product fulfills each of its requirements should be defined precisely. Included therein must be the exact method used when performing each test and the criteria that determine whether or not it has been passed. The number of samples to be tested must also be defined. Where the product can be sold in a number of different configurations, the exact configuration to be tested must be defined. Usually, it will not be possible to devise a qualification program that gives a high assurance of conformance to every requirement. Sometimes it will be technically impossible—even the best accelerated life tests rarely give a high assurance of say a 30 year life requirement. Other times the cost of testing or the time needed for the testing will be unacceptable. In these cases an explicit decision not to perform a particular test must be made and the emphasis for quality assurance directed elsewhere (e.g., by including a conservative safety margin in the design). Even without these limitations qualification testing would be no substitute for good and careful design. On the other hand, its limitations do not prevent it from being extremely useful and important.

Before submitting samples of a product for qualification testing the development team should be confident (from what they know of the design and results of development tests) that the samples will pass the qualification tests. Qualification testing should not be limited to aspects of the product about which the development team has doubts; on the contrary, significant doubt of a product's ability to pass the tests probably indicates that the product is not ready for qualification testing. Experience indicates that, however confident the development team is in a product, usually the product fails one or more qualification tests and corrective action is required. Development team confidence is not a good reason for omitting particular tests.

The timing of qualification testing within the development-manufacturing cycle is a matter on which judgment must be exercised. Ideally, the samples tested should be made by the final manufacturing methods after the development is complete, and large-scale manufacturing and selling should wait until the tests have been passed. This is not usually practical. The overall program cannot be delayed and the manufacturing tools and equipment once made cannot lay idle. The insistence in using exact manufacturing samples for qualification tests also seriously delays the start of corrective action that is required after test failure. However, the samples tested should reflect as nearly as possible the product when normally manufactured. Any deviation will reduce the validity of passed tests and complicate the assessment of failed tests.

Qualification testing is concerned with the design of the product, but all failures occurring during testing are of importance. Most failures will reflect design deficiencies, but others may occur because the samples tested were not made in accordance with the design. However, the latter failures may indicate particular difficulties in manufacturing that *does* conform to the design. In order to know how well the samples tested conform to the design, qualification testing will normally include a formal comparison of the samples against the design drawings. The conformance of the samples to applicable workmanship standards will also be inspected. These particular checks have a very important secondary function: they enable the status of the drawings and standards themselves to be appraised at a defined instant in the development program. In practice, an extremely important byproduct of formal qualification testing is the discipline it introduces to the whole development process. Frequently, it is only the demands of the qualification test program that ensure complete definition of the product's requirements in the product requirement specification, and the completion of other important specifications. Without qualification testing, these problems may be resolved only after major trouble with customers.

Some of the types of test that are often included in a qualification test specification are given in Table 5.5. All products must operate satisfactorily within an applicable range of external environments. Most products must be able to withstand without damage particular kinds of transport and storage conditions. Tests for these characteriatics are given as items 6 and 7 of Table 5.5. Environmental testing has been the subject of much national and international standardization, for example, many tests have been standardized by the International Electrotechnical Commission in its standard IEC 68 for use on electrical equipment and components. Every event occurring during the qualification testing must be formally reported in a properly controlled test log.

Where qualification tests are carried out as a contractual requirement

TABLE 5.5   Tests Included in a Qualification Test Specification

1. Check of configuration
2. Check of conformance of samples to design
3. Visual and mechanical inspection of dimensions and workmanship
4. Complete functional testing under normal operating conditions
5. Functional testing under specified marginal conditions
6. Tests of ability to function correctly in specified environments
7. Tests of ability to withstand without damage specified transport and storage environments
8. Reliability tests for life and failure rate
9. Tests of maintainability.

of the customer it will be usual for the test data to be appraised by the customer's quality personnel. The latter will often want to examine and analyze the primary data and will be prepared to spend a considerable amount of time determining whether a product has passed each of the specified tests. In these circumstances, the qualification test report may be very long and detailed. When qualification testing is done by a manufacturer on its own product the requirements of the qualification test report are different. The results given in the report are a major factor in enabling the division's management to decide that a new product is ready for manufacture and sale. It is therefore very important that results are reported clearly and objectively. The presentation of the report must be such that the important results are highlighted with only enough detail to carry conviction. Also, information should be included that will assure the division manager of the objectivity of the report. However, the report must be as concise as possible; division managers cannot be expected to read large volumes of data, nor should understanding of the report depend on knowledge of various referenced documents, which the division manager will not be familiar with. The report must be self-explanatory. Table 5.6 gives an example of the section headings of such a report. The inclusion of the approval signatures, the names of the people who carried out the testing and those responsible for corrective action, the place where the tests were carried out and the dates of the start and end of the test, give the reader confidence in the report's validity. Also, the fact that the test personnel are named as personally responsible for the tests underscores the importance of product qualification to them.

The summary, in a half a page or less, should list the tests that were passed or failed, the main conclusions of the test, and the status of im-

TABLE 5.6.   Section Headings of a Qualification Test Report

1. Approval signatures.
2. Distribution
3. Summary
4. Contents
5. Qualification test personnel
6. Test venue and date
7. Specifications
8. Test samples and configuration tested
9. Test log
10. Summary of test results and status
11. Corrective actions
12. Repeat of failed tests

portant corrective actions being taken. Under specifications, the number should be given, issue number, date and approval status of the product requirement specification, and the qualification test specification. A one or two page summary of the specifications forms a useful appendix to the report.

The section on test samples and configuration tested should describe precisely the samples tested, their configuration, where and when they were made, whether they were made completely on manufacturing tools, if they were taken from production lots, how the sampling was done, and so on. The test log section gives the whereabouts of the log and names the person responsible for its safe keeping. A typical page from the log can also be given as an appendix to the report.

The heart of the qualification test report is the summary of the test results. It is best given in tabular form. For each test, it should state whether or not the test has been completed—and if so whether it was passed. If it was failed this should be stated with a very brief reason for the failure. The aim here is to provide the reader, in one or two pages, with a clear view of the overall status of the qualification test.

An account of future development or redesign plans is not a logical part of the qualification test report. However, the readers of the report will get an incorrectly pessimistic view of the situation if they are told of failed tests and are given no account of the progress of work to correct these failures. It is best, therefore, to include a short summary of the major corrective actions.

All failed tests should be repeated after the defects revealed have been corrected and, in principle, it is best to repeat all tests, because the changes enabling one test to be passed may have reduced the ability to pass another test. In practice, judgment is usually exercised about the need to repeat all tests. An interim qualification test report should make clear which tests will be repeated and when.

As noted previously, the concept of qualification testing arose from the customer/supplier relationship, and in this context qualification testing applies directly to products that are to be offered for sale. However, even in this context the customer may require, not only that the end item is subjected to qualification testing, but that components and subassemblies are individually approved following qualification tests performed on them separately. The customer recognizes that qualification tests on the end item do not fully assure that a product meets all of its requirements, and for some of the requirements, for example, reliability, the level of assurance may be low.

Any complex product can be thought of as a pyramid made in a number of levels. The basic materials are at the bottom level, components at the next level, subassemblies at the next, and the final end item can be found at the apex of the pyramid. In principle, every part of every level could be qualification tested, but this would yield redundancy and, in practice, judgment must be exercised about which parts and levels should be tested in this way. In any case, major emphasis should be given to the qualification testing of the end item—this is, after all, to be sold to the customer and must contractually meet specified requirements. The only reasons for qualification testing the parts at lower levels are that it may not be possible to test the end item satisfactorily, and that testing at the lower levels may reveal problems sooner.

The need for emphasis on the testing of an end item is not always appreciated by members of the development team. Psychologically, they prefer testing at the lower levels. They are worried that purchased components may not perform according to specification and would like to have this checked. They appreciate the confidence that comes from the testing of their early work—when correction is easy. They are less keen on tests of their finished work—when all of the budgeted time and money is used or has been exceeded.

The simplest way to organize the performance of product qualification is to establish a separate department for this purpose reporting directly to general management either at the division or some higher level of the company. The method only works well for a company with a limited product range and major sales of successive models (e.g., cars or computers). Even for such a company, the cost of a separate organization and facilities is very high. There also can be serious conflicts between the qualification organization and other departments. An alternative, that rarely works well, is to give the quality department responsibility for product qualification. The department's existing resources are fully utilized for other purposes, and it is unlikely that it will be given enough extra resources to do product qualification properly. Another alternative is to make product qualification the responsibility of the design-development department. Only the members of that department are likely to have all the necessary technical expertise, and many of the facilities used for development testing will be applicable for qualification testing. It is also simplest for the costs of qualification testing to be a part—separately identified—of the development budget. However, this approach carries the major objections that it is psychologically difficult for the design engineers satisfactorily to test their own work, and that product qualification will be of secondary importance to them compared with completing the development of the new product. Experience indicates that design-development departments rarely perform product qualification properly without some independent discipline applied.

One way of overcoming some of the objections to having the design-development department responsible for product qualification is to make it jointly responsible with the quality department. Divided responsibility usually leads to confusion and it is therefore important to define precisely the different parts of the overall product qualification process for which the two departments are responsible. In broad terms, the design-development department is financially responsible for the qualification testing as part of the development budget, and must also provide the necessary technical expertise. The quality department is responsible for auditing that all tests are carried out precisely in conformance to defined specifications, that all events occurring during the testing are logged, that no illegitimate interference with the test samples occurs, and for preparation of interim and final qualification test reports. The responsibilities of the two departments are listed in more detail in Table 5.7. It is useful for the design-development and quality departments to appoint qualification managers for each product. Many of the responsibilities listed in Table 5.7 will be carried by the two qualification managers but others, however, will be the responsibility of the respective department heads.

Product qualification, like design review, is one of the subjects covered at the TRW Quality College and Table 5.8 lists six discussion statements devised for this use. Again, the reader may wish to form opinions before reading the consensus view.

Statement 1: False. The only purpose that justifies the cost and formality of product qualification is to prove as well as practicable that a new product (and especially its design) is conformant to all of its requirements before it is handed to a customer. The design-development department can find design defects more cheaply by informal development testing. Only when the design team is wholly confident that the design is right is it worthwhile to perform qualification testing. Experience indicates that even then there are some failures. When ITT Europe started its product qualification program it was two or three years before the first product went through all of its qualification tests (first time) without a single failure. When a design team had reservations about a product, but started the qualification tests anyway, there were invariably major problems and the whole test had to be restarted. The release of a product to manufacturing is not the primary reason for product qualification. The worst that can happen after premature release to the manufacturing department is a lot of scrap and rework.

TABLE 5.7. Responsibilities of the Design-Development and Quality Departments for Product Qualification

Design-Development Department

1. Decides which new products require qualification testing
2. Appoints qualification managers for each product to be qualification tested
3. Includes the cost of qualification testing (and retesting necessitated by initial failures) as an identifiable item in the development budget
4. Includes the necessary time for qualification testing in the development program
5. Includes qualification testing as development "milestones"
6. Defines the product configuration to be tested
7. Defines how the samples for test are to be made and ensures that methods are as near as possible to those of manufacturing
8. Ensures that the required numbers of samples for test are made and delivered according to schedule
9. Ensures that staff to carry out tests is available at the scheduled time
10. Ensures that functional test equipment is available according to schedule
11. Ensures that the product requirement specification defining the requirements that the product must meet has been written, approved, and formally published according to schedule
12. Ensures that the qualification test specification defining the qualification tests has been written, approved and formally published, according to schedule
13. Approves the qualification test schedule
14. Approves (or formally objects to) qualification test reports
15. Corrects the product design to overcome deficiencies revealed by failure of qualification tests

Quality Department

1. Audits lists of products requiring qualification testing and reports to the division manager unresolved omissions
2. Appoints qualification managers for each product to be qualification tested
3. Supplies staff to carry out tests and inspections (e.g., visual and mechanical inspections) requiring expertise possessed by the quality department
4. Takes responsibility for ensuring that all aspects of the qualification tests are performed correctly according to schedule or that delinquencies are reported to the division manager
5. Draws up and publishes the qualification test schedule
6. Audits correct performance of the design-development department responsibilities and reports to the division manager unresolved delinquencies
7. Provides assistance in drafting the qualification test specification
8. Approves or formally disapproves the qualification test specification
9. By auditing ensures that every test is carried out in conformance to the qualification test specification
10. Ensures that the qualification test log is filled in correctly and is retained for reference
11. Reports to the division manager monthly on the progress of the qualification tests against the schedule
12. Writes interim and final qualification test reports and publishes these to the division manager
13. Audits that corrective actions shown necessary by failure of tests are carried out
14. Audits that retesting following corrective action are carried out

TABLE 5.8. Six Statements about Product Qualification

1. Qualification testing is carried out to reveal design defects so that these can be eliminated before delivery to the customer.
2. Product qualification must be the responsibility of the design development department because only they understand the new product and they pay for the tests.
3. The qualification test reports are not written to the division manager because they contain more technical detail than he or she can be expected to understand.
4. An important aspect of qualification testing is that it forces complete specification of the product requirements.
5. Even though the qualification tests are not complete it is sometimes permissible to deliver a product to customers in order to meet the promised delivery dates, provided the quality manager approves.
6. Qualification tests are only cost effective if they are contractually required and the customer pays for them.

The primary reason is the prevention of delivery of a new product that is nonconformant to its product requirement specification to a *customer*.

Statement 2: True. Most people answer "false" to this question because they do not trust the design-development people's objectivity in testing their own product. However, they have not analyzed the practical and cost objections to the alternatives. In this book, I recommend that the design-development department be made responsible, but that the quality department, with strong support from the division manager, also be made responsible.

Statement 3: False. The qualification test reports should be short, crisp documents that reach the division manager within a day or two of the completion of major phases of testing. They are among the most important documents a division manager receives. Nothing is likely to cause more trouble than the release of a defective new product into the market. My experience is that quality departments are often depressingly inadequate in meeting their responsibilities for this reporting—and thereby undermine the whole product qualification system. The report could be written simultaneously with performance of the tests, but the product qualification manager delays publication for weeks, or even months, so that when the report does arrive it has *zero* impact. For interim reports, design-development's delay in clarifying their plans for design corrections necessitated by failed tests is made an excuse for delay, but it is much better to publish without this desirable but unnecessary information. Sometimes quality managers let design-development people take over the reporting—with disastrous results.

Statement 4:   True. It is surprising how often products are designed and developed without a proper product requirement specification. The design-development people talk to their marketing and manufacturing colleagues, but without a proper product requirement specification, subject to formal change control, the different groups inevitably have different perceptions and responses to customer pressures and technical realities. In the end, manufacturing has to be told how to make the product, with drawings, parts lists, and so on, but the six types of specification discussed earlier in this chapter may never be explicitly integrated. Product qualification seems an inappropriate tool for solving this problem but in practice it is one of the most effective.

Statement 5:   False. It is in the answer to such questions that a manager shows whether he or she is serious about quality or is simply building an image. Most groups give the correct answer, but laugh and look sheepish when I ask them: "Why do you do it then?"

Let's take the question piece by piece. First, what about the quality manager's approval? Well, one should *always* say, no. At least this forces the decision up to the division manager. When I am working with groups of quality managers I make them practice saying in chorus, "It hasn't passed. It can't go." The psychological pressures on quality managers are such that some of them have difficulty in saying this even in the protected environment of a classroom. For the final decision maker (the division manager) there are two distinct situations. The first occurs when the development, which happens frequently, has fallen behind schedule. The agreed delivery date has passed, further promises have been made to the customer, but completion of the qualification test schedule, as planned, will cause these promises to be broken also. In the second case, everything is on schedule, the qualification test is completed as planned, but one or more tests have failed. Correcting the design and retesting the product will cause the delivery date to be missed. The second case appears to be more serious than the first; the product has actually failed its qualification tests. In fact, the situation is better. The causes of the failure can be determined and an informed judgment made about the consequences of delivering the product to the customer. In my first draft of the ITT Europe policy, I allowed the division manager to decide whether or not to deliver in such circumstances. The president, M. C. Bergerac, in the only change he made, struck out that clause muttering, "If we give them any loopholes. . . ." The other case is a sheer gamble. It is easy to be optimistic, particularly when the design-development manager is guaranteeing that everything is fine, and the customer is demanding delivery. However, experience shows that new products lacking qualification testing are the reasons for disasters—in too many instances to be accepted by a sensible division manager. (He *may* be lucky this time but what about the next new product, or the one after that?) The griefs of late delivery are soon forgotten, but the consequences of bad quality may last many years. To release a new product to the customer before the tests are complete destroys the whole product qualification system. The schedule time for the qualification tests becomes just a reserve for development delays.

Statement 6:   False. It is sad that most formal qualifications of new products are performed only at the insistence of powerful customers. The introduction of a new product is the most common cause of major quality problems. So, too, the use of product qualification is probably the most cost effective of all quality assurance methods—because it is the best way of preventing such problems. Wise division managers, therefore, insist on product qualification, even when the customer does not pay for it. In fact, when the customer does pay, the tendency is to do only what is demanded. Sometimes this is not what is technically best. The best product qualifications are often performed without customer insistence.

CONCLUSION

In this chapter the application to product design of the three overall methodologies of quality improvement—defect detection, defect prevention, and quality assurance—were discussed, together with the managerial inhibitions which have hampered their general application. This led into a discussion of the six ways of specifying product quality, and their implications for supplier-customer relationships.

A section was then devoted to an introduction to a key defect prevention technique applicable to design—process capability—and it was shown that much bad product quality results from manufacturing processes that are incapable of meeting design requirements (which may also be stated as . . . from design requirements that cannot be met by available manufacturing processes).

The chapter concluded with a description of design review, which is an important defect detection method, and product qualification, which is the main quality assurance technique used to assure that designs are correct before product manufacturing and sale commence.

CHAPTER **6**

INCOMING INSPECTION

Having discussed the marketing and design-development aspects of quality, the next link of the chain of conformance (Figure 2.1) is the quality of purchased items. Companies manufacturing products, on average, buy about as much value from their suppliers as they add through their own manufacturing. It is therefore evident that controlling the quality of purchased items is extremely important to companies that manufacture products. Of course, there are very wide variations with some vertically integrated operations buying as little as 20 percent of their product cost, and some assembly operations buying all of their components, adding only 20 percent of the cost through their own manufacturing activities.

The simplest way to control the quality of purchased items is through incoming inspection. In principle, every item received could be inspected for every feature and characteristic defined on its product requirement specification. The items that passed would go on through to manufacturing. Those that failed would be returned to the supplier. If a substantial proportion passed—90 percent or more—manufacturing would not be held up by the loss of the rejected items. Suppliers would be motivated to minimize their proportion defective by having to deal, at their expense, with the rejected items. This system is very attractive psychologically. The whole responsibility for ensuring the quality of purchased items is given to the incoming inspection section. The members of this section are specialists who like doing incoming inspection. They have a well practiced routine that they perform. The people in purchasing, engineering, and the rest of the quality department have no worry about the quality of purchased items, and can get on with the things important to them.

I am not sure whether the method described was ever used extensively. Certainly, by the time I started work in quality 25 years ago, such testing or inspection of every item at incoming was restricted to special situations and most routine incoming inspection used sampling. Typically, if a lot of, for example, 5000 supposedly identical items were received, instead of inspecting all of them, only a sample, perhaps 80 items, would be inspected. Depending on the result of the sample inspection, the whole lot would either be accepted into manufacturing or returned to the supplier. The problem with 100 percent test or inspection of every feature and characteristic is the cost, which is too high. A division of a few hundred people cannot afford to have 50 or 60 incoming inspectors. Through sampling, though, the number could be reduced to about one or two—what manager could refuse to take advantage of a productivity improvement of such magnitude?

Sampling used in this way—called "attribute" sampling—is the most universally applied statistical quality control technique. All of the other techniques—process capability and control, designed experiments, sampling by variables, regression analysis, and so on—are actually used by only a minority of product manufacturers, but attribute sampling is used by virtually every one for incoming inspection, and it is also used for many other purposes as well. In this chapter, a brief explanation of the theory of attribute sampling will be given with an analysis defining its limitations to follow. In the next chapter a description will be given of the other methods that contribute to a complete supplier quality program.

ATTRIBUTE SAMPLING

This is a typical example of inspection or test by attribute sampling. A lot of 5000 items of a particular product is collected together. The various attributes that the product must have for it to be acceptable are defined. For example, if the product were a resistor the attributes would include the allowed range of resistance, the physical dimensions, the legibility of the branding, the solderability of the leads, and so on. The methods of testing or inspecting for these characteristics would be defined. It might then be decided that the acceptability of the lot as a whole would be determined by inspecting and testing only a sample of the resistors—not all 5000. A common way of doing this would be to take a sample of 80 of the resistors in a random manner from the 5000 and subject them to all the specified tests. If two or less of the 80 were found to be defective (i.e., did not have the specified attributes) the lot of 5000 would be accepted: if three or more were defective, the lot would be rejected.

This example includes the essential features of attribute sampling used to decide whether a lot of items will be accepted or rejected. The required attributes and the methods of test and inspection were defined. It was decided that the lot of 5000 items would be accepted if two or less defectives were found in a sample of 80 items, and would be rejected if three or more defectives were found. The user of attribute sampling is not primarily interested in the quality of the sample; he or she is interested in what it tells about the quality of the lot. Unfortunately, the theory of attribute sampling starts from the assumption that the proportion defective of the lot is known and then works out what will be the likely proportion defective in various samples taken from the lot. This is the opposite of the practical situation in which the proportion defective of a sample is measured, and it is desired to infer the proportion defective of the lot on the basis of that result. In inspection or test of a product by attributes the units of product fall into two categories: "good" units that have all the required attributes and defective (bad) units that lack one or more of the required attributes. Attribute inspection or testing is concerned only with good and bad units.

In order to examine the theory of attribute sampling let us consider another example: a bag that contains 100 balls with certain defined attributes. In the example, this is the lot. We now inspect these 100 percent, or 200 percent, or more if necessary, so that we know exactly how many of the 100 balls are good and how many are defective. Suppose 30 are bad and 70 good.

If, without looking, we take one ball out of the bag and then inspect it the probability of its being bad is 0.3 and of its being good is 0.7.

Suppose we took a sample of five balls out of the lot in sequence and inspected each one in turn and found the first was bad, the second and third good, the fourth bad and the fifth good (i.e., BGGGB). The probability of getting this particular sequence is $0.3 \times 0.7 \times 0.7 \times 0.3 \times 0.7$. Multiplying this out gives 0.03087. If we continued taking samples of five balls out of the lot this particular sequence would therefore appear about 3 times in every 100 samples.

BGGBG is only one of the ways of getting three good balls and two bad balls in a sample of five. In fact there are 10 different sequences:

GGGBB   GBBGG
GGBBG   BBGGG
GGBGB   BGGGB
GBGGB   BGGBG
GBGBG   BGBGG

Each of these sequences has a probability of 0.03087.

The probability of getting any one of these samples containing three good balls and two bad balls from the lot is therefore 10 times the probability of getting one particular sequence. The probability of getting any arrangement of three good balls and two bad balls is therefore $10 \times 0.03087 = 0.3087$. Therefore, if we continued to take samples of five balls out of the lot we would expect to get three good and two bad balls about 30 times in every 100 samples taken.

In the same way the probability of getting the sequence GGGBG, which includes only one bad ball, is given by: $0.7 \times 0.7 \times 0.7 \times 0.3 \times 0.7 = 0.07203$. There are obviously five ways of placing one bad ball in a sample of five, so that if the order is unimportant the probability of getting one bad ball in a sample of five taken from the lot is $5 \times 0.07203 = 0.36015$. Similarly, the probability of getting a sample containing entirely good balls is $0.7^5 = 0.16807$, and there is only one kind of sample like this.

In summary, if we take a sample of 5 balls from a lot containing 70 good and 30 bad balls we have the following probabilities of getting different numbers of bad balls:

Number of bad balls	0	1	2
Probability	1×0.7^5 $= 0.16807$	$5 \times 0.7^4 \times 0.3$ $= 0.36015$	$10 \times 0.7^3 \times 0.3^2$ $= 0.3087$

Adding together 0.16807, 0.36015, and 0.3087 gives 0.83692. The remaining probability of 0.16308 is accounted for by the chances of getting 3, 4, and 5 bad balls. It is a certainty (probability = 1) that the sample of five balls will contain either 0, 1, 2, 3, 4 or 5 bad balls.

It was noted that in carrying out sampling inspection it was necessary to decide what the sample size should be and the maximum number of defectives allowed in the sample for the lot to be accepted (the latter is called the "acceptance number"). The properties of each sample size and acceptance number can be summarized in a graph of "probability of acceptance" against "lot percent defective," and this graph is known as the "operating characteristic" of a sample size and acceptance number.

The operating characteristic for a sample size of 5 and an acceptance number of one is given in Figure 6.1. One point on this graph is marked with a small circle. This point shows that a lot that is 30 percent defective has a probability of acceptance of 0.53. In other words, when a sample of 5 is taken from a lot that is 30 percent defective there is a total probability of 0.53 that the sample will contain either no defectives, or one defective (i.e., satisfy an acceptance number of 1).

The calculations carried out earlier in this section showed that for a sample of 5 taken from a lot 30 percent defective there was a probability of 0.16807 of getting no defectives and of 0.36015 of getting one defective. When added together these yield 0.52822. The calculation therefore gave the means of obtaining the point marked of the operating characteristic. The same calculation using percentage defectives other than 30, enables the rest of this operating characteristic to be calculated.

For practical sampling, tables of operating characteristics are used to describe the properties of various pairs of sample sizes and acceptance numbers. We have just described the essential theoretical basis of the calculation of operating characteristics, and therefore of attribute sampling itself. Of course, to determine the operating characteristic of samples larger than five by the means described here would be impossibly tedious. Fortunately, the numbers 0.16807, 0.36015, and 0.3087 are the first three terms of the binomial $(0.7 + 0.3)^5$ and the known mathematical properties of this and similar binomials facilitate the calculation of operating characteristics. Two other mathematical relationships, the Poisson and hypergeometric distributions, are also used for calculating operating characteristics.

Figure 6.1 gives the operating characteristic of a sample of 5 and an acceptance number of 1. It shows that lots which are 31 percent defective have an even chance of being accepted or rejected by this sampling. It also shows that lots have to be as good as 11 percent defective to have a probability of 0.9 of being accepted and as bad as 58 percent defective to have a probability of 0.9 of being rejected. This means that lots which are better than 11 percent defective are likely to be accepted, lots worse than 58 percent defective are likely to be rejected, and lots with a quality level between these figures may be either accepted or rejected. For most pur-

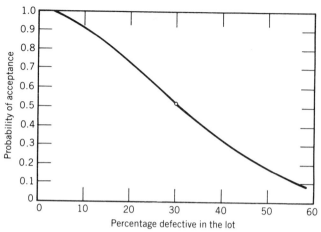

Figure 6.1. Operating characteristic for a sample size of 5 and an acceptance number of 1.

poses, this particular sampling plan gives an unsatisfactory method of determining whether lots are good or bad. The inadequacy arises from the smallness of the sample. Inspection of a sample of five items from a lot is likely to be very inexpensive, but does not give much information and therefore provides a poor separation of good and bad lots.

Figure 6.2 gives the operating characteristic of the sampling plan—sample size 80, acceptance number 2—that we used to introduce this section. For this sampling plan there is an even chance of acceptance for lots which are 3.4 percent defective, a probability of acceptance of 0.9 for lots which are as good as 1.4 defective and a probability of rejection of 0.9 for lots which are as bad as 6.5 percent defective. For this sampling plan the range of percent defective for which either acceptance or rejection is likely is 1.4–6.5 percent.

Attribute sampling is often used to decide whether or not goods supplied by a producer to a consumer have a good enough quality to be accepted or whether they are so bad that they must be rejected. The producer and consumer must first agree on the required attributes of the product and the methods of test and inspection. It is then usual for them to agree on a percentage of defective items which divide acceptable from rejectable lots. For example, they might agree that all lots containing one percent or less defectives are acceptable and lots containing more than one percent are rejectable.

The only way of determining exactly whether or not a particular lot meets the 1 percent criterion is to inspect every item in the lot, continu-

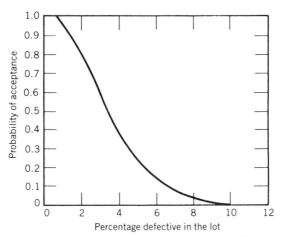

Figure 6.2. Operating characteristic for a sample size of 80 and an acceptance number of 2.

ing until all of the items have been inspected or more than 1 percent of defectives have been found, and, of course, the inspection must be carried out with perfect effectiveness.

Because of the cost of 100 percent inspection the producer and consumer may agree to base their sentencing on sampling inspection. Where the agreed defective level is 1 percent a common pair of sample size and acceptance number is 80 and 2 respectively.

Because sampling cannot determine exactly whether or not any lot is better or worse than the agreed defective level the producer takes a certain risk that he or she will have good lots (better than the agreed level) rejected and the consumer takes a risk that he or she will accept bad lots (worse than the agreed level). From the operating characteristic of Figure 6.2 the producer's risk and the consumer's risk for this particular example can be seen. A lot that is one percent defective (i.e., just acceptable, has a probability of 0.95 of being accepted and a probability of only 0.05 of being rejected). Lots of a quality better than the agreed level have an even higher probability of being accepted—a lot ½ percent defective has a probability of better than 0.99 of being accepted. The producer's risk of having a good lot rejected is quite small for this particular example.

The situation though is different for the consumer. At lot that is 1.1 percent defective should be rejected. However, the probability of such a lot being rejected is only 0.06 and the probability of its being accepted—the wrong decision—is 0.94. Even for a lot that is 2 percent defective or twice as bad as the agreed defective level, the probability of making the correct decision is only 0.2, whereas the probability of the wrong decision is 0.8. It is clear that this particular plan is of high risk to the consumer.

In summary, using an acceptance number of 2 and a sample size of 80 to measure whether or not lots are better or worse than 1 percent defective is good for the producer but bad for the consumer.

Another example will now be considered, where the agreed quality level is 6.5 percent defective (i.e., a much poorer quality than for the first example). However, the producer and consumer could agree to use exactly the same sample size and acceptance number as before, 80 and 2 respectively, for judging the quality. From the operating characteristic of Figure 6.2 the producer submitting a lot which is just as good as the agreed level, 6.5 percent defective, and which should therefore be accepted has, in fact, a 0.90 probability of having the lot rejected. The percentage defective has to be about half the agreed level before the producer has an even chance of getting a lot accepted. The producer's risk of having good lots rejected is therefore high. On the other hand, the consumer's risk of accepting a bad lot is low. If the percent defective is 6.6 percent the chance of making the wrong decision is less than 0.1. Using a sample size of 80 and an acceptance number of 2 to measure whether or not lots are better or worse than 6.5 percent defective is good for the consumer and bad for the producer.

The examples have shown that exactly the same sample size and acceptance number can be used to judge two defective levels differing by 6.5 times, but in one case the consumer's risk is high and in the other the producer's risk is high.

Where acceptance or rejection of lots is to be decided by sampling inspection, two names are used for the agreed defective level. These are acceptable quality level (AQL) and limiting quality (LQ). When the sampling plan to be applied has a low producer's risk, AQL is used: often this is about 0.05 for a lot of a quality just equal to the AQL. In the previous examples the agreed standard of 1 percent defective would be called a 1 percent AQL, because the sampling plan used (sample size 80, acceptance number 2) had a low producer's risk.

Where the sampling plan has a low consumer's risk, often 0.10, the agreed defective level is called the LQ. In the previous examples the agreed level of 6.5 percent defective would be called a 6.5 percent LQ, because for this percent defective the sampling plan of sample size 80 and acceptance number 2 has a low consumer's risk.

It is more expensive to assure a given percent defective by the LQ method than by the AQL. In the examples the same sample size and acceptance number (and therefore the same cost of inspection) were used for an AQL of 1 percent and an LQ of 6.5 percent. If an acceptance number of 2 is used an AQL of 6.5 percent can be measured with a sample size of only 13, instead of the 80 needed for an LQ of 6.5 percent. Similarly, if an acceptance number of 2 is used the sample size must be 533 to measure a 1 percent LQ, compared with 80 for the 1 percent AQL.

In summary, in using attribute sampling for acceptance purposes a sample taken from a lot of product is inspected. If the number of defectives in the sample is more than a preestablished acceptance number the lot is rejected. Theoretically, if the proportion defective of the *lot* is known, the probability of getting *samples* with various defective proportions can be calculated—either by considering all possible combinations of good and bad units of product or by using known mathematical distributions such as the binomial. By relating these sample defective proportions to the preestablished acceptance number, the probability of accepting a lot with a known defective proportion can be calculated (e.g., a lot that is 30 percent defective has a probability of 0.53 of being accepted if a sample size of five is used with an acceptance number of one). By repeating the calculation for lots of different defective proportions, a graph of the probability of acceptance, when using a particular sample size and acceptance number, against the defective proportion of the lot can be derived. Such a graph is called the operating characteristic of the particular sample size and acceptance number.

In using acceptance sampling, the supplier and the consumer agree that a particular defective proportion will divide good lots from bad lots. They then agree a sample size and acceptance number to be used as a means of estimating whether lots are better or worse than the agreed criterion. Acceptance sampling can make this estimate with only limited precision. There is therefore a probability that good lots will be wrongly rejected and that bad lots will be wrongly accepted. The larger the sample size used the smaller the probability of a wrong decision. The sampling can also be biased either to reduce the supplier's risk of having a good lot rejected, or to reduce the consumer's risk of having a bad lot accepted. Sampling plans biased in the former way are called AQL plans and those biased in the latter way are called LQ plans. For a given lot defective proportion and acceptance number, LQ plans require much larger sample sizes, and are therefore much more expensive, than AQL plans.

The most widely used attribute sampling standard—in fact, the most widely used of all statistical quality control documents—was defined by a joint United Kingdom, United States, and Canadian group and was issued as defense specifications, DEF 131A in the United Kingdom and MIL-STD-105D in the United States. It has subsequently been issued as a national standard by many other countries and as international standards (e.g., IEC 410). It is 66 pages long and cannot be described comprehensively here, but Figure 6.3 reproduces its primary table. It shows the relationship between AQLs, sample sizes and acceptance and rejection numbers.

As noted previously, the purpose of an attribute sampling plan is commonly thought to be to enable a producer or consumer to determine whether a lot of product (or a series of lots) has a proportion defective more or less than a predetermined level, and to achieve this at much lower cost than would result from using 100 percent inspection. Certainly, this was the first use of MIL-STD-105D and its predecessors by military agencies buying munitions from their suppliers. For this purpose, it is first necessary to establish the proportion defective that is at the border between acceptable and rejectable. Unfortunately, there is no logical way of doing this. So, all AQLs are established arbitrarily—they are pulled out of the air. Figure 6.3 shows that MIL-STD-105D's AQLs go from 0.010 percent to 1000 percent (i.e., 10 defects per unit) but practically used AQLs are invariably near to 1 percent. This is because on the one hand sample sizes get uneconomically large for AQLs less than about 0.4 percent, and on the other hand human beings feel that proportions defective much above 1 percent are unacceptable.

The simple truth is that every defective item received by a consumer from a supplier is a potential source of trouble to the former. There is no proportion defective below which defective items cause no problem. There is no "acceptable" quality level. Looked at from the viewpoint of incoming inspection, every defective item that goes through incoming inspection into manufacturing must either be screened out during manufacturing, and, for reasons that will be explained in Chapter 8, this requires expensive 100 percent testing or inspection, or it will be incorporated into the product going to the customer, detracting from the quality received. It makes no difference whether the defective item comes from a lot that is 0.1 percent defective or 10 percent defective—that defective item must be screened out or it will go to the customer.

Since its invention before World War II and its development in the years after, attribute sampling has fascinated quality professionals. Scores of papers continue to be written every year on refinements and elaborations of its use. I confess to being a victim of that fascination myself. When I moved from research into industry in 1958 one of my responsibilities was supervision of my division's specification section. I quickly discovered that no one in the section understood attribute sampling and I therefore had to put the AQLs and inspection levels into the specifica-

Master Table for Single Sampling Plans for Normal Inspection

Acceptable quality levels (normal inspection)

Sample size code letter	Sample size	0.010	0.015	0.025	0.040	0.065	0.10	0.15	0.25	0.40	0.65	1.0	1.5	2.5	4.0	6.5	10	15	25	40	65	100	150	250	400	650	1000
		Ac Re	Ac Re	Ac Re	Ac Re	Ac Re	Ac Re	Ac Re	Ac Re	Ac Re	Ac Re	Ac Re	Ac Re	Ac Re	Ac Re	Ac Re	Ac Re	Ac Re	Ac Re	Ac Re	Ac Re	Ac Re	Ac Re	Ac Re	Ac Re	Ac Re	Ac Re

(Table body: Sample size code letters A–R with sample sizes 2, 3, 5, 8, 13, 20, 32, 50, 80, 125, 200, 315, 500, 800, 1250, 2000 and the corresponding acceptance (Ac) and rejection (Re) numbers arranged diagonally across the acceptable quality levels, with directional arrows indicating the use of alternate sampling plans.)

⇩ = Use first sampling plan below arrow. If sample size equals, or exceeds, lot or batch size, do 100 percent inspection

⇧ = Use first sampling plan above arrow

Ac = Acceptance number

Re = Rejection number

Figure 6.3.

165

tions myself. A year or two later I became quality manager of the division which made and sold semiconductor devices, and in that industry attribute sampling has always been a way of life. In those days I wrote a few papers on attribute sampling myself. All of this work, my own included, is based on the false premise that the defined AQLs have some real validity. Once it is accepted that the AQLs are established arbitrarily, any refinement of the system must be seen as a waste of effort.

Having made this clarification, it follows that the purpose of incoming inspection is not to determine whether received lots are better or worse than an AQL. The real purpose of incoming inspection is to reduce the proportion of defective items reaching manufacturing. *Every* defective item reaching manufacturing is a source of trouble. If in a particular year say 10 million units of many different purchased products are received and say 120,000 of these are defective, the important questions for incoming inspection are: how many of these defective units are prevented from going into manufacturing as a result of the incoming inspection and at what cost? Returning to the book's overall theme of planned, long-term quality improvement there is an important follow-up question: is the proportion defective going into manufacturing significantly better this year than it was last year? In the next section an attempt will be made to answer the first two of these questions, and in the following chapter the actions needed to get a positive answer to the third question will be defined.

HOW EFFECTIVE IS ACCEPTANCE SAMPLING?

In this section I will examine the effectiveness of acceptance sampling which is used by incoming inspection to reduce the defective proportion of purchased items entering manufacturing and its cost. Hypothetical populations of purchased items divided into 20 lots will be considered. The various population and lot qualities will be examined, with the lots subjected to various 100 percent and sampling inspections. The effectiveness of the inspections in identifying defective items will be determined and also, the costs of performing the inspections. Where the sampling causes lot rejection, the cost of inspecting such rejected lots 100 percent will be examined as well.

As a first example, the population is assumed to consist of 20 lots each of 1000 units and is 2 percent defective, that is, it contains 400 defectives. The lots are assumed to be randomly drawn from the population, that is, each lot contains about 20 defectives—some having more, and some having less. (Of course, it is an unrealistic assumption, made to help the theoretical analysis, to think that the population quality is known. In real life the quality of the population would not be known.) What happens if the lots are 100 percent inspected? No inspection is perfectly effective, so let us assume the inspection is 99 percent effective:

Number of defectives removed by the inspection point $=$ 0.99 × Number of defectives incoming to the inspection point.

After the 20 lots have been inspected, 396 of the defective units will have been removed and the remaining 19,604 units will contain four defectives (i.e., the outgoing quality is 0.02 percent defective). Twenty thousand units were inspected and 19,604 units were accepted, so the inspection cost ratio per unit accepted is 102 percent. These results are summarized in the first line of Table 6.1. The second line gives the results for another 100 percent inspection, but with an inspection effectiveness of only 90 percent. Even with this low effectiveness the outgoing quality is quite good at 0.2 percent defective. However, the 0.02 percent achieved in the first example is much better than this.

Now let us consider a sampling inspection. Take a sample of 80 from each lot and apply an acceptance number of 2. (Readers who are quality professionals will recognize that this is the result of applying the very common Inspection-level II; one percent AQL condition of MIL-STD-105D to a lot size of 1000.) What will happen? Well, the 20 samples of 80 add up to 1600 units, and, because the population is 2 percent defective, about 32 of these units will be found defective in the inspection. On average each sample will contain 1.6 defectives. Of course, a sample cannot actually contain 1.6 defective units; it can only contain whole numbers of units. In fact, there are many different ways the 32 defective units could be distributed between the 20 samples. One likely distribution is given in Table 6.2. Quality professionals may compute the likelihood of the distribution by using the Poisson distribution.

Sixteen lots were accepted and four were rejected, and the 16 accepted were 2 percent defective (i.e., they contained about 320 defectives). Nineteen of those defectives were removed in the samples. They now contain 301 defectives. The 307 good units from the rejected samples can be added in. The result is 16,307 accepted units containing 301 defec-

TABLE 6.1. Effectiveness and Cost of Different Inspections Performed to Remove Defectives from a Series of Lots of Product

Example	Number of Lots and Incoming Defectives Proportion	Sample Size and Acceptance Number	Accepted Lots			Plus Screened Rejected Lots		
			Outgoing Defectives Proportion	Inspection Effectiveness	Inspection Cost Ratio	Outgoing Defectives Proportion	Inspection Effectiveness	Inspection Cost Ratio
1	20 × 1000 at 2%	100% —	0.02%	99%	102%	0.02%	99%	102%
2	20 × 1000 at 2%	100% —	0.2%	90%	102%	0.2%	90%	102%
3	20 × 1000 at 2%	80, 2	1.85%	7.5%	9.8%	1.52%	24%	26%
4	16 × 1000 at 0.7% 4 × 1000 at 7.2%	80, 2	0.64%	68%	10%	0.54%	73%	26%
5	16 × 1000 at 0.7% 4 × 1000 at 7.2%	13, 0	1.34%	33%	1.5%	1.24%	38%	16%
6	16 × 100 at 0.7% 4 × 100 at 7.2%	13, 0	0.98%	51%	13%	1.16%	42%	26%
7	16 × 1000 at 0.07% 4 × 1000 at 0.72%	200, 0	0.085%	57%	25%	0.07%	65%	40%
8	16 × 1000 at 0.07% 4 × 1000 at 0.72%	80, 2	0.19%	7%	8%	0.19%	7%	8%
9	16 × 1000 at 1.43% 4 × 1000 at 4.28%	80, 2	1.45%	27%	10%	1.13%	43%	31%
10	19 × 1000 at 0.7% 1 × 1000 at 7.2%	80, 2	0.65%	33%	8.4%	0.62%	40%	13%

TABLE 6.2. Sample Defectives from 20 Samples of 80 from a Population 2 Percent Defective

Number of Defectives	Number of Samples	Total Defectives	Sentence
0	4	0	4 Accepted
1	5	5	5 Accepted
2	7	14	7 Accepted
3	3	9	3 Rejected
4	1	4	1 Rejected
5 or more	0	0	—
Total	20	32	16 Accepted/ 4 Rejected

tives. How effective was the inspection? The effectiveness can be expressed as:

$$\text{Effectiveness} = 1 - \frac{\text{Proportion of defectives outgoing}}{\text{Proportion of defectives incoming}}.$$

(Because, after acceptance, the population outgoing from the inspection point is smaller than the population entering the inspection point, it is better to use proportion defective rather than number defective.) The lots incoming to the inspection point were 2 percent defective and those leaving the inspection point after acceptance were $301/16307 = 1.85$ percent defective. The effectiveness is therefore given by:

$$\text{Effectiveness} = 1 - 0.0185/0.02 = 0.075,$$

that is, the inspection was only 7.5 percent effective in improving the quality of the lots (compared with 99 percent and 90 percent respectively for the two 100 percent inspections). What about the cost? Well, only 1600 units were inspected for 16,307 units accepted so the inspection cost ratio was only 9.8 percent compared to 102 percent for the 100 percent inspections. Overall, even though its cost is low, this sampling inspection does not seem very useful.

To complete this example, let us 100 percent inspect the four rejected lots, minus their samples. These 3680 units contain the remainder of the 400 defectives—less the 301 in the accepted lots and the 32 in the samples—(i.e., 67 defectives). Assuming 99 percent effectiveness, 66 of these may be removed by inspection, leaving 3614 units. Adding these units to the 16,307 already accepted, gives 19,921 units containing 302 defectives, that is, 1.52 percent defective. The total inspection effectiveness has now gone up to 24 percent, but now, 3680 plus 1600 equals 5280 units have been inspected. The inspection cost ratio of the inspection is therefore 26.5 percent. Again, this inspection does not seem very useful.

Protagonists of acceptance sampling could rightly claim that this example is not a fair test. Acceptance sampling is best used when dealing with a series of lots that differ in quality; it identifies the good and bad lots. In the preceding example, all 20 lots had the same proportion defective, so it was expected that the acceptance sampling would not perform well. Let us, therefore, examine another example in which the lot quality varies markedly.

In this example we will again consider 20 lots of 1000 units containing a total of 400 defectives. However, 16 of the lots will be of "good" quality containing only 0.7 percent of defectives and the other four will be 10 times as bad in quality containing 7.2 percent defectives. Again, each lot will be subjected to acceptance sampling with a sample size of 80 and an acceptance number of 2. Table 6.3 summarizes what happens and, as before, the "typical sample inspection results" were arrived at using the Poisson distribution. The acceptance sampling gives a correct identification of the good and bad lots. The samples of 80 taken from the 16 good lots contain zero, one or two defectives and all of these lots are accepted. The samples taken from the four bad lots contain 4, 5, 6, and 8 defectives respectively and these lots are rejected.

The accepted lots contain 15,991 units of which 103 are defective. The outgoing quality is therefore 0.64 percent defective and the inspection effectiveness is 68 percent. Sixteen thousand units were inspected to accept 15,991 units so the inspection cost ratio is 10 percent. When the four rejected lots are screened again 100 percent, another 262 defectives are found and three missed. The outgoing quality of the 19,706 units is 0.54 percent defective, the inspection effectiveness is 73 percent, and the inspection cost ratio is 26.8 percent.

In this example, with lots that differ very widely in quality, the acceptance sampling has performed much better than with the homogeneous population. The inspection effectiveness of 68 percent is much higher for the initially accepted lots than the inspection cost ratio of 10 percent, showing acceptance sampling to be a cost efficient method (compared with 100 percent inspection) in removing defectives. However, there is one problem—and it is an important one—the outgoing quality of 0.64 percent defective, although appreciably better than the incoming quality of 2 percent, is not very good; it is worse than those

TABLE 6.3.   Effect of Acceptance Sampling and 100 Percent Screening on 16 "Good" and Four "Bad" Lots

Good Lots	Bad Lots	All Lots
16 lots of 1000 = 16,000	4 lots of 1000 = 4000	20 lots of 1000 = 20,000
0.7% defective = 112	7.2% defective = 228	2% defective = 400
16 samples of 80 = 1280	4 samples of 80 = 320	20 samples of 80 = 1600

Typical Sample Inspection Results

9×0 defectives = 0	0×0 defectives = 0	9×0 defectives = 0
5×1 defectives = 5	0×1 defective = 0	5×1 defective = 5
2×2 defectives = 4	0×2 defectives = 0	2×2 defectives = 4
0×3 defectives = 0	0×3 defectives = 0	0×3 defectives = 0
	1×4 defectives = 4	1×4 defectives = 4
	1×5 defectives = 5	1×5 defectives = 5
	1×6 defectives = 6	1×6 defectives = 6
	0×7 defectives = 0	0×7 defectives = 0
	1×8 defectives = 8	1×8 defectives = 8
Sample defectives = 0	Sample defectives = 23	Sample defectives = 32
Screen 0 lots = 0	Screen 4 lots = 3680	Screen 4 lots = 3680
Defectives = 0	Defectives = 262	Defectives = 262
Total inspected 1280	Total inspected 4000	Total inspected 5280
Defectives found 9	Defectives found 285	Defectives found 294
Defectives left 103	Defectives left 3	Defectives left 106
Outgoing quality .64%	Outgoing quality .08%	Outgoing quality .54%
Inspection effectiveness 68%		Inspection effectiveness 73%
Inspection cost ratio 10%		Inspection cost ratio 27%

achieved by the 100 percent inspections. Screening the rejected lots produces a similar result.

The kind of analysis outlined in Table 6.3 has been applied to a variety of lot qualities, sample sizes, and acceptance numbers, and Table 6.1 gives the results. In example 5, the lot quality is the same as in example 4—16 lots of 0.7 percent defective and four lots of 7.2 percent defective—but the sample size—13—has been made as small as possible, with an acceptance number of zero (another of the 1 percent AQL plans of Figure 6.3). As expected, the inspection cost ratio for accepted lots is very low, 1.5 percent, but the small sample size does not lead to correct sentencing of the good and bad lots and the inspection effectiveness, only 33 percent, is poor. This exemplifies one problem of "accept on zero" sampling plans.

The cost efficiency of acceptance sampling is prejudiced if lot sizes are small. This is illustrated in example 6, where the lot qualities are the same as in examples 4 and 5, but the lot sizes are only 100. The inspection effectiveness is similar to that of example 5, but the inspection cost ratio is much greater.

In examples 7 and 8, the quality of the lots is 10 times better than in the previous examples. This also detracts from the effectiveness of the sampling. In example 7, this is counteracted by using a large sample size. The inspection effectiveness here is fairly good, more than half of the defectives are removed, but the cost is high. In example 8, the sample size and acceptance number of 80 and 2, respectively, do not enable correct sentencing of these better quality lots to be achieved. Here the inspection effectiveness is poor.

The effect of a smaller difference in quality between good and bad lots as well as the effect of having only one bad lot is examined in examples 9 and 10. In both cases, the inspection effectiveness is moderate with about a third of the defectives being identified.

What general conclusions can be drawn from the results summarized in Table 6.1? Well, acceptance sampling is reasonably cost efficient. In five of the eight examples that use sampling, inspection effectiveness was in the range of 2.3 to 6.8 times greater than the inspection cost ratio, and in one other example it was 22 times greater. In the other two examples, the poor cost efficiency was a consequence of poor inspection effectiveness, not high inspection cost.

The main problem with acceptance sampling is its low effectiveness in removing defectives. Under circumstances which favor the system (illustrated by example 4)—large lot size, moderate population quality, and a big difference between the quality of the good and bad lots—about a third of the defectives in the incoming lots still go through into manufacturing. As the circumstances get less favorable, half or two-thirds of the defectives go on to manufacturing, and in some circumstances (illustrated by examples 3 and 8) the system is virtually useless. Under no circumstances is acceptance sampling anything near as effective as 100 percent inspection in screening out defectives.

The overall conclusion then is that, despite its cost efficiency, acceptance sampling is not an effective method of preventing defective product received from suppliers entering manufacturing. This conclusion must be considered in light of the fact that 100 percent test or inspection, which often is effective, has a cost that cannot be borne by most operations. The way around the seeming dilemma posed by these two conclusions will be examined in the next chapter.

STRATEGIES FOR INCOMING INSPECTION

Incoming inspection has two primary purposes: (1) to prevent defective purchased items entering production and (2) to provide information on the defectiveness of items to facilitate production, to control payment of suppliers, to use in discussion with suppliers, and to transmit to customers. Most of the incoming inspection money is spent for the first of these purposes. Defective items that enter production affect the costs and scheduling of production, and the quality of the product going to the customer adversely. Incoming inspection should minimize these adverse effects for the lowest incoming inspection cost.

Some important questions include: How much incoming inspection manpower is optimum? What sampling level is appropriate? What sampling plan is best? In answering these questions the purists say: Count how many lots of particular sizes are received in a week; sample these according to MIL-STD-105, Inspection Level II, and the contractually agreed AQLs; and take account of the requirements for tightened and reduced inspection. Provide manpower and inspection facilities accordingly. Other theorists prefer the use of LQ sampling. In practice, most incoming inspection sections do not work this way. This is not because of incompetence. But they do have to respond to financial and personnel limitations, the effects of earlier catastrophes, and the realities of cost reduction objectives. Table 6.4 summarizes nine different strategies for responding to these pressures. The strategies at the start of the list require a high level of inspection and those at the end require progressively lower amounts.

TABLE 6.4. Acceptance Strategies for Incoming Inspection

1. Identify every defective item
2. Identify lots for which 100 percent screening is cost efficient
3. Reject lots that are worse than a contractually agreed percent defective
4. Reject lots that are worse than the average quality of previous lots
5. Reject lots that are worse than a standard percent defective
6. Reject lots whose percent defective is such that they would cause a major problem in manufacturing
7. Inspect at a level sufficient to keep the incoming inspectors busy, but with no overtime and no inventory of waiting lots.
8. Reject lots in which every item is defective
9. Accept all lots

Strategy 1.   Using incoming inspection to prevent any defective item from reaching manufacturing requires the use of 100 percent inspection. It also requires that every specified characteristic is inspected with perfect efficiency. Even in industries, such as aerospace, where the strategy is not immediately excluded because of its high cost, 100 percent inspection is rarely applied on all characteristics. What is much more common is to 100 percent test a mass produced component, for example, a semiconductor device, for functional defects. The cost efficiency of such testing will be discussed under inspection planning, in Chapter 8. In principle, acceptance sampling could be used to decide for which lots it would be cost efficient to test 100 percent (*Strategy 2*) but, for reasons which will also be discussed in Chapter 8, this is rarely done.

Strategy 3.   This is the classical strategy for acceptance sampling. In order to instill the consumer with the confidence that few lots worse than the contractual agreement will reach production, an LQ plan must be used. A typical sample size and acceptance number for a 1 percent defective level would be 533 and 2 (acceptance numbers of 1 or 0 give a very bad producer's risk). Because this is too expensive, and the LQ is "pulled out of the air" anyway, higher LQs in the range of 5 to 10 percent that require smaller sample sizes are often used, even though such quality levels are obviously worse than what is really required. The AQL plans seem more attractive. For a 1 percent defective level, a typical sample size and acceptance number would be 80 and 2. However, such plans have a high probability of accepting lots worse than the agreed defective level. (A sample that is $2/80 = 2.5$ percent defective—two and one-half times as bad as the agreed quality—requires the lot to be *accepted.*) For a sequence of lots devices like "tightened inspection" are supposed to help, but in practice more often than not they are ignored. The sample sizes become uneconomically large for any quality much better than 1 percent (e.g., 800 for a 0.1 percent AQL). All in all, the classical approach is not very practical.

Two other strategies ignore contractually agreed percent defectives (and often there is no such agreement):

Strategy 4.   Sampling is done to reject lots that are worse by some factor than the average quality of previously received lots. It is argued that there is no point in rejecting lots of a quality that has previously been accepted; conversely, a deterioration in quality, even if within contractual requirements, requires action.

Strategy 5. This is a more common strategy, to use a standard per-cent defective thereby simplifying the work of incoming inspection. To completely protect the consumer requires expensive LQ testing, but in practice AQL plans are almost always used.

Strategy 6. The objective is to prevent lots which have a high percent defective—10 percent or more—from reaching manufacturing. For qualities better than this it will usually be possible to maintain produc-tion. Functional defects will be identified at subassembly and final test and will be eliminated by rework. Production operators will be able to screen out some of the nonfunctional defects. Such palliatives will not work for lots of very bad quality, and the aim of Strategy 6 is to iden-tify such lots.

Strategy 7. The objective here is to keep the incoming inspectors working at a steady rate, with rapid sentencing of lots and a minimum of in-process inventory. These objectives are achieved by adjusting the proportion of lots inspected (by using "skip-lot" methods) and the sample sizes according to the rate of receipt of lots and the availability of inspectors. In periods when many lots are received or the number of inspectors is low, for example, because of sickness, the proportion of lots and sample sizes inspected are reduced. When the rate of lot re-ceipt is less than average a higher proportion of lots is inspected and sample sizes are increased.

Strategies 8 and 9. These last two strategies require, respectively, one item to be inspected from each lot, and no incoming inspection at all. These are obviously very low cost strategies. The first will identify lots in which every item is defective, and is also useful in detecting admin-istrative errors (e.g., delivery of a wrong part number). The last strategy applies when the whole burden of control of the quality of purchased items has been removed from incoming inspection and placed else-where.

A few months after the first quality managers' session of the TRW Quality College, I asked 20 or 30 of the early attendees to tell me about the actual incoming inspection results in their divisions and plants. These particular managers were mainly concerned with mechanical rather than electronic products. The median purchase value was about $10 million a year, comprising some 4500 lots. Most of the inspection was done with sampling; less than a quarter of the units did any 100 percent inspection, and those that did applied it to only one-twentieth of their lots. Lot re-jection rates were mainly in the 3 to 8 percent range but in one or two units the rejection rate was as high as 20 percent. A large proportion of rejected lots were "used-as-is"—particularly by units with a high rejection rate—so that only 1.5–7 percent of lots were returned to suppliers or screened onsite. There was a considerable variability in how quickly the incoming lots were sentenced. Half of the units dealt with 80 percent of their lots in less than two days after receipt and virtually all of the rest within a week. The other half of the units dealt with only half of their lots in two days and 20–60 percent of the lots took more than a week. There was a very wide variation in the amount of incoming inspection performed. This was not just a consequence of the size of the unit; obviously one would expect a large unit buying several times the median value of $10 million a year to do more incoming inspection than a small unit buying less than the median. However, even after normalizing for this parameter, there was a range of 20 times in the amount of incoming inspection performed.

My experience indicates that these results are fairly typical of most incoming inspection operations. Whenever I visit an incoming inspection section, one of the questions I always ask is: What proportion of lots did you reject last month? The answer usually falls within a percentage or two of 5 percent. This applies irrespective of the industry or the types of products purchased. Technically, the consistency of the rejection rate is surprising. I believe the cause is not technical but rather a result of what people expect. They control to this level—by working hard for improvement or relaxing inspection conditions if the actual level should be higher, or tightening inspection conditions if it should be lower. Like most of us, people in incoming inspection like a quiet life. Lot rejection levels near 5 percent help to ensure this.

It is now appropriate to summarize the main points that have been made about incoming inspection and to draw some conclusions. For cost reasons little 100 percent incoming inspection is actually performed. Most incoming inspection uses acceptance sampling with the ostensible purpose of ensuring that the percentage defective of accepted lots is better than some "AQL." However, such AQLs are almost always established arbitrarily and have no real validity. In truth, all defective items that enter manufacturing (not just those in excess of an AQL) are a source of trouble. Incoming inspection should be judged by the proportion of received defective items it identifies, and on its cost for doing so. By this criterion acceptance sampling is an ineffective tool. At best it misses about a third of the defectives but often misses more than half. It is much less effective (though much cheaper) than 100 percent inspection. Even when lots are rejected by acceptance sampling, about half of them are "used as is"—because manufacturing still needs the rejected items. In these days of "just in time" inventory control, manufacturing cannot wait for replacement lots. (It is not sufficient to identify a bad lot; what is needed is a good lot.) The inescapable conclusion of this analysis is that *most of the defective items received by a unit go through incoming inspection into manufacturing.*

Because of this, some argue that incoming inspection should be abandoned, and a few powerful customers have actually done so. My own view is that incoming inspection should be retained but at a low-cost level. A lot should be sentenced on the basis of an average expenditure of no more than half to one person's hour's work. At this rate, the typical unit in my survey of quality managers—which employed several hundred people in total—would have only one or at most two incoming inspectors. To help achieve this low cost level, the basic sampling strategy should be to keep out very bad lots (Strategy 6). One good sampling plan for this purpose is given in Table 6.5. With this plan most lots will be sentenced on the result of the first sample of 20, which ensures low cost. People hate to reject lots because of one defective. The second sample covers this need. Also, without the second sample the "quality for 10 percent producer risk" would be only 0.5 percent, and it does not seem reasonable to have a plan that accepts many bad lots that are 5 to 10 percent defective and which also rejects some lots that are only 0.5 to 1 percent defective. Classical sampling, using MIL-STD-105D's Inspection Level II and single sampling, often requires sample sizes in the range of 80 to 200. Reducing this to 20 may not seem a major change, but it could mean the difference between having only 1 incoming inspector and having 4 or 10.

Currently, many incoming inspection sections are using sampling plans similar to this one because they are so simple and practicable. These users are criticized by the pundits and urged to participate in training sessions where they can learn about the use of "inspection levels" (which vary sample sizes with lot sizes) and the application of "tightened and reduced inspection" (which increase or decrease the amount of inspection on the basis of the results of previous lots in a series). I hope I

TABLE 6.5. Low Cost Sampling Plan

	Sample Size	Acceptance Number	Rejection Number
First sample	20	0	2
Second sample	20	0	1
Cumulative sample	40	1	2

Quality for 10 percent consumer's risk = 11.6 percent defective
Quality for 10 percent producer's risk = 1.7 percent defective

have shown that all of this complexity is largely a waste of effort *because the AQLs have no real validity*, and that the practical people in incoming inspection can go on doing what they are doing without feeling guilty.

As well as using low-cost sampling, flexibility should be exercised (Strategy 7) to keep the inspectors fully, but not over, employed. Having recognized that AQLs and inspection levels have no important validity, there should be no rational inhibition on flexibility. Another important reason for being flexible is to ensure that there is no delay in sentencing (and therefore a minimum of in-process inventory). A good general rule is: If a lot is not rejected by tomorrow it is accepted. This means that for a lot received today if it is not rejected by the end of business tomorrow, it is automatically accepted. At worst there is only a 1 in 20 chance that the lot was rejectable, and then an even chance that the Material Review Board would have allowed its use. Incoming inspection can improve those odds by using judgment about which lots to let through with less inspection than usual when under pressure. In any case, a bad lot adds only a tiny proportion more defectives to those that go through incoming inspection into production anyway every year. I do not exclude special tests, chemical analyses, and so on (often performed by "the lab" rather than by incoming inspection) from the one-day-turnover rule. With the many quick, automatic methods available these days, there is no good reason why adequate tests should not be completed within this time scale.

CONCLUSION

My reasons for suggesting that incoming inspection be retained at a low cost level rather than giving it up completely is that it does allow the systematic accumulation of data on the quality of products from various suppliers (albeit at a slow rate) and it does help to prevent particularly bad lots—which are likely to shatter the quiet life of the quality manager—from entering production.

Perhaps the most important reason for using low-cost incoming inspection rather than some more extravagant approach is that it makes absolutely clear to everyone working for both the consumer and the producer that the required quality of purchased items is *not* being defined or assured by incoming inspection, that incoming inspection is not a magic wand, and that the weight of this quality task must be borne elsewhere. In the next chapter, other methods of ensuring good quality purchased items will be discussed.

CHAPTER 7

QUALITY OF PURCHASED ITEMS

Having shown in the last chapter that incoming inspection using acceptance sampling cannot be relied on to assure the quality of purchased items, the obvious question is: how can the quality be ensured? The answer to that question is very simple:

> *A company that wants to receive good quality parts and materials must buy from good suppliers.*

Good suppliers should have programs that aid in their getting better, and should have an ambition to achieve better quality than their competitors. Customers help their own objectives of being best in quality if they buy from suppliers who have the same objective. Conversely, they seriously hamper achievement of that objective if they are content to buy from average, or worse than average, suppliers. Of course, it is not easy to buy from the best suppliers only. It would be easier if purchased items could be bought from anyone, and that the quality could be assured by incoming inspection or some other magic wand. The reality is that with a good supplier all that the customer needs to do is communicate effectively and give help and cooperation. With a bad supplier, the best that the customer can hope for is that his or her own actions may ameliorate an intrinsically unsatisfactory situation.

MODEL QUALITY POLICIES AND STANDARD PRACTICES

At this stage I shall make a short diversion. TRW sells a wide range of products and services throughout the world. Since its formation it has found that to be explicitly decentralized is the best way of organizing for that mission. Its 80 odd divisions and subsidiaries are given wide powers and responsibilities for their own operations. One consequence of this is that in the quality field TRW has only one companywide mandatory procedure—dealing with the reporting and forecasting of quality costs— and the company's quality policy is defined in a general document, "TRW and the 80s." Beyond this, the company requires that each division shall develop and issue whatever quality policies and standard practices it needs for its own operations, under the authority of its own general manager. To assist the units in doing this, the vice president, Quality TRW, has issued a series of models of such documents. Divisions can use the models essentially unchanged or they can modify them to meet their particular needs. They are not mandatory and, in principle, divisions can ignore them (though the reasons why this is hard to do in a company that is very serious about quality improvement will be discussed in Chapter 13). The model policies are as though written by a division general manager, and the model standard practices are as though written by whichever division department manager the policy makes responsible for implementation. Sometimes guidance documents are issued as well. The models are drafted by one of TRW's quality professionals, usually one of its half dozen staff people at company, sector, or group level, and then, after review by the company's Quality Steering Committee, they are circulated to the divisions for comment. The comments are taken very seriously and cause rewrite of the draft. When the vice president, Quality, judges a document to be satisfactory, it is issued. Because the models are not mandatory, there is no need for the vice president to get a consensus. The models therefore avoid the blandness of many company-written documents, and can also be issued without delay.

The first of these documents dealt with supplier quality, and were written mainly to bring TRW Quality College sessions on that topic into focus. It was TRW's vice president, Materiel, George Harris, who suggested that the models could have a usefulness beyond this initial pedagogic purpose. Table 7.1 lists the policy statements from the model purchasing-quality policy.

The first policy statement deals with the important issue of "trade-

TABLE 7.1.   Policy Statements from TRW Model Policy—Quality of Purchased Items

It is the policy of the division to seek an optimum price and delivery for items that conform to their defined requirements. It is not the policy of the division to trade-off quality, price, and delivery.

The primary objective of the division's purchased item quality system is progressively to reduce the proportion of purchased items that are defective (i.e., that are nonconformant to the defined requirements).

The division will purchase items only from approved suppliers.

The division will establish a relationship of cooperation with its approved suppliers, with the purpose of helping them to supply products conforming to the defined requirements.

The division will approve only suppliers who are honest. It will disapprove suppliers who show they are not honest. The emphasis of the division's purchased items quality program is on cooperating with honest suppliers, and not on policing dishonest suppliers.

In turn the division will treat its suppliers in an ethical, honest manner.

The division's policy of establishing cooperative rather than adversarial relationships with suppliers should minimize the probability of contractual disputes with suppliers. Nonetheless the division will ensure that contractual requirements are clearly defined.

It is the policy of the division to comply with contractual requirements from its customers, which in turn affect its suppliers. It will work with its customers and suppliers to improve the effectiveness of quality systems affecting both.

offs." There is a current management philosophy that is obsessed with the importance of trade-offs. It maintains that each business has to decide whether its success is to be based on cost leadership, customer service, technological innovation, or some other defined factor. Having decided, the business should then cover that factor superlatively well. The philosophy argues that in the real world the total resources available to a business are limited, so it is not possible to do everything well; therefore, except for the selected factor, the aim elsewhere should be for a minimally acceptable competence. Superiority in one factor is traded-off for mediocrity in others. I confess to a prejudice against the philosophy. It obviously has some measure of truth; it is useful for a business to have a strategic thrust, and resources *are* limited. However, my own experience indicates that "nothing succeeds like success," and some well-led divisions seem to be strong in every function, without excessive use of resources, whereas other divisions—who are usually in trouble—have no evident strength. The philosophy can be pernicious for quality. It leads to the erroneous idea that each business has some optimum quality level associated with a minimum cost. The rebuttal of this idea is given in Chapter 9. It also indicates, falsely, that there has to be a trade-off between quality and cost. We have already shown in Chapter 2 that marketing trade-offs do have to be made in defining the product requirement specification of a new product, but that for the rest of the chain of conformance quality and cost are not traded-off but rather are optimized together by superior productivity.

A company that buys products of inferior quality because of their low price is virtually certain to lose more than the cost advantage in extra quality costs. Fortunately, the most efficient and productive suppliers are able to achieve superior cost, quality, and delivery simultaneously. All three are results of making the product properly. (It is up to the purchasing department to convert the supplier's low cost into low price.)

The second statement in Table 7.1 implicitly recognizes the division's aim is to improve on its current quality status rather than achieve some remote ideal.

The third statement relates directly to the primary need to have good suppliers. It also recognizes that a company can deal effectively with only a limited number of suppliers. A formal list of approved suppliers is therefore a key to an effective supplier quality program The next three statements emphasize that quality improvement requires long-term cooperation between customer and supplier, and not an adversarial relationship; and, of course, such cooperation depends on honesty and ethical behavior from both parties. When I have asked purchasing managers about this, they have answered that a large majority of suppliers are honest and do not "play games" with their customers. Unfortunately, a small proportion do not have these proper standards. Unless a division explicitly addresses this issue, it may distort its whole supplier quality program and waste much effort in a vain effort to police a tiny minority of dishonest suppliers. A purchasing division must recognize that its suppliers will differ in competence and that, in any case, they will sometimes make mistakes. The division should be reasonably tolerant of such problems and help its suppliers to solve them. However, it should be completely intolerant of deliberate dishonesty. It should communicate that intolerance to the presidents of its suppliers and to their marketing and manufacturing managers as well as their quality managers. Of course, a customer can make it difficult for its suppliers to be honest. In a well known book on the psychology of human relationships called *Games People Play* (25) Eric Berne categorized such relationships. In his terminology, the business relationship between customer and supplier should be adult-adult. All too often the customer behaves as though it is parent-child. If, when the supplier's quality manager telephones to discuss some problem, he or she is verbally abused as if a delinquent pre-teen, his or her future honesty is not helped. Similarly, a bureaucratic inability or unwillingness to make sensible changes to design requirements or to grant temporary concessions makes it difficult for suppliers to be honest. Of course, when customers play games, for example, pretending the quality is wrong when they want to return excess inventory, they tell suppliers that such behavior is an acceptable way of doing business.

The last two statements are concerned with contractual relationships. Contractual requirements must be clearly defined. However, it is incompatible with a cooperative relationship for a customer to behave as if each interaction will be settled in a court of law, and a great waste of time to continually try to optimize a legal position. In fact, for a series of purchases possibly extending over many years, the commercial pressures a customer can exert on its suppliers make legal action necessary.

The last statement simply means that the division will comply with its own contractual obligations, even though this means it has to do things with its suppliers which are not compatible with its own quality philosophy. A good example concerns "source inspection." Defense agencies often require employees or agents of their prime contractors to inspect the products of their subcontractors at the latters' sites. A prime contractor, for reasons which were discussed in Chapter 2, might think that source inspection was not a good system. Nonetheless, if source inspection is contractually agreed with a customer the prime contractor must perform it, and require suppliers to cooperate.

TRW's model policy on supplier quality concludes with a statement of responsibilities. Three functions are concerned: design-development, purchasing, and quality. The design-development department is responsible for specifying all of the requirements of the items for purchase. (In doing so it should take account of the comments of suppliers, and of its own purchasing, manufacturing, and quality departments.) The design-development department is also responsible for approving or disapproving requests to allow the use of items that do not conform exactly to specification. (Sometimes it is assisted by a "material review board.") Design-development should also constrain its new product program to take account of purchasing needs (e.g., by standardization). One large division I was familiar with some years ago reduced the number of types of electronic components it purchased from over 8000 to less than 6000. This resulted in a massive productivity improvement realized in many different departments. However, the program's implementation took much effort from design-development, and great drive from the senior managers of the division.

The purchasing department must lead the entire supplier quality program. It must believe that a prime requirement of its job is to buy conforming items. It must communicate the division's policy effectively to its suppliers. It must constrain the number of suppliers, and keep a list of approved suppliers.

The quality department is responsible for keeping systematic records of the quality of purchased items, for analyzing the records, for communicating the results to suppliers, and for helping suppliers improve the quality of their products. The quality department is also responsible for acceptance of purchased items by incoming or source inspection, or by other methods.

These three departments must contribute to an integrated supplier quality program, and must participate in the maintenance of the approved suppliers list.

SUPPLIER QUALITY IMPROVEMENT ACTIVITIES

Having defined the supplier quality policy and assigned responsibility for its implementation to the design-development, purchasing, and quality departments, it is now appropriate to discuss the activities these three departments will perform. They are listed in Table 7.2. Because much of the development of quality assurance has come from powerful customers, the impression has been given that actions by the customer can determine the quality of purchased items. In fact, only a limited range of actions are available to the customer, and these do not usually include the fundamental ones, from a quality viewpoint, of designing and manufacturing the product. The supplier, assuming that they are also the designer and manufacturer of the product, has a much wider and more effective

TABLE 7.2. Supplier Quality Activities

Specifications of the items to be purchased
Changes and concessions to the item specifications
Supplier approval
Supplier appraisal
Supplier rating
Changes to supplier approval status
First article appraisal of the items to be purchased
Item acceptance, and disposition of rejected items
Accumulation and analysis of quality data on purchased items
Continuing communication with suppliers

range of activities at their disposal. (Virtually every page of this book is relevant to the work of the supplier, whereas only these few pages are relevant to the customer.) The activities listed in Table 7.2 cannot determine the quality of the products—only the supplier can do that.

The responsibility of the design-development department for the specification of the items to be purchased and for changes and concessions to these specifications has already been noted. These specifications may be in many different forms, for example, specially written purchased item specifications; drawings supported by generic specifications; specifications (often in the form of data sheets) issued by the supplier; and specifications issued by standardization organizations. Whatever its form, the specification should define all of the required features and characteristics of the item, and should be easily usable in the determination of whether or not units that are delivered against it are conformant.

As noted previously, the list of approved suppliers is critical to an effective supplier quality program. A supplier may be approved for some items but not for others. The purchasing department can buy only from approved suppliers (suppliers are approved by a committee consisting of representatives of the purchasing, design-development, and quality departments). Decisions should be by consensus with any of the three departments able to veto an approval.

Conventionally, a supplier approval is usually based on the result of an on-site appraisal of a potential supplier by a team of purchasing, design-development, and quality representatives. Such an appraisal is likely to take at least half a week, taking account of time needed for planning, traveling, and reporting. In a year, a three-member team working full time could appraise approximately 50 suppliers. Most divisions have 100 or more suppliers. Starting from scratch, it would take one team two or three years to appraise all of a division's suppliers; and, of course, very few divisions are able to make available a full time, three-member team for this purpose, In fact, those divisions that do any supplier appraisals at all, usually do only about 5 to 10 a year.

In practice, two other principal methods must be used to complete the approved suppliers' list. First, any supplier who has a history of satisfactory delivery of a particular item to the division can be approved for that item, or similar items. When a division first establishes an approved suppliers' list, it will approve most of its existing suppliers by this method. Second, suppliers who are already approved by competent bodies may be approved by the division. The application of this principle is obvious where the "competent body" is the quality group of a national standardization organization or a major defense agency. However, the method

method should also be extended to utilize the work of competent commercial companies, including customers and competitors of the division. It seems obvious that carrying out an appraisal of a supplier who is already approved by a score or more of other companies is likely to be a waste of expensive effort. The probability of the new appraisal identifying some problem which requires the approval to be denied, or of causing the supplier to improve their methods in some significant way must be extremely low. The division should aim for the completion of a comprehensive approved suppliers' list as quickly as possible, taking a realistic view of the resources available to it for the task.

A supplier should be sent a formal approval document after it has been approved by the division's supplier approval committee. The latter should define the range of items for which the supplier is approved and any limitations on the place of manufacture. The document should state that approval does not imply any obligation to buy, and that approval may be withdrawn if the supplier ceases to be competitive. The approval document should emphasize to the supplier that approval is not an isolated event but rather is the start of a long-term cooperation between the division and the supplier with the objective of progressively improving the quality of the items supplied.

This discussion should not be taken to indicate that formal appraisals for approval purposes are not useful. In fact they are, and many divisions perform 5 to 10 appraisals a year on potential suppliers identified by the purchasing department—who cannot be approved on the basis of existing approvals. Such appraisals need to be well planned, including lists of the main subjects to be covered, the names and titles of the supplier's people with whom interaction is required, and so on. The purchasing member of the team should make the arrangements with the supplier, and obtain agreement to the appraisal plan. During the appraisal the purchasing member will cover necessary aspects of their functional responsibilities. The design-development member should ensure that the supplier's people have a clear understanding of the requirements of the product requirement specification, and should review their suggestions for changes or concessions. An arrangement should be made for these requests to be approved or disapproved in writing.

Traditionally, the quality part of a supplier appraisal has followed a quality assurance approach. In essence, this requires the supplier to define the important systems in writing, and then establish a method of determining whether or not the actual ways the systems are carried out follow the documentation. This seems sensible, because how can the quality of products be controlled if the way they should be made is undefined, or if they are not made the way they are supposed to be? (In fact there *are* other ways.) The main trouble with this quality assurance approach is that it is too difficult and expensive for it to be applied comprehensively. So, in practice, many of the marketing, design-development, purchasing, and manufacturing systems that really determine the quality of the products are ignored, and attention is concentrated on the quality assurance system. The supplier's quality manual is examined to see if it defines such procedures as those for gauge control, calibration of test equipment, use of bonded and quarantine stores, inspection stamps, sampling plans, material review boards, acceptance record keeping, and so on. Checklists for this approach are readily available.

In practice, other subjects are of greater importance than the documentation and comprehensiveness of the quality assurance system. The first of these concerns the overall competence of the supplier's manufacturing system to make the product in conformance to the design. Modern, well-maintained equipment is a prime requirement. Automatic equipment is usually better than manually controlled equipment. A well-trained, stable work-force is another prime requirement. The technical ability and experience of the manufacturing management is a key factor. A supplier who lacks the manufacturing facilities and competence necessary to make the product should not be approved, however good their quality assurance system might be. Another subject of great importance concerns the honesty of the supplier. Much quality assurance effort is wasted because of the implicit assumption that the supplier is dishonest and that policing must be used. In most cases, this assumption is wrong. Where it is right policing will be at best an expensive palliative.

A third subject of vital importance is the supplier's own information about the range of quality of the products being sold, and the willingness to show it to the division. It seems obvious that good suppliers will know about the quality of their products, but, in fact, most suppliers do not know. Suppliers will only know about their quality to the customer if they have well organized systems that give this information. These systems include outgoing quality audit, reliability and environmental tests, and analysis of customer rejections and complaints. Averaged over a period of three months to a year—what proportion of the product, as shipped, is defective, functionally and nonfunctionally? This information is concerned with the total output of the plant to all customers. If the average quality and its range to all customers is good, the quality of the product supplied to a division will also be good. Conversely, if the average quality is bad and uncontrolled, any special quality assurance system imposed by a division may involve increased prices and is unlikely to be effective.

What is the contractual situation? On the one hand a division is likely to be insisting on the responsibility of its suppliers to deliver totally conforming items; on the other hand, it is asking that they show their data, which will indicate that the items are not fully conforming. This seems illogical but the reality is that the division had been accepting items that were not fully conformant, and had not been making any contractual fuss. The division should reassure its suppliers that it is not making the contractual requirements any more onerous than they really were in the past, and will not tighten the accept-reject criteria it actually uses (it would not be practicable to do so). The quality *improvement* the division is expecting will not be enforced contractually (again, it would not be practicable to do so, and the pretense would be counter-productive).

Another subject the appraisal team should cover in detail is the supplier's system for quality improvement. Does the supplier have a well-led and managed multifunctional quality improvement team? Is there a program of statistical process capability measurement? Is statistical process control used? Does the supplier analyze the quality data and then use it to initiate specific quality improvement projects? Are quality costs used as a tool for quality improvement?

Most suppliers will be found deficient in some or all of these criteria. It is not practical to refuse approval of them because of this. However, these criteria should figure largely in the continuing program for improvement with selected approved suppliers. They should be given precedence in the overall appraisal process compared with the conventional quality assurance elements.

Many supplier appraisals are expensive games, played between the quality people of customers and suppliers, which have little effect on the quality of the product supplied. Divisions should ensure that their appraisals are effective—and that the average quality of the items coming from suppliers is significantly better than it would have been if the appraisals were not performed.

Having approved a group of suppliers, it seems logical to take the next step: establishing a system for rating them continually. A closer examination indicates that this is not as logical as it first seems. The approved suppliers' list is fundamental to the whole supplier quality program. It defines the small group of suppliers, perhaps 100, selected from the thousands or millions of possible suppliers with whom the division plans to work for quality improvement. A continuous rating system is just one method that may or may not be effective for facilitating the quality improvement program (and the parallel purchasing improvement program). There are only two purposes for this: to help and motivate suppliers toward improvement, and to assist divisional people in prioritizing their own supplier related activities. All too often, considerable effort is expended in developing a computerized supplier rating system without having this in mind. After a time, the computer print-outs appear and are dispatched "to distribution." Often, no one is singled out to take action on the basis of the reports, and the division generally is not organized to take such action. In fact, the quality manager who wants a quiet life hopes the print-out will indicate stability and peace. Sometimes a better organized division will pick out a few bad suppliers and a quality or purchasing person will be selected to deal with them. Unfortunately, I have to point out a very unpalatable truth:

More defective items come from good suppliers than from bad suppliers

Also, just as it does not matter that a defective item comes from a good lot or a bad lot (it causes trouble in either case), it does not matter that a defective item comes from a good supplier or a bad supplier. The basis of my statement is numerical. A division that has 96 good suppliers (including, almost certainly, its biggest suppliers) and four bad suppliers receives much more material from the good suppliers than the bad ones. This overwhelms the difference in the proportion defective.

Why is this unpalatable? Well, it makes improvement more difficult. Instead of having satisfying, punishment-oriented, parent-child interviews with a few bad suppliers, those responsible for improvement actions have to set up adult-adult relationships with a much larger number of good suppliers. A supplier quality improvement program that addresses only a few bad suppliers is just scratching the surface of the total opportunity.

Conventionally, suppliers are rated for various product quality, support quality, delivery quality, and price parameters. Arbitrary weightings are applied and each supplier is given an overall rating number, usually relative to a maximum of 100. Suppliers are told they are in one of four categories—excellent, average, need-to-improve, or disapproved.

When a powerful customer introduces a new rating system with some fanfare—and implies there will be an increased number of purchases from high-rated suppliers and the disapproval of low-rated suppliers—it does have considerable motivational effect. However, the rating number is, at best, a crude means of sorting. Action should not be taken just because of the number. It would be foolish to disapprove one supplier, or give another supplier a quality award, without the Supplier Approval Committee having made a serious appraisal of the supplier's overall status.

The thrust of this book is directed at quality improvement. For this purpose, the overall rating number has little use. It is necessary to examine the elements that go into it. Suppliers with the same overall rating may need to concentrate their improvement activities in entirely different areas. One supplier may have excellent product quality but slow delivery while another may have good delivery and manufacturing quality but poor design quality, and so on.

Since the rating number has no precise significance there is no virtue in defining it in a complicated way. In fact, it is better to have four numbers, one each for product quality, support quality, delivery, and price, and reduce as far as possible the use of arbitrary weightings. The following issues of product quality might be rated:

1. The supplier's manufacturing excellence
2. The supplier's own product quality information
3. The supplier's quality systems
4. The division's own product quality information

For support quality the following might be rated:

1. The supplier's honesty
2. The supplier's response to technical and quality inquiries
3. The supplier's administrative failures (wrong deliveries, invoices, etc.)

All supplier rating activities must be assessed for value against their two purposes. Do they help the division's prioritization? Do they help suppliers improve? For the latter, a burst of activity over a few months may be more effective than a routine program.

To some extent a supplier rating system is incompatible with the idea of long-term cooperation between customer and supplier. The latter is essentially a relationship between equals; in the former, the rater adopts a position of superiority relative to the rated. (Why do we not have "customer rating" systems?) Therefore, care should be taken that the rating system does not harm the cooperative relationships.

I will say little about the next three supplier quality activities listed in Table 7.2. "Changes to supplier approval status" means that suppliers have to be disapproved as well as approved to keep the approved suppliers' list at its optimum length. The main reasons for taking suppliers off of the list are because of a reduction in the level of purchases from them (possible because the direction of the division's own activities has changed) and because suppliers are no longer competitive—their rate of improvement having been less than that of other suppliers. However, a supplier should not be disapproved as a means of punishment. Rather, the ultimate criterion should be: Is this advantageous to the division?

First article appraisal of the newly purchased product is analogous to product qualification of a new product for sale (see Chapter 5). Ideally, the supplier should do qualification testing and make the results available to the customer.

Item acceptance is normally performed using incoming or source inspection. Both of these have already been discussed.

The last two activities listed in Table 7.2, "accumulation and analysis of quality data," and "continuing communication with suppliers," are related and both are very important. The main thrust of the supplier quality program is to assist good suppliers in becoming better. It would follow then that this objective provides the main reason for accumulating and analyzing quality data. Obviously, this objective cannot be realized without the results being communicated to the supplier. The best way to do this is through a supplier quality engineer. Table 7.3 lists several sources of quality data on purchased items. It is apparent that these are not limited to incoming inspection. In principle, some of the other sources should be more valuable.

In Chapter 4, the importance of the outgoing quality audit was emphasized. For electronic equipment, the results of in-process tests, particularly the ubiquitous 100 percent functional test of the printed circuit board furnished with electronic components, can be a better source of information than incoming inspection by sampling. In practice, the amount of useful analysis of quality data on purchased items performed by customers is very small, and the amount of effective action resulting from the analysis is even smaller.

With the slowly growing recognition within the quality profession that incoming and source inspection do not effectively deal with the problem of the quality of purchased items, the emphasis has moved toward the employment of supplier quality engineers—a very positive trend. However, it is difficult to make supplier quality engineering effective. When-

TABLE 7.3.   Sources of Quality Data on Purchased Items

Supplier's laboratory tests
Supplier's field failure information
Supplier's outgoing quality audits
Customer's laboratory tests
Customer's incoming inspection
Customer's in process and final inspection
Customer's field failure information

ever I go to the shipping area of one of TRW's more customer-regulated divisions, I ask the divisional quality people, "Does the work of these customers' supplier quality engineers really help the quality of the product we sell to them?"

Sometimes the answer is, "no." A customer's representative is just a cog in a paperwork machine. In other cases the answer is, "yes." A good person is acting as an effective communication link between the customer and the division, and is helping to strengthen the division's own motivation for quality improvement. The visits of supplier quality engineers should not be formalities. They should be trying to help the supplier improve, not simply be observers of a static situation. They should meet with the managers who are useful for achieving their goal, but should not spend time in "ceremonial" meetings, unless these have specific objectives.

It is, in fact, very difficult to be effective as a supplier quality engineer. Effective people for this position are hard to find because the necessary balance of maturity and intellectual and technical competence needed for this job fit the bill for easier and more prestigious jobs. Also, the supplier quality engineer requires strong support from the quality manager and all members of the Supplier Approval Committee. This support is often missing and the supplier quality engineer must work in isolation. Finally, there is the question of cost. The 100 odd suppliers of a typical division employing, for example, a thousand people, might take three employees to service them effectively. However, few divisions of that size will be prepared to accept the cost required for such a supplier quality activity. Most divisions will not have a full-time supplier quality engineer. My advice is to appoint one good person, assign approximately 30 key suppliers to him or her, and give complete support. After a year, add another and a few months later promote the first.

CONCLUSION

Many manufacturing companies buy as much value as they add in manufacturing; therefore, the quality of purchased items is of great importance. Unfortunately, the obvious way of ensuring the quality of purchased items—incoming inspection—is insupportably expensive if performed 100 percent and ineffective if performed by sampling. The only way to ensure good quality purchased items is to have good suppliers. This chapter showed how customers can help suppliers work for quality improvement.

CHAPTER **8**

INSPECTION AND TEST IN MANUFACTURING

In Chapter 2, the concept of the chain of conformance (Figure 2.1) was introduced as a means of expressing the concept that making superior quality products was a multistage affair in which concrete and abstract objects—a customer's need, a product requirement specification, a product design and a manufactured product—alternated with marketing, design, purchasing, and manufacturing processes. In principle, both the objects and the processes could be specified, but in practice such specification is usually incomplete. We have now reached the last links of the chain, those concerned with the manufacturing processes (Figure 5.1) that finally realize the design in the manufactured product. In this chapter we shall discuss the manufacturing processes concerned with inspection and test.

INSPECTION AND TEST PLANNING

It is often said that, "You can't inspect quality into a product." Manufacturing people with a background in standard costing also say, "Inspection and test don't add value." They differentiate them in this regard from direct manufacturing operations like fabrication and assembly. Both of these comments have a plausible ring and are easy to remember. However, I do not believe either of them. Table 3.1 shows that in 1983 TRW spent $179 million testing and inspecting its products. Adding in the cost of planning this work brings the total to $211 million. Most of the test and inspection paid for with this money was for improving the quality of the products sold. Without it, many of the products would simply not have worked, and most of them would not have met the customers' expectations. It seems obvious that a product that works and meets the customer's expectation is of higher quality and more value than a product that does neither. One could counter argue that perfect conformance to the customer's need equates to a product quality of unity, and it is not possible to have a quality greater than unity. The nonconformances to the customer's need introduced by less than perfect marketing, design, and manufacturing processes take out quality, thereby bringing the product quality to less than unity. Inspection and testing (by identifying some of such nonconformances and enabling them to be removed) bring the product quality nearer to unity (i.e., they add quality into the product).

In fact, today inspection and test remain, as they have always been, the two principal methods of improving the quality of products. They are virtually the only methods formally and explicitly applied by many companies, and even companies that do apply other methods of quality improvement still use inspection and test as part of the total process for achieving superior quality. Inspection and test have never been fashionable. Right-first-time, zero defects, quality circles, top management involvement, quality and productivity, SPC (statistical process control), SQA (supplier quality assurance), just-in-time, Taguchi methods, and so on, have each had their day in the limelight, but never inspection and test. Nonetheless, literally billions of dollars are spent each year on inspection and test, and without it the quality of most of the products bought and sold in the world today would be unbearably bad.

When my colleagues on TRW's Quality Steering Committee and I were discussing the content of the TRW Quality College in 1981, I emphasized to them the importance of including a session on inspection and test planning. The subject had not been covered by the earlier ITT Quality College in which I had participated, but I felt that these activities which accounted for more than half of TRW's (and ITT Europe's) quality costs, and which also had a profound effect on the company's quality to the customer, comprised a topic of primary importance. My colleagues agreed, but none of them felt sufficiently expert to take the lead, and their inquiries in the company did not produce a volunteer either. I had suggested that a case study would be a good way of dealing with the subject, and one division quality manager did go so far as to offer to collaborate with me in writing such a case.

One day, when I was on the telephone, he came into my office and tipped a great armful of papers onto my already-littered desk. I beckoned him to stay, but he said he was late for a meeting and disappeared. The papers were a set of planning documents and inspection and test results on one of TRW's complex mechanical products. During the next few days, I waded through the pile and gradually wrote the first draft of the "BGP45 Pump" case study. I did not fully understand some of the papers, and many of the results I deliberately changed, so that the case, which is described as the last section of this chapter, finally bore little resemblance to the real product on which it was based. In this way, I avoided confidentiality and approval problems. For some other TRW Quality College cases, for example, quality costs, there were "correct" solutions, but the inspection planning case was deliberately open-ended. However, as group after group worked on it through many different sessions of the college, some general concepts became clear. They form the basis of this section of the book.

The products of the companies I have worked for in the past 27 years, STC, ITT Europe, and TRW, are mainly electrical and mechanical machines and the components from which they are assembled. These included for STC and ITT Europe telecommunications equipment, consumer electronics, defense electronics, measuring instruments, automotive components—both electrical and mechanical—pumps, faucets, electronic components, and special purpose computers. TRW makes many of these classes of products but adds spacecraft, machine tools, and aeroengine parts. In my central staff positions, I have had contact with all of these products, and in developing the ideas of this chapter these are the sorts of products I had in mind. Both TRW and ITT Europe have service businesses, both are heavily concerned with computer software, and ITT Europe was involved to a limited extent in food, cosmetic, and pharmaceutical products, but I have not tested these inspection and test planning concepts for applicability in such areas. The scope is limited to mechanical and electrical machines.

Table 8.1 defines some of the subjects dealt with in inspection and test planning. I have no expertise in metrology or the development of test equipment, so I will not deal with those subjects. My approach will be to examine the overall concepts controlling inspection and test. It is necessary therefore to first define some key terms in ways that clarify their logical relationships.

TABLE 8.1.   Inspection and Test Planning Activities

Determinations of test and inspection equipment requirements
Design and development of test and inspection equipment
Procurement of test and inspection equipment
Planning the calibration and maintenance of test and inspection equipment
Determination of test and inspection points
Determination of inspection levels—100 percent or sampling
Writing of test and inspection specifications and instructions
Development of test and inspection reporting systems
Determination of test and inspection manning levels

First, there are two general terms, product and item, that are used in defining the inspection and test terms.

An *item* is a concrete or abstract object. It is not an action or an activity. Typical item examples include a material, component, subassembly, or product.

A *product* is an item that is sold by a vendor to a customer.

Next, there are four key activities: inspect, test, measure, and use.

A person *inspects* an item by looking at it and comparing it with the specification of a required feature.

A person *tests* an item by applying a specified test equipment, and sometimes a specified stress, to the item, and comparing the response to the specification of a required characteristic.

A person *measures* an item by applying a specified measuring equipment, and sometimes a stress, to the item and comparing the response to a measurement standard.

A customer *uses* a product and compares its features and characteristics to all of the aspects of his or her need.

Inspection is limited to visual inspection, with or without magnification. (Use of a "go, no-go gauge" is a test.) The specified features and characteristics of an item will usually include a specification of the state of the item (e.g., its temperature). Sometimes "preconditioning" will be specified for the item. For a life-test or an environmental test, the item will be stressed for a period of time and then characteristics will be tested. A measurement can be converted into a test by comparing the result of the measurement to the specification of a characteristic.

Next there are five important "failure" definitions.

An item *fails* while being inspected, tested, or used, when it does not conform to a specified requirement, or to an aspect of the customer's need.

A *defect* is the part of an item that caused it to fail.

A *defective* is an item that contains one or more defects.

A person *blunders* when he or she makes a defect.

The difference between the actual and correct values of a measurement is the *error*.

Quality professionals and lawyers have contributed enormous complexity to these five definitions. The former use a large number of synonyms for these terms in a fairly random manner (e.g., imperfection, nonconformity, blemish, bug, fault, mistake, and unplanned event). More often than not, quality professionals leave unclear whether they are talking about a failure or a defect, or a combination of the two. Computer software professionals use the word "error," usually to mean defect (despite the fact that the metrologists had preempted the term error long before there *were* computer software professionals), but sometimes failure or blunder. When product liability (see Chapter 10) became an important cause of litigation, lawyers made things more complex. Their goal was to limit the use of the words "defect" and "failure" as much as possible. When a producer admits that an item has failed or contains defects it leaves him or her legally exposed. This is despite the fact that many items that go into products can fail if they are tested or inspected against their own specifications without causing the product to fail (e.g., a general purpose transistor will have dozens of specified characteristics, some of which will be utilized to the limit when it is incorporated in the design of one electronic equipment, and others when it is used in another equipment; clearly, failure of an irrelevant transistor characteristic will not cause the equipment to fail). This is also despite the fact that only a minority of product failures are dangerous (e.g., it is usually not dangerous if a product fails to look the way it should).

The key terms "fail" and "defect" are intimately connected. Usually, an item fails because it contains a defect (though defect-free items can fail by wear-out or by over-stressing). The existence of the defect precedes the event of failure. However, until the moment of failure the presence of the defect is hidden. It is for this latter reason that "fail" is made the primary term, with "defect" following from it. When an item fails an inspection the defect is usually obvious. When an item fails in use or during a test, considerable analysis may be required to identify the defect that caused the failure.

Sometimes it is possible to determine that a particular person caused a defect. Such a person "blundered." Though both are used more commonly, I do not use "error" for this term, because it has other meanings, or "mistake," because it is not a verb. (To use "mistake" as a verb one has to say "make a mistake." This is wrong. One makes defects not mistakes).

Table 8.2 lists the objectives of inspection and test. What about: to prove that products meet their quality standards? Well, it's hard to prove anything in this world. There is a lot of truth in the old saying, "the only things that are certain are death and taxes." For quality, we can say with certainty that a product has just passed a test, but there is always the possibility that it will fail if the test is repeated, or that it will fail if it is actually used in some way that the test was supposed to cover. So, it is safer to restrict the purpose to that of 2(c) in Table 8.2. We can decide to sell a product only if it passes every one of a series of tests. But that can never prove, with no possibility of being wrong, that the product will work for the customer. Unfortunately, in the quality business, failing just one test always proves that something is wrong, but passing a whole series of tests does not definitely prove that everything is right.

Objectives 1(a) and (b) in Table 8.2 can only be achieved by 100 percent test and inspection, which is called *screening*, because of the low inspection effectiveness of sampling inspection (see Chapter 6). Objectives

TABLE 8.2.   Objectives of Inspection and Test

1. Defective items
   (a) To separate defective items from nondefective items
   (b) To identify the defects in defective items so that they can be scrapped or reworked
2. Measuring the defect level
   (a) To measure the defect level in purchased products to assist decision about their acceptance, to assist decision about payment of suppliers, and to use in communicating with suppliers about quality improvement
   (b) To measure the defect level of items in process to assist decision about whether they will be passed to a subsequent process, and to assist quality improvement
   (c) To measure the defect level of products to assist decision about whether they will be sold, to use in communications with customers, and to assist quality improvement
3. To obtain information about processes used in making items to assist control of the defect level of items made subsequently

2 and 3 can be achieved by either 100 percent or sampling inspection and test. In practice, sampling at levels below 10 percent is commonly used for those purposes because of its low cost. However, when 100 percent test or inspection is being used for Objective 1, information is generated that can be used for the other purposes (though often this source of data is ignored). Most of the money spent on test and inspection goes for Objective 1 because it requires 100 percent application.

INSPECTION EFFECTIVENESS

We have already emphasized the low effectiveness of sampling inspection and test in identifying defective items. One hundred percent inspection and test can have a much higher effectiveness, but the human tendency to go to the other extreme and assume that they are completely effective is not correct. (A reflex reaction to any quality problem is to increase the amount of inspection, and then to blame the inspectors if the problem is not solved. In fact, of course, the responsibility resides with the people—in marketing, design, purchasing, or manufacturing—who caused the problem in the first place). No inspection or test is 100 percent effective, and for inspection and test planning it is vital to remember the known or estimated effectiveness of each test or inspection. There are two types of ineffectiveness—passing bad items and screening out good items—but the following analysis will deal only with the former.

The effectiveness of an inspection, E, is defined by the equation:

$$N_R = E \times N_I.$$

When N_I is the number of defectives incoming to the inspection, and N_R is the number of defectives removed by the inspection.

Another relationship is obvious:

$$N_I = N_R + N_O,$$

where N_O is the number of defectives outgoing from the inspection.

In practice, N_R is what is measured and N_O—the number of defectives left after the inspection—is what is required. The relationship of these numbers which follows from the two previous relationships is:

$$N_O = N_R (1-E)/E.$$

If the effectiveness is 90 percent, $E = 0.9$ and $N_O = N_R/9$. If $E = 0.99$, $N_O = N_R/99$.

The same principles can be applied to more complicated situations. One of the examples in Chapter 8 concerned 20 lots of 1000 units, each lot containing about 20 defects. Samples of 80 units were inspected from each lot, and 32 defectives were found in these samples. Four of the lots were rejected and 16 were accepted. The good units from all of the samples were added in with the accepted lots. What was the inspection effectiveness? The results can be summarized as follows:

	Total	Bad	Good
Incoming units	20,000	400	19,600
Sampling units	$20 \times 80 = 1600$	32	1,568
Outgoing units	$16 \times 920 + 1568 = 16{,}288$	$16 \times 20 \times 920/1000 = 294$	15,994

Applying the equation,

$$E = 1 - N_O/N_I = 1 - 294/400 = .265.$$

However, this does not seem right because many good units were rejected in the four rejected lots. It appears better to use proportion defective, P, rather than number defective in the calculation. Now,

$$E = 1 - P_O/P_I = 1 - \frac{294/16{,}288}{400/20{,}000} = .0975.$$

The inspection effectiveness is only 10 percent, not 26 percent. This example illustrates the use of proportion defective, rather than number defective, in calculating inspection effectiveness.

The main reason for performing inspection and test is Objective 1—to find defects—and for this reason inspection effectiveness is of primary importance.

CATEGORIZATION OF DEFECTS

Conventionally, defects are classified according to their *effect*. They are categorized as critical, major, or minor depending on how serious the failures they cause are. This categorization is most relevant to the end-use customer, and, like so much else in quality management, the categories were established by powerful customers. Customers are interested in the effects of defects. However, what suppliers should be interested in is the causes of defects and how to identify and remove them. For the latter purpose, a different method of categorization is of greater importance. It divides defects into functional, nonfunctional, and reliability defects.

Many of the required features and characteristics of the mechanical and electrical machines that are under consideration in this chapter are functional. They define the ways in which a machine is supposed to work. *Functional defects* cause the products to fail to meet these requirements. Other required features and characteristics are nonfunctional. They are concerned with the products' appearance, size, weight, and so on. *Nonfunctional defects* cause failures of these requirements. The third category of defects, *reliability defects*, do not cause the product to fail functionally at the time of test, or at the time of hand-over to the customer, but will eventually cause functional failures. Tables 8.3 and 8.4 give examples of these different kinds of defects for a mechanical machine, a car, and an electrical machine, a television set.

Functional defects are straightforward. They prevent the product from working and most of them are major. However, I observed a minor functional failure when I took delivery of my previous car. When I got it home, the trunk light failed. It did not come on when the lid was lifted. The defect was a broken light bulb. It is more difficult to think of examples of critical functional defects than minor functional defects. It is immediately obvious that a functionally defective product is not working; therefore it does not usually place the user in a critical situation. An example I use in training programs is that of a person who picks up a new car and drives it out through the showroom window because the brakes are defective. I don't feel it is a very plausible example. How did the car get into the showroom with disconnected brakes?

TABLE 8.3. Examples of Defects in a Car

	Zero/Minor	Major	Critical
Functional	Broken light-bulb filament	Jammed engine cylinder	Disconnected brake linkage
Nonfunctional	Wrong door gap Out-of-tolerance gear cog	Large body-work scratch	Missing number plate
Reliability	Cracked air-conditioning outlet	Defective transistor in cassette recorder	Design defect on steering seal

TABLE 8.4.   Examples of Defects in a Television Set

	Zero/Minor	Major	Critical
Functional	Defective rheostat causing sound degradation	Open circuit solder joint	—
Nonfunctional	Small scratch, out-of-tolerance resistor	Large scratch	—
Reliability	Defective rheostat causing sound degradation	Defective cathode causing tube failure	Defective capacitor causing fire

Nonfunctional defects are more complicated. They can have effects that range from no effect at all to a major effect (but not usually critical). An example of a minor nonfunctional defect in a car is a door gap that is visibly larger on the nearside than on the farside. A nonfunctional defect of zero effect might be a gear-box cog with one of its dimensions outside of the drawing tolerance but, because the meshing cog is well within tolerance, the combination works perfectly. There are many examples of major nonfunctional defects but it is hard to think of critical nonfunctional defects. A missing license plate that results in the driver having trouble with the police again is not very plausible.

Reliability failures are almost always serious, either major or critical. There are two viewpoints with regard to reliability defects. A defect that has actually caused a failure obviously has the same effect level as the failure. If it was a critical failure, the causative defect is also critical. However, *potential* reliability defects can be observed (e.g., during a visual inspection) that have not caused a reliability failure. Their importance—critical, major, or minor—depends both on the seriousness of the possible failures and on their probability of actually occurring. Customer quality representatives often overlook this point when defining defects. For example, they define a surface irregularity on a component, which has no functional significance and which will not be visible in the finished product, as a defect because it might cause a reliability failure. If process improvement reduces the size or frequency of the irregularities, or a better method of observing them is developed, they tighten the standard. Large amounts of money can be spent on process changes and screening inspections addressing such defects. However, very rarely is any money spent on experiments to determine whether the defined defects have significant probabilities of contributing to the unreliability of the product. Often the product's unreliability is controlled by entirely different reliability defects—sometimes unobservable by visual inspection—

and the effect of the visual defect is so small that it is "lost in the noise." Unfortunately, we quality professionals often give unwarranted importance to things we understand—such as visual defects—and close our minds to more important defects—such as a complex stress concentration leading to a fatigue failure, or an ionic impurity in the planar layer of a semiconductor leading to a short circuit—which we do not.

In Table 8.3, the three reliability examples are of actual, not potential, reliability defects. The cracked air-conditioning outlet caused the outlet to break off after the car had been in operation for a few weeks, and the air from that outlet could no longer be channeled in a selected direction. When the defective transistor eventually failed, it put an expensive audio system out of operation. The design defect on a hydraulic seal of a power-operated steering gear caused the steering to fail suddenly, and caused a major accident after some thousands of miles of normal operation.

Table 8.4 shows that the same principles apply to defects on a television set. Functional defects which stop the set from working are usually major. One open circuit among the couple of thousand connections on a typical set will inevitably cause a functional failure as will one nonworking component. Minor functional defects detract from performance in some observable but not serious way—the example concerns the volume-control rheostat. Functional defects are not critical because the failures they cause are obvious. A television set is a piece of furniture as well as an electrical machine, and some nonfunctional defects concern its appearance. Other nonfunctional defects include electronic components that do not conform in all respects to their own specifications but, because the set design is conservative, not in ways that affect the functioning of the set. Critical nonfunctional defects do not exist.

Reliability defects run parallel to functional defects for the minor and major categories. The difference is that failure is not immediate but occurs after a period of normal operation. However, reliability defects are critical much more often than functional defects. Failure of a product after an indefinite period of operation can cause critical situations. The example given concerns an actual case. Several million units of a European-made television set were sold. After several years it became apparent that the capacitor placed across the power input to prevent injection of high frequency noise into the power line was sometimes failing. The failure mode was that the capacitor overheated and sometimes burst into flames. In a proportion of the failures the fire spread to the set, and sometimes the fire spread further. Although, as far as I know, no one was hurt an expensive recall had to be instituted.

The workmanship of the solder joints in electronic equipment gives another illustration of actual and potential reliability failures. If the joint is open circuit or short circuit it is a functional defect. However, if it is neither an open circuit nor short circuit but does not conform to the applicable workmanship standard it constitutes a potential reliability defect. Such joints do actually fail from time to time, though in practice only a small minority of reliability failures in electronic equipment are caused by solder joint defects (most are caused by component defects or design defects). A great deal of quality assurance effort goes into defining the workmanship standards for the solder joints and inspecting against those standards. All of this is important when one percent or more of the joints, as initially made, do not conform to a particular standard, and the number can be halved or doubled by adjusting the standard—and also when there is no experimental data relating different workmanship standards to reliability failures so that definition of the standard is a matter of judgment. The Japanese took a more sensible approach with their consumer electronics. By careful and conservative layout of their printed circuit boards, by attention to the solderability of the component leads, and by close attention to detail in the soldering process, they reduced the proportion of defective joints as initially made—not after visual inspection and "touch-up"—to better than one defect in 100,000 joints. At this level, 100 percent inspection was unnecessary—any effect of solder joints on reliability was completely negligible—and the detail of the workmanship standard became of little importance.

In summary, functional defects are usually major, and nonfunctional defects may have a zero effect, be minor or major. Actual reliability defects are usually major or critical, and potential reliability defects can have any importance depending on how likely they are to cause a reliability failure.

From an inspection and test planning viewpoint, the categorization of defects into functional, nonfunctional, and reliability categories is important because different strategies are used to find the different kinds of defects or to show that they are absent. For functional defects, the process is relatively easy. Functional defects can be indicated, or their absence shown, by a functional test. Such a test can have high effectiveness. Consider the three functional defects given in Table 8.3. Testing the completed new car could easily show the presence or absence of such defects. A minute or two spent in opening and closing doors, trunk lids, and so on, and in operating switches would show whether or not any of the hundreds of possible functional defects in the light circuits were actually there. A brief road test—no more than a 100 yards—would show the presence of the engine defect given in the table and any other possible functional defects in the power system. The same road test would cover virtually all possible functional defects with regards to the brakes, steering system, wheels, and so on.

A key point here is that, when a functional test shows that the required functional output from a system is achieved, it proves that none of the possible functional defects of the system is present because (except for redundancy, which will be discussed in Chapter 11) a single functional defect always prevents the system from working properly. Figure 8.1 shows a product with nine functional subassemblies, A to I. If a functional test across the output is passed, it shows that none of the subassemblies contains a functional defect. However, if the test is failed, one or more of the subassemblies contains a functional defect. The simple pass-fail criterion offers no information about which subassembly failed. More testing and analysis are required to determine this. The defective subassembly (or subassemblies) has to be removed from the product and replaced. The overall functional test then has to be repeated, and again there are pass and fail possibilities. An alternative approach is to functionally test the nine subassemblies before they are put together. The economic advantages and disadvantages of the two approaches will be discussed later in this chapter. Here it will simply be pointed out that a final, 100 percent functional test is a very effective way of identifying a small residual proportion of functional defects in a complex product, or in a population of units of product, or of showing that no such defect is present.

In the television set example of Table 8.4 it is equally easy to show that functional defects are absent. Switching the set on, systematically operating all of the controls, and observing the output is all that is required. However, as with the car, a functional failure does not give immediate identification of the causative defect, and more testing and analysis are usually required for this.

In principle, nonfunctional defects are more difficult to find than

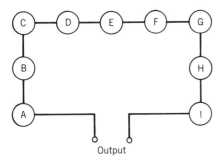

Figure 8.1. Testing for a functional defect.

functional defects because for the former there is no equivalent to the functional test which in one application can show the absence of hundreds of possible defects. Each nonfunctional defect is separate, and a test or inspection addresses such defects one at a time. To determine whether or not defects like the first three nonfunctional defects of Table 8.3 are present, every feature of the car must be visually inspected, one by one. The out-of-tolerance gear cog is even more difficult. It would be impossible to find such a defect on the assembled car, and impracticable to disassemble the car and check every tolerance on every specified dimension on every component—which is what would have to be done to find the defect.

For the television set, the same conclusion applies to its nonfunctional defects. The appearance defects are easily found with a visual inspection, albeit one at a time. The out-of-tolerance components (remembering they have no effect on the performance of the set) could not be found in practice even though, in principle, the set could be disassembled and every component tested for everyone of its specified characteristics.

Reliability defects are the most difficult of all to locate. For the car example (Table 8.3), the cracked air-conditioning outlet might have been found by visual inspection, but the other two defects could not have been found by any normal test or inspection. The three reliability defects in the television example (Table 8.4) could not have been identified by test or inspection of the assembled set—until it failed in use long after the time of sale. The difficulty of testing for reliability defects—the fact that there is no equivalent of the functional test that in one application can show the absence of hundreds of potential reliability defects—together with the seriousness of most reliability failures, has been the main reason for the growth of the separate discipline of reliability engineering, a subject that will be discussed in Chapter 10.

As previously noted, the main reason for performing inspection and test is to find defects. In preparing the inspection and test plan for the manufacture of a product, the key questions are: where in the production process will the defects arise, and where and how is it best to remove them?

The principles of planning for screening are most easily understood if an existing product line is assumed on which measured failure and defect data are available. A production and inspection and test flow chart summarizes the total of all manufacturing process steps and the screening inspection and test stages. It starts with the purchased materials, components, and subassemblies and ends with the dispatch of the product to the customer. It includes any rework and rescreen stages. On the flow chart the addition of defects (divided into functional and nonfunctional) from purchased items, and resulting from production processes, is marked. Also on the flow chart, the subtraction of defects (again divided between functional and nonfunctional) by screening tests and inspections is marked. Defects that may cause reliability failures are included with the nonfunctional defects because they cannot be identified by functional tests.

For a complex product the defect levels can be in terms of defects per unit of product. For simpler products defects per 1000 units of product or million units may be used. In either case, the defect levels should be averaged over a relatively long period, say one month, so that plenty of data is available and short-term variations are eliminated. The last item on the flow chart is the defect level of the product going to the customer.

Figure 8.2 shows an actual flow chart for one complex product (26)— an electronic telephone exchange. It has been simplified to deal only with functional defects. Also, addition of defects by the assembly processes is not separated from addition of defects from the purchased components. The exchange contained six or seven million electronic components of which 4131 failed during the functional testing. These defects are shown as an input at the top of the figure, together with the 29 defects from the connectors and peripheral equipment. The telephone exchange was computer controlled. Much of the software was generic to the whole series of exchanges similar to this one and had been cleared of defects, but the "customer design engineering" and "customer application engineering" software special to the exchange contained 960 functional defects. Another 33 defects came from the power distribution and cabling of the fully assembled exchange (bottom of the figure).

In total, 5153 defects were found as a result of functional test failures. The DC/DC test found 197, the test of hybrid integrated circuits found 1440, the tests of the printed circuit boards furnished with components (the PBA test) found 1773 defects, and so on. Functional tests can be very effective but nonetheless some defects passed through the first stages of testing and were identified at later stages, rack test, factory system test, and finally after reassembly at the customer's site.

It is possible by using such a flow chart to seek cost optimization of the inspection and test plan. It is often said that "it is cheapest to find a defect as early as possible." It is certainly true that the cost of a failure is higher at a late stage of testing than at an early stage. In the previous example, the defect causing a failure of the factory system test might involve any one of millions of electronic components or tens of thousands of lines of software code, and might take a while to find. For a failure of a

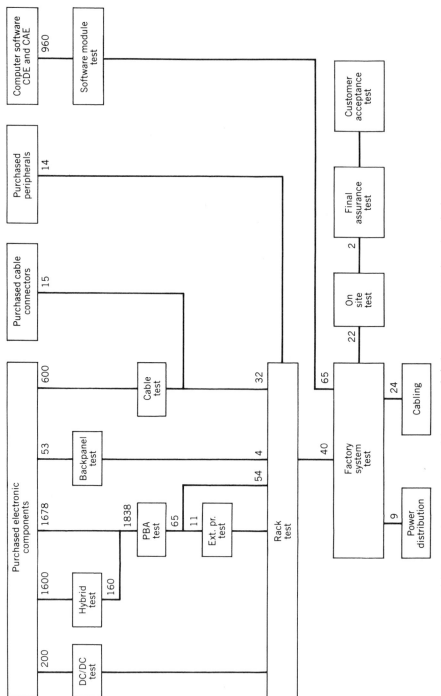

Figure 8.2. Addition and subtraction of functional defects in a 10,000 line local electronic telephone exchange.

PBA test, the defect is already isolated to, at most, several hundred components, and could be found relatively easily. However, the performance of any test costs money and a test that results in only a few failures may best be omitted.

An example will illustrate how cost optimization can be approached. In electronic telephone exchanges like that illustrated in Figure 8.2, the "line circuit" may be repeated thousands of times. Let us assume that in a particular type of exchange each line circuit consists of one printed board assembly (PBA) and each of these PBAs contains four units of a particular type of semiconductor integrated circuit (IC). At incoming inspection, which was performed by sampling, it was found that on average 0.8 percent of the ICs were functionally defective. Because of its very low effectiveness, the sampling test did not find many of the defects, and these went through to assembly and caused failures of the 100 percent test of the completed PBAs. The failed PBAs were tested further to identify the defective ICs. The latter were removed from the PBAs, replaced with new ICs and the PBAs were retested. Would it be cost efficient to introduce a special 100 percent test of the ICs to screen out the 0.8 percent of defective units before they were assembled into the PBAs? The answer to that question depends upon an analysis of the costs.

Assume for each IC that the cost of 100 percent test is 13 cents. Similarly, after failure of a PBA test, assume that the average cost of identifying the defective component, removing it from the PBA and assembling a replacement component, and then retesting the PBA is $25. (Cost differences like 13 cents to $25 make people believe it is economical to find defects as early as possible). Each IC costs $1.10.

The cost equation seems simple. Screening one IC eliminates a 0.8 percent probability of having to rework a PBA.

Cost of screening = $0.13 + $1.10 × 0.8% = 0.14.
Cost of rework = $25 × 0.8% + $1.10 × 0.8% = $0.21.

It appears clear that the screen *is* cost effective.

However, closer examination showed that, although 0.8 percent of the ICs were nonconformant to their specification and failed the IC test, only 0.66 percent failed the PBA test, presumably because the line circuit did not fully use all of the characteristics of the IC. When the screen was put in (applying the IC specification, because the detail of what the line circuit needed was not known) it did screen out 0.8 percent; but another 0.12 percent still failed at the PBA test. The cost picture was now as follows:

With screening:
  Cost of screening = $0.13 + $1.10 × 0.8% = 0.14.
  Cost of rework = $25 × 0.12% + $1.10 × 0.12% = $0.03.
  Total cost = $0.017
Without screening:
  Cost of rework = $25 × 0.66% + $1.10 × 0.66% = $0.17

With these figures the cost effectiveness of the screening test was marginal, but it was kept in because it might have eased testing at later stages (because some of the ICs responsible for the difference between the 0.8 percent and the 0.66 percent might cause failure of these tests) and it might have increased the reliability of the telephone exchange.

This description shows that, provided the appropriate costs are known, it is not difficult to calculate the cost effectiveness of various 100 percent tests—though an overly simplistic approach may give the wrong answer.

In this example, it was stated that the quality of the ICs was known to be 0.8 percent defective as a result of sample tests at incoming inspection. The calculation showed that 0.8 percent was about the breakeven point for the 100 percent screening test of the ICs. It might seem sensible to retain the sampling test at incoming inspection, and perform the 100 percent screen when the sampling indicated the quality was worse than 0.8 percent defective and omit it when the quality was better than 0.8 percent. Unfortunately, the sampling adversely affects the economics. The sampling plan should have an even chance of rejecting lots of ICs that are 0.8 percent defective, a higher probability of rejecting lots worse than this, and a lower probability of rejecting lots having a quality better than 0.8 percent defective. One such plan uses a sample size of 80, an acceptance number of zero defectives, and a rejection number of one defective. Unfortunately, this plan has a 10 percent probability of rejecting lots as good as 0.13 percent defective and an equal probability of accepting lots as bad as 2.8 percent defective. Suppose a lot of 1000 ICs that is 1.6 percent defect arrives. If the 100 percent screening test is performed the cost is as follows:

Cost of screening = $1000 × 0.13 + $1000 × 1.10 × 1.6% = $147.60.
Cost of rework   = $1000 × 25 × (1.6/0.8) × 0.12 + $1000 × 1.10 × (1.6/0.8) × 0.12% = $62.63.

Total cost with screening = $210.20.
Without the 100 percent screening of the ICs, the cost is as follows:

Cost of rework = $1000 × 25 × (1.6/0.8) × 0.66% + $1000 × 1.10 × (1.6/0.8) × 0.66% = $344.52.

Screening the thousand ICs saves $134.

However, if the lot had been 0.4 percent defective, not 1.6 percent, the screening would have lost money. The sampling can be used to decide whether screening is appropriate or not, but it has two problems. First, there is the cost of the sample test itself, which will be more than 80/1000 of the cost of the screening because of the fixed costs associated with any test. Second, is the fact that this suggested sampling plan applied to a defective level of 1.6 percent will indicate the lot should *not* be screened—the wrong decision—30 percent of the time. Because of these two effects the cost saving on the 1000 pieces will be much less than $134. One could work out the actual cost saving for our example, but it does not seem worth the effort, since sampling is rarely used in this way. In fact, 100 percent screens of either purchased products or in-process subassemblies, in practice, are usually applied arbitrarily rather than as a result of economic calculations. Once the decision is made to use a screen, it is much easier to apply it to every lot, rather than to mess about with sampling as well. In principle, the screen can be deleted if the results indicate that the quality of a series of lots has improved to the level where it is no longer economic to perform it. However, once an inspection plan is defined it will usually be maintained without change unless there is some major problem. Nonetheless, the underlying theory applicable to such screens is as described previously. Obviously, all of the relationships could be expressed algebraically, but arithmetical examples are easier to understand, and when economic calculations *are* made (infrequently) they are usually done arithmetically.

In preparing the inspection and test plan for a product, the aim should be to realize the two overall objectives, given in Table 8.5 for a low cost. The first objective is not some mystical, ultimate end. It is a simple consequence of the fact that a product with even one functional defect will not work, and as soon as the customer tries to make the product work he or she will find this out. If 100,000 units are bought and just one unit

TABLE 8.5. Overall Objectives of Screening Inspection and Test of a Manufactured Product

1. Reduce the number of functional defects in the product to zero
2. Reduce the number of different kinds of nonfunctional defects in the product below defined quantitative levels

contains a functional defect, when it comes time to use that unit, it will not work. Fortunately, 100 percent functional tests can have high effectiveness. Their application to the finished product is therefore a straightforward way of helping to achieve the first of the overall objectives.

A customer is primarily concerned with failures, not defects. Until the product fails the customer does not know it is defective. One reason that functional defects must be eliminated is that they always cause failures. This is not true for nonfunctional defects. Some types of nonfunctional defects are so obvious that they almost always cause failures while other types of nonfunctional defects (and reliability defects, too) will not be noticed by the customer until they reach a certain quantitative level, and will not therefore cause failures below that level. For example, I mentioned that Japanese television sets may contain one in a 100,000 solder joints nonconformant to the applicable workmanship standard. At that level the defect is invisible to customers. They will not be visually inspecting the PBAs so the sets will not fail visually, and the overall reliability of the sets will be such that most customers will discard their sets for other reasons after 10 or 15 years without ever having suffered any reliability failure. There is really no way to know if a product contains zero nonfunctional defects. Therefore, zero failures is a more practicable objective than zero defects (see Chapter 11). However, it is possible to measure the nonfunctional defect level (see "outgoing quality audit" below) and ensure that it is less than some applicable standard, one percent, 0.1 percent, 10 parts per million, and so on.

In preparing the inspection and test plan for a manufactured product, the key determinants are where the defects are added and where they are subtracted. Figure 8.2 gave an example of an actual product. But how can these numbers be known in the planning phase, before the product is actually tested and inspected? In principle, the numbers of defects which will be added can be predicted by a method analogous to reliability prediction (see Chapter 10) and the number subtracted can be predicted from the expected inspection efficiency of the planned inspections and tests. For 10 types of electronic components, Table 8.6 gives the proportion found to fail functionally in tests during the manufacture of consumer electronic equipment (27). These results are not concerned with the proportion defective to the component specifications; they are the proportion that failed the PBA test and subsequent tests during the equipment manufacture. The data was obtained in 1979 on European and Japanese components (U.S. components scored similarly to the European).

As an example of using such data, consider a printed board (PB) fur-

TABLE 8.6. Component Functional Defective Rates (parts per million)

Component Type	European	Japanese
Resistors (fixed carbon)	15	1
Potentiometers	250	15
Capacitors (ceramic, polyester)	200	8
Capacitors (large electrolytic)	800	15
Diodes	400	4
Rectifiers	1000	4
Transistors (less than 3w)	250	7
Digital ICs	1500	—
Digital ICs (after 100% test)	—	180
Coils, relay coils	500	9
Printed boards (PBs)	6000	60

nished with 34 resistors, 8 ceramic capacitors, 43 digital ICs, 4 transistors, and 10 diodes. The failure proportion of the PBA due to component failures when using the European data of Table 9.8 is given by:

$$1 \times 6000 + 34 \times 15 + 8 \times 200 + 43 \times 1500 + 4 \times 250 + 10 \times 400 =$$
77,160 parts per million.

So, 7.8 percent of these PBAs might be expected to fail on test, with 6.5 out of the 7.8 percent due to IC failures. The data of Table 8.7, for the particular manufacturing processes applied, could be used to predict another group of failures. The predictions could then be used to compare various possible inspection and test plans (e.g., alternatives that do and

TABLE 8.7. Printed Board Assemblies—European Process Defect Rates

Process	Defect Category	Defect Percentage
Crop and form (semiautomatic)	Nonfunctional	0.1
Manual kit selection	Functional	0.1
Computer kit selection	Functional	0.03
Automatic sequence kitting and component insertion	Functional	0.03
Manual component assembly	Functional	0.1
Manual manufacturing of interconnection cable	Functional	0.2
Wave soldering (single sided PB)	Nonfunctional	1.0
Wave soldering (double sided PB)	Nonfunctional	0.3
Hand soldering of wires	Functional	0.1
Terminal insertion	Nonfunctional	0.1

do not apply a screening test to the ICs before they are soldered onto the printed board).

Thus far, it has been implicitly assumed that the two objectives of screening inspection and testing given in Table 8.4—zero functional defects and quantitatively acceptable levels of nonfunctional defects—can be achieved by screening. In practice, achievement of those objectives comes at least as much from better purchasing and manufacturing—reducing the input of defects into the product—as from better screening. In our example, using the Japanese component defect rates of Table 8.9, including the screened ICs, the proportion of PBAs failing on test would be only 0.8 percent. If the effectiveness of the PBA test is 99.9 percent, less than 1 in each 100 thousand of the Japanese PBAs would be defective after the test compared with 1 in 10 thousand of the European PBAs. A European manufacturer who wanted to achieve virtually zero failures of PBAs could achieve this objective by using Japanese components rather than by increasing the effectiveness of the PBA test. (Of course, in addition this manufacturer would have to communicate as effectively with the Japanese component makers as do the Japanese equipment makers, and also improve his or her own manufacturing processes so that they were contributing no more than ppm functional defect levels.) In fact, Table 8.6 embodies one of the principal reasons why the Japanese have been able to dominate the consumer electronics markets of the world. A television set produced in 1979 contained about 700 components. In Europe, the kit of components was functionally defective at a level of about 500 ppm. This sounds quite good; it corresponds to an AQL of 0.05 percent, much better than the AQL of many military components. However, 700×500 ppm is 35 percent, which means that one out of every three European sets would fail functionally. Because of this failure proportion, all sets had to be tested functionally, and a third of the sets had to be expensively analyzed, reworked, and retested. Apart from the cost and disruption of all of this, the inspection effectiveness was about 99 percent, so that approximately half a percent of the sets failed as soon as the customer switched them on. By 1979, the Japanese, through close cooperation between television and component makers, had reduced the average functional defect level of the components of the kit to about 10 to 15 ppm, and improved the assembly processes correspondingly. Through these efforts, only one percent failed the functional test. Analysis and rework became minor activities, and the "dead-on-arrival" failure rate was a factor of 10 better than the European sets.

The same principles can be applied to predict the defect proportion of a complex mechanical piece after a series of machining processes, or of a mechanical assembly. Each process will make defects at a rate dependent on its capability of achieving the design tolerances (see Chapter 5) and how well the process is controlled. Less than 0.3 percent of the units are defective for a capable and controlled process. In addition, because of the shape of the normal distribution (see Figure 8.3) most of the defective items are only just defective (97 percent of them are within one further standard deviation of the tolerance limit). In practice, this is very important. Because most assembly designs have built-in safety factors, a small proportion of components that are only just out of tolerance will usually constitute nonfunctional defects of zero effect, whereas components that are much further out of tolerance will constitute functional or reliability defects of major or critical significance. Because there is always some imprecision in a test, a "guard band" should be applied to help to ensure that units passing the test are within specification. In testing the product from an incapable process, many good pieces can be scrapped because of the guard band. A capable process does not suffer from this problem. Use of a guard band causes negligible losses because there are very few pieces near the tolerance.

Table 8.8 summarizes the interaction of screening inspection and test, and process capability and control. For a product made by capable and controlled processes, any small proportion of functional defects can be screened out by a final 100 percent functional test on the completed product. For example, capable and controlled processes used to manufacture a particular type of product might result in only one unit in a thousand being functionally defective; application of a final functional test

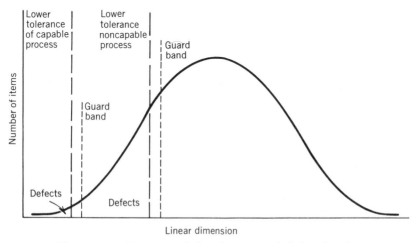

Figure 8.3. The normal distribution and defect levels.

TABLE 8.8. Interaction of Process Capability and Control, and Screening Inspection and Test

Capable and Controlled Processes

Less than 0.3 percent defective as made; most defects near to the tolerance.
Functional defects: screen by final 100 percent test.
Major and critical nonfunctional and reliability defects: achieve higher capability.
Minor nonfunctional and reliability defects: pass to the customer.

Incapable or Uncontrolled Processes

Many defective items made; many defects well beyond the tolerance.
Functional defects: screen by successive in-process and final 100 percent tests.
Nonfunctional and reliability defects: screen by successive in-process and final 100 percent inspections.
Residual functional, nonfunctional, and reliability defects: pass to the customer.

with an effectiveness of 99.9 percent would reduce the functionally defective level to one ppm. Most types of nonfunctional defects should be at an "invisible" level and can be passed to the customer. If there are any major or critical types of nonfunctional or reliability defects, 100 percent visual inspections can be used (keeping in mind their low inspection effectiveness), or a higher capability process can be used.

For products made by incapable or uncontrolled processes a whole battery of in-process and final 100 percent screening tests and inspections must be applied. These may be reasonably effective for functional defects, but are unlikely to reduce nonfunctional and reliability defects to low levels. The residue of these will remain in the product going to the customer.

One of the major disadvantages of conventional *ad hoc* inspection and test planning, particularly for a complex product, is that no one comprehends how the resulting inspection and test plan actually works. All that is known is that, possibly after one or two initial improvements to solve obvious problems, the plan has been applied for a period of time and everything has been quiet. Because the plan is not understood people fear that a change may result in catastrophe. The ensuing reluctance to change the inspection plan is particularly onerous for a division that is actively working on quality improvement. Quality improvements in design, purchasing, or manufacturing should all give opportunities for improving the effectiveness and reducing the cost of the inspection plan (and inspection and test may account for more than half of the quality costs), but apprehension about unknown consequences may prevent the division from taking advantage of those opportunities. On the other hand, if the test plan includes quantitative knowledge of how the defects are added and subtracted, and also, by means of an outgoing quality audit (see Chapter 4) the defect level of outgoing products, as the number of added defects is reduced, the amount of inspection and test can also be reduced in a controlled manner without fear of adverse consequences.

THE BGP45 PUMP—AN INSPECTION PLANNING CASE

David Kramer gazed at the pile of papers on his desk. Three months before he had been promoted to senior quality engineer in the Power Pumps division of RPU. One of the projects he was responsible for in his new position was the BGP45 pump. This was a hydraulic pump used in aircraft. It was a new development for a particular customer. It had entered production just before David had taken up his new job and to date 60 units had completed manufacture and test. The entire first order was for 2000 units. The selling price of each unit was $22,640 so the overall order was of major importance to the division.

The pump was a very complex, mechanical assembly. The main housing was an aluminum casting with many machined faces. Another complex, machined casting formed the cover which was bolted to the housing. Inside of the casing were numerous gears and bearings, the main impeller, and various oil pressure relief valves.

In manufacture three subassemblies, the valve subassembly, the flange and filter subassembly, and the booster stage and shroud subassembly were put together separately and then assembled together.

Kramer's attention was directed at a schematic diagram of the pump. This showed how the hundreds of parts came together in the three subassemblies and how they were then integrated.

The reason that Kramer was studying the pile of papers so intently was that he had decided that it was important for him to become fully familiar with the inspection and test plan of the BGP45, which had been developed by his predecessor. Now was a good time. Various inspection and test sheets that detailed the results of the examination of the first units were available. It should be possible to use this information in determining whether or not the inspections and tests were achieving their objective of giving the customer an assured defect-free product. It might be possible to improve the plan to make the assurance more complete—or to reduce the cost. The latter was an important item. The Power Pumps division had quality costs of about $1 million a month—34 percent of the added manufacturing cost—and nearly 60 percent of the total was appraisal cost.

Although Kramer had been looking at the schematic for about 10 minutes, it was so complicated that he could not fully comprehend it. However, he thought he saw the pattern. He decided to redraw the diagram in a simplified manner. This would give him the double advantage of having something easier to work with and of clarifying the overall picture.

He took out a pad of squared paper and picked up a ball point pen, but immediately changed his mind. A pencil would be better—it had an eraser. Kramer's powers of concentration were good and an hour later the job was done (Figure 8.4). It looked a bit dirty because of the many erasures, but the manufacturing flow was clear. Six different inspections were performed on various subassemblies in addition to incoming inspection of purchased parts and the final test and inspection of the main assembly.

Next, Kramer looked at the part inspection results. Although most of the parts were purchased outside and subjected to incoming inspection, the more complicated ones were fabricated in the division's machine shops where Kramer had inspection result sheets called "Characteristic Inspection Record." He studied the first one in detail (Figure 8.5). It seemed fairly clear that there had been four lots. They were 100 percent inspected for inspections designated 700 and 701 and inspected at Inspection Level II, AQL 6.5 for inspections 702 and 703. Some parts had failed and been scrapped or reworked. The inspections were detailed on an inspection instruction called a "Standard Operating Practice"—particular to the part number. Kramer searched for the relevant standard operating practice in the pile of these documents (Figure 8.6). He also had a look at the drawing, which gave dimensions and additional inspection information.

Kramer looked further into the stack of records. He sorted out a considerable number of "Discrepant Material Notices" (Figure 8.7) which showed the actual inspection results that were summarized in the characteristic inspection records. He methodically clipped all corresponding sheets together and wondered why no one had analyzed these data before. Surely they would suggest some useful improvement actions.

The volume of paper was devastating and on an impulse Kramer decided to count it. He had 94 sheets of characteristic inspection records, 67 discrepant material notices, 159 sheets of standard operating practice, 35 drawing sheets, and a stack of final test records. Incoming inspection

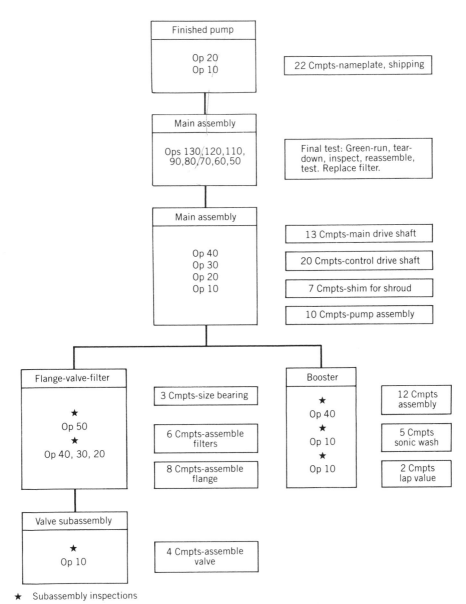

★ Subassembly inspections

Figure 8.4. The BGP45 assembly flow diagram.

Characteristic Inspection Record—Supplementary Sheet

By | Date

Oper No 30 | Comm 54 | F R No 5717-01 | Part Name CAV. OF | Insp Group 1358-00 | Sheet 1 | Of 1

	Qty in Lot	Chg Ltr	S Q L P	Chg Print Ltr	Insp	100% 700		100% 701		6.5% 702		6.5% 703		Characteristics																		Number	Comments Col	Disposition	
						Size	Def	Size	Def	Size	Def	Size	Def	Size	Def	Size	Def	Size	Def	Size	Def	Size	Def	Size	Def	Size	Def	Size	Def	Size	Def			Code	Qty
Lot No 4084	25	A			1st	25	0	25	(2)	8	0	8	0																			DMN	2 SCRAP	4	2
					2nd																														
Insp By 85381																																RWT		1	23
Sample Plan																																			
Date Insp 9-24-80																																			
Lot No 4108	25	A			1st	25	0	25	0	8	0	8	0																			DMN			
					2nd																														
Insp By 85471																																RWT		1	25
Sample Plan																																			
Date Insp 11-10-80																																			
Lot No 4223	64	A			1st	64	(14)	64	0	13	0	13	0																			DMN	14 REWORKED	3	14
					2nd																														
Insp By 29877																																RWT	PIECES OK-TO		
Sample Plan																																	STOCK 4-4-81	1	50
Date Insp 4-1-81																																			
Lot No 4250	100	A			1st	100	(100)	100	0	20	0	20	0																			DMN	100 REWORKED;	3	100
					2nd																														
Insp By 29635																																RWT	ALL OK-SENT TO		
Sample Plan																																	STOCK 7-8-81		
Date Insp 7-2-81																																			
Lot No					1st																											DMN			
					2nd																														
Insp By																																RWT			
Sample Plan																																			
Date Insp																																			
Lot No					1st																											DMN			
					2nd																														
Insp By																																RWT			
Sample Plan																																			
Date Insp																																			
Lot No					1st																											DMN			
					2nd																														
Insp By																																RWT			
Sample Plan																																			
Date Insp																																			
Lot No					1st																											DMN			
					2nd																														
Insp By																																RWT			
Sample Plan																																			
Date Insp																																			

TRW 2732 Rev 2 Printed in USA

Figure 8.5. Characteristic Inspection Record.

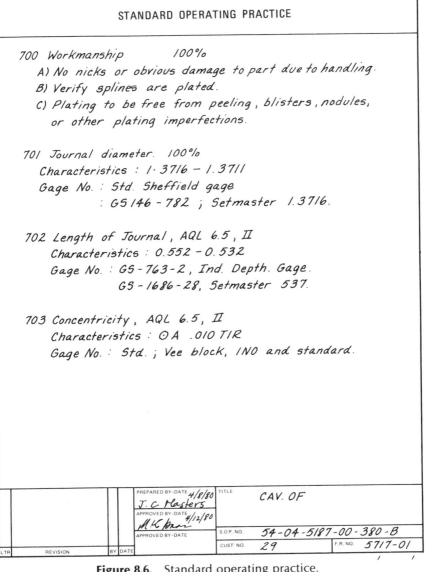

Figure 8.6. Standard operating practice.

had promised him their results on the purchased parts and their analysis, but asked for two weeks to get the information together.

Part by part, Kramer started to go through the inspection sheets, summarizing the results on a chart. After a couple of hours, he took a break and went over to the cafeteria for lunch.

When he got back and saw that only about half of the stack of sheets

Discrepant Material Notice	TRW Inc. Power Accessories Division			P.O. No.			Sheet ___ of ___ No. 99797

Part Name				Commodity	Part No		Chg L
Impeller				5450	215374-00		B

Point of Rejection	Mfg	Assy	Lot No & Qty	Pcs Received	Acceptance Sample	Disc Pcs in Sample	Pcs Accepted	Pcs Rejected	Rework Pcs	Pcs to M R	S.O.P No & Rev
	✓		0001	15			13	2		2	

Last Comp Oper	Mfg Signature		Date	Initiator		Date
30	Miken		12-20-79	18165		12-20-79

Discr No.	No of Pcs Ser Nos	Oper Causing	Dept Chg'd	Char No	Characteristic	Drawing Zone	Discrepancy	Cause Code	Disposition* Prel	Eng	Qual
1	A41	HANDLING			VISUAL		TIP OF BLADE BENT		D/P	D/P*	
2	A49	HANDLING			VISUAL		TIPS OF BLADES BENT		D/P	D/P*	
3							REQUIRED OK 1-22-80				
4											
5											
6											
7											
8											
9											
10							* REMOVE BENT TIP AND				
11							HAND BLEND TO PRINT				
12											

Inspection Supervisor	Date	Prel Signature		Date	Engineering Signature	Date	Quality Signature	Date
Ted Stroud	12-20					1-22-80	S Groth	1-22-80

Rechecked and Found Acceptable Nos	Contract Govt /Com	Case Record Data Lot Size	Qty Discr	Govt Signature	Date

Accepted on Past Material Review Board Action Nos B ✓

Visual Discrepancies Incidental and Acceptable Nos. Remarks

C.A.R Required ___ Yes ___ No

TRW Responsible for Discrepancies Nos.

Sub Assy. Rej ?
Vendor Lot Rej ?
Mfg Rej (Bad Casting)
Inv Code 9/Sub Contract

Pcs. to (Stock) (Further Processing)	Signature	Date

	Pcs		Pcs
___ Return to Vendor for Credit		___ Scrap Here for Credit	
___ Return to Vendor for Replacement	Pcs	___ Scrap Here — No-Credit	Pcs
___ Other ___	Pcs	___ Rework	Pcs

Signature & Date J. Monkman 2-3-80   Stock Room Signature   Date Received/Issued   Stk. Rm. Bal

Physically Scrapped	Teardown	Return to Vendor	Repair/Rework	Stock/Reinstate 2	Inventory Write-off
Material	Labor	Mfg Expense		Total Value	

*Disposition Code
A-Accept as is   D/P-Rework to print   C Scrap   RTV-Return to Vendor   M.R.B Mat Rev Board Act   U Repair

TRW 3346 Rev 6/84
Printed in USA

MRB/RTV

Figure 8.7. Discrepant material notice.

222

was examined he was tempted to abandon the whole project. After all, the division had been doing inspection and testing for many years and the work on the BGP45 was proceeding in an uneventful way. What was there to prove? Then a thought struck him. He had been told that King, the division's quality director, had arranged for the quality director of the General Equipment division to do an informal audit of Power Pumps. They had dreamed up the idea at the group quality council. Later on, King was going to audit the General Equipment division. The Power Pumps' audit was to begin tomorrow and Kramer was slated for an hour in the afternoon.

Why not present the whole problem to the visiting expert? Perhaps together they could settle on some really useful actions. Kramer was not concerned about sharing the glory. He was a smart young man and had already learned that when there was a success there was enough glory for everyone. (Conversely, he had learned that after a failure, bosses do not want to listen to excuses, no matter how good). He might, at worst, impress the visitor with his conscientiousness, and receive independent confirmation that the present inspection plan was alright.

Inspired with this thought, he continued with his labor. By mid-afternoon he had summarized all of the inspection results. He thought that it would be best to have them typed for tomorrow's discussion (Figure 8.8).

Of course, a key part of the whole inspection and test system was the final test of the completed pump. This was a complex 100 percent test with the following stages. First, the pump was attached to a test gear and allowed to pump fluid in simulation of normal operation for 78 minutes. Then the pump was completely disassembled and each part visually examined for any improper wear. After reassembly the pump was operated for an additional 30 minutes in the simulation mode to check that the disassembly and reassembly had given no problems. During this operation the flow-rate was measured and compared with its specification. Finally, a new oil filter was inserted.

Looking at his summary of the inspection results of the parts, Kramer had the uneasy feeling that the fully assembled pumps might be loaded with nonfunctional defects. (But what about functional defects?) Had the various part and subassembly inspections and tests cleared out all of the functional defects—so that the final test could simply be a clean assurance of good performance—or was it just another screen for removing functional defects?

Kramer spent the rest of the afternoon with a stack of final test sheets trying to get an answer to that question. The results could be summarized briefly. Sixty units had been through final test, 54 had passed completely,

Number	Part (FR) Number	Quantity	Failures/100% Inspection	Failures/Sampling Inspection	Number Accepted
1	5 370-01	169	4/169		165
2	5 371-00	265	5/265	0/13, 0/3, 0/1	260
3	5 372-00	298	0/298		298
4	5 374-00	166	0/166		166
5	5 376-95	443	0/443		443
6	5 534-01	275	0/275	1/104, 2/25	275
7	5 535	249	6/249	29/185, 7/164, 19/133, 55/116, 0/64, 0/21	106
8	5 717-01	214	114/214	0/164	100
9	5 788-00	320	207/320	0/108, 0/32	113
10	5 893-00	299	0/299		299
11	6 081-01	124	0/124	0/23	124
12	6 082-01	157	121/157	0/82	36
13	6 083-01	184	78/184	16/135	90
14	6 084-01	125	69/125	0/72	56
15	6 085-01	139	25/139	0/42	104
16	6 089	271	49/271	0/32	222
17	6 155-00	148	0/148		148
18	6 157-00	256	256/256		0
19	6 158-01	116	0/116	0/22	116
20	6 159	285	0/285	0/96, 0/34	285
21	6 160	686	248/686	0/76, 0/21	438
22	6 203-01	157	5/157		152
23	6 263-01	155	40/155		115
24	6 276-00	243	3/243		240
25	6 443-01	161	35/161	0/42	126
26	6 450-01	211	44/211		167
27	8 606-01	273	0/273		273
28	8 607-01	302	0/302		302
29	8 608-02	26	0/26		26
30	8 610-02	122	0/122		122
	Totals	6839	1309/6839 19.1%	129/1810 7.1%	5367/6839 21.5%

Figure 8.8. Piece-part inspection results.

and 6 had failed. Four failures were for "low flow," the output of the pump being below specification. (For one of these, the impeller shaft had shown scoring on the teardown inspection.) The other two failures were for "seal leak." The answer was clear: the pumps, going into final test, *did* indeed contain functional defects.

The following day, Kramer was in his office when King opened the door and ushered in his visitor. King was tall and thin with a saturnine face. Although he was actually the kindest of men, he had not quite thrown off the shyness of his youth, and Kramer always found him somewhat intimidating. The visitor was in marked contrast. He was less than average height, thick-set, with crisp grey hair. He had bright, intelligent eyes and greeted Kramer with a cheerful grin. Without waiting for King's introduction, he said, "You must be David Kramer. My name's Bob Perron," and offered to shake Kramer's hand. Kramer immediately felt at ease. Perhaps he really would get some useful help with the BGP45.

Sometime later Kramer had completed his account of the BGP45 pump and the results he had analyzed. Perron was speaking.

"There are two ways of getting a high quality product. The first is to make it right. To be sure that all of the machines are capable, that the operators know what they are doing—and want to do it—and so on. The second is to be much less sure about the way it is made and to have a comprehensive inspection and test system to filter out the functional and nonfunctional defects. Well David, which do we have here?"

Kramer thought for a moment, "I guess most high quality products rely on a mixture of the two methods. I'm sure from the information I've shown you that you think that for the BGP45 the main emphasis is on inspection and test. I don't really think that is true. We've got some excellent equipment and our workforce is really skilled. Most of them have been here for years. Of course, we have got a proportion of younger people who don't have quite the same work attitudes."

Perron's grin, which was never far away, reappeared. He knew he must be 20 years older than Kramer. If the latter thought some of the operators were "younger people," they must be really young.

Perron continued, "That's good David. Skilled operators are very important but what about the machines; are they capable?"

Kramer answered readily, "I was working on the floor when most of the new machines were brought in for the BGP45 pump. We went through a series of cutting and drilling operations to qualify each machine. They checked-out fine—no problems. Besides, most of the machining operations are computer controlled so I'm sure that they're capable. A lot of the other machining is done with the same equipment that we use for other pumps, so I'm sure that it must be capable also."

Perron went on, "If you are really making the product right, then often the amount of inspection and test is reduced and you finish up having a quality better than you can measure with the amount of inspection you are doing. Despite your thoughts on capability, the number of inspection failures show that you don't have this situation with the BGP45. How many defects do the pumps contain when they go to the customer?"

Kramer blustered a bit, "Well none. The customer won't allow it. This is a very critical item. If one of these pumps failed it could really be serious. Of course, this is a new pump, but we have never had a failure with similar pumps . . . not for years anyway. Now and then we get a chance to compare with pumps made by competitors and ours are the best. Our mean time between failures averages over 10,000 hours and the spec is only 6000 hours. And the customer's inspectors always accept them. They may find one or two things but we put those right before they go out."

Perron persisted, "All that means is that the first 60 pumps had no functional defects and that you have been lucky so far that the nonfunctional defects have not included any serious reliability defects—though there is always the worry that one of these days the reliability might go haywire. Even with their small sample, the customer's inspectors are finding some nonfunctional defects. Don't you do your own outgoing audit?"

Kramer perked up, "We do better than that. Because this is a critical item, we tear down each pump after 78 minutes operation and visually inspect each part. Then we put the pump back together and test it to make sure that it meets our customer's requirements. After we've got more experience with the pump, we shall probably reduce the tear-down frequency to one in three, but right now we inspect them all 100 percent."

Perron was interested in this run, inspect, and test routine. He asked Kramer if there were any dimensional measurements taken during the tear-down inspection. Kramer replied that this was done only if a visual check showed an abnormal wear pattern.

Perron went on, "Let's see if we can make an estimate of defects from the inspection results. With duplicated pieces, each pump contains 52 in-house-fabricated parts. Your sheet shows 6839 of these parts inspected and 5367 accepted, almost 22 percent rejected. . . ."

"But that 22 percent didn't get into the pumps," Kramer interrupted. "The rejects were all reviewed by the MRB. Some would have been scrapped, others reworked to print, and they would only have been used "as is" if the product engineer was sure they would have no effect on performance or reliability."

"How does the MRB work?" asked Perron.

"Well, its contractually required both for commercial pumps like the BGP45, and for military pumps. The main difference is that a government representative sits in on the MRBs for military pumps. For commercial pumps the customer is only brought in if a nonconformance might affect the interface with the rest of the aircraft. . . . The members of the MRB are quality, product engineering, and reliability. They meet every week, and every now and then, more often—to get the MRB area cleared out."

Perron went back to his earlier point, "I still think it would be useful to estimate how many defective parts go into the pump because inspection missed them. Any approved by the MRB would be extra to that. How effective do you think the inspections are?"

Kramer felt a great reluctance to answer that question. He knew that, like everyone else in the division, he had been pretending that the inspection effectiveness was 100 percent. But he also knew that if he said that to Perron he would be faced with a kindly smile—the sort that a good school teacher gives to a conscientious but dim pupil who has come up with another wrong answer. He forced himself to bite the bullet, "I guess it couldn't be better than 90 percent."

Perron grunted and asked to see the final test results. "It looks like the major failure mode is low-flow. What were the primary causes of these failures?"

Kramer was stumped. He hadn't found any failure analysis records which would enable him to specifically answer Perron's question. He finally replied, "I'm not really sure what the causes of the functional failures were, but for each in-process discrepancy we issue a discrepant material notice [DMN] that shows the disposition of the part involved."

Kramer showed Perron one DMN as an example (Figure 8.7).

"You see here that 15 impellers were checked and 2 were rejected for handling damage. Both parts were repaired. Whenever we find a part out of print, it's corrected before it goes into the final assembly. . . ."

A short time later King returned to take Perron to the next appointment. But Perron was so interested in Kramer's exposition that he arranged to return the next morning. During the evening Perron made a list of questions to discuss with Kramer (Table 8.9).

At the TRW Quality College these seven questions have been debated many times. A brief account of some of the conclusions reached at these sessions will now be given.

TABLE 8.8.   Questions about the BGP45 Test and Inspection Plan

1. What are our impressions of the inspection and test planning process in the Power Pump division?
2. Do the "characteristic inspection record" and "discrepant material notice" give good data for defect prevention purposes?
3. What is an estimate of the average number of defective parts of own manufacture in each pump going to the customer?
4. Why were inspections 702 and 703 performed to a 6.5 percent AQL?
5. What do the final test results suggest with regard to: (a) the probability of good immediate performance to the customer; and (b) the continuing reliability of the pump? Should any changes be made to the final test?
6. How might the inspection cost be reduced while maintaining the existing quality to the customer?
7. What key actions should be taken as a result of the analysis of the inspection plan?

1. *Inspection Planning Process.*   Power Pumps division used conventional *ad hoc* methods for its inspection and test planning. An overall manufacturing flow chart with inspection and test points marked did not exist. No one had determined where or how many defects were entered, or where they were removed, or again, how many.

2. *Inspection Records.*   The characteristic inspection record and discrepant material notice were the sort of documents that quality assurance people love to file with the thought that such records may help to protect them from blame in some future disaster. The documents were also used for procedures of the material review board, which was a key instrument for legitimizing the use of defective items. Long-term defect prevention was not one of the reasons for these documents.

3. *Estimate of Defective Parts.*   The effectiveness of the 100 percent inspections of parts is not known, but its order of magnitude may be guessed. It is unlikely to be as high as 99 percent; 90 percent is a reasonable guess. Figure 8.8 shows that the proportion of defects received was 19.1 percent. Using the formula:

$$P_O = P_R \ (I\text{-}E)/E,$$

where P_O is the proportion of defects outgoing and P_R the proportion removed,

$$P_O = 19.1\% \ (0.1)/0.9 = 2.1\%.$$

The failures of the sampling inspections are additional to this. Guessing that the sampling inspections have a 50 percent effectiveness gives:

$$P_O = 7.1\% \ (0.5)/0.5 = 7.1\%.$$

Use "as is" decisions by the MRB would add some more defectives to the product. All in all, it is not unreasonable to estimate that 10 percent of the parts of own manufacture assembled into the pumps might be defective for one or more dimensions or workmanship requirements. With each pump containing 52 parts, there were five defective parts per pump.

4. *Why 6.5 Percent AQLs?*   High AQLs like 4, 6.5 and 10 percent are rarely specified because someone has actually determined that such high defective levels are acceptable, or that such levels optimize costs. They are just an artifact of the sampling plan. Table 8.10 shows some numbers extracted from MIL-STD-105D, applicable to "normal" inspection. If a test is expensive or destructive, it is often decided that only a very small sample can be inspected from each lot (e.g., two or three). Once this is decided the AQL has to be 6.5 or 4 percent, because smaller AQLs require bigger samples. So, in reality, the reason that 6.5 and 4 percent AQLs appear on specifications is because someone has decided that they cannot afford to test large sample sizes.

5. *What Do the Final Test Results Suggest?*   Many of the groups that have used this case study in the past produced essentially correct answers to question 3 about the number of defective parts in the pumps after part inspection. Few groups gave correct answers to question 5, which, in fact, is very similar. The groups flinched from applying the analysis of question 3 to question 5. There could be at least two reasons for this. The first is that it is more difficult to force oneself to recognize that the effectiveness of a functional test is less than perfect than it is to recognize that a visual inspection has limited ef-

TABLE 8.10.   Sample Sizes for High AQL's

AQL (%)	Acceptance Number	
	C = 0	C = 1
4.0	3	13
6.5	2	8

fectiveness. The second is that the consequences of that recognition are so much more serious and unpleasant for the functional test than for the visual inspection that people, even in the protected environment of a classroom, are reluctant to face up to them.

To apply this analysis, one must estimate or guess the effectiveness of the final test. It should be much better than the 90 percent used for the inspections. But how much better? 99 percent? 99.9 percent? The latter percentage (99.9) seems a bit optimistic. Let us assume 99 percent is correct. Using the formula for the outgoing proportion defective:

$$P_O = P_R (1-E)/E,$$

gives

$$P_O = 0.1 (1-0.99)/0.99,$$

because P_R, the proportion defective removed was 6/60; therefore

$$P_O = 1/990,$$

that is, 1 in 990 of the pumps may fail as soon as the customer uses it (i.e., two pumps will fail out of the total order of 2000). The division might be lucky though and the effectiveness of the final test might be better than 99 percent. It seems overly optimistic to assume this. What will be the nature of the failure? Well, this is a functional failure, not a reliability failure. Functional failures are usually major but not critical—these failures will not cause aircraft to crash. The aircraft manufacturer will usually find, through their own tests, that the flow rate is below specification, or they will notice oil dripping out of a seal. In either case, they will not be pleased with this $22,640 purchase.

What about the long-term reliability? The case has very little information—only a good history on similar pumps, and worries engendered by the high proportion of nonfunctional defects and the final test failures.

Should the final test be changed? Some groups, because of its high cost, have wanted to reduce the frequency of the final test from 100 percent to sampling. (Kramer suggested one in three for the teardown part of the test.) This would be most unwise. The inspection effectiveness would drop to 50 percent or worse and the 2000 pumps might contain 100 that would fail functionally, and 15 or 20 with a scored impeller or something similar—which might result in a critical reliability failure.

6. *Reduce the Inspection Cost.* It is useful to differentiate between three reasons for changing the inspection plan: to improve the product quality while increasing the inspection cost; to improve the product quality without increasing the inspection cost; and to reduce the inspection cost without decreasing the product quality. This question addresses the third objective. In the short term, completing the manufacturing and inspection flow chart and determining where the defects are added and subtracted might suggest economies. In the long term, however, measuring process capability and applying process control should allow considerable reduction in the inspection and test cost (and also improve the quality) but such a program takes several years to implement and the 2000 pumps will be completed long before then.

7. *What Are the Key Actions?* Some of the required actions have already been discussed. However, there is one key action that stands out from the others—yet few of the groups who have worked on the case identified it—and that is to find out the causes of the three major failure modes that appeared on the final test—low flow, seal leak, and scored impeller shaft—and take whatever actions are necessary to prevent those failures from ever appearing in the future. The effectiveness analysis on the final test makes this obvious. However, without this analysis, those responsible can fool themselves into believing that the final test is cleaning out all important defects and that it is not vital to prevent them.

CONCLUSION

In this chapter, the idea that quality cannot be inspected and tested into a product was refuted, and the importance of inspection and test in achieving superiority in product quality was emphasized. The principles of inspection and test planning were described, through definitions of the key terms: fail, defect, and functional/nonfunctional. The inspection and test objectives of zero functional failures and low, quantitative levels of nonfunctional defects were discussed in relation to process capability and control. The practical application of inspection and test planning was illustrated with a case study.

CHAPTER 9

MANUFACTURING QUALITY

Process control using statistical techniques is perhaps the most important of all the statistical quality control methods. It is closely related to statistical process capability which was discussed in Chapter 5. The fundamental ideas were established by W. A. Shewhart in the 1920s and published in his 1931 book, *Economic Control of Quality of Manufactured Products* (24). Although there are innumerable examples that show the effectiveness of the methods, throughout industry only a tiny proportion of the potential level of application has actually been achieved. In 1948 a group of Japanese engineers became aware of Shewhart's work and as a result, Dr. W. Edwards Deming visited Japan in 1950 to address meetings of Japanese managers. From that beginning, in 1950, until today the Japanese have achieved a high level of application of statistical process control methods, and have trained literally millions of managers, engineers and workers in the techniques. In 1980 statistical quality control in the United States was given new impetus when Deming participated in the NBC television program, "If Japan Can ... Why Can't We." Since then the level of activity has continued growing.

The quality professionals of TRW recognized the validity and importance of the trend toward statistical process control, and from the beginning in 1981 incorporated major sessions on the subject in all versions of the TRW Quality College. Dr. Tom George, director materiel and quality for TRW's Industrial and Energy Sector, took responsibility for preparing and presenting these sessions, which include a computer-simulated case study. By 1982, some of TRW's major customers, including the Ford Motor Company and Pratt & Whitney, were pressing their suppliers to apply statistical process control. In addition, Ford, who had employed Deming as a consultant, made the application of statistical process control the primary requirement for consideration in the company's "Preferred Supplier Award" which was announced in 1982.

An important skill for a senior functional staff member to possess is knowing when the company is ready for a particular program. Over the past 20 years, I have had this sense many times—for quality cost improvement in 1966, 1973, and 1981; for product qualification in 1972; for quality to the customer in 1984; and so on. A strong push from the center at the opportune time can help set a key program in motion, and similar pushes at later times may help to sustain programs that have not yet achieved their full benefits, but which may be ready to run down. Conversely, the same level of emphasis and activity applied at the wrong time can be dissipated without effect. Toward the end of 1982 I suggested that 1983 be the year that TRW pushed for the implementation of statisical process control. Some divisions were, of course, already working actively on the subject—either through their own initiative or in response to customer pressure. Once verbalized though, the need for company-level encouragement seemed obvious. The matter was aired at one of the company's "small management meetings" involving the group vice presidents. Then the president of the company wrote to the sector executive vice presidents, "about the need for a TRW-wide effort to measure the capabilities of our manufacturing processes to meet our engineering designs and to implement statistical control of these processes," and asked for a summary of plans. Later in this chapter the results of these initiatives will be given, but first the technical concepts underlying statistical process control will be described. Since Shewhart's 1931 book many other books have examined the theory and in addition major companies have issued handbooks describing its technical application (e.g., *Statistical Quality Control Handbook* issued by Western Electric Company, Inc., in 1956 and *Continuing Process Control and Process Capability Improvement*, issued by the Ford Motor Company Inc., in 1983); therefore, in this book my purpose is only to give readers a general idea of the key concepts.

STATISTICAL PROCESS CONTROL

First, it is useful to recall some of the points made about process capability in Chapter 5. Manufacturing processes are inherently variable so

that successive items of product are not identical. If there are many different causes of the variability of a manufacturing process and each cause
contributes about the same amount of variability as every other, the process will be stable and the variation of resulting product characteristics
will be approximately normally distributed. The distribution will be defined by two parameters, the mean and the standard deviation. If the design tolerance is greater than six times the standard deviation, the process
will be capable of achieving the design tolerance if properly centered. In
addition to the ordinary causes of process variation there may be one or
two special causes of variation which contribute more to the product
variation than each one of the ordinary causes. The product characteristics resulting from a process with a special cause of variation are unlikely
to be distributed normally. Such a process is inherently unstable; therefore, it is necessary to eliminate any special causes of variation before determining the capability of a process.

As a process with no special causes of variation continues to be used,
its product will have a random variation confined within the limits of the
process' capability. The first objective of statistical process control is to
prevent adjustment of such a process. Any adjustment will increase the
product variation; the narrowest possible product variation results from
leaving the process alone. The point can be illustrated by using the process capability data of Table 5.1. The last column in this table simulates
the variation in the diameter of 50 cylinders made by a process with nine
ordinary causes of variation and no special cause. Figure 9.1 shows these
results plotted sequentially. Figure 9.2 shows what happens if process adjustments are made. One obvious method of doing this is for the operator
to measure each piece as it is made and then adjust the process before
making the next piece. The operator takes some diameter (e.g., 1.0040
inch) as the target. Table 9.1 shows how this works for the first 10 pieces.
The first completed piece had a diameter of 1.0038 inch. The second
piece would have had a diameter of 1.0018 inch, but an adjustment of
+2 10-thousandths was made (because the first piece was 2 10-thou-
sandths smaller than the 1.0040 inch target). So its diameter was 1.0020
inch. This caused an *additional* +20 10-thousandths adjustment for the
third piece, making 22 in total. So, the third piece, instead of having a
diameter of 1.0013 inch, was 1.0035 inch. The same procedure is applied
to all 50 pieces, in each case the additional adjustment is added to the
previous cumulative adjustment to give the new cumulative adjustment.

The scatter of points is appreciably wider in Figure 9.2 than in Figure
9.1 and the total range of the diameters in inches for the whole 50 points
is increased by the adjustments from 1.0013–1.0061 to 1.0005–1.0085. A

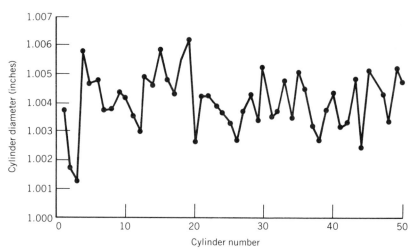

Figure 9.1. Sequential plot of product variation from a controlled process— without adjustment.

laborious attempt to reduce the scatter has failed completely; just leaving the process alone and doing nothing gives a better result. This is the first key point derived from statistical process control: the variation of the product made by a process which is under control is a minimum if the process is not adjusted.

The second objective of statistical process control is to indicate when a special cause of process variation is starting to affect the variation of a product characteristic. Analysis that determines the nature of the special cause can then be undertaken and followed by corrective action. Some special causes, such as tool wear, can be predictable and progressive, and little or no analysis is required to determine the appropriate corrective action. Others will be unexpected and the appropriate response will not be immediately clear.

It was noted in Chapter 5 that the variation of a product characteristic resulting from a controlled process will have an approximately normal distribution, and that any normal distribution can be defined by two parameters, the mean of the values of the distribution, and their standard deviation. The former defines the average of the values and the latter defines how widely the values are dispersed from the average. A special cause of variation entering a process can cause either the mean or the standard deviation of the product characteristic variation, or both to change. In determining whether or not such an event has occurred it is

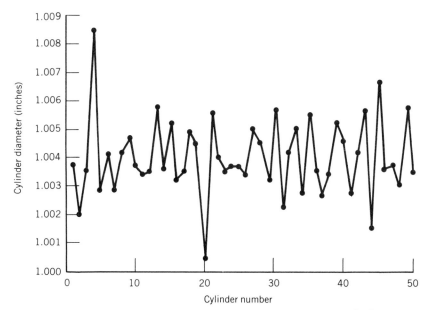

Figure 9.2. Sequential plot of product variation from a controlled process—with adjustment.

useful therefore to have continuing measures of both the mean and standard deviation of the product characteristic. A sequential plot of the values of the product characteristic, such as the measurements of cylinder diameter given in Figure 9.1, can indicate whether or not the mean has remained constant. Variation in the mean may cause the scatter of points to move up or down either as a trend or a sudden jump. Such a chart does not give a clear indication of changes in the standard deviation. "Control limits," which indicate the bands of likely values for the characteristic when the process is under control, can be drawn on charts like Figure 9.1 (for example by the "moving range" method) so that such charts can be used to indicate the onset of a special cause of variation. However, in practice, it is much more common to use successive small samples of values, for example, five, to obtain estimates of the mean and standard deviation of the distribution, and to use these to indicate the onset of a special cause. The most widely used of these, mean, $\overline{X}$, and range, R, charts, will now be illustrated.

The last column of Table 5.1 simulates how much the diameters of 50 successive cylinders made by a controlled process exceed one inch. Figure 9.1 shows these results plotted. The next to last column of Table 5.1

TABLE 9.1.   Effect of Process Adjustments on a Controlled Process

Cylinder Number	Unadjusted Diameter (inch)	Cumulative Adjustment (10-thousandths inch)	Adjusted Diameter (inch)	Additional Adjustment (10-thousandths inch)
1	1.0038	—	1.0038	—
2	1.0018	+ 2	1.0020	+20
3	1.0013	+22	1.0035	+ 5
4	1.0058	+27	1.0085	−45
5	1.0047	−18	1.0029	+11
6	1.0048	− 7	1.0041	− 1
7	1.0037	− 8	1.0029	+11
8	1.0038	+ 3	1.0041	− 1
9	1.0044	+ 2	1.0046	− 6
10	1.0041	− 4	1.0037	+ 3

gives similar results but for a process with the addition of one special cause of variation. Table 9.2 shows these 100 results divided into 20 successive samples of five values, and the means of each sample taken—as an estimator of the population mean—and the range of each sample also taken—as an estimator of the population standard deviation. Figure 9.3 shows these results plotted. In practice, such samples of five values would be taken after defined time intervals (e.g., one hour, or defined numbers of pieces, e.g., 100). Both the $\overline{X}$ and R charts show a substantial change

TABLE 9.2.   Values of $\overline{X}$ and R for Successive Samples of Five Units from a Controlled Process and an Out-of-Control Process

	Controlled Process			Uncontrolled Process	
Sample Number	$\overline{X}$ (Inch)	R (10-Thousandths Inch)	Sample Number	$\overline{X}$ (Inch)	R (10-Thousandths Inch)
1	1.00348	45	11	1.01068	129
2	1.00416	11	12	1.01376	177
3	1.00434	27	13	1.01394	185
4	1.00348	35	14	1.0155	174
5	1.00388	10	15	1.01308	156
6	1.00384	25	16	1.01584	190
7	1.00410	15	17	1.0093	120
8	1.00368	19	18	1.01488	126
9	1.00376	27	19	1.01016	127
10	1.00448	18	20	1.01528	168

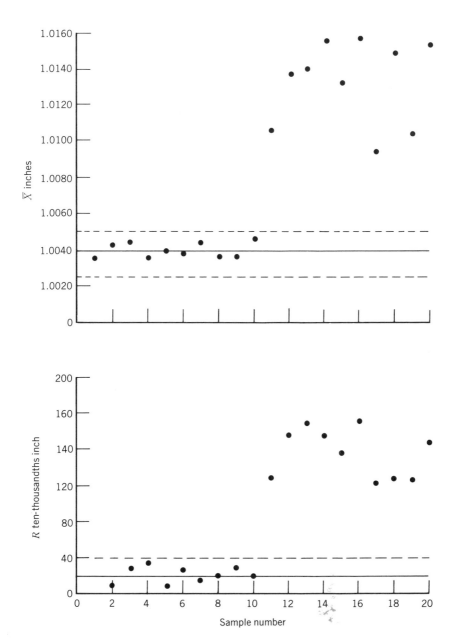

Figure 9.3. $\overline{X}$ and R plots showing onset of a special cause on a previously controlled process.

between the tenth and eleventh samples—which is due to the effect of the special cause present in the second 10 values. This special cause of process variation has such a big effect on the product characteristic that the change between the tenth and eleventh samples is obvious. However, for a smaller special cause, there might be a problem in differentiating between the effect of the special cause and the variation due to ordinary causes. Control limits are added to the charts to help solve this problem.

Control limits for the R chart are obtained as follows. First the mean of the ranges, called $\bar{R}$, of the samples is calculated. For the first 10 values of Table 9.2, $\bar{R}$ is 20.7 10-thousandths of an inch. The upper and lower control limits of the range are obtained by multiplying $\bar{R}$ by standard factors, given in Table 9.3. For the sample size of five, the lower R factor is zero, and the upper R factor is 2.11 which means that the lower control limit is zero and the upper control limit is 2.11 times 20.7 which equals 43.7 10-thousandths of an inch. The mean of the ranges of the samples and the upper control limit of the ranges are marked as full and dotted lines respectively on the R chart of Figure 9.3. It is clear that the eleventh and all successive points are outside the upper control limit. This indicates the onset of a special cause of variation.

Control limits for $\bar{X}$ charts are obtained in a similar way. The mean, $\bar{\bar{X}}$, of the $\bar{X}$ is first calculated. For the first 10 values of Table 9.2, $\bar{\bar{X}}$ is 1.0039 inch. The width of the upper and lower control limits is given by multiplying $\bar{R}$ by the $\bar{X}$ factor of Table 9.3. In our case, using a sample of five, gives 20.7 times 0.58 which equals 12.0 10-thousandths of an inch. This is added to and subtracted from $\bar{\bar{X}}$ to give 1.0051 inch and 1.0027 inch as the upper and lower control limits of $\bar{X}$ respectively. $\bar{\bar{X}}$ and the two control limits are marked on the $\bar{X}$ chart of Figure 9.3. As with the range chart, the eleventh and all subsequent points fall well beyond the upper control limit, indicating the onset of a special cause of variation.

One may ask how the factors given in Table 9.3 are derived? The answer is that they come from the mathematical properties of the normal distribution. They indicate the probabilities of extreme values of the dis-

TABLE 9.3. Control Limit Factors for X and R Charts

Sample Size	$\bar{X}$ Factor	Lower R Factor	Upper R Factor
2	1.88	0	3.27
5	0.58	0	2.11
10	0.31	0.22	1.78

tribution going beyond ± 3 sigma limits in the absence of special causes of variation. A few times in a thousand a value will go beyond the upper or lower control limit in the absence of a special cause. Higher frequencies than this indicate the onset of a special cause. The actual calculation of the factors is beyond the scope of this book. Table 9.4 lists other indications of the onset of a special cause of variation. (One and two sigma limits divide the three sigma zone into three equal zones.)

In summary, statistical process control determines the likely variation in the characteristics of a product made by a controlled process (one with no special cause of variation). A controlled process should not be adjusted because any adjustment to the process will increase the variation of the product characteristics. The variation in the product characteristic of a controlled process will have an approximately normal distribution defined by particular values of two parameters, the mean and the standard deviation. The state of control of the process can be followed by plotting two estimators of the mean and standard deviation, the mean and range of small samples. Control limits can be calculated for each of these estimators. When either the sample mean or range goes outside of the control limits, it indicates that a special cause of variation is now affecting the process. Corrective action to eliminate the special cause is required, and may or may not need to be preceded by analysis to determine the nature of the special cause.

In this chapter and Chapter 5, brief accounts have been given of the theories of statistical process capability and control. Neither are very difficult. The difficulty lies in carrying through the steps which are necessary for the theoretical ideas to be converted into practical implementation. In discussing this, let us consider a multiplant, operating division of say a thousand or so people. It designs, manufactures, and sells a particular range of mechanical products. Heretofore the products' design tolerances have been established without any regard to the statistical capability of the manufacturing processes, and the manufacturing processes have been controlled by craftspeople who are guided by routings rather than detailed process specifications. Screening inspections have been applied in a pragmatic way. Then the division manager decides that he or she wants

TABLE 9.4. Control Chart Indications of the Onset of a Special Cause of Variation

1. One point outside of the 3 sigma limit
2. Two of three successive points outside of a 2 sigma limit
3. Four of five successive points outside of a 1 sigma limit

statistical process capability and control to be introduced in his division. This decision may be a result of customer pressure, company policy, persuasion by the division's quality manager, the division manager's own reading, or a combination of any or all of these influences. What must take place for this decision to be implemented? Basically, a very complicated series of psychologically and technologically directed actions. First, the division manager has to convince the plant and product engineering manager, as well as the manufacturing engineering, human relations and quality managers that the program is really important, and that he or she is going to assign it a sufficiently high priority—in competition with all of the division's normal work and other improvement programs—so it will actually be implemented. Then a multifunctional plan has to be established that defines all of the activities that have to be performed to move the division from its present status to the required status. A realistic assessment of the resources that are required to implement the actions must be balanced against the time required, and then a detailed schedule of the key "milestones" must be prepared. Often this planning is not performed, or it is carried out in a perfunctory manner by the quality manager, and the result is ignored by the other key managers. The consequence is such that the resources needed are grossly underestimated and the rate of progress is very slow. TRW experience indicates that it takes at least 2 years for a division to implement process capability and control. If the resources supplied are less than half of what is really necessary, the time scale will spread out to five or more years. At such a rate of progress, it is highly probable that the objectives will never be achieved. The high level of drive ncessary from the division and plant managers to keep the program moving will not be maintained, the rate of progress will slow down, and the program will fizzle out—with most of the resources that *have* been expended wasted.

Why is so much drive required? In any division, most of the available resources are devoted to the normal work—designers design, salespeople sell, purchasing agents buy, and so on. Such activities happen virtually automatically. Changing something always takes effort, but some changes are relatively easy because they are interesting. Introducing new "toys"— computers, test equipment, process equipment, and soon—is in this category. But other changes are different and, however important, have to be implemented by the drive and persistence of champions. Even when such improvements are successfully implemented, relaxation by the champions allows for a slip back into the old, natural ways. Statistical process capability and control are especially unnatural. It is natural for a craftsperson to control a process like a racing driver controlling a car—by feel, experience, and flair. It is not natural, hour after hour, day after day, week after week, to measure the pieces, plot the points, perform the arithmetic, and constrain all personal actions by the results. Some operators will have difficulty with arithmetic. Many will feel a reluctance to plot points that show the process is out of control and to seek assistance in solving problems. Others will be disinclined to put written accounts of problems and actions on the charts. Statistical process capability and control apply similar constraints to the natural behavior of first line supervisors (e.g., by requiring them to stop a process and lose output while a special cause is investigated), design engineers, purchasing agents, and many others. So, the introduction of process capability and control is a major challenge to management—because of these psychological factors, technical difficulties, and financial constraints.

Table 9.5 lists some of the actioins that have to be planned, scheduled, provided with resources, and implemented so that a division can complete a program of statistical process capability and control. The list indicates the complexity and difficulty involved in successfully implementing such a program. It may be salutary to summarize TRW's experiences. Early in 1985 I asked TRW's division managers to describe the status of their statistical process control programs, plant by plant, as of March 31, 1985, and their plans for the rest of the year. The survey was most applicable to the company's automotive and industrial and energy sectors, and its electronic components group, 53 divisions in all. Since mid-May, 1985, responses have been received from 50 divisions with only three overseas divisions outstanding. In total, information was provided on 120 plants. The responses indicate that before 1982 only five units had significant programs for application of statistical methods to the capability and control of their manufacturing processes. During 1982 another 12 plants started programs, possibly as a result of participation of their managers in the TRW Quality College, but more likely as a result of customer requirements. It was previously noted in this chapter, that at the end of 1982 we started a strong company-led drive on statistical process control. Twenty-eight more units started programs in 1983, bringing the total to 45. During 1984 and 1985 the impetus for statistical process control was maintained and the number of units with active programs rose to about 120.

The respondents were asked to indicate how many of their manufacturing processes were judged appropriate for statistical process control. Some plants used a "macro" definition of a process and a typical number of processes reported was 100. Other plants defined each controllable parameter as a process and gave responses in the thousands. Either defini-

TABLE 9.5. Activities for Implementing a Statistical Process Capability and Control Program

Responsibility	Activity
Division manager	Decide to implement program.
Division manager	Convince department heads he is serious.
Division manager	Establish multifunctional implementation committee and appoint program manager.
Program manager	Prepare initial implementation schedule.
Functional managers	Agree schedule and assess resources required.
Division manager	Agree schedule and resources.
Human relations manager	Get support of supervisors.
Consultants or internal trainers	Determine numbers of managers, engineers, supervisors, operators, and inspectors who require training. Conduct training, taking account of education level of trainees.
Quality and manufacturing engineering	Identify all existing processes. Determine: which have had capability measured; which are incapable; which are under statistical process control; which require capability measured; and which require statistical control.
Purchasing and quality engineering	Communicate to suppliers of materials and components the desirability of instituting statistical process capability and control.
Quality and manufacturing engineering	Conduct process capability studies on all designated processes.
Manufacturing and quality engineering	Provide necesssary additional and better gauges.
Manufacturing and quality engineering	Determine special causes of variation. Improve processes. Remeasure capability.
Manufacturing engineering	Revise process specifications.
Product engineering and marketing	Examine tolerances of designs, which are beyond the capability of processes, and widen when possible. Conduct necessary negotiations with customers.
Manufacturing engineering	Establish statistical process capability requirements with vendors of machines.
Purchasing	Convince machine vendors of seriousness of this requirement.
Manufacturing engineering	Provide new machines and processes as required.
Manufacturing and quality engineering	Perform acceptance capability tests of new machines.

TABLE 9.5. *Continued*

Responsibility	Activity
Quality and manufacturing engineering	Provide statistical process control methods for machine operators. Change time standards as necesssary.
Manufacturing supervisors	Institute start of statistical process control and continually evaluate application.
Machine operators	Change from traditional to statistical methods of process control.
Supervisors, manufacturing and quality engineering	Respond rapidly and effectively to operator problems.
Manufacturing engineering	Determine need for and institute: improved machine maintenance, tool change, cycle time, and so on.
Quality engineering	Monitor defect levels from the original and modified processes of items, and of the outgoing product.
Quality engineering	Modify inspection and test plans.
Inspection supervisor	Implement modified inspection and test plans.
Quality manager	Each month report progress of the implementation versus the scheduled milestones to the division and plant managers.
Marketing and quality managers	Inform customers about progress made in implementing the program and the resulting improved product quality.
Division and plant managers	Follow progress of program and continually communicate to all levels—managers, engineers, supervisors, operators, and inspectors—the importance of the program.

tion clearly shows that TRW had a vast number of processes to control. One obvious first step was to train the involved design, manufacturing, and quality engineers and the production supervisors, operators, and inspectors. By March 31, 1985 over 10,000 TRW employees had received this training, and plans had been made to train another 6000 over the course of 1985.

What about actual implementation of the programs? The respondents were asked to indicate the numbers and percentages (relative to the total number of applicable processes) of charted, controlled and capable processes. The results indicated that less than half of the reporting units had yet made substantial progress toward the final objective of having controlled and capable processes. By the end of 1985 a high proportion of the plants planned to have their processes charted, but by then many plants would still have a long way to go in control and capability. Thirteen units have made excellent progress and already have most of their processes both controlled and capable. Many units, not just the 13 furthest ahead, reported major benefits from their programs in reduction of scrap and other failure costs, better outgoing quality, reduced needs for inspection, improved operator job satisfaction and quality awareness, and customer recognition leading to reduced customer quality assurance activities, and increased competitiveness.

This example indicates how much drive and persistence, in addition to resources and effort, is needed to implement such a program.

THE ECONOMICS OF QUALITY

The economics of quality is of interest, because it gives an example of two conflicting business philosophies. One of these holds that, to a major extent, business is a matter of making trade-offs between the achievement of competing objectives. The other contends that if a business is operated efficiently it will simultaneously achieve the optimum result for a number of apparently competing objectives. In quality terms the conflict is between the argument that high product quality has to be traded for high cost and late delivery, and the alternative that when a product is made "right the first time" the best product quality is obtained at the lowest cost and with the shortest delivery time. Many controversies of this kind persist because these simple statements fail to address the real situation which is far more complicated.

P. B. Crosby, who is perhaps the most perceptive intuitive thinker working in quality management today, asserts that "there is no economics of quality" (1). Ten years ago, in my book, *The Cost of Quality* (20), I gave my view that "these hypothetical relationships between quality and price are not very useful," and briefly discussed my reasons. However, the topic continues to fascinate writers and teachers on quality. A widely circulated textbook, *Quality Planning and Analysis* (28), published in 1981, devotes three pages to it. The lead article of a special issue of *Quality Progress* (29) devoted to quality costs made it a major topic, and there are many other indications that it is still of general interest.

The discussions just referenced usually relate price, cost, or quality cost to quality. They all conclude that there is some optimum level of quality at which the other parameters have their ideal value. They imply that a quality better than the optimum is undesirable. They conclude that it is important to determine the optimum level of quality. These discussions are deficient in at least three respects. First, they do not always define the terms they use. For example, as different definitions of quality radically change the analysis, it is not surprising that the logic gets confused. Second, their analysis is qualitative not quantitative. Third, they do not give data on real products—or even attempt to imagine real products—as the focus for their analyses. They assume that all products can be treated in the same way. Figure 9.4 gives three typical graphs from the referenced sources. All appear to have linear scales from zero to 100 percent for their quality axes, and imply that costs are rising very rapidly when the quality is within a few percent of 100 percent quality.

A few examples will show that for many products this is an incorrect conclusion. For more than 20 years I have bought my shirts and underwear from a British retail chain famous for its quality control and reasonable prices. On no occasion did I judge one of these products to fail. To this customer they are zero-failure products at the 100 percent quality level, and with a price and, I assume, a cost at a moderate level. Sugar is a simple product. My wife has never had a failure with a packet of sugar. Even more complicated products like butter, milk, and eggs virtually never fail. When did you last buy rancid butter, sour milk, or bad eggs? All of these products have quality at the 100 percent level and moderate prices.

A favorite example of mine is gin and tonic. I have been drinking one or two each week for the past 35 years. Again, I have habitually bought two famous English brands (one gin, one tonic) of moderate price. My gin or tonic has never failed to meet my quality expectation. We can make a quantitative estimate: 100 drinks a year for 35 years. If the defective proportion for either gin or tonic is 1 in 1000, I should have had a failure by now; at 1 in 10 thousand I might just be lucky; at 10 ppm my result was virtually assured and I can drink gin and tonics for the rest of my life with high confidence.

Twenty years ago the mean time between failures of most types of color televisions was less than a year. The customer suffered considerable expense and trouble in coping with this problem. The mean time between failures of the better makes of set is now as long as the amount of time that most people have their sets. This important improvement in quality has been achieved without cost or price increase. An even more

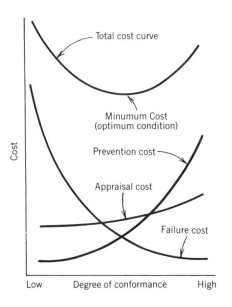

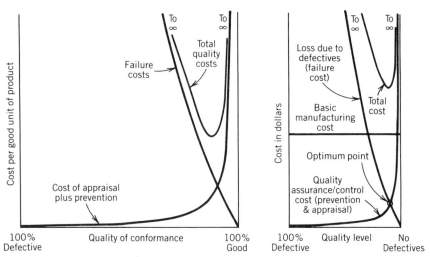

Figure 9.4. Hypothetical relationships between cost and quality.

striking improvement has been achieved in the quality of the electronic components from which the sets are made—from 0.1 percent defective to a few ppms—with no major cost increase.

What do these practical examples tell us? First, the emphasis has been on "failures" not "defects." Products may contain invisible defects but if they do not cause failures they are no problem to the customer. (Of course, there is always the possibility that the customer will use, inspect, or test the product in a new way that discovers such a defect. Then at the moment of failure the invisible defect is revealed as an actual defect.) Second, none of the products had a significant number of failures in a life time of buying and use—and none had the high cost and price that the exponential rise of the graphs in Figure 9.4 would indicate as inevitable.

Let us consider a more difficult example. Some time ago I bought a new car. I first decided how much money I was prepared to spend, and how long I was prepared to wait for delivery, I then had to decide which of the available cars, in my judgment, had the highest product quality. The cars did not match my ideal dream. In order to get a new car for my price I had to limit several of the "aspects of my need." I had to trade off the aspect concerned with good control in snow (which I think is helped by front wheel drive) for the aspect concerned with comfort (which is helped by large size). I had to trade-off the aspect concerned with the need to overtake with facility (which requires high acceleration), with the aspect of wanting to be able to carry a lot of luggage and get in and out easily myself (which determines the size of the trunk and the arrangement of the doors). The car company, whose marketing people made the trade-off of various features and characteristics which best corresponded to my need trade-offs, got a head start for my purchase. Into my decision I then added judgment about how well I thought the various companies had realized their marketing specification through the design, purchasing, manufacturing, and test/inspection phases. Of course, if I had been prepared to pay, say $50,000, the limitations on my need would have been much less, but I would still have these trade-offs to make. It seems clear that in deciding what aspects of a need to satisfy, and therefore what product features and characteristics to require, trade-offs must be made and a customer unwilling to make trade-offs will have to accept higher and higher prices as need-aspects are added (whose satisfaction requires a product with ever more features and ever improved characteristics).

I noted that the economics of quality can be discussed effectively only if quality is defined clearly. In Chapter 2, the following definition of quality was introduced:

The quality of a product is the degree of conformance of all of the relevant features and characteristics of the product to all of the aspects of a customer's need, limited by the price and delivery he or she will accept.

It was also suggested that the customer's need and the features and characteristics of the product to satisfy that need were linked by a chain of conformance. Figure 9.5 is a shortened version of this chain. The previous definition of quality spans the whole length of the chain of conformance, as does Juran's definition, "fitness for use." Crosby's definition, "conformance to requirements," covers the part of the chain from the product requirement specification to the product. Neither Crosby's nor Juran's definition deals explicitly with price or delivery. Trade-off is essential in the first half of the chain of conformance. This could imply that a customer might enter into the fairyland of infinite cost and price when their need can only be satisfied by features and characteristics beyond the state-of-the-art. In our definition, the clause, "limited by the price and delivery he or she will accept," keeps the customer firmly in the real world.

However, the graphs attempting to illustrate the economics of quality are not concerned with the marketing aspects of quality. They clearly imply the existence of a defined product requirement specification and the quality they deal with is "the degree of conformance" to that requirement specification, (despite the fact that our shirt, butter, sugar, milk, eggs, and gin and tonic examples, showed that achievement of complete conformance to the customer's need can often be achieved and that, in such cases, nonconformance to some product requirement specification

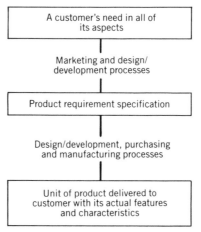

Figure 9.5.   Shortened version of chain of conformance.

that merely reflects that need is trivial). Even for the complex product, the car, the fact of trade-off in the marketing aspects of quality does *not* require trade-off or high cost in achieving virtually complete conformance to the requirement specification; there is no law of nature that always makes it very expensive to manufacture a product that conforms to a practical product requirement specification. Manufacturing nonconformance does not inevitably give a cost saving that could be used to provide, say, an extra feature at the same cost. The principle of "making it right the first time" potentially gives a practical method of achieving exact conformance to the product requirement specification at moderate cost.

To progress further in the analysis of the economics of quality it is useful to attempt a quantitative analysis of a product, albeit a hypothetical one (30). Assume that a mass-produced mechanical component is sold by a component manufacturer to an equipment maker. The component manufacturer and the equipment maker have agreed on a product requirement specification of the component. Quality can be defined then as, "the degree of conformance of the actual features and characteristics of the product to the specification of the features and characteristics," and it can be conveniently measured as the reciprocal of either the proportion defective or the proportion failed. The product supplied to the equipment maker will be a mixture of items for which the degree of conformance is complete, and items for which it is not.

Assume only one characteristic has a tight tolerance that is difficult to achieve. The manufacturing cost at 100 percent yield is $10 and the selling price is $13. The equipment maker receives them in lots of 1000 each week. They sometimes accept them by sampling inspection at incoming using MIL-STD-105D, Inspection Level II, AQL 1 percent, at a cost of $250 per lot. The component manufacturer has been provided with a piece of manufacturing equipment that, associated with a defined manufacturing process, is just capable of achieving the specified tolerance at $\pm 3\sigma$. When held in control, therefore, 99.7 percent of the items will meet the equipment maker's specification. The equipment maker's design is such that the probability of the part failing functionally (not fitting with a mating piece) is zero when it meets specification and becomes unity at $\pm 4\sigma$. Such functionally defective parts are found in the equipment maker's assembly operation at a cost of $20. The manufacturer does not always keep the process under control. The manufacturer can then do 100 percent inspection with 90 percent efficiency at a cost of $1 per piece. The rejected parts have to be scrapped. We can now consider the cost and quality relationships for various scenarios.

Scenario 1. The component manufacturer holds the process just in control. The equipment maker has found that lots always pass incoming inspection and has ceased to do it. The lots that go to their assembly line are 0.3 percent defective, but only those beyond $\pm$ 4σ (2.5 percent of the 0.3 percent) always fail to fit as do another 7.5 percent of those between $\pm$ 3σ and $\pm$ 4σ. So, 0.03 percent (300 parts per million) fail functionally. The equipment maker is not organized to charge the manufacturer for these.

Scenario 2. The component manfacturer lets the process go out of control, so that on average the lots are 2 percent defective. They ship them that way. The equipment maker does incoming inspection; they reject 10 percent of the lots back to the manufacturer, but what is accepted is still one percent defective and 0.1 percent fail the assembly process. The manufacturer 100 percent inspects the rejected lots.

Scenario 3. With the process out of control the component manufacturer averages 10 percent defective and does 100 percent inspection. This improves the quality to one percent defective. The equipment maker does incoming inspection, rejects 5 percent of the lots, but this has little effect on the quality and still 0.1 percent fail in the equipment maker's assembly.

Scenario 4. The equipment maker decides to discontinue accepting items that yield even as few as 0.03 percent functional failures in the assembly process (e.g., because another supplier can do better). Although the component manufacturer has the process under control (giving 0.3 percent defective and 0.03 percent functional failures) they have to do 100 percent inspection (at 90 percent efficiency) as well.

Scenario 5. With the new requirement passed down by the equipment maker, the component manufacturer decides to improve the capability of the process. A new machine is purchased which enables the process to achieve $\pm$ 4σ within the equipment maker's tolerance. The process is similar to that used before and the rate of production is the same but the machine requires an extra $10,000 per year of depreciation, equivalent to $0.5 per piece on one-shift operation. With $\pm$ 4σ capability only 0.006 percent is defective. Only 5 percent of those out of specification now fail on the equipment maker's production line, because most are only just out of tolerance (i.e., 0.0003 percent, or 3 ppm). The equipment maker buys only 1000 per week, and has zero failures in the first year. He or she is able to use "just-in-time" methods and saves 60 cents cost per unit. This savings will be shared with the manufacturer.

For each of the previous scenarios it is possible to calculate the component maker's cost and the equipment maker's cost. It is also possible to calculate the quality, expressed either as proportion defective to specification or as proportion failing during inspection or use. Table 9.6 shows the results. (Details of the calculations are given in reference 30.)

In Figures 9.6 and 9.7 the results are put into price/quality graphs similar to those in Figure 9.4. In Figure 9.6 quality is expressed as proportion defective. As the originator of this example, I know what the proportion defective is. However, in real life this would not be known unless especially measured. The proportion failed is easily known—it requires only to record the failures as they occur and to add them up—so Figure 9.7, which expresses the degree of conformance as the proportion failed, is more realistic.

What do these graphs show? First, we need to use a log scale for quality. We can then go from 100 percent failure to failures measured in ppm. Linear graphs measuring quality from 0 to 100 percent do not enable us to plot the results. Second, the prices and costs go up and down by significant amounts depending on exactly how a particular quality is achieved. The costs are changed by the interplay of screening inspection, sampling acceptance, and how the product is made, but there is no indication of any continuous, smoothly curved relationships. The range of cost in this example is about 20 percent—which is enough to convert a profit into a loss—but there is no impression of costs rising toward infinity even though we have continued the graphs to very high quality levels. In this example, failure proportions that approach one ppm do not require exceptionally high costs. Of course, if the tolerance had been above the state-of-the-art the costs would have been infinite, but this is an unrealistic requirement.

Figures 9.6 and 9.7 could easily be redrawn with the costs expressed as

TABLE 9.6. Manufacturing Costs and Quality Levels of a Hypothetical Product Made by Five Different Methods

	Scenario				
	1	2	3	4	5
Component maker's cost per piece accepted ($s)	10.00	10.12	12.15	11.03	10.20
Equipment maker's cost per piece used ($s)	13.01	13.28	13.28	13.00	12.70
Proportion defective supplied to equipment maker	0.003	0.020	0.010	0.00033	0.00006
Proportion failed by equipment maker	0.0003	0.101	0.051	0.000033	0.000003

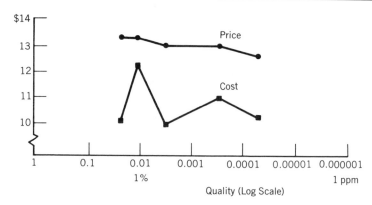

Figure 9.6. Graph of equipment maker's cost-per-piece-used (price) and component manufacturer's cost-per-piece-accepted (cost), against proportion defective delivered to equipment maker (quality).

quality costs instead of total costs, and for some of the scenarios the quality cost is just $10 less than the total cost. However, it does not seem useful to do this.

The so-called economics of quality have been examined. It was shown that the freqently published graphs of relationships between cost and quality that are supposedly applicable to all products, have no general validity. Unless the various terms are carefully defined such graphs have no meaning. Even when the terms are defined each product will have its own cost versus quality relationship which follows no general pattern. In establishing the marketing aspects of product quality—deciding what the product requirement specification will be—trade-offs have to be made, and these are best done initially in terms of a predefined price, with iteration to different prices if necessary. Once the product requirement specification is determined further trade-offs should be unnecessary, and for many products very high quality, measured as proportion observed by the customer to fail in ppm, can be achieved at no higher cost than for much worse quality. An example showed costs varying irregularly by only 20 percent with quality varying by a factor of 100,000—and one of the lower costs was associated with the highest quality. The advantage resulting from superior quality might have been illustrated even more dramatically if the example had included other costs which might have resulted from poor quality—in product recalls, inability to deliver, lost orders, liability litigation, and the many hidden costs of manufacturing disruption due to poor quality. The main reason why earlier analyses of the economics of quality are pernicious is not because they contain defects of logic and lack realism (though they do), but because they suggest to makers of products

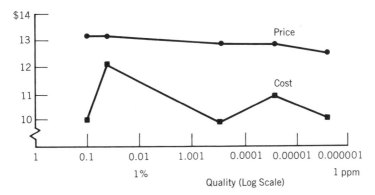

Figure 9.7. Graph of equipment maker's cost-per-used (price) and component manufacturer's cost-per-piece-accepted (cost), against proportion failed by equipment maker (quality).

that they should stop their quality improvement efforts when they have reduced their defect levels to one percent or a little lower, rather than striving for ppm and better.

CONCLUSION

Products are manufactured by processes and the essence of manufacturing defect-free products is in having processes that are capable of achieving the requirements of the designs, and in controlling the processes effectively. In practice, process control has to be reinforced by 100 percent inspection and testing to screen out defects. It is practicable through these means to sell products which are virtually free of functional defects, contain levels of nonfunctional defects which are invisible to the customer, and have acceptable reliability.

CHAPTER 10

RELIABILITY AND PRODUCT LIABILITY

Reliability is often regarded as a separate topic from quality. In this book, the term "product quality" embraces all of the features and characteristics of a product including its reliability characteristics. Delivery quality and support-service quality, but not reliability, have been differentiated from product quality. We, therefore, would speak of "quality including reliability" not "quality and reliability." Reliability is concerned with all of the characteristics of a product which may change with time. When a product does not conform to its requirements the first time it is tested or used the failure is not referred to as a reliability failure; reliability is concerned with failure to conform after some period of conformance.

My own reliability experience has been mainly with electronic equipments and components, and I shall concentrate on these in the following discussion. However, this restriction is not much of a disadvantage because many of the advances in reliability began in electronics.

THE RELIABILITY PROBLEM

There are many different measures of reliability. For a complete product that can be repaired the most common reliability measure is "mean time between failures." The product is operated under specified conditions and after some time it fails to meet one of its specified characteristics—usually a functional characteristic. The product is repaired and operation is restarted. After a further period of time it fails again. The procedure is continued and the time between failures is measured. The average of these time intervals is the mean time between failures (MTBF). More than one unit of the product can be operated under the stated conditions. The MTBF can then be calculated from the results of all of the units. One way of doing this is to divide the sum of the times on test of all of the equipments, ("equipment hours") by the number of failures. The larger the MTBF, the better the reliability. In defining the product requirement specification the minimum MTBF can be one of the specified characteristics of the product.

Another common measure of reliability applied to mass-produced, nonrepairable products—such as electronic components—is failure rate. To determine the failure rate of a population of components a sample of the components, say 1000, is operated under specified conditions, and specified functional characteristics are tested either continuously or at predetermined time intervals. The accumulated number of failures is graphed against the product of the number of components on test (which will decrease as components fail) and the time on test, (this product being called "component hours"). The slope of this "survival" curve at a particular time gives the instantaneous failure rate of the component sample at that time. Alternatively, the total number of failures divided by the component hours gives the average failure rate up to that time. The lower the failure rate the better the reliability will be. The MTBF and failure rate measured in these ways are subject to sampling error. The magnitude of the error, which can be calculated by statistical theory, decreases as more failures occur. Customarily MTBF is measured in hours and failure rate in reciprocal hours.

The concept of the chain of conformance (see Chapter 2) shows that many marketing, design, purchasing, and manufacturing activities contribute to the making of a new product. Three particular groups of these activities are the following:

1. Establishment and specification of the required features and characteristics of the product.
2. Design, purchase, and manufacture to achieve the required features and characteristics.
3. Test to show whether or not the required features and characteristics have been achieved.

These three groups of activities do not occur in consecutive order. The marketing, design, purchasing, and manufacturing processes almost always contain many iterations since testing at various stages shows that all of the required features and characteristics have not been achieved. There are continual feedback loops of redesign, rework, and even changes to the product requirement specification because of test failures. Testing of the immediate features and characteristics of a product can usually be carried out in minutes or hours. Even qualification testing, which is the most thorough and elaborate stage of testing, rarely takes more than a few weeks. When a product has passed a well-planned and implemented test program there is usually a good probability that it possesses all of its required immediate features and characteristics.

However, what about a product's reliability characteristics? Can its reliability status be tested in the same way as its immediate functional status? Well, in principle the MTBF of an equipment or the failure rate of a population of components can be measured by life testing. Then, if the result is worse than specified, further redesign or rework can be undertaken. One fundamental difficulty with this is that many electrical and mechanical machines are required to work for a period of 10 years or more, and it is unlikely that the MTBF at the end of this period will be the same as at the beginning. Solution of this problem seems to require life tests of 10 years' duration. There is another problem. An MTBF, for example, of one year is specified. To measure this level with reasonable accuracy requires say five machines to be tested for a year, or 10 machines for six months, or some other test of similar magnitude. Apart from being very expensive, the results from such a test will arrive too slowly to give enough feedback to help design-development or manufacturing rework. They need the sort of speed that comes from functional tests. Another difficulty is that life tests may be destructive or may change the state of the units being tested. They are different from functional tests which normally leave the units tested unchanged, so that functional tests can be used 100 percent to screen out functional defects. In Chapter 8, functional tests on a car were discussed, none of which involved more than driving the car 100 yards. Contrast this with a 1000 hour operational life test which might involve 50,000 miles of driving. Such a test would wear out the car to some extent. There would then be no assurance that the car's behavior over the next 50,000 miles of use would be the same (minus the corrected defects revealed by the test) as during the test. "Burn-in," which will be discussed next, is not a direct equivalent to functional testing for screening out defects.

The fact that reliability testing is not as effective as immediate functional testing raises two fundamental questions:

1. How can one design and manufacture products of specified reliability when one cannot rely on feedback from test failures to correct problems?

2. How can one have confidence that a product is of specified reliability when one cannot easily measure the reliability by testing?

A whole new discipline, reliability engineering, has evolved over the past 30 years to respond to these two questions. Although, in some ways, it would seem more logical to deal with reliability immediately after Chapter 5 (Design Quality), I felt that it was necessary to leave the subject until after test planning had been covered (Chapter 8) because of the importance of testing to the subject of reliability.

Table 10.1 lists some of the techniques that have been invented to help in making reliable products and measuring how reliable they are.

Besides measuring a product's reliability by testing, one can predict it by examining its design. In Chapter 8, data on the proportion of electronic components known to be defective (Table 8.5) were used to predict the proportion of television sets that would fail a functional test. The television contained 700 components that had an average functionally defective proportion of 500 ppm. As any one defective component would cause the set to fail, $700 \times 500/1,000,000 = 0.35$ of the sets were predicted to fail (i.e., about one in three). If, in addition, the reliability failure rates of the components were known the MTBF of the television set could be predicted in a similar way. Let us assume the average component failure rate is 0.0000001 per hour. The MTBF for this would be $1/0.0000001 \times 700 = 14,286$ hours, which is just over a year and a half. I chose the failure rate of 0.0000001 per hour in order to get a realistic value for the MTBF of the television set. It means that 1 in 10 million of the components is expected to fail every hour. To avoid using such com-

TABLE 10.1.   Reliability Techniques

Reliability prediction
Standardization
Redundancy
Physics of failure
Overstress and accelerated life testing
Stress analyses—electrical, thermal, and mechanical
Failure distributions
Burn-in
Failure mode and effect analysis
Fault tree analysis

plicated decimals, reliability engineers use a unit called a *fit* which is one billionth of one per hour. In this unit our components had an average failure rate of 100 fits.

Predicting the reliability of equipment seems very easy. Just multiply the number of components used to assemble the equipment by those same components' average failure rate, and then take the reciprocal to get the MTBF. One important consequence of this approach is that it shows that the more components in an equipment the less reliable it will be. If we had used 7000 components to make a computer instead of 700 to make a television set the MTBF calculation would have been $1/0.0000001 \times 7000 = 1428$ hours (i.e., about 8½ weeks) not 1½ years. If we had wanted the computer to have an MTBF of 1½ years, we would have used components with an average failure rate of only 10 fits; the 100 fit components would not have been reliable enough.

In practice, performing a reliability prediction is more complicated than the examples discussed previously indicate. First of all, the failure rate of each different type of component must be used, because the average failure rate of the whole set of components is not known, and also the various interconnections (e.g., solder joints) must be treated as if they were components. Secondly, each type of component will have many different failure rates. If the equipment design puts a low stress on a component the latter will usually have a lower failure rate than if it is highly stressed. For example, a transistor may be rated by its manufacturer to dissipate up to one watt of power; however, its failure rate would likely be much less if it were called on to dissipate only one-tenth of a watt. A well-performed reliability prediction includes a very careful analysis of the equipment's design from the viewpoint of the stresses—both expected and unexpected—it applies to the components. Similarly, a component's failure rate will be lower if the equipment's design allows its characteristics to degrade well beyond their specified limits before it causes an equipment failure, than if its full specification is utilized by the equipment. Nonetheless, performing the calculations is not exceptionally difficult—particularly since computer programs are available which do most of the work.

The main reason that reliability prediction cannot do for reliability characteristics what functional testing does for immediate functional characteristics is not the difficulty of calculation. It is because of the difficulty of establishing the component failure rate data. The two examples, the television set and the computer, called for average component failure rates of 100 fits and 10 fits respectively. A typical life test to measure a 100 fit failure rate would be 5000 units tested for 10,000 hours (over one year). A type of component with a 100 fit failure rate would suffer about five failures on such a test, giving a statistically accurate measure of the failure rate. The 10 fit failure rate would require a test 10 times as big, say 50,000 units for 10,000 hours. If the equipment contained 100 different types of components, 100 similar tests would have to be performed. It is clear that such an approach is impracticable; it is worse than measuring the MTBF of the equipment directly. Reliability predictions are actually made using a different approach. Standard compendia of component failure rates, of which the best known is MIL-HDBK-217, are used. These are based either on extensive component life tests in the past, or on the results of past operation or test of equipments. The use of such compendia is based on the assumption that the failure rate of components of a particular type being assembled today into an equipment, which will stress them and utilize their characteristics in certain ways, will be the same as the failure rate of some similar components made years ago by different manufacturers, and stressed and utilized in similar but different ways. The error resulting from that assumption can be a factor of ten or more, and it is therefore surprising how often a prediction, validated long after, turns out to have been fairly accurate.

The theory of reliability prediction indicates why the second of the reliability techniques listed in Table 10.1, standardization, is so important. The simplest way of making new pieces of reliable equipment is to pattern them (both in design and manufacturing processes) after old pieces of equipment whose reliability has been confirmed by years of customer use. Of course, this straightforward method is often impracticable because of the need for improved performance. An intermediate approach would be to use well-established components, for which good failure rate data was available, in a new design, which also had a satisfactory reliability prediction. A similar method takes advantage of the fact that many complex equipments consist of a number of modules, each made from components. The more that modules, which have proved to be reliable in long-term use, can be used in equipments of new design, the more likely are the latter to be reliable. Unfortunately, the use of such standardization is foreign to the psychology of many design engineers. They prefer to start every new design from scratch and to introduce all of the latest component innovations. I remember a particular example, which concerned a major type of equipment for which a new design generation appeared every 10 or 20 years. One such transition changed the equipment's electronics from analogue to digital, and from discrete electronic components to specially designed integrated circuits. The computer control went from centralized logic, with one computer, to distributed logic which used a series of microprocessors. To me, steeped in the old quality manager's dictum "every innovation is a source of trouble," that seemed enough. But the designers were not satisfied. Although these changes accounted for virtually all of the performance improvement, they also changed the equipment practice (the racks and frames on which the modules were mounted), the air conditioning, the cabling method, the teleprinters; they went to multilayered printed boards, they introduced reflow soldering, and so on. Of course, many of the unnecessary changes *were* sources of trouble. Also, much of the innovation destroyed the confidence in the accuracy of the reliability prediction, and rendered the reliability methodology a "wait and hope" situation.

The third reliability technique listed in Table 10.1 is redundancy. For an equipment with a nonredundant design every functional failure of a component or connection causes the equipment to fail. The design can be made deliberately redundant, so that some components or modules fail without the equipment failing. One extreme form of redundancy is to have a complete standby equipment, which is brought into action when the primary equipment fails. In principle, such redundancy can greatly increase product reliability, although it has obvious disadvantages in cost, weight, and so on. In addition, redundancy increases complexity, and that in turns reduces reliability. One of the important uses of reliability prediction techniques is the estimation of the reliability improvement that results from the introduction of a particular kind of redundancy— taking into account the adverse effect of the added complexity.

An important question is: Why do reliability failures occur at all? It is easy to understand why immediate functional failures occur. If a component is left out, a connection is missing, or the design is wrong it is obvious that the equipment will not work. But why should an equipment that was working stop working? Analysis after such a failure may reveal a specific reliability defect. But before the failure it was only a potential defect, and for it to have caused an actual reliability failure it must have changed in some way. In a fundamental way such failures are examples of the rundown of the whole universe expressed in the Second Law of Thermodynamics. Sooner or later everything decays from an ordered state to a disordered state. The perfectly ordered working equipment, with every functioning component in its proper place, becomes disordered in some way and suffers a reliability failure. In practice, there are innumerable processes of failure. Every component or connection has its own set. Some of these are physical decreases or order (e.g., a chip of waste metal moves and short-circuits an electrical path). Others are the results of chemical processes which, unless externally driven, always take a system to a less ordered state. Such chemical processes are often greatly accelerated in rate by application of extraneous energy—vibration or temperature cycling causing fatigue failures, increased temperature accelerating the diffusion rate of one material through another, potential differences causing movement of charged ions, and so on. Knowledge of failure processes (or failure mechanisms as they are usually called) often enables actions to be taken to eliminate their effect or at least delay their onset. In this way the reliability of a component, and hence the equipments in which it is used, can be improved. "Physics of failure" is the title given to such work. The problem with this approach is the vast number of different failure mechanisms, the considerable amount of chemical and physical research needed for an analysis of each one, and then the difficulty of devising and implementing improvement strategies on the basis of the analysis. Therefore, the rate of progress is slow.

In performing a component life test it is necessary to adjust the scale of the test so that a statistically valid number of failures is obtained. The more failures observed, the more precise is the measure of failure rate. In our television set example, to measure a failure rate of 100 fits, we tested 5000 components for 10,000 hours and got five failures. For cost and time reasons it would have been very desirable to end the test after 1000 hours (six weeks) but then there probably would have been no failure or, at most, one, and the measure of failure rate would have been imprecise.

However, if, as a result of physics of failure studies, the failure mechanisms were understood, the life test could be carried out under an over-stress condition that would cause failures to occur at an accelerated rate compared to that of the actual-use condition. In our example, if a particular over-stress condition produces an acceleration of 10 times in the failure process, five failures would occur in 1000 hours instead of 10,000 hours, which would enable the failure rate to be measured with reasonable accuracy in six weeks instead of a year. An even greater advantage would result from an acceleration factor of 100. Using that same over-stress condition we could measure the failure rate in a few days. Unfortunately, in any real case there are usually many different failure mechanisms (all with their own acceleration factors) none of which is known accurately. In practice a pragmatic approach is adopted. Judgments are made about the types of stress—temperature, vibration, voltage, and so on—expected to accelerate the failure mechanisms of the component type under consideration. Failure rates are measured at a series of stress levels (sometimes using "step-stress" methods), and extrapolations are made from the high-stress, short-time results to lower-stress, long-time conditions, and finally to the real-use, very long-time condition. Most chemical processes are accelerated by increased temperature, and many such processes follow the Arrhenius equation:

$$\log (\text{rate}) = A - B/T$$

where A and B are constants and T is the absolute temperature; this relationship is often used in making extrapolations. It is clear that accelerated life tests can be very useful, but the quantitative value of results depending on acceleration factors of more than 10 is very doubtful, despite the temptation to use 100 or 1000 because of the time compression obtained.

The fact that failure rates can be accelerated by applying over-stress conditions to components is useful for life testing. However, if the design of an equipment is such that overstress conditions are applied to some of the components during actual use, the reliability of the equipment will be adversely affected. In designing equipment for high reliability it is important, therefore, to carry out careful analyses of the electrical, thermal, and mechanical stresses to which every component will be subjected, and then to ensure that no component is overstressed and that, when useful, components are understressed.

It was previously noted that the MTBF of an equipment or the failure rate of a population of components may not remain constant with time. In principle, one might expect the failures of a sample of components all of which started a life test at the same time to follow a normal distribution (see Figures 5.4 and 5.6) with respect to time. (An equipment is more complicated because failed components, which will have aged in use, are replaced by new components when the equipment is repaired.) For example, such a distribution would result if the dominant failure process occurred at a constant rate and the amount of deterioration required to cause individual components to fail was normally distributed. We also learned in Chapter 5 that a combination of several distributions, even if they themselves are not normal, often results in a normal distribution— and this also might lead us to expect failure distributions to be normal. In practice, failure mechanisms that affect the whole population of a particular component type (often called "wear out" mechanisms) often do result in normal (or log normal) instantaneous failure rate distributions, and cumulative normal survival curves. On the other hand, failures resulting from external, accidental events are likely to cause a constant instantaneous failure rate and an exponential survival curve. Another possibility is that a proportion of the components in the population contain potential reliability defects not present in the rest of the population.

These may fail earlier than the other components. These three different types of failure distributions can be illustrated for a hypothetical population of people. People who survive all other causes of death finally succumb to old age (wear out) in the 80s or 90s according to a normal distribution. A small minority will survive beyond the three sigma level and live perhaps for more than 100 years. People die at earlier ages at a constant rate due to a constant-danger-level environment causing accidents, infectious illnesses, and so on. Initially, embryos and infants die at a higher rate because of potential "reliability" defects. Real human populations have different quantitative mixtures of these three distributions, for example, the middle, constant death rate is higher for primitive than for advanced populations, and have additional features, for example, a high accident rate for young adult males and an extra death rate due to the diseases of middle-aged people (these diseases are different from the causes of death in old age). Electronic components show all of these patterns of failure as well as many more. This complexity greatly increases the difficulty of measuring failure rates. If it could be known that the failure rate of a particular component had a single constant value, this could be measured by a test resulting in only a handful of failures. However, to determine whether the failure rate was increasing or decreasing and then to characterize the different parts of the overall failure distribution would require a test with a size and duration sufficient to cause hundreds of failures. A failure rate will often be assumed constant, simply because there is not enough failure data to show that it is not.*

"Burn-in" is a very widely used method of attempting to improve the reliability of components based on the use of accelerated life testing and failure distributions, which themselves depend on a knowledge of the physics of failure. Some populations of electronic components contain a small proportion which, because it contains potential reliability defects which are not present in the rest of the population, fails early. Such component populations are similar to human populations whose infants have a higher death rate than adults. The reliability of equipments made from such components will be better—their MTBF's will be longer—if the components are operated for a long enough period so that the "infant mortality" is over before they are assembled into equipment. Alternatively, the equipments can be operated for a period, during which failed components are replaced, before they are handed over to customers. Such processes are called burn-in.

---

* In practice, the Weibull distribution is often used for the analysis of component failure rates.

Burn-in is principally used as a means of upgrading the reliability of components that have been made by uncontrolled processes. The potential reliability defects that cause failures during the burn-in are often similar to functional defects that have already caused failure of functional tests or nonfunctional defects that caused failure of visual inspections. Burn-in is so widely used because it is about the only method available to a purchaser of electronic components to improve the reliability of the components. Manufacturers of components can apply the more satisfactory method of making the components properly, but this method is not available to users, and, on the whole, users of components have found it much easier to rely on burn-in than to face the cost and difficulty of persuading component makers to control their processes.

Unfortunately, burn-in is only marginally effective. Typical burn-in times are one day or one week. For human beings this time would be much too short; 1 to 5 years would be needed to pass the infant mortality period. The same is true for most components. The problem is addressed by over-stressing the burn-in, so that one week is the equivalent of a longer period—how much longer is usually not known. An over-stress that is too high could put the components into the wear-out region where the failure rate rises instead of falls. Quantitatively, the amount of improvement available is limited. Suppose an equipment is burned-in for one week under an accelerated condition that is equivalent to 10 weeks of normal operation and there are four failures. Suppose this decreases the failure rate by a factor of 10. This indicates that in subsequent normal operation there will be 4 failures in 100 weeks (i.e., an MTBF of 25 weeks). This improvement is not bad, but it is equivalent to about the best that could be achieved by a one week burn-in. A burn-in of reasonable duration cannot give an MTBF of 10 years, such as achieved by Japanese television sets. High reliability requires the components be made reliable and used conservatively, or that the equipment contain extensive redundancy.

Three consequences can result from burn-in. The first is no failures are caused and the burn-in therefore has no effect on the reliability of the components so treated (other than the use of some of the wear-out life). The second is that, a few failures occur and there may be a consequent useful improvement in the components' reliability. Third, many failures occur and it is likely that the components' reliability will be inadequate even after the burn-in. Burn-in is often applied as a routine without any analysis of the results. It may then give considerable comfort to those requiring its performance. But it often is either a waste of effort or ineffective.

THE SUBMARINE CABLE TRANSISTOR CASE

I will leave discussion of the last two reliability techniques listed in Table 10.1 until the next section on product liability. Instead, I will illustrate the use of the others by describing a particular project (31) I was involved in some years ago. At that time I was the quality manager of the Transistor Division of Standard Telephones and Cables Ltd., (STC), which was ITT's main company in the United Kingdom. For many years STC has been the leading maker and installer of submarine cable communication links. More than half of the world's cable links, spanning the seas and oceans of the world, have been made by STC. Despite the competition of satellites, submarine cables continue to be a main method of international communications.

Signals are attenuated as they pass along a submarine cable. To overcome this effect they have to be amplified by a series of "repeaters." A long link, crossing an ocean, includes hundreds of repeaters resting on the ocean bed. The reliability requirements for such repeaters are extreme. A typical life requirement is 20 years, and any failure during that time necessitates sending a ship into the ocean to retrieve and repair the repeater. Meanwhile, the cable's revenue of thousands of dollars per minute is being lost. For technical reasons, redundancy is not practicable for repeaters so the components have to be very reliable. In repeater design, great emphasis is placed on standardization, and people are reluctant to use an unproven component. Despite the invention of the transistor many years before, special, high reliability vacuum tubes continued to be used in submarine repeaters until the mid-1960s. Early transistor technologies, based mainly on germanium, were not inherently suitable for high reliability components. It was only with the invention of the silicon planar technology that a change from vacuum tubes to transistors seemed judicious.

In 1961 STC started to make silicon planar transistors for civil and military applications. By 1966, they had considerable experience with the technology. When STC's Submerged Repeater division in conjunction with its customers decided that transistors might be used in the control circuits (but not the speech circuits) of a major new system, appropriate technology was available. The system was for 480 two-way, 4-kilohertz circuits between the United Kingdom and Portugal. The repeaters would include 1200 transistors and 2400 diodes. The reliability requirement was for no more than one transistor failure and one diode failure in four years of operation—24 fits and 12 fits respectively.

In supplying these semiconductor devices, STC's transistor division had two tasks: (1) to make devices which would have the required reliability and (2) to obtain evidence, before installation, that the reliability would be achieved.

For the first task, many studies in the preceding five years had shown that STC's normal methods of making silicon planar dice were appropriate for high reliability applications. The same was true of the normal methods used for mounting the transistor dice: in a hermetically sealed, gold-plated metal can, in which the external contacts were made via glass-metal seals. Such an encapsulation enabled the gas ambient in which the die was immersed to be defined and kept constant. The division decided that no departure would be made from these methods. Especially high reliability would be achieved by meticulous attention to the materials and manufacturing processes, and by 100 percent screening of the devices. It was believed that this approach was much more sound than the alternative of introducing new methods which had not been proved by a longer period of production. The same principle was adopted with regard to the assembly operations. These would be carried out by a few of the normal production operatives, of known superior skill, rather than by engineers or some other special group. It was also decided that the diode dice would be mounted and encapsulated in the same way as the transistor dice. It was believed that conventional methods of diode assembly were not as good for reliability as the selected transistor method, and this standardization also reduced the number of processes to control.

The manufacture of the transistors involved 78 manufacturing and inspection processes from the input of the purchased silicon slices to the completion of the encapsulation. These processes were defined in 124 specifications. The devices were moved rapidly through these processes with a minimum of waiting time. A complete record was kept of each silicon slice through the diffusion stages and of each lot of dice through the assembly stages. One typical inspection was performed at 50 times magnification after completion of the assembly. Twenty-four defined features were inspected, including the post bonds, the aluminum bonding wires, the die bond, the die, and the header. This was done to screen out devices with visual nonfunctional defects that might be potential reliability defects.

On completion of the assembly the devices were subjected to a series of 100 percent tests. First, they were tested electrically to their specification. Those passing were subjected to five temperature cycles between −55 and 150 degrees Celsius. The devices were then subjected to 20 drops on a tumble test which imparted shocks of greater than 10,000g, a procedure which had been found to be more effective in identifying defective bonds in such devices than other tests such as centrifuging. The devices were then hermeticity tested using helium to a limit of 5×10^7 atmosphere cubic centimeters per second. The results are given in Table 10.2.

The hermeticity test was a functional test, and the thermal and mechanical tests were overstress reliability tests. The effectiveness of overstress tests depends on the ability to select stress levels that are significantly greater than those the devices will suffer in actual use, but are significantly less than would damage a properly made device. In fact, submarine repeaters, once installed, have a shock-free, constant temperature environment. The test stress levels employed were well within those levels which would damage the devices.

Similar considerations were applied to the 100 percent electrical life test that was used. Several years' reliability testing experience with commercial devices of similar construction indicated to me that wear-out failures affecting all of a sample could be induced in a few days or weeks by accelerating the failure mechanisms. This was done by bringing the case temperatures to levels in the range of 200 to 280 degrees Celsius. In a typical experiment, 1000 devices were taken from five production lots. They were randomized and half stored at 275 degrees Celsius and the other half at 300 degrees Celsius. The devices were tested periodically by using relevant electrical characteristics for the failure criteria. The results showed that the failure rate was increased 3.8 times by changing the temperature from 275 to 300 degrees Celsius. This corresponded to a value of 38 kilocalories per mole for the constant B in the Arrhenius equation that was previously discussed.

An attempt was made to check this acceleration factor by testing 50 samples of each of the submarine repeater transistors at 240 and 280 degrees Celsius. However, these devices were so much more stable than the commercial devices that they gave no complete failures and showed little change in electrical characteristics during the six months of testing. Im-

TABLE 10.2.   Results of Thermal, Mechanical and Hermeticity Tests on Submarine Repeater Transistors and Diodes

Device Type	Number Tested	Number Failed		
		Thermal	Mechanical	Hermeticity
Transistor	2642	0	0	1
Diode	4793	0	0	7
Both	7435	0	0	8

posing higher stress levels was not practicable because it was known that this induced failure mechanisms irrelevant to normal operation.

The results achieved were used to define the conditions for a three months' duration burn-in. The given failure rate requirement was no more than one failure in four years. An acceleration factor of 16 was therefore needed for four years of life to be realized in three months. Using the 38 kilocalories per mole value showed that a case temperature of 70 degrees Celsius would give the necessary acceleration relative to the use-condition ambient temperature of 10 degrees Celsius and the case temperature of 30 degrees Celsius. The burn-in applied the repeater electrical conditions to the transistors and diodes (the acceleration came from the elevated case temperature). The power for the electrical conditions was supplied by lead-acid storage batteries, which were physically disconnected from the transistors and diodes during charging, and the condition of the devices was monitored periodically using isolated, low-energy probes. The purpose of these two precautions was to eliminate any possibility of wrongly induced failures. The results are given in Table 10.3.

No devices failed. Statistical calculations showed there was a 90 percent confidence that the failure rate of such devices would be no higher than 26 fits (10^{-9} per hour) in the transistors, or nine fits if the same failure mechanisms were assumed to apply to both the transistors and the diodes. At 60 percent confidence a failure rate as low as four fits was assured. On removal from the racks all of the devices were remeasured for characteristics previously measured before the burn-in. (In each case the measurements were made three times to ensure the identification of blunders.) Although the actual usage of the devices in the submarine repeaters did not require great stability of characteristics, it was reassuring that the changes had normal distributions and low standard deviations.

For the mechanical, thermal, and burn-in tests there was no failure, and therefore no defective device was screened out. These tests indicated

TABLE 10.3. Results of Three Months Burn-In (Equivalent to Four Years Operation) on Transistors and Diodes

Device Type	Transistor	Diode	Both
Number tested	2557	4743	7300
Number failed	0	0	0
Failure rate in fits:[a]			
90 percent confidence	26	14	9
60 percent confidence	10	6	4

[a] One fit = 1×10^{-9} per hour.

how well the devices had been made, and gave a measure of their reliability. Specifically, the burn-in offered evidence that the required failure rate would be achieved, provided that: (1) the acceleration factor used was not grossly optimistic; (2) the failure distribution did not show a marked rise in the next 20 years compared with the first four years (covered by the three months accelerated burn-in); and (3) some external accident did not occur. Provision (2) was addressed by the high-temperature life tests which showed that wearout failures, and consequently increasing failure rates, would not occur for times much longer than 20 years.

The only failures occurred on the nondestructive hermeticity test. This test was repeated after the burn-in using a radioactive krypton method with a sensitivity of better than 10^{-11} atmosphere cubic centimeters per second. One device, with a leak rate of 7.3×10^{-10} atmosphere cubic centimeters per second, was excluded.

This example has shown how the reliability techniques of prediction, standardization, overstressing, accelerated life testing, failure distribution analysis, and burn-in were used to help satisfy a particular high-reliability requirement. The submarine cable system went into operation in 1969 and, as far as I know, none of the transistors or diodes have failed since then.

In Chapter 8, it was pointed out that effective 100 percent functional tests could contribute to the manufacture of "PPM" components (i.e., populations of components which contain proportions of devices which are functionally defective at the ppm level). Reliability sets a limit to this process. New functional defects will appear in a population of components according to the reliability failure rate of the population. Potential reliability defects will become functional defects or wear-out will cause functional failures. In round numbers, a population of components can only sustain a functionally defective proportion of one ppm if it also has a failure rate of one fit. The reason for this is as follows. At a one fit failure rate, during 1000 hours the proportion failed will be:

$$1 \times 10^{-9} \text{ per hour} \times 1000 \text{ hours} = 1 \times 10^{-6}.$$

In 1000 hours, which is about six weeks, a population of components which have a reliability failure rate of one fit will have accumulated one ppm of functional defects. There is little reason in performing exhaustive functional testing to screen out ever smaller proportions of functional defects, if similar proportions of new defects will build up in a few weeks as a result of reliability failures. Progress beyond this limit, both in ppm level failure proportions and fit-level failure rates, requires reliability improvement using methods based on physics of failure studies and process capability and control.

Many advanced technological products include computers, and the quality of such products depends on both the "hardware"—the concrete components and modules from which the product is made—and the "software"—the abstract programs controlling the operation of the computer. Quality improvement of computer software is a special part of the total subject of quality improvement. Quality improvement is particularly important for the preparation of computer software because more than half of the total cost of such preparation results from not performing various activities right the first time (i.e., more than half of the total cost is quality cost). One of the principal activities of computer software preparation is to "write code"; and "lines of code" is one common measure of the size of a computer program. A program with 100,000 lines of code would be considered moderately large. The code for a program of that size would normally be written by several programmers, and it would not be unusual for their work to contain about one percent of functional defects (usually called "errors" or "faults"). A whole series of inspections (e.g., "code reading") and tests (e.g., module tests and simulation tests) have to be used to identify these defects. In practice, if the proportion of defects initially introduced into the system is too large it will prove impossible to find them, and the system will never be made to work. This critical proportion decreases as the size and complexity of the system increases.

In the preparation of computer software, there has been surprisingly little explicit work on defect prevention—reducing the input of defects into the system—though many general computer software advances, such as strong emphasis on "top-down" system design, the use of high-level languages, and the incorporation of proven modules in new systems, have had a very positive effect.

From a reliability viewpoint, computer software, which is an abstract set of numbers, cannot have potential reliability defects. There is no failure mechanism whereby one number can change into another number. Computer software failure has nothing analogous to an electrical connection going open circuit because temperature cycling or vibration causes an incorrectly made bond to break. It might be thought, therefore, that computer software could not suffer reliability failures in use. This is not so. The reason for reliability failures is that software programs, when brought into use, may still contain functional defects. In using a computer, a series of input conditions are applied and a series of output conditions result. Except for simple programs the number of possible input conditions and resulting output conditions is so large that it is not practicable to test every one (i.e., 100 percent functional testing cannot be performed). In use, a reliability failure occurs when a particular input-output condition that has not been used before exercises a defect in the program. Analysis of such a failure can than be used to indicate the correction that needs to be made. Unfortunately, such a correction can possibly introduce new functional defects. In extreme circumstances, the reliability of a program can deteriorate rather than improve because of such "corrections." In principle, reliability failures of this kind can be found in hardware products. Imagine a car working satisfactorily for a long time in a country with a conservative speed limit, but failing as soon as it is driven in a country without a speed limit—an existing functional defect was revealed for the first time.

One last point about the quality of computer software will be mentioned. For complex systems it is often very difficult to define "all of the aspects of the customer's need" and to formulate the product requirement specification defining "all of the relevant features and characteristics" of the software product to meet that need. One method of tackling this problem is to define a draft of the product requirement specification in software language and then to design a model of the system that meets the specification. The customer is able to simulate with the model the way he or she will use the actual system, thereby clarifying his or her need, and evaluating whether or not a system made in conformance with the draft product requirement specification will satisfy all of the aspects of that need. If the simulation indicates that a system conforming to the draft product requirement specification is not going to meet all of the aspects of the customer's need, the product requirement specification is revised and the process repeated.

PRODUCT LIABILITY

Until about 20 years ago a person who suffered injury as a result of using a product could legally recover damages from the product's manufacturer if there was a contractual relationship with the manufacturer—in most cases because the customer had purchased the product directly from the manufacturer by proving breach of express or implied warranty. An injured party with no contractual relationship with the manufacturer could establish a case against the manufacturer only by proving that the manufacturer had been negligent—which could not usually be done.

Then in 1963, California established different grounds for a lawsuit, called "strict-liability," which made it much easier for an injured person to recover damages from a product manufacturer. Since 1963 most other states of the United States and several Western European countries have adopted strict liability. American federal legislation and a directive from the European Economic Community, both of which would unify strict liability laws, are now in process. The details of strict liability law, which differ from state to state and country to country, are matters for lawyers. I will merely indicate the general principles. First, strict liability applies to commercial products. If an amateur carpenter makes a chair and gives it to a friend, the latter cannot sue under strict liability when the chair collapses and causes him injury. Second, any injured person can sue; he or she does not have to have a contractual relationship with the defendant. Third, the plaintiff has to prove: that the product was defective in a way that made it unreasonably dangerous; that the defectiveness of the product caused the injury; and that the defect was present in the product when it left the defendant's control. The plaintiff does not have to prove that it was the defendant's negligence that caused the defect. The presence of the defect is enough; its cause is irrelevant. Fourth, the plaintiff can sue any one or more of the parties concerned with the design, manufacture, or distribution of the product (and one of the factors considered will be the ability of the possible defendants to pay substantial damages).

Obviously, a key point that may be at issue is whether or not a product that caused an injury was defective. A person may suffer a cut with a sharp carving knife, without the knife being defective. The person in question would not have a product liability case. On the other hand, the knife might shatter while being used to pry off a lid and blind the user. In this instance, the customer might have a case ("foreseeable misuse" is not excluded from strict liability) if it could be shown that the steel of the knife was nonconformant to the manufacturer's design specification.

There are three kinds of product liability defects.

Manufacturing/purchasing defects

Design defects

Warning defects

The manufacturing/purchasing defects are the most straightforward. If the actual product, as manufactured, does not conform to the design drawings or other design specifications, or purchased components, and so on, do not conform to the designer's purchasing specifications, the product is clearly defective. There are many ways that such defects can arise, but one that is frequently overlooked is when a process has been deliberately changed, or custom and practice has drifted away from a process specification without adverse (and sometimes with positive) effect, but the specification has not been changed. A claim that what was actually done was correct and the specification was incorrect, makes for a poor defense in court.

When there is no clearly established purchasing or manufacturing defect, the plaintiff will claim there is a design defect. The chain of conformance (see Chapter 2) shows that what the design of the product has to conform to is not as clear as what the manufacture of the product has to conform to. This opens up legal argument. Sometimes the design will be nonconformant to established safety standards or to internal design rules, or may not require incorporation of reasonable safety devices. Other times there will be no obvious nonconformance and the plaintiff will simply claim that any failing product must be defective. Deciding whether or not a product contains design defects is often a matter of judgment. Sometimes it is necessary to decide whether the product's benefits to the consumer outweigh its risks.

The third class of defect covers warning defects. The manufacturer of a product is required to supply appropriate warnings about hazards associated with the product and its uses. For the carving knife example, the manufacturer would have been safer if a prominent label was attached stating, "This carving knife is made from hard steel. You must not use it to prize off lids because it may shatter and injure you." A supplier must not only instruct the consumer about the safe ways to use the product but also warn of the consequences that may result if the instructions are not followed; therefore every warning should:

1. Identify the nature of the danger
2. Indicate the severity of the danger
3. Instruct how to avoid injury
4. Describe the likely consequences of ignoring the instructions

Products are dangerous because they have hazardous features. Table 10.4 lists the most common of such hazards. Electrical products may be dangerous if they utilize high voltages or currents. Products made from inflammable materials may be dangerous, particularly if their combustion emits toxic fumes. Products that utilize solid, liquid, or gaseous materials which may explode are dangerous. Products that contain poisonous materials which may be inhaled, eaten, or touched, are dangerous. Products

TABLE 10.4. Product Hazards

Electricity	Poison
Fire	Radiation
Toxic fumes	Noise
Explosion	Physical condition

emitting electromagnetic radiation, spanning the whole spectrum from gamma and X-rays, through ultraviolet, visible, and infrared radiation to microwave and other radio-frequency radiation, are dangerous. Products producing high levels of noise are dangerous. Finally, products may be dangerous because of their physical size and weight, their sharpness, their method of fixing, and their motion. The design and manufacture of safe products requires attention being given to such hazards.

THE RECALL OF THE NOVA FRITEX

Some of the quality improvement principles applicable to product liability can be illustrated by a case I was involved in some years ago (32). *Nova*, one of ITT's companies in Belgium, manufactured and sold electrical domestic appliances. Included among the range of products it produced was the Fritex 3, a deep-fat fryer for cooking such things as potato chips. In construction, the Fritex 3 consisted of an aluminum casting in the form of an open can that held vegetable oil. In operation, the casting was electrically heated by a separately manufactured heating element, a resistance wire heater contained within a metal tube and insulated from it. In the original Fritex design the heating element, in the shape of a toroid, was fused into the base of the main body unit as part of the casting. The rest of the Fritex included the outer cover, an adjustable thermostat, the electrical flex, and the connectors for the heating element and the thermostat. Units like this worked without any problem.

However, the manufacture of the casting, with the inclusion of the heating element, was difficult and costly; an independent consultant employed by Nova therefore suggested that a channel should simply be cast into the base of the aluminum can. The heating element would then be clamped into the channel as a separate operation rather than be cast in (Figure 10.1). Production of the Fritex 3 to this design started in August 1975.

On January 6, 1976 Nova after-sales services received a defective Fritex

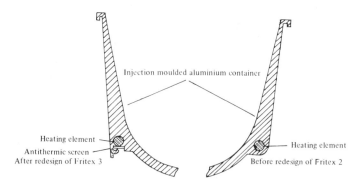

Figure 10.1. Incorporation of heating element before and after cost reduction.

3 from a customer. An analysis of the product showed that the heating element had moved in the groove so much that one of the ends made contact with the aluminum casting. A test on 10 Fritex 3s heat-cycled without oil confirmed that this was a potentially repeatable failure mechanism. On January 10 a second customer complained that he had received electric shocks from his Fritex 3.

Nova management stopped production of the Fritex 3 on January 14 and, after review of the problem with the Appliance Division director (ITT Consumer Products Group, based in Brussels) a letter was sent later in January to all Nova's dealers informing them of a possibly serious defect in the Fritex 3. It asked them to return all of their stocks to Nova, and wherever possible, to get them back from final customers.

By early February the consumer products group executive, the ITT Europe product Safety Council (involving the quality, legal, technical, marketing, and safety departments, and having close contact with the insurance department) in Brussels, and the chairperson of the ITT product safety council in the New York headquarters had all been informed of the progress of the recall—which had been extended to the United Kingdom where a substantial number of Fritex 3s had also been sold.

Nova's technical department conducted an urgent investigation of the problem and made a comparison between the original design and the new design of the Fritex 3. They showed that in two respects the new design was worse than the old. First, the thermal contact between the heating element and the aluminum casting was much less effective. In operation, the power input was the same, as was the final temperature reached by the casting, which was controlled by a thermostat, but the extra thermal resistance had to be overcome and this caused the heating element to reach a higher temperature, about 180 degrees Celsius higher in the new design. Second, the expansion and contraction stresses caused by this excessive temperature, together with the less firm anchoring of the element given by the clamp system, allowed the heating element slowly to creep around the channel when the Fritex 3 was switched on and off. Life tests on 10 Fritex 3s indicated that a high proportion might fail in this way.

This failure mechanism markedly reduced the useful life of the Fritex 3. The design was clearly unsatisfactory. However, the Fritex 3 was always sold in Belgium with a three-lead flex terminating in a standard European plug with a grounded connection. The enclosed instruction sheet expressly stated the need for the product to be properly grounded. In the United Kingdom the Fritex was supplied without a plug, as is customary, but the instructions required the use of a grounded plug on the three-lead flex. Obviously, if used correctly in this way the failure would not be dangerous. At worst the heating element at mains voltage would touch the grounded casting and cause a fuse to blow. Unfortunately, the standard European plug could readily be forced into a two-pin socket and it was believed that many kitchens in Belgium did not have properly grounded outlets. It was this deficiency that made the failure dangerous.

The ITT Europe product Safety Council set up a special working party to monitor the management of the problem. It assigned overall responsibility for coordinating all required actions to A. K. Mueller, director quality, Consumer Products Group. It also asked him to take the lead in performing a risk analysis. Table 10.5 summarizes these results.

The proportion of Fritex 3s expected to short-circuit was derived from life-test experiments. Later results indicated that this initial assumption was somewhat pessimistic. One thousand cycles up to operating temperature and then cooling gave no more than 25 percent of short-circuit failures. For larger numbers of cycles the predominant failure mechanism was the wear-out of the heating element resulting in a safe, open-circuit failure.

Peter Clifton of the ITT Europe marketing department determined

TABLE 10.5. Risk Analysis of Nova Fritex 3

	Minimum (%)	Maximum (%)
Proportion of Fritex expected to short circuit	25	50
Proportion of Belgian kitchens with no ground	50	75
Proportion of short circuits giving electric shock	100	100
Proportion of shocked users requiring medical attention	2	8
Overall product of the above proportions	0.25	3

the expected proportion of kitchens in Belgium in which the electrical supply did not include a ground connection. Official data did not exist but the electricity and gas distribution company's own estimate was that only 25 percent had a ground meeting legal standards, 25 percent had a nonlegal makeshift ground, and 50 percent had no ground at all. The figure of the proportion of shocked users requiring medical attention came from a market research initiated by Clifton especially to supply the information. Finally, it was simply assumed that a Fritex in the short-circuit condition, working on a nongrounded outlet, would sooner or later give someone an electric shock. Overall, the risk analysis showed that electric shocks from about one percent of the Fritex 3s that remained in the selling market might cause a customer to seek medical attention. It was also determined that 18,703 Fritex 3s were in the field in Belgium and 7798 in the United Kingdom.

In neither Belgium nor the United Kingdom is there a government agency, like the United States' Consumer Product Safety Commission, that must be informed of unsafe products, like the Fritex 3. The sole responsibility for deciding whether or not to recall a product therefore rests with the management of the company concerned. Under these circumstances, arguments in favor of conducting a recall include:

1. A conscientious regard for the well-being of users of the product
2. The possible total of damages and other costs that might result from product liability claims
3. The adverse publicity that might ensue if the media perceived that there was a serious product safety problem and no recall action had been taken

Arguments against conducting a recall include:

1. The possibility of destroying a reputation for quality built-up over many years, with an adverse effect on future sales
2. The high cost of conducting an effective recall and its very adverse effect on profitability
3. The futility of conducting an ineffective recall

This last point is particularly important. In the United States it may be necessary to go through the motions of conducting a recall to comply with the instructions of a government agency even when good judgment indicates that most of the units of unsafe products are unlikely to be returned—and therefore there would be little actual improvement to the safety of consumers. In the absence of such instructions an assessment of the likelihood of achieving a successful recall is a key input in making the decision. For the Fritex 3, there was no record of the names of the ultimate customers, so they could only be reached by broadcast communications.

After considering these factors the management of Nova and ITT Europe decided that a full recall should be attempted. The main weight was given to the results of the risk analysis.

Accordingly, three announcements were made in all of the newspapers in Belgium (a country with a large number of local papers) in both French and Dutch on February 17, March 12, and April 14, 1976. A similar announcement was made in the United Kingdom national newspapers on March 3. In addition, in Belgium a statement was made about the recall on a television consumer program. With the later notices, a simple policy of making them as effective as possible, irrespective of any adverse effect on product image, was adopted and professional marketing was applied to that end.

Market research was also conducted to determine the effectiveness of the advertising. This showed that 10 from a sample of 15 understood the message of the second advertisement. The research also showed that fears about an adverse effect on market image were apparently groundless; on the contrary Nova received credit for conducting the recall honestly, this being the first time any company had conducted such a recall in Belgium. However, the market research also showed that, despite the extensive advertising, most consumers remained unaware that there ever was a defective product. For example, from a sample of 25 telephone subscribers in Flanders who owned deep-fat fryers, only nine had seen a further advertisement especially directed at that group on July 13 and only 10 saw yet another advertisement made on August 15.

Nonetheless, in the end after a number of repeats of the press advertising and additional publicity on radio and television the recall was extremely effective. The forty-seventh report issued by Nova on May 6, 1977 showed that all but 1570 of the Fritex 3s had then been accounted for in Belgium and all but 719 in the United Kingdom. In both cases well over 90 percent of the number sold had been recovered. This is an exceptional achievement; in the United States a return rate of 25 to 50 percent for a recall is considered very satisfactory. The professional marketing view was that "The remaining portion of the population of owners of defective Fritex 3s are a residual fragment that it is impossible to reach." Fortunately, as the population of Fritex 3s aged it became progressively more likely that failures would be by safe open circuit rather than unsafe short circuit.

In the end there were only two accidents with the Fritex 3: one involving personal injury and one involving damage to property, and the probability was that neither of them was in fact caused by a defective unit. The June 1977 issue of the Dutch consumer magazine *Consumentengids* gave an improved, safe Fritex the only "good" rating among the seven types of deep-fat fryers that were tested.

MAKING SAFE PRODUCTS

How could the problem with the Fritex 3 have been prevented? Well, proper application of design review and product qualification (see Chapter 5) would have greatly reduced the probability of its occurrence. Since 1972 ITT had had a policy, QU 11-0, requiring each new product to be subject to defined qualification tests. ITT also gave guidance to its units on design review. However, Nova was a small company which at that time had staffing weaknesses in its technical and quality departments, and the design change was suggested by a consultant unfamiliar with the requirements for product qualification. The fact that the Fritex 3 had been tested and approved by approval authorities in several countries only emphasizes that there is no adequate substitute for well-conducted internal qualification tests.

If design review had been conducted it would have revealed the lack of two important reliability analyses, "failure mode and effect analysis" and "fault tree analysis." If a product is dangerous it is usually because of a reliability problem. If a product is dangerously defective before it leaves the factory where it is manufactured, this will likely become apparent during inspection or functional testing. However, if it becomes dangerous only as a result of a reliability failure, it is much less likely to be detected. For example, the Fritex 3 was not dangerous until movement of the heating element allowed mains voltage to reach the aluminum casting, and the condition leading to this failure could not be observed by functional testing. Reliability improvement techniques, such as failure mode and effect analysis, are therefore valuable for safety improvement.

Table 10.6 shows the start of a failure mode and effect analysis as it might have been made on the Fritex 3. It is a "bottom-up" analysis. A primary component is selected and all of the possible ways it can fail—its failure modes—are envisioned, and also their causes. Then the effect of

TABLE 10.6. First Part of a Failure Mode and Effect Analysis of the Fritex 3 Deep Fat Fryer

Component Name	Function	Failure Mode and Cause	Effect of Failure on		Corrective Action
			Next Item	Product	
Heater coil	Heat heater unit	Break (Open circuit): (1) defective coil; (2) excessive voltage; (3) overheating due to bad thermal path	Heater unit: can heated	Inoperative	(1) None (2) None (3) Measure thermal resistance; improve design if necessary
Heater unit	Heat aluminum cast can	Open circuit: (1) broken coil; (2) detached lead connection	Aluminum cast can: not heated	Inoperative	(1) See above (2) Examine lead connection; improve design if necessary
		Short circuit to can: (1) detached lead connection; (2) heater unit rotates in casting channel	If main fuse blows, not heated; if main fuse does not blow, reaches main voltage	Inoperative

Becomes dangerous | (1) See above (2) Temperature cycle to examine likelihood; return to previous design if necessary |

each failure mode on the next item into which the primary component is assembled is determined, and the effect on the product itself. The analysis is repeated for the next item, and so on until the last item is the product itself. A second primary component is then selected and the analysis repeated until all of the primary components and all of the intermediate items have been examined. For each failure mode, possible actions to prevent the failure are examined. A decision is then made regarding whether or not to implement one or more of them. This decision is based on the probability of the failure occurring, the seriousness of its effect, and the cost of the correction and its probability of eliminating the cause of the failure. Some forms for recording the results of a failure mode and effect analysis include a column for probability of failure. However, usually this probability can only be guessed. Since most of the failures are reliability failures, the problem is compounded by the need to judge the ways in which the product may be used, and for how long. In practice, the best that can usually be done is to make some semiquantitative grouping of likely and unlikely failures. Obviously, the primary consideration is whether or not a failure mode is dangerous. If there is a practicable method of eliminating a dangerous failure mode that has been revealed by the analysis, it should be taken even if it is judged that the probability of failure is low.

Fault tree analysis is complimentary to failure mode and effect analysis. It is "top down" rather than bottom-up. It starts with a possible accident and defines the sequence of events necessary for the accident to occur. Figure 10.2 shows part of a fault tree analysis as it might have been performed on the Fritex 3. It uses symbols which are commonly applied to the logical analysis of electrical circuits. An AND gate indicates that the output will result only if one input AND another input are both present. An OR gate indicates that the output will result if either one input OR another input is present. NAND and NOR gates are similar to AND and OR gates respectively, but the output does not result rather than does result. The purpose of fault tree analysis is to enable identification of dangerous sequences of events so that corrective actions, such as improving the design or warning users, can be taken to break the sequences.

As with all other quality improvement activities the actions necessary to make products safe and reliable are unlikely to happen spontaneously or as a by-product, for example, of normal design activities. Rather, they must be explicitly managed. One important first step for product safety involves a division manager's appointment of one department head to be the division's Product Safety Coordinator and the establishment of a di-

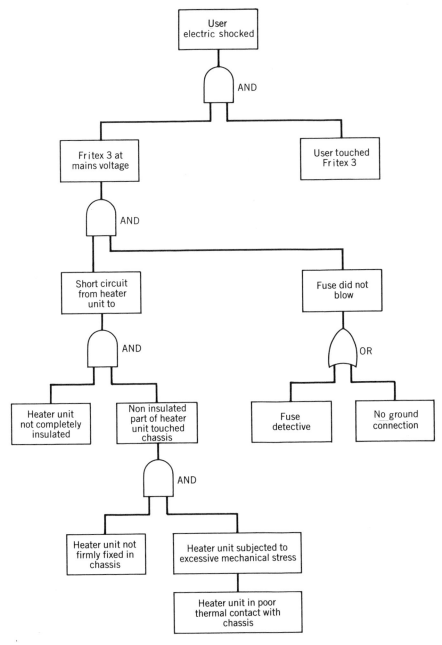

Figure 10.2. Part of a fault tree analysis of the Fritex 3 deep fat fryer.

TABLE 10.7. Departments Represented on Division Product Safety Improvement Committee

Marketing	Design/development
Manufacturing	Quality
Legal	Insurance
Public relations	Purchasing

vision Product Safety Improvement Committee. Table 10.7 shows the possible membership of such a committee. There should be meetings on a regular basis, monthly in the beginning and quarterly later on, to plan an examination of the safety aspects of current and future products. The committee also should review insurance provisions and the division's response to legal requirements. It should prepare contingency plans for dealing with a product recall or any other major product safety problem—because an actual problem requires urgent effective responses which are unlikely to occur if a division is unprepared. This committee should examine the training needs of division people and implement and manage the necessary program.

CONCLUSION

Perhaps the most common reason for a product falling short of the needs of the customer is its inadequate reliability or safety. There are two explanations for this. First, it is more difficult for a customer to determine the safety or reliability of a product than it is to assess its functional performance, appearance, and other immediate characteristics. If such characteristics are unappealing the product will not sell. The manufacturer, therefore, is forced to satisfy these particular aspects of the customer's need. However, the manufacturer may well be able to sell products with unsatisfactory safety or reliability because the customer cannot recognize this at the time of sale. Also, because reliability and safety are probabilistic, the majority of customers may have no problem with the product. This is no comfort though to the unlucky minority that do. The second reason for inadequate product reliability and safety is that making safe and reliable products, and measuring how safe and reliable they are, is difficult because functional testing does not usually work effectively for these characteristics. A company that is serious about quality improvement, therefore, has to give special attention to reliability and safety.

CHAPTER 11

MULTIFUNCTIONAL QUALITY IMPROVEMENT PROGRAMS

In previous chapters, evidence for the importance of product quality in determining business success has been presented and stressed, the two methods of measuring quality have been defined, the chain of conformance has shown the roles of the marketing, design-development, purchasing, and manufacturing functions in achieving superior product quality, and then in turn the quality aspects of each one of these functions was discussed. In contrast to this separate-function method of organizing the book, one of its continuing themes has been the need for multifunctional and cooperative approaches to quality improvement. In this chapter three specific quality improvement programs, each with a multifunctional emphasis, will be discussed. Two of these, zero defects and quality circles, are very well known, and reasons for discussing them again are partially for completeness—any book on quality improvement is seriously incomplete if it ignores these important subjects—and partially to present my evaluations since I have had experience in their application. The third program discussed is the engineering-based approach to quality improvement introduced by TRW's automotive sector.

"14 STEPS TO QUALITY IMPROVEMENT"

Zero defects was perhaps the earliest formal quality improvement program having as a major objective the involvement of all of the people in a business. Zero defects started in the Martin Company in 1961, applied to missiles for delivery to the U.S. government (33), and was formalized by P. B. Crosby (1). Crosby extended the concept after he became director quality of ITT. He defined an overall program of quality improvement in 14 steps, which incorporated the original zero defects ideas and went beyond them. He summarized his program in a booklet entitled, *Quality Improvement through Defect Prevention* published by ITT in 1967. In 1966 Crosby had shown me a draft of this work and later that year, when I became director quality of STC, ITT's main U.K. company, I suggested that the 14 step program be implemented as part of STC's contribution to the United Kingdom's 1966–67 "Quality and Reliability Year." Accordingly, work was started in a number of STC's divisions. Progress was made but, for reasons that will be discussed next, the divisions balked at first at the explicitly zero defects activities. It was another of ITT's companies, LMT in its Laval, France plant that actually conducted the first zero defects day in Western Europe. With that example, the switching division at New Southgate in London and then other STC divisions followed. Meanwhile, ITT's main West German company had picked up the program energetically. For the next 12 years, during the time that I was director quality, ITT Europe, Crosby's 14 step program was a major part of the company's quality activities. Outside of ITT, the program had an impressive vogue, including its adoption by Japanese companies (e.g., the Nippon Electric Company). In 1979, Crosby described the 14 step program in his book *Quality Is Free*, and after leaving ITT, started to introduce it to major companies through his new, highly successful, consulting business. As a consequence, in 1985, nearly 25 years after its inception, zero defects is in a new resurgence.

Before discussing Crosby's 14 step program it is useful to examine another important expression of his quality philosophy: the "absolutes of quality management." As defined in *Quality Is Free*, these are:

Quality means conformance not elegance.

There is no such thing as a quality problem.

There is no such thing as the economics of quality; it is always cheaper to do the job right the first time.

The only performance measurement is the cost of quality.

The only performance standard is zero defects.

This book has already taken a position on most of these statements, but it is useful to summarize them here. A detailed discussion of the meaning of quality can be found in Chapter 2 that concluded that product quality was indeed the "degree of conformance," but not just to the product requirement specification. Conformance had to be directed to the customer's need (and that need must be limited by price and delivery considerations).

With regard to quality problems, Crosby's statement is useful in emphasizing that quality problems are caused, not by the quality department, but by one or more of the other functions whose activities input into the chain of conformance (see Chapter 2), and only these departments can solve such problems. However, customers may legitimately refer to quality problems; it is not their responsibility to determine which of their supplier's departments caused a quality problem.

This book agrees with Crosby's statement about the economics of quality. Unfortunately, much of the quality profession and a number of business consultants do not. Hopefully, the detailed discussion given in Chapter 9 will help to convince them.

A major point of disagreement is Crosby's fourth statement about the cost of quality being the *only* performance measurement. This book emphasizes two measures of quality improvement: quality to the customer as well as quality costs. The major thrust of product quality improvement must be directed at the customer's need. Crosby rightly contends that a measurement must be measurable, and in Chapter 4 we showed how quality to the customer could be measured by comparison with competing products.

The last of Crosby's absolutes is that, "The only performance standard is zero defects." Many people have difficulty with this. The position of this book is that as a general statement of final purpose and as an expression of a refusal to compromise in establishing quality standards it is excellent. A careful semantic analysis reveals some problems, but such an analysis is not relevant to Crosby's purpose. (Such an analysis was made in Chapter 8 because it was needed to give a basis for a discussion of inspection and test planning. The difference between defects and failures was examined; it was shown that achievement of zero functional failures was not only practicable but necessary, and that achievement of "ppm" failure proportions was now a practical requirement for some products.)

Table 11.1 lists Crosby's 14 steps and I will now give my comments on each one in turn, based on 12 years of experience in the application of the program under Crosby's guidance, and six years of further experience since our association ended. The first step, management commitment, is fundamental to any effective philosophy of quality improvement. In this

TABLE 11.1.   Crosby's 14 Steps to Quality Improvement

1. Management commitment
2. Quality improvement team
3. Quality measurement
4. Cost of quality evaluation
5. Quality awareness
6. Corrective action
7. Establishment of an ad hoc committee for the zero defects program
8. Supervisor training
9. Zero defects day
10. Goal setting
11. Error cause removal
12. Recognition
13. Quality councils
14. Do it over again

book it has been emphasized repeatedly that quality improvement never happens automatically but must be planned and managed. It has also been pointed out that most of the energies of a real operating division go to performing its day-to-day tasks, and that only a small proportion is available for improvement, any improvement. Without real, tangible commitment and personal involvement from the division manager, it is virtually certain that the rate of quality improvement will be lower than that of any competitor whose management has that commitment.

A premise of this book is that quality improvement is the responsibility of a number of departments—it is not just a task of the quality department. Another premise is that improvement action is the most difficult part of the total process. Establishing a policy, performing training, motivating people, writing procedures, making measurements, performing analysis, drawing conclusions and so on, are all necessary and have their own difficulties and problems. But they do not cause actual improvement; they are precursors to the ultimate stage—the improvement or corrective action, that changes a design, that gets a new supplier, that improves a manufacturing process, that buys a new gauge of better sensitivity, and so on. Any division that is serious about quality improvement must have an organizational framework to manage and coordinate this difficult, interfunctional activity. Step 2, the quality improvement team (which may have other names) provides this framework. It is needed to establish priorities for action, record commitments, assign resources, and monitor progress. Its responsibilities embrace the unit's whole quality improvement program and it needs to be chaired by someone in authority (e.g., a plant manager).

Step 3 is quality measurement. Most quality improvement depends on the systematic accumulation and analysis of quantitative data. The importance of such measurements has been discussed throughout this book. It is the basis of both statistical process capability and control and it is the means by which good suppliers are identified from bad, and it enables the progress of good suppliers to be monitored as they improve. The opportunities for quality measurement in the marketing and design-development parts of the chain of conformance were described (more as a hope than an actuality). In the last chapter of this book the possibility of quality measurement and improvement away from activities directly associated with the product will be covered. Crosby embraces this wide scope for the use of quality measurement.

Step 4 is cost of quality. A detailed description of this subject has been given in Chapter 3. The next step is quality awareness. This is the first lead-in to the zero defects parts of the program. One aspect is a low-key, continuous advertising program, that uses posters, articles in the unit's newspaper, and so on, to raise awareness about quality improvement. Equally as important is the completion, under the supervision of the quality improvement team, of management controlled quality improvement projects, and discussion of successes between management and employees. In doing this, the employees will gain confidence in management's genuine dedication to quality improvement; otherwise, the quality awareness activities may lead them to believe that they are involved in some short-term motivational gimmick.

As previously noted, corrective action is central to any quality improvement program, and Step 6 gives a specific approach. Encouraged by the quality awareness program, employees bring problems that are causing them to make defects to the attention of their immediate supervisors. Where possible, the supervisors effect solutions. Wherever the solution is beyond their capability, others are involved, with some problems going to the quality improvement team.

The next two steps—ad hoc committee for the zero defects program, and supervisor training—are where the 14 step program becomes specific about zero defects, and where many units start to have problems. The first six steps of the 14 step program cover in a well thought-out, systematic way, activities that are important for any serious quality improvement program. Readers of this book may recognize that they provide only a framework for many of the subjects covered in earlier chapters, but it is a valuable and largely noncontroversial framework. Zero defects *is* controversial. I believe most quality professionals are opposed to it. The reasons given include dislike of the ballyhoo associated with zero defects day, opinions that such activities are not a proper part of a "serious" quality program, intuitions about the "impossibility of zero defects" (of the kind I analyzed in the context of inspection and test planning, but which I think are irrelevant to zero defects programs), and, in some countries, "because zero defects is incompatible with our national culture." My opinion is that these "reasons" are just rationalizations. I have said before that people do the same things week after week, and when they select the small proportion of new activities, a key consideration in their decision is what they want to do. But for the vast majority of quality professionals (and I write as one of them), running a zero defects program is not one of those things. It does not turn them on at all. On the contrary, the whole idea usually generates negative emotions. In fact, having personally seen zero defects day operated successfully in many different countries (each with its different, national flavor, but in none a serious problem) I can testify that the employees always had a good time, the managers found it to be a great opportunity for exercising visible, personal leadership, and customers and local government officers participated willingly with approval. Provided the managers of the division really were serious about quality improvement, and had proved this by their previous actions, there were no negative effects. Zero defects day gave a valuable ceremonial boost to the quality improvement program and provided a useful planning milestone which helped to keep the overall program on schedule. One small point: the zero defects pledge often causes alarm to the ad hoc committee, and many units avoid its use. This is unimportant since alternatives, such as personal letters from the division manager to every employee, seem to work just as well. Perhaps, a practical approach is to delegate the management of zero defects day to people in marketing or human relations who may be more comfortable with such occasions than quality people. In any case, the full involvement and training of the first-level supervisors in the part they play in the zero defects activities (Step 8) is vital to the success of the program. Crosby also properly emphasizes the need for participation of the employees' representatives.

Despite my experience with the successful application of zero defects in Europe, I have not felt it useful during the past five years to push the idea at TRW. The climate of opinion has been much more conducive to quality circles than zero defects, and, following the precept that a staff person should facilitate programs whose time is right, we have supported the former. At the same time, many of the non zero defects steps of Crosby's program have been an intrinsic part of the TRW quality philosophy—management commitment, quality improvement teams, quality costs, quality measurement (called "quality performance indicators"), corrective action, recognition, and quality councils.

After zero defects day, there is a need to take advantage of the high level of quality awareness created. The next two steps give specific methods for achieving this. In goal setting, each group within the unit establishes its own targets for defect level reduction, using the already established quality measurements. The goals must be measurable and the targets must have specific achievement dates. Each group should reach a consensus with the supervisor managing the process (rather than imposing an objective). The other method is called error cause removal. In the terminology of this book, employees are asked to define the problems that cause them to blunder, thereby making defects. They are not required to propose solutions to the problems—though, if they wish, they may do so.

Step 12 is recognition. Unfortunately, it is human nature to criticize people when they blunder and take it for granted when they do things correctly. In the work context, this attitude is sometimes rationalized by saying people are "paid to do the job right," thereby removing any credit for doing so, and making it a duty to punish any failure to do so. Whatever its logic, this is poor management. Professional managers suppress their natural tendency to criticize unnecessarily and train themselves to give recognition. The 14 step program formalizes this important concept. It emphasizes nonmonetary methods of recognition. There is little advantage in complicating normal wage and salary increase and bonus methods of giving recognition—and such methods are no substitute for expressions of thanks and public praise. At ITT, recognition methods ranged from a little ceremony conducted by a West German plant manager every Friday to great, annual "ring of quality" dinners in New York City and Brussels. In the former, the plant manager toured his manufacturing lines and presented a red sticker to any operator who had made no defect that week; a defect-free month received a gold sticker. Such was his charm and good humor that this was a happy and positive end to the week.

Because the 14 steps comprise explicit completeable activities, the end of the program is eventually reached. What should then happen? Crosby's answer is given in the fourteenth step: Do it over again. I suggest that the quality improvement program be allowed to enter a quieter phase: to concentrate on retaining the lower defect levels that have resulted from the program, and develop new specific projects for improving quality to the customer and reducing quality costs under the continuing management of the quality improvement team, but not to continue to emphasize the more public steps. Then, two or three years later, the whole program can be reestablished with a new ad hoc committee planning a new zero defects day in its own way, and conducting the supervisor training, target setting, error cause removal and recognition steps.

Crosby's thirteenth step, quality councils, has been left to the end because it differs from the others. These steps are all concerned with conducting a multifunctional quality improvement program within a particular unit of a company. Quality circles are a means of establishing peer level communication between the unit quality managers of a company. When I was a division quality manager during the 1960s my company had no quality councils. Thus, I never met its other quality managers. The two other divisions on the same site had quality managers, but we never talked. I knew the quality managers of competitors and customers, but not those of my own company. Later on, at Crosby's suggestion, we established quality councils. In ITT Europe we had perhaps a dozen such councils. These were a principal means of communication across the function, of enabling the quality managers to know each other personally, and of establishing a functional esprit de corps. We have used the same system in TRW.

As conceived by Crosby, quality councils are self-managing. They elect their own chairpeople and secretaries and arrange their own programs and meetings. For an organization as large and complicated as ITT Europe, it was the practice to have a top council whose membership was the 10 or 15 staff quality directors of the major national companies and international groups. There was a matrix of regional councils, West German, Scandinavian, British, and so on, and product councils, electronic switching, consumer products, and so on. In practice, it took considerable effort from the four-member quality staff in Brussels to keep the system operating and viable. It was not necessary for us to participate in every meeting, but the quality council system is inherently fragile, and without staff support, most councils will cease to operate in a year or two. It is not so much that they are killed by management decision—though this does happen in times of budget stringency—as that they are undermined by their membership. The members get little positive credit for their participation from their local line managers, though the good managers give necessary support, and the effort required is extra to that required by normal duties—and to be chairperson or secretary of a council is a significant responsibility. Some quality managers are unwilling to supply that effort and may feel inadequate in the presence of their peers. Another problem is one of unrealistic expectations. Only occasionally will a quality council carry through a serious project to completion, and in some of these cases the reality is that an important part of the work is done by the quality staff. The benefits of quality councils are mainly in shared experience, emulation, as a forum for communication between line and staff, and for psychological support.

QUALITY CIRCLES

Quality circles started in Japan, and a very good history of their application in that country is given by Professor Ikuro Kusaba (34) of which this paragraph is a summary. A quality control research group, set up by the Japanese Union of Scientists and Engineers (JUSE) in 1949, started to study statistical techniques for quality control. Quality control was promoted strongly by visits of Dr. W. E. Deming in 1950 and Dr. J. M. Juran in 1954. Before 1960, efforts in promoting quality control were oriented at managers and engineers. In 1960, JUSE published *QC Text for Foremen,* and started in 1962 the periodical, *QC for Foremen.* The objective of the latter's editorial board was to get foremen and workers to study the concepts and techniques of quality control. To this end they suggested that their readers establish groups named QC Circles to read the periodical together. They also asked each QC Circle to register with the JUSE. The first QC Circles were registered in 1962 and by 1980 the number of registered circles had risen to 120,000. Kusaba estimated that there were at least 10 times that number of unregistered circles, which would suggest that Japan has perhaps 10 million circle members.

Japanese writers always emphasize that QC Circles is only one aspect of their country's quality activities and Kusaba includes it among the following:

1. Companywide QC with all the members participation.
2. Diagnosis and audit of QC, especially made by the top management of the company.
3. Vigorous education and training.
4. QC Circle activities.
5. Excellent application of statistical methods.
6. Nationwide QC promotion activities.

Kusaba states that the foreman is usually the leader of a newly established QC Circle, but when it is well established it may elect its own leader with the foreman acting as advisor. Circles typically meet once or twice a month for half to one hour.

Through the meeting, understanding of their own jobs is deepened, better human relations and the leader's leadership is established, and the members' participation-consciousness and fellowship-consciousness are highly developed. Furthermore, the ways to solve the problems by using quality control techniques are rightly understood by them.

Although Japanese QC Circles do not work exclusively on product quality it is their prime focus. Kusaba quotes a study of one set of meetings which showed that quality was the subject of the meeting 53 times, cost 32 times, and other topics a smaller number of times. National and regional QC Circle conferences are held in Japan. In the presentations at these conferences the use of simple quality control techniques has been a main topic. Kusaba states, "Without the QC techniques the QC Circles could not attain the objects of their activities." He lists the Ishikawa diagram,* graphs, and Pareto charts as the most-used techniques.

In the United States, no single body, like the Japanese JUSE with its central registry, has participated in the introduction of quality circles. Nonetheless, the level of adoption of quality circles has been very high. As many as half of the large manufacturing companies of the country have used quality circles, and this makes it the most widely used of all such systems.

There are important differences between its application in the United States and Japan. One difference is that in the United States leadership has come from people with a human relations or productivity background not from quality professionals. In Japan, JUSE, despite its name, is primarily a quality organization, and it has always emphasized the professional quality aspects of the program. In the United States, the orientation of quality circles has often been toward personal interactions and group dynamics, and as much attention has been given to quality of work life and productivity as to product quality. Wayne S. Reicker, of Quality Control Circles, Inc., in a paper presented at the American Society of Quality Control's 1982 conference, said that the "ASCQ has not been a particularly strong supporter of QC Circles, nor has it helped to give the movement a quality thrust." Another U.S. innovation has been the use of "facilitators." When the managers of a company or division wish to establish quality circles they normally appoint one person to be the facilitator. This person receives training from specialized consultants and then works with the various groups who have volunteered to establish circles. The facilitator trains the circle leaders (in TRW for 20 hours), participates in the circle meetings, and acts as a link between the circle members and the company's management. In U.S. industry most such facilitators have previously worked in human relations or communications, not quality.

On the whole, quality circles have been enormously successful. The fact that such a high proportion of companies employ quality circles shows that, using the facilitator approach, they are relatively easy to in-

---

* For cause and effect analysis.

troduce. TRW has several hundred quality circles. An early application was in the high technology, defense units based on Los Angeles. These circles helped by their facilitator, Dale Miller, have worked successfully for up to five years. More than half of them are for white-collar employees, and several are exclusively for engineers.

At the TRW Quality College, we ask different groups to be protagonists and antagonists of Crosby's 14 step program and quality circles respectively, and, after a period of analysis and reflection, to debate their positions. Some of the results are as follows. The success of both is dependent on "management commitment." This is explicit for 14 steps, but is equally important for quality circles. Some people believe that quality circles can succeed without management support. This is fallacious thinking. Also, one of the important limitations on the growth of quality circles is management's capability to respond to problems that are identified by the circles. Some problems are solvable by the people in a particular circle, using the resources available to them, but others will not be. They require the work of engineers, expenditures on capital equipment, cooperation with other circles, and so on, and all of these require action from management. Again, the 14 steps require establishment of a multifunctional, management-level quality improvement team. Quality circles do not; but in practice, such a team is virtually essential for responding to issues raised by the quality circles. Both systems emphasize the accumulation and systematic display of quality data, typically the number and categories of defects. In the 14 steps, such data is thereby brought to the attention of the workers, and they establish targets for reduction in the number of defects—mainly by exercising extra care. Defect causes that cannot be addressed by this method may be addressed through the error-cause removal step. In quality circles, especially the Japanese variety, defects are attacked by standard quality control techniques such as Pareto analysis and cause and effect analysis.

The quality circle methodology does not include quality costs. The use of quality costs, to define, prioritize, and monitor quality improvement projects, is a major advantage of 14 steps. One of the problems with quality circles is that energy may be wasted on trivialities, and major opportunities may not be addressed. Again, "recognition" is an explicit part of 14 steps, but is equally important for quality circles. One opportunity for members of a quality circle to receive recognition is by presenting the results of their work to the division or plant manager. Such a prentation may be the only chance first-level employees have to communicate directly—in a very positive setting—with a senior company manager.

Training is a topic where the two approaches significantly differ. The

14 steps includes only "supervisor training," where concentration is given to their gaining an understanding of the concept of zero defects and the part they must play in zero defects day. Quality circles places major emphasis on training in both human interaction skills and simple quality control techniques, with U.S. circles emphasizing the former and Japanese circles the latter.

Overall, many of the TRW groups that have contrasted the two approaches conclude that it is most practical and effective to utilize elements from both 14 steps and quality circles. But they also conclude—as the Japanese have always emphasized—that either 14 steps, quality circles, or a combination of the two, is not enough for a rich and comprehensive quality philosophy.

TRW AUTOMOTIVE'S "TOTAL QUALITY OBJECTIVE"

The third approach is one developed by R. M. Lynas, executive vice president and general manager of TRW's automotive sector, and codified by the sector's director, quality, R. A. Jones in a handbook (35) published in August 1985. For a number of years Lynas has managed TRW operating divisions in North America, Europe, and Japan. His approach to quality is based on his observations of the different managerial approaches in the three areas, and their effect on quality. He discusses his total quality objective under the headings, management, engineering, and control. Lynas contends that in the United States, work on quality has concentrated on control, and the balance needs to be redressed by changing management practices—not just quality management practices—which are detrimental to quality, and by emphasizing engineering. In the past, the automotive industry used "control" as a synonym for inspection and test. Lynas is obviously correct in his contention that a company that utilizes only inspection and testing for quality improvement has a very limited program for achieving that objective. However, he goes further. Even statistical process control will have limited effectiveness unless proper management practices are applied, and the product, process, and workplace are all properly engineered. Lynas emphasizes the critical importance of thorough work practices by all of the engineering functions (see Table 11.2) for the achievement of superior quality. In many instances, significant quality improvements can be realized, even with an existing plant or an existing product line, by a detailed engineering review of prod-

TABLE 11.2.   Activities Included in "Engineering for Quality"

General
    Design review
Product engineering
    Design failures modes and effects analysis
    Contact point analysis
    Product design interrelationship
    Identification of critical characteristics
    Product qualification
    Reliability prediction
Manufacturing engineering
    Process balance analysis
    Process failure modes and effects analysis
    Locating point analysis
    Capability index analysis
    Tool life cycle development
    Machine tool set-up analysis
    Operator responsibility for tool quality
    Tool breakage analysis
    Analysis of variables
Plant engineering
    Preventive maintenance program
    Machine start-up and shut-down procedures
    Machine/tool overload monitoring
    Machine build/rebuild capability
Industrial engineering
    Material handling
    General process analysis
    Performance standards
    Capital justification verification
Quality engineering
    Source selection and supplier development
    Operator responsibility for quality
    Test and inspection planning

uct and equipment design, workplace layout, material handling, tool control, and preventive maintenance, coupled with better training of operators and use of their talents. He contends that statistical process control—identifying and correcting special causes of variation—might not effect many of such improvements.

Clearly, even better results are likely when Lynas' principles are applied in setting up new processes or making new products, particularly when they are coupled with determinations of the capabilities of every manufacturing process before designs are frozen or equipments purchased.

The total quality objective requires each division to review the effect of all of its management practices on product quality. It categorizes such practices in three tiers: shop floor, plant/division, and group/sector/company. Table 11.3 lists examples of practices in each tier. Priority should be given to items in the first tier, because these are the easiest to change.

The handbook recommends that many tasks now performed by specialists in the interests of job simplification should be returned to operators. It lists: inspection, tool inspection, equipment calibration, machine set-up and adjustment, machine maintenance (lubrication and cleaning), tool grinding, and machine and equipment repair. As operators diversify their skills, they can be organized in self-sufficient work cells, and can rotate between different functions. Such an objective requires major programs of training, skill evaluation, and compensation enhancement. Performance measurement for individuals and groups should be changed to emphasize quality rather than quantity. Unnecessary distinctions between groups of employees, and unnecessary restrictions on their activities should be eliminated. In particular, practices which imply mistrust of employees—time clocks, cafeteria buzzers, and so on—should be abandoned. Employee involvement programs, which follow the principles discussed earlier in this chapter, are strongly encouraged.

Lynas recommends avoidance of three-shift operation unless essential, because it results either in curtailing preventive maintenance or waste of resources while it is performed in production time. Two-shift operation with a three hour period after each shift for maintenance, tool changes, and so on, is preferred. The section on management practices concludes with requirements for supplier quality improvement and quality strategic planning (see Chapters 8 and 12).

The total quality objective emphasizes "engineering for quality," but it also states:

> It is important that every opportunity be taken by the engineering departments to invite and make use of contributions from operators and first level supervision. These individuals are often the most knowledgeable of all concerning the manufacturing processes, and their input must not be ignored.

Table 11.3 shows the list of activities concerned with engineering for quality. Many of these topics have been discussed already. Those that have not include contact point analysis and product design interrelationship. For contact point analysis, "the product engineer carries out a formal study of the fit at each point of contact between components in an

TABLE 11.3.   Management Practices Affecting Product Quality

Tier I	Shop floor
	Timekeeping
	Timing/compensation
	Work rules
	Skilled trade rules
	Operator responsibilities
	Classification system
Tier II	Plant/division
	Standard cost system
	Organization
Tier III	Group/sector/company
	Labor contracts
	Purchasing policy

assembly taking into consideration the tolerances of each component dimension contributing to that fit." The criteria for acceptability of the range of a fit must take into account not only the ability to assemble the components, but also the performance characteristics of the resulting assembly. For the latter, "product design interrelationship requires the product engineer to search for and review the use of existing parts in new applications. Also new designs should be reviewed to identify interrelationships with prior designs." Similarly, commonality with previously (and successfully) used manufacturing processes is recommended.

Several of the manufacturing engineering activities not already discussed are concerned with tools—life cycles, set-up analysis, operator responsibility, and breakage analysis. The total quality objective requires the manufacturing engineers to "establish tool life cycles and replacement schedules which will ensure that tools are replaced before the possibility of defective product occurs. . . . Where possible life cycles sufficient to permit tool changes only between shifts or during meal breaks should be developed." Set-up analysis is used to prevent set-up blunders which "result in poor quality parts" and long set-up times which "result in low productivity due to machine downtime and also cause large work in process inventories and scheduling difficulties." In order to give operators responsibility for tool quality, "the manufacturing engineer should provide the necessary equipment, gauges, and prints; and operators should be trained in the evaluation of tools." To prevent tool breakage the:

Manufacturing engineer must be knowledgeable of critical tool applications and should clearly define the limits of correct usage beyond which tool breakage will occur. [He] should develop shop floor reporting systems to report on and investigate all tool breakage incidents from which a history of tool breakage can be complied . . . (and) engineering resources can be directed to solving the problems.

Under plant engineering activities, a similar theme covers preventive maintenance, start-up and shut-down procedures and machine and tool overload monitoring.

Some industrial engineering practices can be detrimental to quality. To prevent this the industrial engineer should plan for a minimum of material movement and handling, with little or no movement of material out of and back into a technology cell.

All systems must be designed to prevent damage to material and to prevent any possibility of material mix. . . . Any performance measurement system should emphasize first-time-through quality, and not pieces per hour. Industrial engineering should develop performance measurement systems which give maximum credit for continuous production of acceptable product.

A powerful incentive for application of these precepts is the requirement that large capital investment programs will only be approved after industrial engineering has verified "that all designated engineering-for-quality technologies have been addressed."

These extracts illustrate the special flavor of the total quality objective. The quality engineering part of the engineering for quality section, and the quality control systems section both cover activities—statistical process capability and control, quality performance indicators, quality to the customer, quality costs, inspection and test planning, usage of multifunctional quality improvement teams, and so on—that are discussed in detail elsewhere.

CONCLUSION

Three distinct, important approaches to quality improvement have been described in this chapter. Although they differ in many ways, and reflect the ideas and personalities of their originators, they include many common themes: the preeminent importance of quality improvement, its never-ending nature, the necessity of management commitment and leadership, the need for universal involvement, the requirements of effective horizontal communication, and finally, the need to achieve a balance between the technological and people aspects of quality improvement.

CHAPTER **12**

ORGANIZING AND PLANNING FOR QUALITY IMPROVEMENT

Current high-circulation books on business management fail to address the issue of the organization of large companies. They write of the importance of a "simple elegant structure." They discuss the need for elimination of staff and approvingly mention some major companies which have reduced the number of staff employees to 100 or less. But, they do not define the functions of these people.

I will discuss the subject from the perspective of one who has been a member of such organizations for many years. The companies I have worked for have been explicitly decentralized. I believe that all large companies are actually decentralized whatever their organizational philosophy, because people at the lower levels continue to function the way they always have, change in ways that suit them, and are influenced by the upper levels of the company only in particular ways.

Large decentralized companies consist essentially of two parts, operating divisions and a superstructure of line and staff managers. Companies which design and manufacture products usually have a classic hierarchical organization. Matrix, task force, and other types of organizational approaches usually apply only in companies that are working on large-scale projects.

ORGANIZATION OF AN OPERATING DIVISION

One simple, elegant structure for an operating division in a manufacturing company is illustrated in Figures 12.1 and 12.2. In establishing this structure the following rules were used:

1. Everyone is either a supervisor or a worker
2. First level manufacturing supervisors have a standard span of control of 20
3. All other supervisors have a standard span of control of six
4. Workers can appear at all levels in the organization, not just the bottom level
5. Workers have no more than two people reporting to them, and these people have no one reporting to them

Other schemes of this kind often use the categories: managers, supervisors, workers, and "individual contributors." At the start of my career I worked as a scientist. An important scientific principle, called "Occam's razor," states that if two theories explain the same experimental results the simpler explanation is the better of the two. Similarly, it is better to use two categories, workers and supervisors, instead of four if the result is the same. Also, it does not seem proper semantics to exclude individual contributors from management. For example, I have been responsible for managing the quality activities of major companies for many years, but as a worker, not as a supervisor. Another advantage of the categorization into workers and supervisors is that the output of the division can be seen as the result of the total activity of the workers. The supervisors do not contribute directly to the output; they have their positive effect by increasing the effectiveness of their subordinate workers, both those supervised directly and those reporting to subordinate supervisors, and by representing the results of their workers' efforts to their own bosses and peers. When a manager contributes directly to output (e.g., when a sales manager deals personally with a customer, he or she is acting as a worker not a supervisor).

The organization that is illustrated in Figures 12.1 and 12.2 employs over 1000 people. If the division manager and operating manager are allowed to be considered as an "office of the division manager," there are only four levels from this office through the bottom level workers in the division headquarters, and five through the workers in the plants. By including secretaries, and adding another plant and extra plant depart-

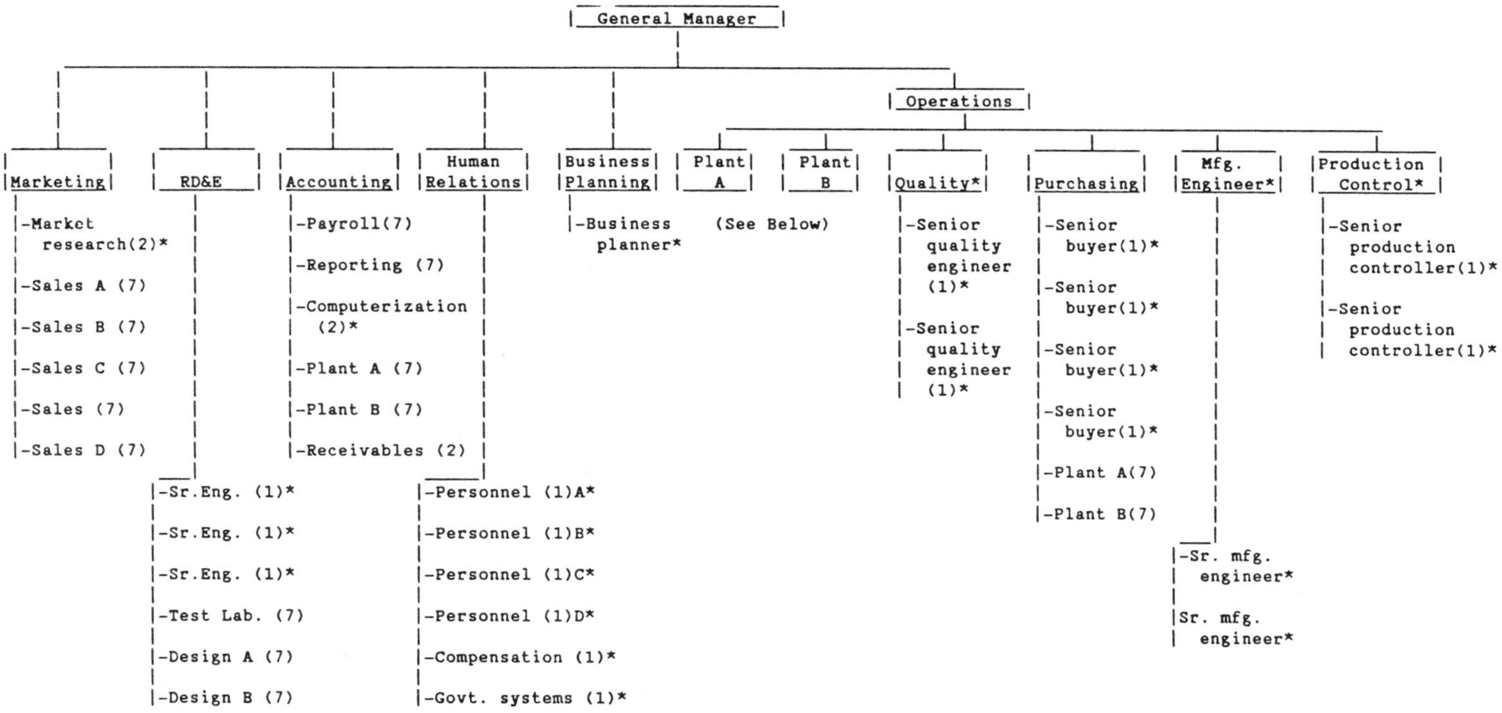

Figure 12.1. Model divisional organization.

( ) Numbers of people

* High-level workers

Total number of people on chart - 142

305

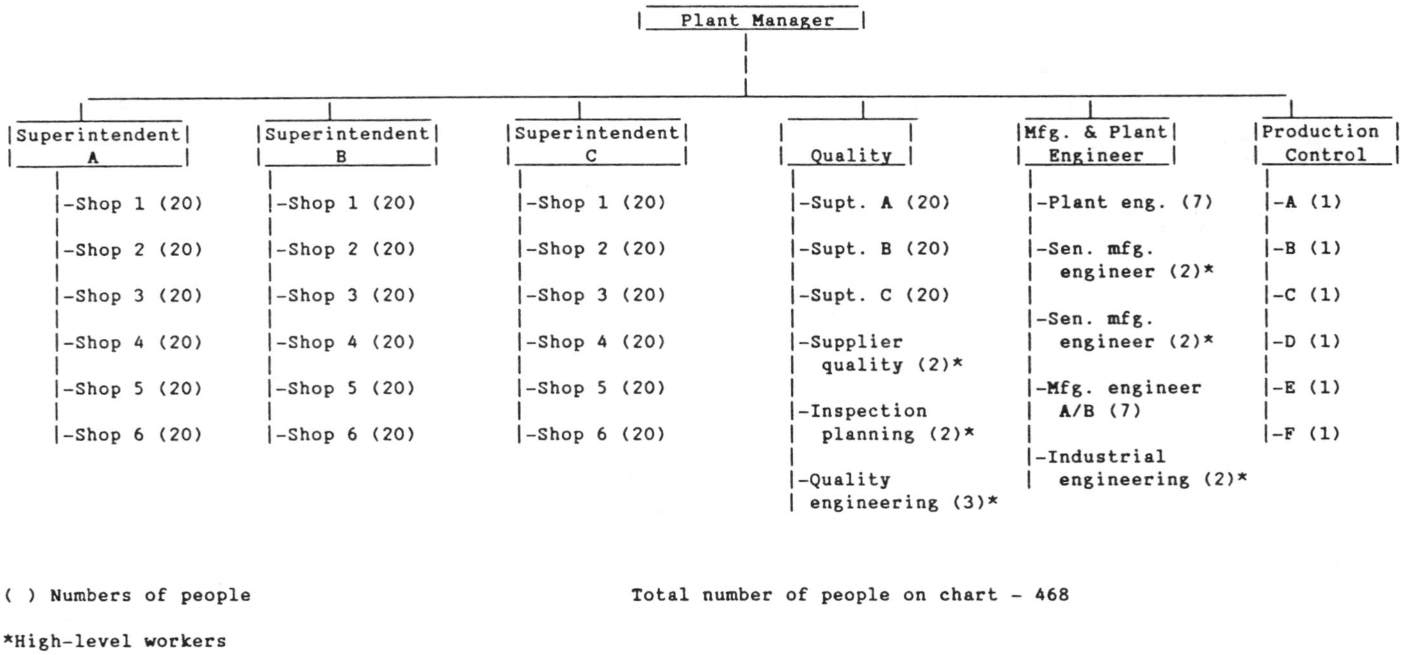

Plant Manager

Superintendent A
- Shop 1 (20)
- Shop 2 (20)
- Shop 3 (20)
- Shop 4 (20)
- Shop 5 (20)
- Shop 6 (20)

Superintendent B
- Shop 1 (20)
- Shop 2 (20)
- Shop 3 (20)
- Shop 4 (20)
- Shop 5 (20)
- Shop 6 (20)

Superintendent C
- Shop 1 (20)
- Shop 2 (20)
- Shop 3 (20)
- Shop 4 (20)
- Shop 5 (20)
- Shop 6 (20)

Quality
- Supt. A (20)
- Supt. B (20)
- Supt. C (20)
- Supplier quality (2)*
- Inspection planning (2)*
- Quality engineering (3)*

Mfg. & Plant Engineer
- Plant eng. (7)
- Sen. mfg. engineer (2)*
- Sen. mfg. engineer (2)*
- Mfg. engineer A/B (7)
- Industrial engineering (2)*

Production Control
- A (1)
- B (1)
- C (1)
- D (1)
- E (1)
- F (1)

( ) Numbers of people

*High-level workers

Total number of people on chart – 468

Figure 12.2. Model plant organization.

ments, the number of people accommodated could increase to 1500 or more with no extra organizational levels. Such a division could have sales of $100 million. A four/five level organization of considerable size is achieved in spite of using only a moderate span of control number, six, and filling many of the places with high-level workers.

It is important to minimize the number of levels in an organization. Doing this greatly aids communication from top to bottom and vice versa. At least as important is that it helps horizontal communication by increasing the number of peers at each level, and the formal and informal communications between networks of peers are key means of organizing and coordinating the execution of complex tasks. In the organization shown in Figures 12.1 and 12.2, the 11 people reporting to the division and operating managers obviously form one important communication network, and the 50 odd people at the next level another.

It is noteworthy that the chain of conformance (Chapter 2) can be put on its side and then superimposed on an organizational chart—showing that *products* move horizontally across the chart from the marketing department, to the design-development department, to the purchasing department, and then to the manufacturing department. Of course, there must be a corresponding flow of information between peers in these departments. It is also likely that communication between peers is the easiest and most creative of all business communications. Because of the influence that pecking order has on human psychology, supervisors communicate very freely with their subordinates, but subordinates are somewhat inhibited in their communications with their direct supervisors, and will communicate with their boss's boss only in strictly limited ways. The fewer the number of levels there are in an organization the less communication is restricted by the effect of such inhibitions, and the more peers there are at each level to communicate freely. This discussion also reinforces the perception of the importance of formal quality improvement devices for horizontal communication, including design review meetings, quality improvement teams, quality councils, and quality circles.

Another reason for minimizing the number of organizational levels is because of the special importance of three-level and five-level organizations. This importance arises from the fact that people two levels apart in an organization will know each other personally and are likely to have direct communication fairly often. We all know our boss' boss and we all know the people working for our direct subordinates. Conversely, personal contact between people separated by more than two levels in an organization is likely to be infrequent and formal. Approval activities are very important at two-level separation. We approve (or disapprove) the key actions that affect the people reporting to our own direct subordinates, and our boss's bosses do the same for us. Additional approvals by levels that are further removed give rapidly diminishing returns. With a three-level organization everyone knows everyone personally. Even for a five-level organization, the people at the third-level know up to the top manager and down to their own workers—and they have their peer network for horizontal communication.

These organizational principles seem theoretically sound. Why is the practice usually so different? It is because the theoretical organization is very unnatural and it will exist only if some champion has managed effectively to make it exist. Most company organizations arise pragmatically rather than in response to theory. It is hard to change this bias because in the United States and the United Kingdom pragmatism is admired more than theory.

Organizations build up more than the optimum number of levels for several natural, pragmatic reasons. First let's assume that the division illustrated in Figures 12.1 and 12.2 is very successful. Its sales grow rapidly and it makes good profits. The number of people increases from 1000 to 1500 and it opens another manufacturing plant. It continues to grow and reaches 2000 people. Clearly, some organizational change must take place. Theory indicates the division should split into two, a second division manager should be appointed reporting to the group vice president or company president depending on the size of the company, the plants should be assigned to one or other of the two new divisions, and the functional departments should each be split. What is much more likely to happen is that the division manager will appoint three subdivision managers who are responsible for the RDE and marketing of particular groups of products for particular customers, and that the other functions including manufacturing will provide services to the three subdivisions. (It is interesting to note that usually three subdivisions rather than two are formed. This could be because a line span of control of two is so obviously wrong, or it could be that the division manager does not want to make the subdivision managers too powerful.) Changing in this way directly adds a level to the organization, and some of the functional departments may add another level because of their growth in size. The only person who really cares about the division organization is likely to be the division manager, and he or she has no motivation at all to give away half of the empire. Another involved party, the group vice president, knows that this is a very successful division run by a strong-minded, highly competent division manager. Why should the vice president antagonize the latter by forcing the relinquishment of half of the operation, and entrust that half to an unproven manager who might turn out to be incompetent? What sensible person would incur all of that trouble for a theory?

Another reason for complex organizations is that it is natural to establish organizations on a functional basis. Consider a plant quality department. Functionally organized it might have a test section, an inspection section, and a quality engineering section. The first two sections would have supervisors between the section heads and the workers, and the quality engineering section head would have a couple of quality engineers working for him or her. The organization could be changed so that four inspection or test supervisors and three quality engineers all reported directly to the plant quality manager. The reorganization eliminates an organizational level, and would undoubtedly work better than the alternative, but it seems very unnatural and experience indicates it would probably not be adopted.

A third reason concerns high level work. I have suggested that organizations are made up of workers and supervisors. Supervision involves a limited number of activities whereas work can have countless different forms. Work activities are performed not only at the bottom level of the organization; many work activities are performed at higher levels. In Figure 12.1, for example, I show the activities of business planning, market research, and accounting computerization all being actually performed, not supervised, at high levels in the divisional organization. Most managers perform some mixture of generalized supervisory activities and specialized work activities. In a natural organization most high level work is done as a part time activity by supervisors. It seems that the majority of managers like that arrangement. After all, they studied for many years to become an engineer or an accountant, and then practiced their profession for several more years. Do they want to withdraw from all of those activities and just be a supervisor? If they have 6 to 10 people reporting directly to them (and the latter control many people also) they will have little choice because their supervisory responsibilities will take up almost all of their time. On the other hand, with only three or four direct subordinates, significant time will be available for the practice of their profession. With a minimum level organization, it is necessary explicitly to incorporate individual high level workers or groups of two or three such workers. (A senior professional with a younger professional assistant can often output an extraordinary amount of work if both are able and energetic.)

In his book, *Management in Action*, W. D. Hilt (36) states that the "functions of the manager are fairly well agreed upon by the management theorists" and gives them as planning, organizing, staffing and staff

TABLE 12.1.   List of Activities of a Supervisor

1. Select and appoint direct subordinates
2. Participate in selection of, and approve, next level subordinates
3. Conduct similar activities for dismissals
4. Define scope of direct subordinates within own scope
5. Review and approve work plans and specific proposals (e.g., capital investments) of direct subordinates
6. Monitor subordinates' work (e.g., by discussion and by reading monthly progress reports)
7. Reward subordinates doing good work and punish those doing bad work (more often by praise and criticism than materially)
8. Coordinate activities of direct subordinates (e.g., by conducting weekly "staff meetings")
9. Cause subordinates to respond quickly, effectively, and in a coordinated way to changed external circumstances
10. Train, guide, and counsel direct subordinates and subordinates one level removed
11. Give leadership and motivation to whole department
12. Represent department in activities analogous to numbers 4 to 9 with own boss and peers

development, motivating, and controlling. On the whole, supervisory activities are easier to comprehend—I have listed a typical set of such activities in Table 12.1—and the nonsupervisory aspects of management are likely to be specialized. All managers are familiar with supervision—they give it and receive it—and I do not feel I have any special perceptions to impart, except to make one comment about motivation and leadership. My experience is that most people are self-motivated to do a good job, and that that is certainly true of the best workers. The leaders and supervisors of such people more often than not demotivate them rather than motivate them—by carelessly revealing their lack of appreciation for good work, giving recognition to one peer and not to another equally deserving, arbitrarily changing assignments or organization, by criticizing unjustly or in public (even if justified) and so on. After such an incident, it may take days or weeks before a subordinate's self-motivation returns to its natural high level. Perhaps, leadership is as much the professional avoidance of such negatives as positive charisma.

ORGANIZATION OF A QUALITY DEPARTMENT

Within an operating division, are there organizational factors special to the quality department? Should there be a quality department at all, or should quality activities be carried out within other functional departments? If the division's quality philosophy is one of quality assurance the answer is clear cut. In its essence, a philosophy of quality assurance requires that all activities affecting product quality must be defined in process specifications. The people performing these activities are supposed to follow the specifications. To assure that they do, an *independent* group of people is made responsible for checking. Similarly, all of the requirements of the product must be defined in a product requirement specification, and, when all of the design, purchasing, manufacturing, testing, and inspection activities needed to achieve conformance of the product to this specification are completed, an independent group of people check that it does. (A quality assurance system is no panacea because it is difficult to define many key activities or to get people to follow the definition—e.g., in design—and the methods of independently checking activities and products for conformance can be either costly or ineffective.) The independent group doing the checking is normally either the customer (or agents of the customer) or the supplier's quality assurance department. If the supplier's quality assurance department is doing the checking, the department should clearly be as independent as practicable, which means that the division quality manager must report to the division quality manager. In principle, 100 percent screening inspections and tests to find defects should be done by manufacturing, with the quality assurance people doing separate, independent assurance tests and inspections. In practice, such duplicated inspection is very expensive even if it is done by sampling (when it is not very effective). Sometimes the quality assurance people will take over the 100 percent screening inspections and tests and omit the acceptance sampling.

For quality improvement, which is what this book is about, unlike that for quality assurance, the best organization for quality is not obvious. If superior product quality is established as a primary objective of the division, and it is accepted that everyone in the division is working toward that objective, it does not seem appropriate to have one group policing others, checking up on them, and being their conscience. Alright, it may sometimes be useful to do a secondary set of inspections or tests, but not because people cannot be trusted. Unfortunately, sometimes people cannot be trusted—particularly if they are not given good leadership. Another dilemma is that the policing makes the untrustworthiness more likely, and is not very effective in neutralizing it. A pragmatic view would be that it is best to have separate quality departments in the division and plants with the quality managers reporting directly to the division and plant manages respectively, and a close functional link between the division quality manager and the plant quality managers. The quality department should do all inspection and testing—incoming, in process, and final—of manufactured product, except that done as a part time activity, for example, by a machine operator. The quality department should do outgoing quality audits for information, but acceptance sampling should be avoided. Reasons for this are that most manufacturing managers are not very interested in inspection and test and do not supervise it very well. The control of inspection and test makes the quality department seem more important which helps its other activities, and including inspection and test in their job descriptions helps the recruitment and compensation of effective quality managers. Another reason is that the suggested organization is sufficiently close to the one derived from quality assurance principles to be accepted by all but the most dogmatic of customers—and perhaps this organization, which makes the quality department fairly independent, helps to remind people in other functions that they are just as involved in achieving superior product quality as the members of the quality department.

QUALITY IMPROVEMENT BUSINESS PLANNING

The reader of this book will have performed a complicated set of activities in the past month—some concerned with work and others with private life. Why did he or she do that particular set? The answer is human motivation, for which the best known theory is Maslow's. He claims that motivation is the attempt to satisfy needs in the following hierarchy: physiological; safety/security; social/affiliation; esteem/recognition; and self-actualization. In practice there is a much simpler answer to the question: Why did I perform that particular set of activities last month? Because I performed the same set the previous month. Human life patterns are firmly constrained by nationalities, jobs, education, habits, interests, obligations, responsibilities, the activities of those around us, and so on. Our room for maneuver is very limited by both our environment and our psychology.

So, the key question is not: Why will I perform a particular set of activities this month? It is: What will cause me to do something different this month from last month?

Most people have some scope for change, but why do they select one change in preference to another? Maslow's hierarchy could give an explanation, but in a work context there is again a simpler explanation. People change:

1. Because *they* want to
2. Because their boss wants them to
3. Because someone else wants them to

Usually, the myriad of detailed changes needed for quality improvement to occur are not the kinds that people want to make. There are many other more interesting innovations: design a new product, get a big order, change a business strategy, select a new machine, and so on. Therefore, a rapid rate of quality improvement can be achieved only if it is planned and managed. It is important therefore that every division prepare an annual quality improvement plan as a formal part of its overall business planning process. Because quality improvement is multifunctional, the planning must be multifunctional, and the draft plan must be evaluated seriously and approved by the division manager. The planning must involve the marketing, design-development, purchasing, manufacturing, and quality departments, with necessary assistance from the controller department.

The plan must start with defined premises: the definition of product quality, the multifunctional nature of quality improvement, and the use of the "two measures of quality improvement" to record the current status and to be the means of expressing planned improvements quantitatively. The plan must establish long-term objectives, for example, to be better than competitors in quality to the customer and quality costs, and it must define quantitative targets for the coming year.

The main part of the quality improvement planning concerns the specific programs and projects to be worked on—the acceptance of responsibility, the identification of needed resources, and the establishment of the dates for reaching defined "milestones."

For marketing, the emphasis of the plan will be on quality to the customer and on how an increasing proportion of the division's sales can be moved into the "best quality" category compared with competing products. Plans for improving support quality may also be included. For design-development, plans will involve quality cost improvement of existing products—participation in statistical process capability programs, manufacturing process improvement, and so on. For new products, emphasis may be put on evaluation of the design of competing products, design for manufacturability and testability, and planning of design review and product qualification.

For purchasing, the quality improvement plan should aim for a drastic reduction in the proportion of defective items received, as a consequence of ensuring that purchases are made only from good suppliers, that effective communication is maintained with them, and that help and motivation for continuing improvement is given. For manufacturing, the objectives should emphasize the conformance-to-design aspects of quality to the customer, and quality cost improvement as a result of improved and better controlled manufacturing processes. For the quality department, projects might involve improved inspection and test and improved quality data reporting and analysis.

General programs that might be planned include the establishment and organization of a multifunctional quality improvement team or a product liability board, the start of quality circle or zero defects activities, or implementation of quality-directed training programs for engineers, operators, testers, and so on.

A main requirement of the quality improvement business plan is that it be based on a realistic view of the resources, priorities, and resolution of the division. All too often plans include ambitious targets that are not achievable. If a realistic plan were drafted the division manager—along with managers in the superstructure of the company—could decide whether the slow progress indicated was acceptable, or whether they were prepared to pay for more resources or change priorities in order to obtain more rapid progress. An over-optimistic plan hides the need for such decisions, and wastes months of time.

CONCLUSION

This chapter has discussed the organization of operating divisions in decentralized companies. It has given reasons why it is important for such divisions to have simple, elegant organizations—mainly to facilitate vertical and horizontal communication—and why many real organizations do not follow this ideal. The organization of quality departments that follow, respectively, quality assurance and quality improvement philosophies, is discussed, and the importance of multifunctional quality business planning is emphasized.

CHAPTER 13

THE ROLE OF STAFF MANAGERS

Having briefly discussed the organization of operating divisions in a decentralized company, the management superstructure of such a company can be discussed. Typically, this superstructure does not itself earn revenues or make profits, and its costs are paid for by levies on the operating divisions which do. This fact greatly reduces the apparent power of the people in the superstructure, and makes it important that their costs and numbers are controlled. Anyone who is located at a company, sector, or group headquarters is likely to be called "staff" although such people perform at least the seven very different classes of activities listed in Table 13.1.

The top management of the company, the chairperson, the board, and the chief executive officer perform legally required activities. They are also the focus of outward looking activities for the shareholders, the financial community, and local and national government, and they supervise the company's senior managers. They and the operating divisions are the two essential parts of the company. In principle, the top management could be comprised of a couple of people supported by part-time, external board members. In any case, top management's total costs are usually less than one-tenth of a percent of the company's total revenues.

The other senior general managers function mainly as the supervisors of the operating division managers and perform activities similar to those listed in Table 12.1. If their span of control is small they may also act as high-level workers performing, for example, strategic planning and mar-

TABLE 13.1.   Classes of Activities Performed by the Company Superstructure

1. Activities of top management—chairperson, board, chief executive officer
2. Activities of senior general management—chief operating officer, sector executive vice presidents, group vice presidents
3. Personal assistance to top and senior management
4. Legally required centralized activities
5. Centralized operational activities
6. Functional leadership of the operating divisions
7. Service to other company staff

keting activities. With a span of control of six of more, such senior general managers should be small in number and cost less than one tenth of a percent of the revenues of the operating divisions they supervise.

Personal assistance to the top and senior general managers of a company is the classic staff activity. It consists of public relations assistance, speech writing, and so on, and financial, legal, marketing, human relations, and operations advisors performing analyses and making recommendations with regard to acquisitions, divestitures, the approval or disapproval of operating divisions' strategic plans, capital expenditures and high-level appointments, and so on. Again, the number of people and their costs should be small. The senior managers can deal directly with only a limited number of people and their advisers can be high-level workers, not supervisors of large departments.

The next category of staff work covers legally required centralized activities, such as the preparation of the quarterly and annual financial results and reports, a necessary minimum of internal financial auditing, preparation of legally required personnel reports, and so on. Once again, by taking advantage of computerized data processing, the numbers of people required for these activities should not be very large.

The fifth category consists of operational activities which the top management of the company has decided shall be performed centrally. Typical activities are the borrowing of money by the treasury department, the implementation of stock option and other incentive plans by the human relations department, the centralized implementation of computerized management information systems, centralized selling and purchasing, centralized research and development, centralized legal services, centralized advertising, and so on. The first four categories of staff work listed in Table 13.1 should cost well below one percent of a company's revenues, but this fifth category can easily cost several times that amount. It is in this category that costs can get out of control and cost effectiveness can become low. The costs of an operating division, in principle, are controlled automatically by the requirement to make a profit and to grow— two parameters that are easily measured. (In practice, for operating divisions with benign markets and high profits these constraints may be insufficient to prevent costs increasing in ways that would not be tolerated for staff groups.) The costs of centralized operational activities are controlled only by the managers of these activities and their supervisors. It is they who decide what level of surcharge shall be placed on the operating divisions to pay for centralized activities. It could be that in a decentralized company operational activities should only be performed at group, sector, or company levels, when it is certain that such centralization will aid efficiency. In any case, centralized operational activities should be organizationally separate from other staff activities (e.g., personal assistance to top management and functional leadership) otherwise it becomes extremely difficult to monitor if centralization of the activity continues to be cost effective.

The sixth type of staff work consists of support of the operating divisions. It is the type of staff work most relevant to quality improvement and it will be discussed in more detail below. It will be suggested that staff support of the main divisional functions can be provided effectively for a cost of a few tenths of a percent of the company's revenues. The seventh category of staff work is the provision of services, such as recruitment, office services, payroll and so on, to the other staff departments. Obviously, its costs are likely to be proportional to the magnitude of the other departments.

In practice, the size and costs of the superstructure of a company tend to grow progressively and then to be subjected to sudden arbitrary cuts, usually when the company has a period of adverse performance, or when there is a change of top management. (Even while the staff members are being dismissed, some of the operating divisions are adding organizational levels and surreptitiously changing into groups with their own staff.) The cycle, which is inefficient from the viewpoint of the company and unpleasant from the viewpoint of the staff, could be prevented if the seven types of activity listed in Table 13.1 were separately identified and controlled systematically. This knowledge would also help to solve the span of control problem which always besets top management. If it wishes to minimize the number of organizational levels in the company and aid communication, top management has to have six or more line sectors or groups reporting directly to it. However, the addition of a similar number of staff departments also reporting directly can appear to overload the top managers. Part of the answer to this problem is to recognize that staff departments—if they consist mainly of high-level work-ers—should not require the same level of supervision as major line organi-zations.

STAFF FUNCTIONAL LEADERSHIP

Compared with an independent company of the same size, what advan-tages does an operating division of a large company have? Well, it has some obvious advantages like borrowing money more readily, surviving temporary losses that might bankrupt an independent company, getting marketing advantages from the company's overall reputation, and having synergy with other divisions.

The division's main advantage, however, should be that its managers receive help from the superstructure of the company that enables them to run the division more effectively than managers of an independent com-pany who do not receive such help.

That may seem a surprising statement. Some common perceptions are that the division general manager is a genius who is hampered by bureau-cratic interference from headquarters and that he or she is not completely trusted only because of the paranoia of some staff people. If that were the case, large companies could instantaneously improve their profitability by eliminating much of their headquarter's costs, retaining only enough staff to operate as a holding company but making no attempt to influence the management of its divisions. The top line-managers of most companies believe that their division managers are competent people, not necessarily geniuses, and that the performance of these division managers is im-proved by guidance and motivation provided by themselves. They also believe that the results of errors of judgment by division managers can be prevented by approval requirements on plans and projects. The same rea-soning suggests that the performance of the functional managers—mar-keting, manufacturing, accounting, and so on—in the operating divisions is also improvable by appropriate guidance and support. Some of this ob-viously is provided by the division manager but he or she cannot be an expert in all of these functions, and senior functional staff at headquarters is another possible source of such help. The importance of improving functional performnce—functional excellence, in current business jar-gon—results from the fact that the vast majority of people employed in business work in functional departments. Only a tiny minority is con-cerned with general leadership and setting strategic direction. Strategic planning may be little more than a complex game if an ambitious and desirable plan is developed with insufficient functional capability to implement it, and may be very frustrating if a realistic view is taken of the scope of the strategy as defined by a limited functional capability (see Chapter 14).

Once it is accepted that division managers and their department heads are people whose performance can be helped and improved, the only remaining issue is the amount and quality of help. Poor quality "help" will cause deterioration, not improvement. A better kind of help may effect some improvement but not commensurate with its cost. Only the best help will cause improvement and be fully cost effective. The importance of such help varies with the function. It depends on the size of the function in the operating divisions (which is often in the order manufacturing, marketing, design-development, quality, accounting, etc.). In a large company, such functions will comprise thousands of people and the central functional staff may require only one-tenth of a percent of the total manpower. (For the quality staff, which will work with the divisional marketing, design-development, purchasing and manufacturing people as well as the quality departments, the ratio to the total of people they help may be even smaller). The importance of functional help also depends on how much of the functional activity is common to all divisions and how much is special to individual divisions; central functional help may address virtually all of the activities in accounting, a high proportion in quality and purchasing, and progressively smaller proportions in manufacturing, design-development, and marketing. Nonetheless, for all of these functions there is worthwhile scope for improvement as a result of centralized functional help.

Functional staff in the company superstructure can have three different relationships with the company's operating divisions as follows:

1. Authoritative
2. Service
3. Leadership

In an authoritative approach the staff people either have, or behave as if they have, the right to give orders to the divisional people. If orders are not obeyed, the disciplinary methods of the company can be invoked. In a decentralized company, which invests its line division managers with great power and responsibility, the authoritative approach may appear to be inadmissible. In fact, there are at least two practical authoritative methods the staff can adopt. The first method involves the imposition of mandatory requirements for the supply of information by the operating divisions. The operating divisions are so conditioned to supplying essential financial data that they will also supply various kinds of extra data. The second method is when a division is in serious trouble and a team of staff people is imposed on it by senior management to "help" it solve its problems. The authoritative relationship between staff and line is intrinsically adversarial. Despite these two techniques, an authoritative approach can be only a limited part of the mode of operation of a functional staff in a decentralized company.

The opposite relationship is one of service. The functional staff's role is to provide specialized services to the operating divisions. The initiative is with the operating divisions. When they want service from the staff, they ask for it. Sometimes the staff will go so far as to attempt to sell their service to particular operating divisions, but the decision whether or not to buy the service rests with the divisions. All information that is obtained by the staff is confidential and is not reported outside of the concerned division. At the limit, the operating divisions using the staff will pay the latter's full costs—the staff receives no central funding. Many staff people like the service approach. It places no responsibility on them other than to practice their profession conscientiously and competently in the positive environments provided by division managers who have asked for their services. The staff have a role similar to independent consultants. Staff people who have previously spent many years in the line often feel that the service approach is the only proper one. They believe that the line people inherently have sole responsibility for achieving the company's objectives, and that the staff role is subordinate to that responsibility. The service approach by functional staff, even though it is nonadversarial, is not completely viable over the long run. If an operating division has to pay the full cost of the staff, they are not likely to get value for money. Only occasionally will the technical expertise of the staff be better for dealing with a particular situation than that available from the full range of independent consultants. On the other hand, if the staff costs are paid centrally and confidentiality is maintained, top management, which controls the costs, may see little evidence of value and axe the activity— and if confidentiality is not maintained the operating divisions will have another good reason for preferring external consultants.

In the leadership approach, top management gives the functional staff the responsibility for making significant improvements to the functional effectiveness of the operating divisions. As stated by TRW's CEO, R. F. Mettler, the functional staff share "the burden of the initiative" with the line people. The staff are given no right to order line people to do things, and final responsibility for accepting or rejecting staff initiatives remains with the division managers. However, the staff decides which divisions—often all of them—will benefit from particular activities, and the company accepts that they have various legitimate methods of applying pressure to the divisions. Information about a division obtained by the staff is explicitly available to the senior management of the company; it is not confidential to the division. Even though the staff will often perform valuable services for divisions, the latter do not have to pay for such services. As the role of the staff is leadership not service, they are funded centrally so that they are not under the control of those they are required to lead. There is always a significant adversarial element in the relationship of functional staff operating in a leadership mode and line managers. However much a division manager may like a staff member personally and however much respect the division manager may have for this employee's integrity and competence, the staff member places limitations on the division manager's freedom of action and, because of his or her channels of communication to the company's top management, can also be viewed as a threat. All things being equal, division managers would be more comfortable if staff members with functional leadership roles did not exist, and they could satisfy any perceived functional needs by hiring their own consultants. Such functional staff need to be positioned high in the company organization and have prestigious titles, otherwise the division people will not take them seriously. Functional staff with leadership responsibilities are specifically a tool to be used by the company's top management. They survive only so long as they have the explicit support of top management. Division managers may tolerate them if they are of unimpeachable integrity and great competence, but will use any displays of incompetence or self-serving behavior as a rational means of undermining them. Of course, many staff people survive for a time by keeping a low profile.

Functional leadership is a very special kind of job. Most of the other staff positions involve activities that are either very similar to the corresponding activities in an operating division, or involve only the high level practice of a professional skill. Personal assistance to the senior line managers, legally required line activities, centralized operational activities, and services to other staff groups all fall into these categories. Centralized purchasing and marketing are not intrinsically different from the same activities performed at the division level, and giving legal advice to a CEO may involve complexities beyond those likely for giving advice to a division manager, but the difference is of degree only. Success in such activities in an operating division is therefore a good predictor of success in a corresponding position in the superstructure, and divisional experience is directly applicable.

For functional leadership the situation is different. Compare my last line job—quality manager in STC's semiconductor division—with my present job as vice president, quality of TRW. In the former, I was head of a department of nearly 100 people. I had four section heads reporting to me, and much of my time was devoted to supervision. I was an important cog in the division's operating machine. Most of my responsibility was to react effectively, and cause my department to react effectively, to the needs of the rest of the machine—to inspect, test, and accept the output of manufacturing, to participate with design-development in the design review and qualification of new products, to help the sales department deal with commercial customers, to respond to the requirements of the quality assurance system requirements of military customers, and so on. The need for proactive work was small compared to the need for effective reaction—and each proactive requirement could be delegated to one or more of my 100 subordinates each one of whom would do what I asked. Communication, with my boss, my subordinates, and my peers in the 1000 person, one-site division, was simple.

As vice president, quality TRW, I am supposed to increase significantly the rate of quality improvement of the company's 80 operating divisions comprising overly 90,000 people working in several continents and many countries. I have one director and a secretary reporting to me directly—the only people I can tell to do something—and a close functional relationship with three sector staff people having quality responsibilities. I perceive that the rate of quality improvement in the divisions is largely dependent on the actions of their division managers and their marketing, design-development, purchasing, and manufacturing functions, and in these areas I have not even a tenuous functional authority. I have very little to react to; if I just wait for my telephone to ring I will probably wait a long time. My job is to be proactive, to accept the burden of the initiative, and I have no one to whom I can delegate that burden. The technical aspects of quality that I learned as a division quality manager are relevant to my position, and the knowledge I gained of how an operating division works is also important. But the managerial skills I learned as a division quality manager—as a supervisor, peer and subordinate in a compact, focussed operating organization—are largely irrelevant to and completely inadequate for the performance of my current job. Fortunately, I have had two other experiences as a senior staff man and I think that I am now beginning to get the hang of the job.

The primary task of a functional-leadership staff member at the company level is to help the operating divisions become more effective. This staff member is also responsible for helping the top and senior line managers of the company. Because the functional staff in the rest of the company superstructure are nearer to the operating divisions than he or she is, they also perceive that he or she should help them. In some companies, there is a much less clear recognition of the responsibility of the other managers in the superstructure to assist the functional staff member. This staff member, like they are, is performing a job for the company and will produce a better output for the company if he or she receives cost-effective help.

One managerial philosophy suggests that during his or her career a star manager should alternate line and staff positions. This philosophy does not work well in practice because it is much easier to get promoted to division general manager from positions as division department head or general manager of a smaller division, than from a functional staff position. For those making the appointment, there is much more risk involved in the latter step than promoting an internal department head of known ability or an already successful general manager. Also, it is so difficult to be a successful functional-leadership staff manager that more people damage than enhance their reputations in the attempt. Thus, ambitious line managers are wary of taking staff positions. On the other hand, a division manager's experience is not an especially good preparation for the position of a senior, functional staff man. The managerial requirements are very different, and most general managers do not even have a deep knowledge of the technical aspects of the function. The latter is essential if they are to perform as high-level workers and not just be supervisors of small staff departments. The main advantages a division general manager has in a functional staff position are personal—the fact that most division general managers are mature, intelligent, energetic, and well respected. From the functional staff viewpoint, if such positions are felt to be important, it is a problem if people are promoted back into the line after two or three years when they have learned the necessary staff techniques and have become effective.

The senior line managers face some of the difficulties of senior functional staff. A division general manager promoted to group vice president no longer has 1000 people at beck and call, and the ability to cause things to happen by direct instruction or by the coordination of a team of department heads. He or she is still a supervisor who in principle can command subordinates, but in practice the staff member's techniques of questioning, suggesting, and persuading are more appropriate. In my years in Brussels I participated in hundreds of the famous ITT management meetings that were conducted by the company's legendary chief executive officer H. S. Geneen. Geneen has a—no doubt deserved—reputation as a strong, authoritative manager. I was impressed though that at the end of every series of penetrating questions directed at clarifying particular issues, Geneen always emphasized that the relevant local manager must make the decision, that it was this manager's responsibility, and that Geneen could not know enough about the detail of the local situation to usurp that responsibility. Each group vice president, in dealing with division general managers, is essentially in the same staff-like position as Geneen. It would, therefore, be very useful for a senior line manager to have had four or five years experience as a functional staff manager, but for a career-oriented individual, it would probably not be worth the risk.

THE ROLE OF QUALITY STAFF

In Chapter 2, I discussed the necessary elements of quality improvement under the headings policy, honesty, priority, and capability. The same headings can be used to give a framework for a discussion of the work of quality staff, as an example of a functional staff in a leadership role. The quality policy of a company is determined by its top management. Unless the top management of a company has a policy that actually places strong emphasis on quality it is unlikely that they will establish a staff quality activity—they will leave quality to the operating divisions—and if they do (perhaps for image reasons) the staff cannot be effective. At the time of appointment of the staff the quality policy may be inexplicit, and the staff may then help to clarify it—for example, by emphasizing quality improvement rather than quality assurance—but the key issue is whether or not the top management is serious about quality. If they are, the quality staff can reinforce that conviction by quantifying the advantages of quality improvement and by managing practical programs to achieve it. But it is asking more than is reasonable of a functional staff to place them in the position of having to convince their own unreceptive leaders of the importance of their function.

Following from the policy, the quality staff should take the lead in developing the quality philosophy of the company. A great company should have a specific quality philosophy particular to itself. I shall make no attempt to define what I mean by a quality philosophy because I believe the definition is best left vague. A quality philosophy starts with a quality policy, but is much more than that. It includes principles and methods, specific programs and measurements, it strongly reflects the ways real quality-related situations are actually dealt with. It is as much a matter of people and their relationships and motivations as abstract ideas. It is a permanent part of the company's culture, continually evolving, but not constrained within a specific time period like a program. In a decentralized company every operating division will have its own quality philosophy reflecting the attitudes of its thought leaders and the ways it actually performs. The company quality philosophy should not be imposed on the divisions. Rather it should influence and enrich their own quality philosophies and itself evolve in response to their needs and ideas. The whole of this book reflects a particular quality philosophy which has drawn elements from the quality philosophies of the companies by which its writer has been employed.

Turning to honesty, this, or some lack of it, is a part of a company's overall business philosophy. Unless exact attention to legal and ethical principles is an unequivocal part of a company's business philosophy, it has little chance, for reasons that were discussed in Chapter 2, of achieving superiority in quality, and the effect of its quality staff, if appointed, is likely to be small. However, the converse is not true. Like so much in business, a clear position of principle is only the first step in the achievement of a desired end, and for honesty the quality staff may have an important role in clarifying its difficult, practical implications for quality, and educating the managers of the operating divisions.

Most of the efforts of the quality staff will be devoted to increasing the priority accorded to quality improvement in the operating divisions, and in helping them to improve their quality-related capability. The former is of major importance. The benefits of quality improvement do not come quickly, and it complicates and makes more difficult the achievement of what they see as their normal objectives, by the division managers, and the marketing, design-development, purchasing, and manufacturing people, who primarily determine its rate. For these and other reasons, the priority accorded to quality improvement must always be enhanced by managerial action. If it is just left to achieve its natural level in competition with other business activities, its priority will invariably be less than the optimum for the long-term advantage of a division or company.

A minority of division managers, perhaps because of their familiarity with the PIMS results or because of customer pressure, will themselves lead the priority enhancement. The quality staff can help such division managers by working with their functional managers. For the rest of the division managers, the quality staff can use various direct methods of raising their level of involvement in quality improvement, and in addi-

TABLE 13.2. Activities of Quality Staff Related to Policy, Honesty, Priority, and Capability

Activity	Policy	Honesty	Priority	Capability
1. Developing the company's overall quality philosophy	x	x	x	x
2. Developing the company's overall quality programs		x		x
3. Conducting a quality communication program	x	x	x	x
4. Conducting a quality education and training program	x	x	x	x
5. Managing the quality measurement program—quality to the customer and quality costs			x	
6. Managing the self-audit program			x	x
7. Conducting independent audits		x	x	x
8. Managing the competence of quality managers			x	x
9. Consulting for specific divisions				x
10. Participating in team-assistance to problem divisions			x	x
11. Assisting in quality related public relations activities				
12. Participating in extra company activities				

tion, they can support, with data, questions, quality summaries, and so on, the similarly directed efforts of the senior line managers in the company superstructure.

Table 13.2 lists a set of typical quality staff activities which bear on quality improvement. The development of the company's quality policy and quality philosophy have already been discussed. This activity leads naturally into the formalization of particular quality programs. In TRW, these programs are sometimes covered in mandatory company policies, but more often in nonmandatory model policies and standard practices (see Chapter 7) or in informal guidance papers. The number of subjects covered increases steadily with the passage of time and in mid-1985 includes the following topics:

Competitors quality evaluation

Quality cost reporting, forecasting, and improvement

Design review

Product qualification

Legal and ethical issues

Supplier quality, including incoming inspection

Inspection and test planning

Acceptance sampling

Statistical process capability and control

Quality system audit

Quality business planning

The third activity listed in Table 13.2 concerns communication, and obviously one of a functional staff's main tasks is to communicate effectively. A staff of one or two people cannot give functional leadership to people without communicating with them by one medium or another. A list of all of the groups of people the head of such a staff has to communicate with is as follows:

1. Top management of the company
2. Direct subordinates
3. Members of the functional hierarchy
4. Rest of the company
5. People outside of the company

Effective communication with the top management of the company is vital. In fact, it is a matter of survival. If the top management of a company has serious doubts about the cost effectiveness of a functional staff group, it may consider it has a duty to eliminate that cost. Most of the benefits of the work of the functional staff appear in the operating divisions, but the staff cannot rely on positive comment rising up from that source to the top management. It is not the responsibility of the operating divisions to say how useful the staff are—and the semiadversarial relationship between staff and line will inhibit such communication anyway. So the staff must communicate directly with the top management. Formal reports (e.g., a monthly written report) is one way, but probably better ways include the top management actually seeing the staff in action with the senior managers of the company, or the staff providing the top management with data and ideas to assist the latter in playing its part in the functional improvement of the company.

A functional staff member, who is a high-level worker, will have at most three direct subordinates, and will have no problem in communicating with them. Communicating with the functional hierarchy is a different matter. Figure 13.1 shows TRW's quality function hierarchy for the company, sector, and group levels in mid-1985. The line quality managers, who supervise quality departments comprising 8000 people, include four group product assurance directors (shown in Figure 13.1), 80 division quality managers, and about 150 plant and project quality managers. The quality staff comprise seven high-level workers and three secretaries, the company vice president quality and director quality, a quality director for one sector, a vice president product quality for another, a director quality and materiel for another, and two group quality directors for particular groups. The policy of TRW is *not* to fill every place in a functional hierarchy, but to add only enough staff people to perform the essential tasks. For example, the two groups with quality directors are more complex than the others and have special needs which the other groups do not have. When there is no group quality director the functional link is directly from the sector to the divisions. This organization works satisfactorily.

Functional staffs often issue regular newsletters to the line people.

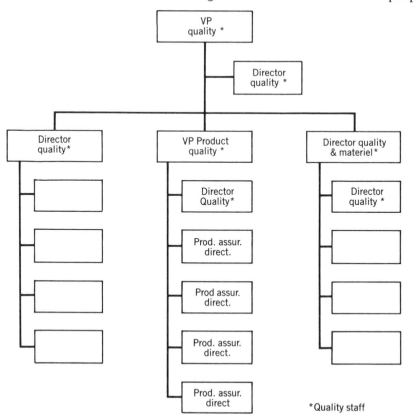

Figure 13.1. TRW's quality functional hierarchy at company, sector, and group levels.

Some staffs will have a budget that enables them to employ a full-time editor. For others, the responsibility is given to an administrative assistant. In either case, the methodology is to seek snippets of information about personnel changes and individual achievements. These are supplemented from time to time by accounts of functional meetings, and so on, and reprints of selected articles from magazines or technical journals. Often, the newsletter is glossily printed. *TRW Quality Communication* is different. It is not a newsletter; each issue deals seriously with a single topic, usually in five to seven typewritten pages. Many of the ideas presented in this book were first addressed as *TRW Quality Communications*. When used in this way, it is part of TRW's quality education program. Table 13.3 summarizes the contents of the issues of the communication during 1982–1985. It also deals with the progress of TRW's quality programs, quality to the customer, quality costs, statistical process control, and so on, giving not only an analysis of the company's overall status, but also reporting the individual progress of each division. Such issues of *TRW Quality Communication* go to division managers and the top management of the company, as well as the quality managers, in an explicit attempt to exercise peer pressure to enhance the priority accorded to quality improvement. Other issues of *TRW Quality Communications* are devoted to "success stories," in which divisions describe their achievements in quality-program implementation—with the purpose of giving recognition to the people involved and of encouraging emulation. One rule is followed: that every *TRW Quality Communication* is written entirely by TRW people. Also, there is no editor or administrative assistant. Editing is done by myself or TRW's quality director, Tom Hughes, and typing and publication is done by our secretary, Ann Landfield. These practices prevent our readership from being overwhelmed by "junk" copies. Although we are not committed to any defined schedule, we have issued a *TRW Quality Communication* on average every three weeks for

TABLE 13.3.   Subjects of "TRW Quality Communication" 1982–1985

TRW quality policies and practices	16
Status of TRW quality programs	12
Development of TRW quality systems	11
TRW unit success stories	9
TRW top management quality statements	6
TRW evaluations of external papers and so on	4
TRW papers presented at external conferences	3
Special Christmas issues	3
Total number of issues	64

the past four years—and it has become an important tool for implementing TRW's quality programs.

Communication to the rest of the company can fan out from the quality function at all levels, but this is not sufficient. Direct communication from the quality staff has to be used also. As noted, selected issues of *TRW Quality Communications* go to division, plant, and functional managers throughout the company. All key managerial groups are addressed by the TRW Quality College, the company's large management meetings and small management meetings give other opportunities, and various ad hoc methods are used as well. Direct communication between the quality staff and line managers also occurs during division and plant visits. Communication outside of the company is yet another task for the quality staff. Part of a company's benefit from achieving superiority in quality is lost if it does not communicate this fact to its customers and the financial community. Of course, many companies try to convey an image of quality but this is much less useful than communicating real quality achievements.

Perhaps the most effective way of inculcating a quality philosophy as a means of changing the total culture of a company is for the quality staff to conduct a high-level education and training program (activity 4 of Table 13.2). My first experience with such a program came with ITT. Around 1967, P. B. Crosby, who was then director quality of ITT, suggested that it would be useful to conduct training in quality management for the divisional quality managers of STC, ITT's main company in the United Kingdom. I agreed and Crosby arranged for Dr. Max Astrachan, who was then the director of the ASQC's Education and Training Institute, to come over to the United Kingdom to conduct a one-week duration course in STC's training school. We also invited participation from two or three quality managers from ITT's other European companies. The course was successful, and it led me to believe that I, with the assistance of my STC colleagues, could conduct similar sessions with a modified and extended syllabus for the rest of STC's quality managers, and this we did. Some time later, Crosby recognized that such training programs were an extremely powerful tool for quality improvement, and named them the ITT Quality College. He also established a syllabus emphasizing his "14 Steps to Quality Improvement." During the next decade the ITT Quality College was taught by ITT's quality staffs in Brussels and New York, under the leadership of myself and R. W. Vincent, respectively, in many sessions on both sides of the Atlantic and in other parts of the world. When Crosby left ITT, his Quality College became a key part of his highly successful consulting business, and, when I also left ITT, I introduced the same concept into TRW, though with a different syllabus.

TRW's Quality College has four objectives:

1. To develop and communicate TRW's quality philosophy

2. To cause participants to perform differently and more effectively when they return to their operating divisions

3. To enable a group of peers from different TRW divisions to get to know each other, and also for them and TRW's quality staff to get to know each other personally

4. To give participants a good time

The importance of a company having a coherent quality philosophy has already been discussed. The TRW Quality College is structured to be very participative, using case studies and discussion sessions, so that attendees have many opportunities to input their own ideas and thereby influence the development of the company's quality philosophy.

Table 13.4 summarizes the syllabus of the one week duration college for quality managers. The two and two and one-half day colleges for division managers, marketing managers, design managers, purchasing managers, and manufacturing managers are based on the same quality philosophy but are tailored to address the needs and interests of each particular group. It could be argued that too much material is covered in the time available. However, in conducting education and training programs functional staffs have different objectives from consultants or training experts. Consultants want to spread out their material. If they have three days' worth of material they would rather get paid for three days than compress the material into a two-day program. Training experts are concerned with making it as easy as possible for participants to establish and maintain interest which leads to emphasis on low information content participative methods. Functional staff are trying to change the future behavior of the participants—by utilizing as effectively as they can the strictly limited time available to them. As the participants are being paid by the same company, the staff believe they have a right to expect effort from the participants as well as from themselves. The functional staff's position is intermediate between that of my old college lecturers who included a couple of Nobel Prize winners and who appeared to believe that their information was so important that no care at all needed to be taken in its presentation, and that of professional entertainers who cannot assume that their audiences will make any effort at all.

TABLE 13.4. TRW Quality College—Syllabus of One-Week Duration Session for Quality Managers

Day 1

Introduction and objectives of the college	Lecture/discussion
The strategic importance of quality improvement	Lecture/discussion
Quality to the customer	Lecture/discussion
Quality costs	Lecture/discussion
"Smithson relay"—part I	Quality cost case
"Smithson relay"—part II	Quality cost case

Day 2

Product liability—prevention	Lecture/discussion
Design review and product qualification	Question and answer
"TRW semiautomatic thread grinder"	Computer exercise on process control
Process capability and control	Lecture/discussion
Statistical process control implementation	Lecture/discussion
Automotive total quality objective	Lecture/discussion

Day 3

Acceptance sampling	Lecture/discussion
Inspection and test planning	Lecture/discussion
"The BGP45 Pump"	Inspection planning case
Supplier quality	Question and answer

Day 4

"Quality circles or zero defects?"	Quality improvement case
Quality performance indicators	Lecture/discussion
Legal and ethical policy on product quality	Lecture/discussion
System quality audit	Lecture/discussion
College dinner	

Day 5 (half day)

Quality business planning	Lecture/discussion
Division/plant quality	Exercise/discussion
Improvement programs	Participant response
Closing remarks	Lecture

The most important purpose of the TRW Quality College is to cause participants to change and improve the ways that they actually do things back in their own divisions. If, on their return, they only feel that they have been through an interesting educational experience that may in some undefined way cause them to be better managers in the future, the college may be judged a failure. The purpose is to effect specific improvements. For this reason, the participants are trained in defined quality programs as well as educated in underlying principles. The subjects covered at the college are addressed in many other ways, through *TRW Quality Communications*, at quality councils, by mandatory company, sector, or group requirements, by publicity and peer pressure, and so on. The belief is that no one method is likely to be effective in causing change and improvement, but that many methods together should support and reinforce each other. A similar concept applies to the participants themselves. When all of the managers of a division have participated they also should reinforce each other. The TRW Quality College therefore has the target to reach *all* of the company's key, product-quality determining managers. (We were not so ambitious in ITT Europe.) As of mid-1985, this objective has been achieved for division general managers, division, plant, and project quality managers, and purchasing managers. (In each case one session a year is now being conducted for new appointees.) About 40 percent of the population of marketing, product engineering, and manufacturing managers has also been reached. Also, a fair number of TRW's divisions have requested that a special session of the TRW Quality College be conducted at their site so that all of their managers can attend simultaneously.

In TRW, as in ITT, we decided that education and training of managers in quality should be conducted by the company's quality staff rather than by consultants. This is obviously much more difficult for the staff. It requires them to be confident that they have the necessary skills in quality management and teaching to instruct senior people. The benefits are that a company quality philosophy can be developed rather than a consultant's quality philosophy be received, that a high level of commitment to change and improvement can be maintained, that consistency can be achieved with other implementation methodologies, and that key personal relationships within the company can be established and developed.

The fifth set of quality staff activities listed in Table 13.2 concerns the management of quality to the customer and quality cost improvement programs. These programs, including the part played by staff, have already been discussed in Chapters 3 and 4. However, it may be useful to cover one further aspect of the quality to the customer program. Many years ago P. B. Crosby coined the sentence, "Make ITT the standard for quality, worldwide," but it remained only an exhortation. When Crosby left ITT I put together the idea expressed by that phrase, the quality conclusions from the PIMS data, and my own analysis of the definition of product quality into the quality to the customer concept discussed in Chapter 2. When I joined TRW, I felt this approach brought into focus the ideas on quality expressed by the top management of TRW, and accordingly presented it briefly at the company's management conference in the autumn of 1981. The concept became part of the syllabus of the TRW Quality College and I wrote and talked about it at every opportunity, but for a time no actual implementation occurred. During this period I was accused of being obsessed with quality cost improvement, a program that was then making much more rapid progress, but I always emphasized the primacy of quality to the customer. A first breakthrough came in 1983 when Mike Ryan, then director quality of TRW's automotive sector, convinced A. W. Reynolds, then the sector's executive vice president, that all of TRW's automotive divisions should perform competitors' quality evaluations as part of the sector's strategic planning process. Using the automotive sector experience as a lever, the next year, with the help of Tom George and Jack Isken, their respective quality directors, we persuaded the executive vice president of the industrial and energy sector, and the vice president of the electronics components group to have similar evaluations performed. In 1985, four years after its initiation, we are still nursing this fledgling program which is by no means institutionalized.

This anecdote illustrates the way that functional staff can work. Many programs go through a series of stages:

1. An initial intuitive idea
2. Analysis, amplification, and correction of the idea
3. Expression in a workable program
4. Approval to implement the program
5. Development of communication methods
6. Communication to the implementors
7. Motivation of the implementors
8. Monitoring of the implementation
9. Pressure for more effective implementation
10. Refinement and institutionalization

Commonly, different people work on the various stages. A senior manager has the initial idea, assistants or consultants work it out, a top manager or a high-level committee approves the program's implementation, communication or training experts develop necessary material, professional trainers (internal or consultants) teach it, and functional staff monitor implementation. An alternative is for two or three high-level-worker functional staff to do the whole thing. If they have the competence and commitment, this is much quicker, cheaper and more likely to be effective. There is no requirement to manage dozens of people, and seek stage-by-stage approval—with the possibility of the program being slowed down or stopped. (My approach is not to ask anyone to approve a program. I first think hard about whether or not it will benefit the company, whether it is going to cause real trouble to particular people, and whether it has a good probability of success. I also ask the company's director quality to critique the idea. If it passes those hurdles, I start to go ahead in an open way, informing relevant people, but not asking their permission. By this approach they are not exposed if the program goes wrong, and are not placed in the position of having to decide if they want to take that risk.) The method was successful with quality cost reporting, quality to the customer measurement, quality college teaching, and so on. Of course, it is psychologically demanding. Seeking formal approval, hiring consultants to do the technical work and training, using specialists for the logistics, and so on, drastically reduces the burden carried by any one person.

Activities 6 and 7 listed in Table 13.2 concern auditing, which is the subject of Chapter 14. The next activity is managing the competence of the company's quality managers. In a decentralized company three possible approaches can be taken. The first is to leave the matter entirely to the line managers to whom the quality managers report. The second is to expect the headquarters human relations function to cover the matter as part of its general responsibilities for management development. The third is for the quality staff to be proactive. My own experience is that the first approach gives, as would be expected, a very heterogeneous result, and that the second suffers from the disadvantage that quality managers are far down the priority list of human relations departments.

The third approach, quality staff participation, is most useful when a company is giving a new emphasis to quality. It could be that a company has had a traditional approach to the responsibilities of its divisional quality departments, concentrating on the use of inspection and test to sort out defective product. Over the years the costs of inspection might have been reduced by sampling but with a serious loss of effectiveness. Manufacturing might have taken over functional testing, so that it largely determined the quality that went to the customer. The quality department might have added assurance activities, by which it was supposed to "police" manufacturing (but not marketing or design-development) and started to cooperate with the customers' quality people on formal documentation systems. Some of the quality department's people might have been retitled quality engineers and worked on simple troubleshooting, progressed concessions, and served on the Material Review Board. Managers of such departments might have difficulty in responding to new challenges—for statistical process capability and control, design review, new product qualification, supplier quality improvement, quality to the customer measurement and improvement, quality cost improvement, quality data analysis, automatic testing, rational inspection and test planning, and coordination of a multifunctional quality improvement team. As the quality staff encouraged the application of these methods, it might also help the division managers not only by educating and training their quality managers, but also by giving them judgments about their quality managers' ability, in comparison with their peers, to cope with the new requirements. This is another of the difficult and delicate responsibilities that a quality staff has to accept if it has a functional leadership role, but not if it has a service role. Other similar tasks are to keep a record of talented quality people, advise on appointments and participate in decisions. My own experience is that this personnel area is a very difficult one that I have not always felt that I was covering very well.

The next two quality-staff activities listed in Table 13.2 concern assistance to specific divisions either as individuals or as part of a multifunctional team. The purpose can be to catalyze introduction of a specific program (e.g., systematic inspection and test planning) or to help solve a major problem. Some companies give considerable emphasis to this kind of work by their staff. My own view is that it is less cost effective than other kinds of quality staff activity. It is a matter of arithmetic. A company like TRW has 80 divisions and twice as many plants. At any one time there may be several of those units having significant problems; therefore say 5 or 10 quality staff people might need to be continually in action with them. Meanwhile, the other 90 percent or more units are getting no quality staff assistance at all. Conversely, for the other activities listed in Table 13.2 two or three quality staff can have an affect on all of the divisions. Other difficulties with the troubleshooting approach are that the staff are unlikely to have deep expertise in all required fields, that considerable effort is wasted by unit people at the start of the staff's participation as they ask for necessary information, and that the managerial and technical weaknesses in the division that caused the problem may remain when the task force leaves. On the other hand, from the staff's viewpoint an important advantage is that an appropriate proportion of this type of work keeps them in touch with the "real" world of the operating units.

An examination of quality costs is another illustration of the point. Imagine a large company with 100 divisions of the same size, and quality costs of $500 million *per annum*. Assume five of the divisions are in trouble and have twice the average quality cost to manufacturing added cost ratio, so they each have quality costs of $10 million. If there are a couple of quality staff members, they can adopt one or other of two different strategies. They can concentrate their efforts on one, two, or all five of the problem divisions, or they can devote their efforts to establishing a company-wide quality cost improvement program. Suppose they decide to work with all five of the problem divisions. There is $50 million of quality cost available, half of which is "excess." Without their help the rate of improvement in one year on the normal $25 million might be 5 percent and on the excess $25 million, 10 percent, together saving $3.75 million. Their help might cause an extra $3.75 million to be saved, a 10 times or more return on their costs. With the other strategy, the staff could introduce quality cost reporting in all 100 divisions (the company did not know it had $500 million of quality costs), conduct training programs, establish forecasting and project definition requirements, report results, establish peer pressure, involve top management and so on. There is now $500 million available for improvement. Without the staff's efforts, at an improvement rate of 5 percent per year, the saving might be $25 million; with their efforts it might go up to $50 million, a 50 times or more return on their costs. (Of course, it can be argued that the staff's efforts add costs beyond their own direct costs, but so do their efforts when working in particular divisions.) This analysis seems to lead to a conclusion contrary to that reached by application of the Pareto principle, which indicates that it is most cost effective to concentrate effort on "that 20 percent of the problems that cause 80 percent of the total loss." The reasons for the difference are perhaps because divisions' problems do not follow the Pareto distribution (because the "top 20 percent" divisions would have gone out of business if they did), and because the staff members are performing different actions in the two strategies.

The last two subjects listed in Table 13.2 concern activities of quality staff outside of the company. These can be part of the public relations program of the company, and also participation in trade associations, professional society, and civic duties. All of these activities are important in communicating the quality work of the company, in meeting the company's civic responsibilities, and in keeping the quality staff in touch with up-to-date professional trends. However, they can become ever more time consuming, and, except in special circumstances agreed by the company, they should be controlled to consume less than one-tenth of the staff member's time.

This chapter ends with another of the Christmas issues of *TRW Quality Communication*. It deals with the Toledo syndrome which besets staff people trying to help operating divisions to change.

THE TOLEDO SYNDROME

Some years ago when I was the vice president, quality of a major European multinational corporation, I was visiting our Spanish subsidiary. It was a large company with about 15,000 employees, that developed and manufactured an extensive range of telecommunications equipment. Its headquarters was in Madrid and it had manufacturing plants both in the suburbs of the city and in several other parts of Spain.

On the second day of my visit I was driven from Madrid to Toledo. I had made the same journey before and I did not enjoy it. It is years ago now and I do not remember too clearly, but I think the drive takes nearly two hours. The road goes across a flat, uninteresting plateau. The surface of the road I remember as not being good, and the conditions for overtaking other vehicles difficult. When I was a child I suffered from motion sickness, and the road to Toledo always made me remember this. (It was the habit of my friend, the quality director of the company, to provide me with a dinner of superb food and wine, starting at 10 o'clock. He had followed this habit the previous evening, and this reinforced the recollection of my childhood problem.)

Nonetheless, we arrived in Toledo without mishap. Toledo is one of the most beautiful towns in the world. I have little faith in my memory so I will not try to describe it, except to say that one's first view from the Madrid road is across a parched canyon. The medieval wall and houses are displayed in terraces across the side of the mesa on which the town is built. The shapes are arranged so perfectly that it seems like a painting by a Renaissance master. The predominant colors of amber and ochre glow in the Spanish sunshine.

The company had built a large plant outside the town two or three years before. It was making telecommunications equipment currently for "transmission," but it was planned to add electronic telephone exchanges. About 1000 people were putting electronic components onto printed circuit boards, performing flow soldering, doing automatic testing and fault finding, assembling the boards into frames and racks, making cable harnesses and soldering them into place, and doing all of the other processes typical of the manufacture of complex electronic equipment.

We had recently completed documentation of a 200 page "model quality system" for manufacture of printed board assemblies. My friend, the quality director of the Spanish company, had offered the Toledo plant as a guinea pig for its application. As I said, it was a new plant and, except for a nucleus that had transferred from Madrid, it was staffed entirely with local people to whom electronics, or indeed any high technology product, was unfamiliar.

A senior quality engineer on the staff of the quality director had accompanied me from Madrid. He was a charming man in his mid-30s, very intelligent and of excellent technical education. The fact that my companion spoke very good English was, from my viewpoint, even more important than his other talents.

We had a good day in the plant. Americans believe that all problems can be solved if you involve the right people, and get some action. The English have pretty much the same philosophy, though we also believe that many problems go away on their own if you give them a little time. Nations to the south and east tend to be more fatalistic, to believe a person has less control of his fate and that some problems must be endured with dignity. In Spain I always felt that 700 years of Moorish rule had left an imprint of the Arabic concept of "kismet"—destiny—on its people. However, the Spanish have infinite courtesy, and a Spanish plant always seems to have many managers and engineers who have time to talk to a visitor. So, it was a good day.

I saw so many improvement opportunities, so many places where the model quality system could be applied with benefit, that I insisted on going back to the plant after the lunch that started at two and finished at four (another great meal in a restaurant with a different unbelievable view from its terrace of that beautiful, old town). But, "insisted" is the wrong word. They appeared pleased at my unusual request. Traditionally, in Spain most of the work is accomplished in a long morning, and few visiting staff people have the enthusiasm or the stomach to return to the plant after lunch, but I convinced them that I was serious. Whether their pleasure was real or whether this was another example of their unfailing courtesy I do not know.

After another two or three hours, and many dignified farewells, my companion and I climbed into our car for the return to Madrid. I was very dependent on him. I was going back to Brussels the first thing the next morning. I had little confidence that, without assistance, the Toledo plant would make the many improvements that were possible. Although the word was not used, I felt that they viewed 12.6 percent of the joints coming defective from the flow soldering machine (they had a wealth of quality statistics) as kismet. The 16 girls reworking those joints were seen not as the consequence of a soluble problem, but as a contribution to the solution of another problem—unemployment in central Spain.

The quality director had appointed my companion as his agent to effect quality improvement in the Toledo plant, and to spend as much time there as was useful for the achievement of that objective. I started to describe to him methods of better controlling the flow soldering machine. I spoke of measuring and recording its temperature, of the need to assign clear responsibility for its scheduled maintenance, I spoke. . . .

Gently, he interrupted me. "Dr. Groocock," he said, "unfortunately, the main problem is with the solderability of the leads of the components we buy here in Spain, and as you know government regulations require a large local content in our production. If only we could buy our components in Germany . . . or England," he added, giving proper regard to my nationality.

I started to speak to predipping, but a mental picture of 16 more solemn-eyed girls, each with her solder pot, restrained me. I changed my tack. More quality statistics had shown that 2.7 percent of the components assembled into the printed boards were wrongly placed, causing a massive failure rate at the subsequent test, and another large team of girls doing rework. I spoke of the virtues of clear engineering information, of auditing of the performance of each individual operator, of the need for "recognition." Tentatively, I mentioned the possibility of initiating a zero defect program.

He let me finish. It was dark outside. I could no longer see the flat plain of the central plateau. He said, "Yes, but the only real solution is to have automatic insertion. . . ." He told me at length about a visit he had recently made to Antwerp, Belgium and the prototype automatic insertion machine he had seen there. We both knew there was no possibility of such a machine being installed in Toledo within five years.

I realized that I was playing what ever afterwards I called the Toledo syndrome game with one who I guessed was a consummate master. The game in its classical form is played between a visiting staff member and a local manager. In this pure form the time period is defined by the inevitable departure of the staff member. The latter's object is to get the local manager to commit to one or more realistic, achievable, improvement actions. The local manager's objective is to show that all such suggested actions are not possible. It was his fine consecutive use of, "If only . . ." and "Yes, but . . . ," that had hinted at the mettle of my opponent.

He confirmed his master status. As the car swayed along the uneven surface, we played the game. My concentration was absolute. I no longer noticed the shine of the headlights or the swish of the tires. He destroyed one suggestion after another. I mentally turned the pages of my model quality system manual, and attacked again and again. He never flinched or even made a foul stroke. He never said, "If only it rained as much in Spain as in England . . . ," because that is impossible and therefore against the rules. Over the last 20 kilometers he used all of the classic end games of: "Our customer would not allow it . . ."; "If only we could make people redundant like they do in America . . ."; "Yes, but the union would never agree . . . ," and "If only you could get the president (of the whole multinational corporation) to order our managing director to. . . ."

For one awful minute, I felt a warm glow of peace and fellowship stealing over me, and heard myself agreeing that a particular suggested action was impossible. That in itself was not bad. In fact, often it is good tactics for the staff member to agree quickly to the impossibility of some action and pass on to the next. No, my discomfort arose because I had joined my opponent. I was playing for the other side. I was starting myself to think creatively and imaginatively of reasons why nothing could be done. I was drifting into that cozy, comfortable, fairy-tale land where no improvement is ever possible and no new effort or action is ever required.

I was so shaken that I allowed him to use up nearly 10 minutes of play time by a deep, philosophical discussion of the interrelationship of product quality, the quality of work life of the entire population of the world, and the quality of the total environment of planet earth. (He actually used the term.) If I had been alert I could have declared this diatribe illegal on the grounds that in no conceivable way could it have anything at all to do with a real action, but, as I said, I was shaken and I let him continue.

Of course, I lost. We parted at my hotel. He seemed genuinely sorry when I refused his invitation to dinner, pleading fatigue and that I had an early start in the morning.

I never again met his equal. No Briton or American, growing up in a society that values change and believes in the possibility of improvement, can hope to match a master from such an older culture. A Briton or American, particularly one with the intellectual capability to play the game at the highest level, will feel embarrassed to reveal too blatantly that he or she is afflicted with the syndrome. Many such persons, once the negative emotion, engendered by hearing someone else's good idea, has run down enough, will implement the suggestion. Many another will implement the suggestion when it finally reemerges from their subconscious as their own creation.

I have never played the Toledo syndrome game with a Tibetan monk or an Indian mystic. Perhaps after a lifetime spent in conservation of a 1000-year-old tradition they would be unable to play. Maybe my Spanish opponent played so well because, with the rising tides of technology and democracy in his country, he knew that change was inevitable, and he feared it.

I have described the classic game, but there are many variations. The only definitive symptom of the Toledo syndrome is the thinking deeply, imaginatively and creatively of reasons why suggested changes and improvements cannot be effected. Anyone whose job requires the implementation of change will have met many people suffering from the Toledo syndrome, because it is endemic in all changeable human organizations.

I have told this as though it were a true story. I was driven from Toledo to Madrid and I did play the Toledo syndrome game, but the details of the plant, the character of my opponent, and the game we played, are a composite of many similar events that occurred before and after my journey from Toledo.

CONCLUSION

This chapter was concerned with the work of staff in a large decentralized company. It first described briefly the total range of staff activities, and then discussed the role of staff made responsible for providing functional leadership to operating divisions. The specific activities of quality staff were then defined in detail. The chapter concluded with an account of the pathology of the Toledo syndrome.

CHAPTER 14

SYSTEM QUALITY AUDITS

Product quality audits and their importance have already been discussed in Chapter 4. They are used to measure, not control, the quality of product going to customers. Their purpose is to indicate the direction and progress of long-term improvement actions, so that future product going to customers will be better in quality than current product. System quality audits are used to determine the status of the quality system, consisting of the processes and procedures which determine the product quality. System quality audits are performed for a number of different reasons, which will be discussed here.

SYSTEM AUDITS FOLLOWING MIL-Q-9858A

In December 1963, the U.S. Department of Defense published MIL-Q-9858A, "Quality Program Requirements," replacing an earlier version issued in 1959. It is a relatively short document of about 5000 words, but for over 20 years it has had a profound effect on virtually all suppliers to the Department of Defense and the Army, Navy, Air Force, and the Defense Supply Agency. It has also influenced military purchases by other governments (e.g., members of NATO) and other agencies, and has significantly affected the development of quality practices throughout indus-

TABLE 14.1. Section Headings of MIL-Q-9858A, "Quality Program Requirements"

1. Scope
2. Superseding, supplementation, and ordering
3. Quality management
4. Facilities and standards
5. Control of purchases
6. Manufacturing control
7. Coordinated government/contractor activities
8. Notes

try generally. Table 14.1 gives its sector headings. Under scope, which includes "Contractual Intent" and "Summary," the specification states,

> This specification requires the establishment of a quality program by the contractor to assure compliance with the requirements of the contract. The program and procedures used to implement this specification shall be developed by the contractor. The quality program, including procedures, processes and product shall be documented and shall be subjected to review by the government representative . . . The program shall assure adequate quality throughout all areas of contract performance; for example design, development, fabrication, processing, assembly, inspection, test, maintenance, packaging, shipping, storage and site installation.

The essential philosophy of the specification is illustrated by another quotation from section 3, Quality Program Management:

> 3.3 Work instructions. The quality program shall assure that all work affecting quality (including such things as purchasing, handling, machining, assembling, fabricating, processing, inspection, testing, modification, installation, and any other treatment of product, facilities, standards or equipment from the ordering of materials to dispatch of shipments) shall be prescribed in clear and complete documented instructions of a type appropriate to the circumstances. Such instructions shall provide the criteria for performing the work functions and they shall be compatible with acceptance criteria for workmanship. The instructions are intended also to serve for supervising, inspecting and managing work. The preparation and maintenance of and compliance with work instructions shall be monitored as a function of the quality program.

> 3.4 Records. The contractor shall maintain and use any records or data essential to the economical and effective operation of his quality program. These records shall be available for review by the government representa-

tive and copies of individual records shall be furnished him upon request. Records are considered one of the principal forms of objective evidence of quality.

MIL-Q-9858A requires a contractor to define and document the way all processes must be performed from design through site installation, the way all tests and inspections of product must be performed, and then record the results of all of these operations. The contractor is required to control his or her suppliers and subcontractors in the same way. The thrust of the specification is one of rigid control and quality assurance: define, document, perform in conformance to the document, independently check conformance, record the results. The implication is that if this system is followed the product will be correct. There is no emphasis on quality improvement, or on a philosophy of never ending improvement. Improvement is addressed only in a short section on corrective action, "Design, purchasing, manufacturing . . . operations, which . . . have resulted in defective supplies . . . must be identified and changed as a result of the quality program. . . ." Quality costs are mentioned but not as a tool for quality improvement. A brief subsection on "Statistical Control and Analysis" deals mainly with acceptance sampling, and makes no mention of statistical process capability or control, which are key techniques for quality improvement.

System quality audit is a major and essential part of a quality program based on MIL-Q-9858A. The contractor must establish an independent product assurance activity whose major task is to audit the system—to ensure that every process affecting product quality is fully defined and documented, and then to check by witnessing and inspection that those performing or conducting the processes do so in exact conformance to the documentation. Then the government, through one of its quality assurance agencies, DCAS, AFPRO, and so on, may have 100 or more people resident at the contractor's site performing another level of auditing. Occasionally, the local residents will be supplemented for two or three weeks by another team of auditors making a further independent check.

The purpose of system quality audits under MIL-Q-9858A is to confirm that everything relevant to product quality is defined and documented, and that the actuality conforms to the documentation. For a competent contractor, the level of conformance may be very high. Exhaustive audits will reveal, even in a very large operation involving thousands of people, only a finite number of specific nonconformances, each of which can be the subject of a documented corrective action. A major problem may be that the system is closely defined in some areas (e.g.

manufacturing) but is much less defined in other areas such as design-development (and perhaps not at all in marketing, which is not mentioned in MIL-Q-9858A).

MIL-Q-9858A is effective to a very considerable extent. It is worth noting that it has remained unchanged for over 20 years, despite continuous, extensive application. Its major weakness is that it lacks emphasis on quality improvement. Its great virtue is that it helps to ensure that processes are defined and controlled, though there is no emphasis on statistical process control. The considerable cost of its implementation is magnified by its implicit assumption that no one can be trusted. Industry in areas unaffected by MIL-Q-9858A has the opposite problem: a plethora of ill-defined and uncontrolled processes.

PRINCIPLES OF SYSTEM QUALITY AUDITING

In the previous section a particular kind of system quality auditing—that conducted by a strong customer, the U.S. government, on its military equipment suppliers—has been described. Such a customer can impose requirements for a defined quality program (e.g., MIL-Q-9858A) on a supplier as a condition for doing business. Its own auditors can then check whether or not the supplier is performing in exact conformance to the clearly defined requirements. Assuming, as is usual, some nonconformances are discovered, the auditors will formally report them to a manager who has been designated by the supplier as responsible for corrective action. The auditors have no responsibility for ensuring that the corrective action is taken; that is the job of the supplier. The latter defines the corrective actions and the time schedule. After the appointed time, the customer's auditors repeat the audit. If the corrective actions are not complete, the customer punishes the supplier through its contract/purchasing department by stopping progress payments, canceling orders, removing the supplier from the approved suppliers' list, and so on.

The reality, however, is not as simple as the preceding description would indicate. The supplier will always have some level of concern, greater or lesser, that the customer will exercise power to cause trouble and will therefore be encouraged to respond to the auditors' requirements, but the auditors are not usually in a position of overwhelming strength. They have several different problems. The first is that most suppliers will be reasonably good, from a quality viewpoint, but not excellent. Corrective actions performed by a supplier will improve the situation but by no means make it perfect. Auditors will feel unjustified in asking for major sanctions against such a supplier, and other parts of their organization (e.g., purchasing) are unlikely to support sanctions in such circumstances. Another problem for the auditors is that the customer-defined quality program requirements are often so wide and comprehensive, that genuine differences in judgment are virtually inevitable. It becomes impossible to characterize disagreements between the supplier and the auditors in black or white, conformance or nonconformance terms. A related problem is that, in practice, the quality program is usually very well defined in some areas (e.g., gauge control, the use of bonded and quarantine stores, final test and inspection) but largely undefined in other areas (e.g., design rules, process capability, development testing). The auditors may recognize intuitively that, as has been emphasized in this book, outgoing product quality is largely determined by how well the product is defined, designed, purchased, and manufactured. They may recognize that over emphasis on control of certain aspects of the total process while largely ignoring others, or concentration on secondary quality assurance procedures which only modify the outcome of the primary activities, reduces the system's legitimacy and weakens their ability to insist on complete conformance. However, to define and document all of the essential marketing, design-development, purchasing, and manufacturing processes of the total system, to establish an effective method of auditing for conformance, and then to define corrective actions for all nonconformances, is obviously extraordinarily difficult. It may well be impossible to define such requirements in any general way, separate from specific applications and, in practice, audit systems do not attempt such a comprehensive approach.

Finally, most auditors are normal people who want a quiet life. They do not want crises with the supplier, their own purchasing or contract people, or their own top management, most of which groups are higher in the pecking order than they are. They know that they are not going to get perfection—exact conformance to some ideal system. Their hope is less ambitious: that their efforts result in useful improvement.

SYSTEM AUDITS FOR QUALITY IMPROVEMENT

The system quality audits discussed so far have had the ostensible purpose of determining whether or not an actual "quality program" (in MIL-Q-9858A terms) is in exact conformance to the defined and documented program, so that it may be approved or disapproved, or corrective actions to bring it into conformance may be initiated. However, it was concluded that the real purpose shaded toward general improvement rather than exact conformance. Other types of system quality audits are conducted explicitly as a tool for quality improvement. One such type is conducted in the operating divisions of a large company by members of the quality staff at the vice president or director level. Such an audit is not conducted against defined quality program requirements. The auditor may have some standard practices in mind but these will not have been communicated formally to the division under audit. Nor will conformance of the division to its own standard practices be an essential part of the audit.

The auditor, drawing on long experience and high-level analytical skills, will determine some key areas in which improvement should have a major effect on the success and profitability of the division. The auditor will define some actions and frame them as specific recommendations, discuss these actions with relevant, functional managers and, in an exit interview, with the division or plant manager as applicable. The auditor will address a report, listing the recommendations, to the division manager, and will copy the report to group and executive vice presidents (after giving the division manager an opportunity to ask for changes). Figure 14.1 gives an example of such a report. In practice, some of the recommendations will be adopted and others will not. There is no follow-up system; to require the division to report in writing would change the relationship between the auditor and the division in an adverse way, as would a follow-up audit. Very infrequently, a serious problem will persist, the recommendations will not be followed, and the auditor will hear of this. Then, in a personal way, the auditor can choose to approach the division manager again or to ask the group vice president or executive vice president to intercede.

The purpose of the audit is to help and pressure the division into improving. The effectiveness of the system depends on the auditor actually doing a high-level job in identifying important problems and opportunities and making practical, useful recommendations. It depends on the prestige of his or her position giving access to key managers, and the experience to deal with them effectively. The implied threat of ready access to group and executive vice presidents adds some immeasurable weight to the audit's effectiveness.

A major problem with this type of audit is that there can be only a limited number of high-level staff people and only a small proportion of their time is available for audits; therefore, only a small proportion of units can be audited within a limited time period.

TRW Interoffice Correspondence

To:
Division Manager
XYZ Division
From:
J. M. Groocock
Subject:
Trip Report—Visit to TRW XYZ Division
July 1–2, 1981

Date:
July 9, 1981

1. *General Subjects*

I endorse your emphasis on customer service and quality as indicated in your memo of June 29th. The PIMS analysis indicates the extreme importance of these two factors to a business' growth and profitability. One of the two major quality programs I am currently pushing has a similar thrust. You may find the "Competitors' Quality Evaluation" I left with you of some help. I also suggest you involve your quality managers in the product quality half of your program.

Action Recommended

1. Involve quality managers in your "Customer Service and Quality" program.

2. *Plant A*

2.1 *Quality of purchased supplies*

An incoming inspection activity has recently been started at Plant A on forgings and now involves four inspectors. A visit has been made to one of the three suppliers of forgings.

The whole emphasis of the supplier-quality activity should be to help and encourage the suppliers to deliver more good product. It should not put emphasis on screening out bad product at incoming because: the plant has survived without such screening in the past and as the product delivered improves problems in manufacturing will be less than in the past; to make an incoming inspection screen effective would take many more than four inspectors and would be very expensive; rejecting bad product at incoming still causes manufacturing a problem because of supply shortages and inventory problems (you need good product).

Actions recommended

2. Do not proceed with the plan to appoint a fifth incoming inspector.
3. Ensure that all lots are processed through incoming inspection within 24 hours of receipt. Increase sample sizes when number of lots received is small and decrease when number is large, so that inspectors are kept working at optimum rate and there is no build-up of backlog (selection of sample sizes is arbitrary anyway).
4. Assign effort to analyze the results of the inspections, adding up the results over hundreds of samples. The analysis should indicate what *actions* by particular suppliers on particular parts, dimensions, and so on, will have the most effect in improving quality into manufacturing.
5. Assign effort to visit suppliers, armed with the results of defect analysis, to help the suppliers achieve better quality. This is the most difficult part of the process.

Figure 14.1. Trip report following a system quality audit.

The emphasis should be on persistent cooperation with the suppliers: there should not be an adversary relationship. Do not start rejecting lots (the plant survived without doing this in the past—and you will accept far more defective parts in the "good" lots than you could reject).

6. Use the analysis of incoming inspection results to monitor the suppliers' progress in improvement.

2.2 *In-process quality control*

Although there is little formal quality control in-process at Plant A this, in fact, is the vital stage where the quality is built-in and the quality to the customer is determined. As noted above, supplier quality control is just starting and final inspection is likely to be rather ineffective despite the high scrap cost (see below). So, that puts the emphasis on in-process quality control.

There are two general approaches: bring some of the inspection earlier so that defective product is screened out before all value is added; progressively reduce the proportion of defective product made. The second of these potentially has much more benefit. Both require accumulation of defect data, and its analysis and then action.

Actions recommended

7. Select a number of processes, which are thought to contribute significantly to final inspection failures.
8. Perform process capability studies and institute statistical process control (you will need consultant help).
9. Take action, by operator training, design-tolerance adjustment, process improvement, tool improvement, gauge control, and so on, to significantly reduce the defect level. Again, this is the difficult part. An interfunctional quality improvement team assigning actions, establishing schedules, and monitoring progress is needed.
10. When *success actions* have been implemented extend the system to more processes and machines.
11. Determine how much effort is required (particularly for improvement actions) to cover the whole plant.

2.3 *Final inspection*

The final inspection section consists of 25 people but only 12 do inspection. Lot sizes range from 5–1000 (typically, 300). Inspection is by sampling, typically a sample of 80, reject on 1 defect. Failed lots are 100 percent inspected for only the failed characteristic. Information was not available on the proportion of lots failed, but it was guessed to be about 10 percent. In one experiment, 1108 units of different types were inspected and 179 (16 percent) were defective (not fully to print). The cost of scrapping items failing the inspection was 6 percent of manufacturing added cost (MAC); the cost of reworking failed items was not known. The quality of the units going to the customer (percentage defective) was not measured or known. The cost of customer rejections was 1.02 percent of MAC (May year-to-date).

The above information, supplied by the final test section, seems inconsistent with regard to the percent defective. The incoming quality would have to be no worse

Figure 14.1. *(Continued)*

than 0.13 percent defective for only 10 percent of lots to be rejected by an 80-0 sampling plan (MIL-STD-105D, Table X-J-1). 0.13 percent is a factor of 100 different from the 16 percent measured in the special exercise. My feeling is that the 16 percent is nearer the actuality than the 0.13 percent.

Sampling inspection of this kind is often ineffective, with the average quality (percent defective) in lots after the inspection being little different from the percent defective coming to the inspection. (The Appendix,* which is intended for your quality people, gives the reasons for this.)

Actions recommended
12. Tabulate the number of lots inspected and the number rejected. Tabulate the number of units inspected in the samples and the number found defective. Tabulate the defect types causing your product to be defective.
13. After say a month, for the total final test activity, calculate:
    Percent of lots rejected;
    Percent of units found defective in the samples.

    The second percentage measures the quality made by manufacturing. A principal objective of the quality program is to improve that percentage. It should receive much publicity: everyone should know what the number is each month.
14. Do a "Pareto" plot of the different kinds of defects and their *causes*. Have a multi-functional team attack the causes.
15. Assign part of the final inspection activity to reinspect product to measure the quality going to the customer. Take small samples from different lots totaling say 1000 units per month. This will take only a small fraction of the effort of the section and can be made available by reducing the sample sizes of the usual inspection.
16. Calculate the percentage of units found defective in the samples. This is a measure of the quality going to the customer, which is vital information for any serious quality program. Comparison with the number given by Action 15 will show the effectiveness of the final inspection activity. I will be surprised if the outgoing defective level is better than half of the incoming level. This will emphasize the importance of Action 16 to improve the incoming quality; it should *not* be seen as a reason to increase the final inspection cost.
17. Do a Pareto plot of the different kinds of defects. Relate these to the defect types which cause most customer rejections (from an analysis of customer rejections). Take action to improve.
3. *Plant B**
4. *Quality Cost Improvement*
    There are opportunities for massive quality cost improvements at both Plants A and B. Both plants should start formal quality cost reporting as soon as possible, using the draft SPI that I left with you. The latter should be frozen on July 27th and is unlikely to change significantly from the draft. It should become a company requirement form September 1981 (report due October 15th). Although the Forecast is not required until the beginning of 1982, this is really the heart of the program and you should start to develop specific projects, which are targeted to save particular amounts of money, as soon as possible. A normal overall target is that such projects should add up

* Not reproduced.

Figure 14.1. *(Continued)*

to 10 percent of the quality costs (e.g., if your quality costs in 1981 are $5 million you should plan specific projects to save $500,000 in 1982). In fact for XYZ Division, 10 percent would be a very unambitious target and you should not wait until 1982 to start.

Actions recommended
18. Start quality cost reporting according to the draft SPI as soon as possible.
19. Develop a major program of quality cost improvement projects for inter-functional improvement teams at both Plants A and B.

Opinion
With a good market and profit position XYZ Division is well situated to take its major opportunities for quality cost reduction and for measurement and improvement of its quality to the customer. However, my impression is that the total activities at both the A and B plants have settled down to a complex "equilibrium" which is comfortable to many people. You and your new managers are disturbing this equilibrium with the purpose of achieving rapid improvement—but it will take a lot of persistence and resolution to do this.

cc:
Group Vice President
Sector Executive Vice President
Sector Staff
XYZ Division Functional and Plant Managers

Figure 14.1.   *(Continued)*

Another problem is that the audits have many difficulties for the staff auditor. They involve tiring travel. The fifty-third audit performed ought to be a crushing bore. The pressure to perform at the expected high level and the ever present possibility of antagonizing a line manager or getting into other serious trouble make them nerve-wracking. The requirement to write a report is a chore and its high-level distribution is another source of possible trouble. So, time constraints and psychological pressures drastically limit the number of such staff audits. (Only a "high-level worker" can perform them. A staff manager who is a supervisor not a worker will not be able to perform such audits alone. They could lead an audit team, but not conduct a solitary audit.)

As a company develops model quality policies and standard practices, it becomes possible to audit against each division's actual policies and standard practices, and to judge whether or not the spirit of the models is realized in them. A similar situation exists for a division having its own comprehensive quality policies and standard practices independent of company models. Such an audit can be performed by a staff person who is less prestigious and experienced than the judgmental audit just discussed. The exit interview can be with the quality manager, not the division manager, and the audit report, even if addressed to the division manager, will usually be actioned by the quality manager. Copies go to the auditor's boss, the high-level staff member, not the group and executive vice presidents. (Although the boss may send a summary of all audits to these vice presidents each quarter "for information.")

It can be argued that it is not legitimate to audit conformance to a new company-inspired quality system until the relevant division managers have been trained in its application and been given a reasonable time to implement it. When conducted prematurely, a first audit is likely to be a training exercise. (But, why not? The answer is that auditing for this purpose is a less efficient training method than an explicit training program, e.g., a quality college.) When they have been trained, the division people know what they should be doing, they know how to do it, and they know whether or not they are in fact doing it (because it is a codified system and they have been to a quality college, or received a "training" audit, or because it is their own system that is being audited). Such an audit, conducted by a low level staff man, is more like a customer's audit (though without the customer's clout) than the consultant-type audit of the high-level staff member.

Usually, the audit will show nonconformances to the quality system. The auditor will discuss these with the quality manager and try to get him or her to agree to initiate improvement actions. If, as is likely, the quality manager is unable or unwilling to respond to all important points, or a follow-up audit reveals that some actions have not been taken, what can the auditor do? Well, the auditor may seek to involve the high-level staff member. Various actions are open to the latter. They can write to the division manager. They will feel insecure in doing this (Was the audit really right?) and in any case this action has a high probability of just making the division manager defensive. They can telephone—that could be a beautiful conversation. They can speak to the group vice president. (What is the answer, when the latter asks if the audit has been reviewed with the division manager?) They can do a follow-up audit. Again, they are going to have a great time. They are no longer in a consultant role. They are now analogous to a captain of police following up on the sergeant.

After a while, the low-level staff audits become a routine attracting little attention, and the high-level staff member stops trying to progress the unsatisfactory ones. Then someone says, "The division people are capable of doing the audits themselves. They make most of the improvement actions without any help from us. Why don't we make it a self-audit?"

QUALITY SYSTEM SELF-AUDITS

The purpose of a system quality audit can be any one of the following:

1. To determine whether or not a supplier meets a required standard, so that he or she can be approved or disapproved by a customer
2. To identify nonconformances by a supplier against a customer-required quality program specification, so that the supplier can correct these and avoid penalties imposable by the customer
3. To provide a tool for quality improvement

It has already been argued that purpose (2), in reality, may often have a strong content of positive quality improvement, thereby going beyond simple elimination of defined nonconformances. Except when the customer is directly involved, purpose (3) is the only reason for performing a system quality audit. As a tool for quality improvement, there is much to recommend a self-audit. As always with quality improvement, the most difficult part of the total process is to perform effectively the improvement actions. Establishing the audit system and performing the audit are not as difficult as the improvement actions. The latter have to be carried out by the people of the unit being audited. If the audit has been conducted by the same people, they will believe the results and have "ownership," and these two factors are strong motivators for action. They are likely to more than compensate in overall effectiveness for any lack of objectivity or expertise in performing the audit. The unit under audit is most likely to improve if its general manager wants quality improvement enough to give it high priority. External pressure for improvement is less effective than a general manager's own commitment.

In TRW we developed a system quality audit procedure mainly for self-audits by the company's operating divisions, though it can also be used for independent audits. When it was first issued, the covering note suggested that there would have been little value in developing a quality audit procedure that merely copied material from existing customer-imposed audits. Instead, the TRW audit addressed the company's own quality philosophy as expressed at the TRW Quality College. However, the cover note also restated the principle that each TRW division would have its own quality philosophy which would rightly differ to a greater or lesser extent from the company's philosophy. The company audit might therefore have only partial relevance to any particular division and it was suggested that, after applying the company audit, each division quality manager should think about additions needed to make an audit comprehensive for his division's own quality improvement purposes.

The overall quality and quality improvement status of an operating division are defined by the two measures of quality, quality to the customer, and quality costs. Criteria for judging that status can be established, for example, the following:

> For quality—all sales to be from products best in quality compared with competing products; and for the quality cost to manufacturing added cost ratio to be half what it was at the start of the program.

> For quality improvement—products representing 10 percent of sales to move up two grades of quality to the customer in one year; and quality cost improvement projects to save 10 percent of the quality costs in one year.

It can be argued that to audit the quality system that causes the improvement in quality, as well as to measure the quality directly, is redundant. If the measurements indicate a superior status, any apparent inadequacy in the system achieving the result may not be significant. However, in practice, I have never seen measurements showing such clear-cut superiority. Always there has been scope for improvement in quality to the customer and quality costs. Audit of the system is then a valuable source of information about how to get improvement. Nonetheless, the results of the system audit must always be considered in the light of the measures of overall quality.

Figure 14.2 gives the TRW System Quality Audit modified to follow the order of the quality programs described in this book. It starts with the quality to the customer and quality cost measurement programs (audited for their effectiveness as measurement systems, not for the actual values of the measurements, which were previously discussed). Then marketing and design-development quality programs are covered, followed by purchasing, manufacturing, and inspection-test programs. Finally, multifunctional and employee-involvement quality programs are covered.

For a customer-type system quality audit, in which the purpose is to determine that an actual program comforms exactly to a required quality program specification, or to identify every nonconformance so that it can be the subject of a specific corrective action, it is necessary to audit every aspect of the quality program specification—to do a 100 percent audit. For a system quality audit to assist in quality improvement, it is only necessary to audit a sample of the aspects of each program, enough to determine whether the program should be the focus of improvement action.

1. *Quality to the Customer*
    1.1 Manufacturing conformance quality is measured quantitatively every month by an outgoing audit. The audit result is related to customer rejections and complaints. _____
    1.2 The quality of product requirement specifications has been compared with the quality of specifications of competing products. The design quality of the products has been compared with that of competing products, by laboratory evaluations, market research, and so on. _____
    1.3 The post-delivery performance quality of the products has been compared with that of competing products, by life and environmental tests, market research, and so on. _____
    1.4 A multifunctional team has done a formal Competitors' Quality Evaluation within the past year. _____
    1.5 A multifunctional team has developed specific quality to the customer improvement projects with assigned people and dates. _____ _____
2. *Quality Costs*
    2.1 Quality costs are measured accurately (including rework) by the Controller according to SPI 01-15-15. _____
    2.2 A multifunctional team identifies quality cost improvement projects. Responsible people and target dates are clearly assigned. _____
    2.3 The quality manager, assisted by the controller, produces an annual quality cost forecast, taking account of changes, for example, volume and compensation, external to the quality system, and the effect of quality cost improvement projects. The forecast is approved by the division manager as compatible with his strategic goals. _____
    2.4 Actual savings from the improvement projects are measured at defined intervals (e.g., quarterly). _____
    2.5 The quality cost report is examined monthly by the division's quality improvement team and corrective actions are taken for adverse variations due to slippage of quality cost improvement projects, or due to deteriorations. _____ _____
3. *Design Review*
    3.1 The division has issued a policy on design review, which includes definition of responsibilities, and requires participation of marketing, design-development, manufacturing, purchasing, and quality. _____
    3.2 In the past year all new products, for which good judgment indicated that design review was appropriate, were so reviewed. _____
    3.3 Useful information was supplied to participants before the meetings, chairpersons were properly assigned and agenda and minutes were issued. _____

Figure 14.2. System quality audit statements.

3.4 Relevant analyses such as safety, reliability, mechanical stress, thermal, failure mode and effect, and dimensional tolerance, were carried out and the results were examined at design review meetings.   _____

3.5 Design-development took appropriate action as a result of design review recommendations, or absence of such action was reported to the division manager.   _____   _____

4. *Product Qualification*

4.1 The division has issued a policy on product qualification, which includes a definition of the responsibilities of the design-development and quality departments.   _____

4.2 In the past year all new products or products with a significant level of change were subjected to formal product qualification, based on qualification tests.   _____

4.3 Qualification tests were conducted according to properly-issued qualification test specifications, and the results were reported by quality in timely qualification test reports.   _____

4.4 No new product was delivered to a customer, before the qualification tests (planned to be completed and passed before such delivery) were actually completed and passed.   _____

4.5 For products which failed qualification tests, design-development improved the design, and relevant parts of the qualification test were repeated and passed before the products were delivered to customers.   _____   _____

5. *Product Liability*

5.1 One of the division's department heads has been appointed as product liability coordinator, and chairs a product liability committee including marketing, design-development, legal, quality, and insurance.   _____

5.2 All of the division's products have been subjected to appropriate product safety analyses (e.g., failure mode and effect analysis, fault tree analysis, etc.). Labels, warnings, and instructions have been similarly analyzed.   _____

5.3 Design, manufacturing, and documentation improvements, as indicated by such analyses, have been implemented, or are planned.   _____

5.4 The division's record keeping has been analyzed from a product liability viewpoint and improvements indicated have been implemented or are planned.   _____

5.5 The product liability committee has prepared written contingency plans for dealing with a major product liability problem (e.g., a major recall or a major law suit).   _____   _____

6. *Process Capability*

6.1 The division has issued a policy for measuring the capability of its existing manufacturing processes and for achieving full

Figure 14.2.   *(Continued)*

capability for all existing and new processes in a defined
time.   _____

6.2 Process capability has been measured for all of the division's
existing manufacturing processes.   _____

6.3 The results of process capability studies have been used by
design-development and manufacturing to make corrections
to the design or process so that all processes are capable.   _____

6.4 In the past year the designs of all new products were evaluated by design-development, manufacturing, and quality
and necessary actions were taken to ensure that the designs
are compatible with the known/projected capability of ex-
isting/new manufacturing processes.   _____

6.5 In the past year all capital equipment authorizations, requests for quotation, and purchase orders for new or rebuilt
machinery, required statistical capability measurements (2
points). Formal acceptance tests were completed in all cases
to verify machine capability (2 points).   _____   _____

7. *Incoming Inspection*

7.1 Low cost sampling is used (20, 0; 40, 1), or a written quantitative analysis of failure data has shown that another plan is
better.   _____

7.2 Over the past year the average time per lot to determine acceptability (total hours of incoming inspection—including
supervision and support staff—divided by number of lots)
was: less than ½ hour (4 points); less than 1 hour (2 points);
less than 2 hours (1 point).   _____

7.3 The proportion of lots for which acceptability was determined in the day following receipt (including laboratory
tests) was more than 99 percent (4 points); more than 95
percent (3 points); more than 90 percent (2 points); more
than 85 percent (1 point).   _____

7.4 Each month an analysis of incoming quality is made and reported: percent lot rejections; proportion of failures in samples inspected; and analysis of results for individual
suppliers. All three were analyzed (4 points); two (2 points);
one (1 point).   _____

7.5 Systems, facilities, and equipment are excellent.   _____   _____

8. *Supplier Quality*

8.1 The division has issued a policy on supplier quality, which
includes definition of the responsibilities of the purchasing,
design-development, and quality departments.   _____

8.2 The division has a properly-constituted committee of purchasing, design-development, and quality people who determine which suppliers are on the approved suppliers list (2
points). The committee also coordinates the supplier quality
improvement program (4 points).   _____

Figure 14.2.   *(Continued)*

8.3 The division has one or more full-time supplier quality engineers, working to a well-structured program and fully supported by the supplier approval committee.   _____

8.4 The proportion of purchased items which were nonconformant to design specifications in the past twelve months is known quantitatively in terms of individual pieces (4 points), or delivered lots (2 points).   _____

8.5 The proportion nonconformant in a recent period (e.g., past three months) is measurably lower than in a base period (e.g., one year ago); 20 percent, (at a yearly rate) (4 points); more than 15 percent, (3 points); more than 10 percent (2 points); more than 5 percent (1 point).   _____ _____

9. *Process Control*

9.1 The division has issued a policy for controlling its manufacturing processes with statistical methods. There is also a written plan that implements statistical process control in a defined time for all applicable operations.   _____

9.2 The division has a training program in statistical methods (1 point), and a plan has been established to train operators, supervisors and engineers in a defined time (1 point). Training in statistical methods is complete (2 points).   _____

9.3 Statistical process control is used on all of the division's manufacturing processes.   _____

9.4 Product measurement, data recording and control charting is done by manufacturing operators (4 points), operators/inspectors (3 points), inspectors (1 point).   _____

9.5 The results of process control charting are regularly reviewed by manufacturing, design-development, and quality, and necessary corrections are made to eliminate special causes of variation and achieve ongoing conformance to design requirements.   _____ _____

10. *Inspection and Test Planning*

10.1 For all products an inspection and test plan has been prepared and every inspection and test point is marked on a flow chart of the manufacturing processes.   _____

10.2 After a period of production, the number of defects added by purchased components and manufacturing processes, and subtracted by inspection and test points have been marked on the flow chart. The inspection and test plans have been optimized, based on this data.   _____

10.3 There is a defined schedule for calibration of every piece of inspection and test equipment, that takes account of effort available, and no piece of equipment is beyond schedule. The proportion of equipment out of calibration when calibrated is measured, and is less than a specified percentage (e.g., 10 percent).   _____

Figure 14.2. *(Continued)*

10.4 Except where it is impossible, every product is subjected to a final 100 percent functional test, and the failure rate is less than a specified percentage (e.g., 1 percent). _____

10.5 For every product, a sampling outgoing quality audit is performed (for information, not for acceptance) and the content of nonfunctional defects is determined each month. _____ _____

11. *Quality Performance Indicators*

11.1 The quality department regularly publishes a report of quality performance indicators to other functional departments of the division. _____

11.2 Performance indicators are included for design quality, manufacturing quality, reliability, supplier quality, and support quality. _____

11.3 The performance indicators are segregated by product or process and are analyzed to identify opportunities for improvement projects (quality to the customer or quality costs). _____

11.4 The report of performance indicators is used to track responsibility for problem correction and verification, and project implementation. _____

11.5 Performance indicators are used by the quality improvement team to identify quality issues. _____ _____

12. *Employee Involvement Program*

12.1 The division has quality circles (or similar groups with a different name) in place (2 points). They are active in areas beyond manufacturing and quality (3 points), and involve more than half of the division's total manpower (4 points). _____

12.2 The division has a trained "facilitator" and each circle has a leader, who has been trained in meeting management and human relation skills. First level supervisors and workers' representatives have received training, and have been positively involved in the activities of the circles. _____

12.3 The circle members have been trained in simple quality control techniques: Pareto analysis, cause-and-effect analysis, control charts. _____

12.4 The division has an effective system for quick management response to problems raised by circles, which require resources outside the circle for resolution. _____

12.5 The division has a working system for giving nonmonetary recognition to persons or groups achieving significant successes. _____ _____

13. *Multifunctional Quality Improvement Team*

13.1 The division and each of its plants has a formally-constituted, multifunctional quality improvement team. It is chaired by a senior manager (e.g., the plant manager) and

Figure 14.2. *(Continued)*

has membership from design-development, manufacturing supervision, material/purchasing, and quality. _____

13.2 The team meets at least once per month. It evaluates quality performance indicators. It assigns specific projects to working parties, defines dates for completion, minutes this, and follows up. _____

13.3 The team's activities are in accord with a long-term quality business plan, which projects that the division will be superior to its competitors in both quality to the customer and quality costs in a defined number of years. The team's activities and achievements are sufficient in magnitude to give a good prospect of realizing that object. _____

13.4 As a result of the work of the quality improvement team significant improvements have been made in nonquality activities (e.g., inventory reduction and just-in-time methods) productivity improvements, worker and first-level supervisor involvement, and participation. _____

13.5 The division manager is personally involved in the work of the division and plant quality improvement teams (e.g., they attend some meetings, they read and comment on minutes and they give recognition for achievements). _____ _____

14. *Quality Business Plan*

14.1 The division produced a formal quality business plan which was approved by the division manager, as an input into its strategic plan. _____

14.2 The plan was produced by a multifunctional team including quality, marketing, design-development, manufacturing, and material/purchasing. _____

14.3 The plan included the results of a competitors' quality evaluation, and defined actions for the first plan year to increase significantly the proportion of the division's sales in the "best" category, and to get all of its sales into that category during the plan period. _____

14.4 The plan included the results of a year by year projection of quality costs—taking account of planned volume, compensation, and other changes, and quality cost improvement projects—which will get the division to a best quality cost to manufacturing added cost (or to sales) ratio, compared with competitors, during the plan period. _____

14.5 The plan included the quality improvement plans of the marketing, design-development, manufacturing, material/purchasing, and quality departments, and a personal overview by the division manager.

Figure 14.2. *(Continued)*

We found that a sample of five statements was sufficient to measure the status of each program. Standardization in this way helped to simplify the next step: the rating itself. For each statement, the rating was in the range zero to four credits.* For some statements specific rating criteria were given; for the rest the following criteria were used:

The division is completely conformant to the statement   4
The division has some minor nonconformances to the statement   3
The division has serious nonconformances to the statement,
    but the program is good enough to have some value   2
The division has a small activity on the program   1
The division has no, or negligible, activity on the program   0

With five statements per program and four credits maximum for each statement, up to 20 credits can be received.

When the audit is complete the number of credits received for each program can be marked in a quality improvement profile, as shown in Figure 14.3. This gives a pictorial impression of the division's quality system status and a first indication of the programs needing improvement. Of course, the division manager and the functional department heads will determine the priorities of specific improvement actions. Some programs may be of little importance to a division and, even though they get a low audit rating, will receive a lower priority than more important programs even though the latter have a better rating. The quality improvement profile does not include a space for an overall total, and no arbitrary standards of "good" or "bad" ratings are given. The purpose of the audit is not to establish pass or fail criteria, but to indicate where improvement may be required and help to establish the priority for utilization of the division's limited quality improvement effort.

In use by TRW divisions, the system quality audit has been found to be very easy to use. The division or plant quality manager, or a working party of quality, marketing, design-development, purchasing, and manufacturing managers, can complete the audit in half a day or less. Because the statements are so specific there is little room for well-informed people to reach contrary conclusions. In some units, different people performed the audit independently and obtained remarkably consistent results. TRW's Electronic Components Group, under the leadership of its quality director, J. R. Isken, supplemented the self-audits by independent

---

* Ray Wachniak, Firestone, pointed out to me the benefit of using the positive word credit rather than some neutral or negative word.

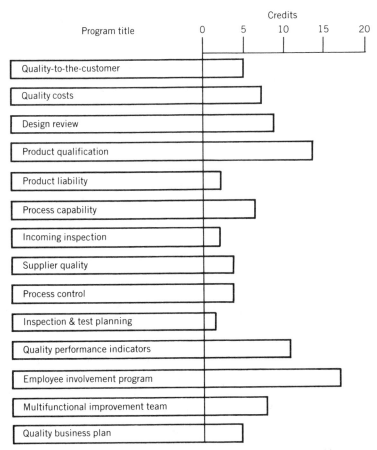

Figure 14.3. Hypothetical quality improvement profile.

audits conducted by division quality managers from other divisions. Such units, of course, took longer than half a day, but the results confirmed the validity of the self-audits.

FUNCTIONAL REVIEWS AND STRATEGIC PLANS

A multidivision company can extend the concept of functional self-audits into functional reviews. A functional self-audit is an audit of the people and systems of a particular function of a division, which is carried out by its own people. A functional review is a series of functional self-audits carried out simultaneously by all of the divisions of a company (or some other integrating unit of the company, e.g., a group) with the results reported outside of the individual divisions, and with integrated conclusions determined for the company. The self-audits may be supplemented by independent audits but this is not essential. A functional review has the purpose of identifying actions that, if taken, should markedly improve the effectiveness and efficiency of the function in the divisions reviewed.

In performing a functional review, data is gathered and analyzed, and possible improved actions are determined together with the resources needed to implement them. The actions are recommended to the company's president who should determine whether or not they will be implemented. The preceding defines the logical scope of a functional review but to be useful it has to go further. The evaluation of the recommended actions by the general managers of the divisions must lead to a set of agreed actions at the division level, which are carried out and verified for effectiveness. Similarly, the president and the company functional staff must establish a practical implementation plan, for interdivisional programs.

Many different line and staff managers at division, group, sector, and company levels, contribute to strategic plans. However, the actions necessary for the execution of these plans (except for acquisitions and divestitures) are mainly carried out by the operating divisions. Each division therefore needs an operational plan defining the complex series of actions—and the people who are responsible for performing them, and the schedule of their performance—which must be carried out, if the strategic plans relevant to the division are to be realized.

In practice, divisions are organized on a functional basis and most of their people are assigned to particular functions. For divisions which design and manufacture products for sale, most of its managers and other people will be within the following functional departments: marketing-sales, design-development, manufacturing, material, quality, controllers, and human relations. In practice, the operational plan of a division will be made up of separate subplans for each of these functions—though, of course, these subplans must all be consistent with each other and they must all be integrated together to give a coherent total plan.

In principle, when developing its part of the operational plan, each divisional functional department could first determine whether or not it had the capabilities to perform the series of actions required of it by the strategic plan. If it did not, additional actions could be added to get the needed capability. In practice, this system would usually not work, because the requirements of the strategic plan would not likely allow enough time to build up much capability. So, in practice, the strategic plans are not the primary documents from which all else is derived. The assumed functional capabilities of the divisions are a key input into the strategic plans. Most company strategic plans do not address functional capability in any detail and usually implicitly assume that key divisional functions are fully competent (other than for divestitures, it would be an unusual plan that was predicted on functional incompetence).

This argument might suggest that functional review is primary—that a series of functional reviews would determine the capability of the divisions and that the strategic plans would be designed to best exploit that capability. The reality is that neither strategic plan nor functional capability, as determined by functional review, is primary with regard to the other—they interact with each other. In performing a functional review, all of the involved divisions start a self-audit at a prearranged time, either under the leadership of their own functional manager, or by other methods suitable to the unit. The audit team assesses the current adequacy of their division's functional operating systems. They cover such things as the education and experience of their managers, engineers and supervisors, the quality to the customer and quality costs of their products and services, the status of their manufacturing processes relative to the state-of-the art, and the record of new product creation of their design-development teams.

The divisional functional managers then determine what actions are needed and what resources have to be applied to meet standards set by the best of their competitors and to meet the requirements of strategic plans. At the same time they extrapolate into the future, predicting the adequacy of their systems, and determining the actions and resources needed to maintain competitiveness. The division manager reviews and amends, as necessary, the report of the audit team.

The local ownership of this part of the program is a key reason for success. Added up over the whole company, the local improvements made as a result of functional reviews may be the larger part of the company total.

The division manager then sends the audit report to the group vice president, and makes copies available to group and company functional staffs. Group vice presidents, assisted by their own functional staffs, consolidate the reports of their divisions, draw overall conclusions, and prepare a report which they send to the company president, again making copies available to functional staff.

Line management has the responsibility for determining when functional reviews shall be carried out and their scope: which functions shall be reviewed in which divisions and in how much detail. Obviously, some degree of simultaneity is important (e.g., a company can only form a view about its overall level of competence in a particular function if most of its divisions review that function at a particular time). In making these decisions line management will take account of the emphasis of relevant strategic plans, preconceptions about the status and importance of particular functions, and the opinions of functional staffs. Because functional reviews are carried out by existing people, there is virtually no extra cost to the company. The real cost is the set-back to other improvement programs which will not receive the same attention while people are working on functional reviews.

Functional staffs can help to clarify the principles of functional review. They can also provide "model standard practices" to assist the divisions in the actual performance of functional reviews. These models will draw on experience and ideas from different parts of the company. They should not be mandatory documents; rather they should give divisions the freedom to take account of their own special situations and to implement their own ideas. However, they should make it unnecessary for every division to develop its own methodology, and should give enough standardization at the divisional level to facilitate the analysis at higher company levels. The models are likely to be improved in light of experience and may help to institutionalize functional reviews. Functional staffs are likely to have an important part in integrating the divisional reviews and assisting their line managers in drawing overall conclusions and establishing overall action plans.

Most company employees work in defined functions in operating divisions. Only a minority of people work in general management and in the company superstructure. Functional excellence is therefore of paramount importance to a company's success. However well the strategic direction of the company and its constituent units is set, the company's potential is limited by its functional capability. Functional review is also an important method of achieving the consensus of large numbers of managers which is a necessary precursor of successful action programs. However, it is not realistic to believe that the incremental improvements made to the divisions' functional activities by the effort that their own people make available from current operations will alone be sufficient to bring them all to a competitive state of excellence in a reasonable time. To have any reasonable hope of achieving that objective it is essential that periodically the magnitude of the task is determined in its totality, and then company-wide plans for action are established.

TRW carried out functional reviews of its technology functions—design-development, materiel/purchasing, manufacturing, quality, productivity and information systems—in 1984–1985. For quality, 80 divisions and their groups and sectors were assessed using quality to the customer and quality cost data for current status and future plans. In addition, all of the units performed the system quality self-audit (modified for the defense-business divisions). Major improvement actions resulted from these reviews, including marked strengthening of managerial and engineering capability, and increased emphasis on key programs, such as the use of statistical methods, and quality in engineering.

Functional review is another example of a functional-staff initiative that causes operational divisions to do what they otherwise would not. I published the *System Quality Audit Procedure* to TRW's quality managers early in 1984 and suggested that they might use it for internal improvement purposes. I also wrote that I, "would obviously be very interested to hear about such applications—in confidence if the respondent wishes. . . ." Half-a-dozen managers did use the audit and commented favorably on it. However, my impression is that the majority performed the audit only when we built up the momentum by means of the overall functional review—despite the fact that it could be performed in only a few hours.

CONCLUSION

In this chapter the purposes and methods of system quality audit have been discussed. Such audits had their genesis in the desire of strong customers to have a method of determining whether or not suppliers should be approved, and whether or not they conformed to defined quality program specifications. However, I argued that achievement of this latter objective had considerable difficulty because it was impracticable to define comprehensively all system and process requirements related to product quality, and to establish conformance or nonconformance in black and white terms. A major purpose of system quality audit, therefore, was quality improvement—starting with the current status as determined by the audit and establishing a priority list of actions achievable by limited resources—rather than conformance to an arbitrary requirement. This then led to a discussion of various types of improvement-directed audits—high and low level staff audits, self-audits and functional reviews.

I will end this chapter on quality auditing by highlighting the Japanese "executive audit." In Chapter 11, I pointed out that QC Circles is just one aspect of the Japanese company-wide quality philosophy, and quoted five other aspects listed by Professor Kusaba. The second of these was, "diagnosis and audit of QC, especially made by the top management of the company." In many Japanese companies this is a reality—their top executives do spend an important part of their time personally auditing their operating divisions. Jim Pratt, Director of Statistical Programs, ITT, who lived in Japan for some years and has visited the country several times recently, included the following statement in a paper he presented at a Michigan State University conference in August, 1985:

> Executive audit—Several Japanese executives who amazed me with their knowledge of detail in a factory of a multiplant division explained how they came by this level of knowledge. In one case it was called slicing down through the organization. As I recall, we were told this gentleman spent three days of every other week personally auditing operations in his factories. These were not operations reviews; these were meetings with small groups at every organizational level. The objective, it was explained, was to insure the endorsed methods and techniques were being used—that they were aimed at the common goal—to learn what projects were being worked on—and, most importantly, to offer help.

Such top management involvement is the best method of achieving the level of priority for quality improvement necessary for business success.

CHAPTER 15

WIDER APPLICATION OF QUALITY IMPROVEMENT

In this book I have concentrated on the quality improvement of products sold by suppliers to customers. My reasons for limiting the scope are that quality improvement is most advanced in application to products—and most of my experience is with products. However, the need for quality improvement in services is, on the whole, greater than that for products, though the incentive is usually less. This is because service businesses are exposed to less international competition than product businesses, so that a service business's success is determined by its quality status relative to local competition, not international competition. It seems useful in this last chapter to indicate that many of the concepts and techniques for product quality discussed in earlier chapters are also applicable to service quality—and to other areas of the business not found on the product chain of conformance.

QUALITY IMPROVEMENT IN SERVICE BUSINESSES

In general terms, products are objects and services are activities, though some service businesses are much involved with objects (e.g., the car in a car rental business and the food in a restaurant business). However, whether a service business provides an object or an activity the ideas underlying the definition of quality used in this book, and the chain of conformance (see Chapter 2) are equally applicable. For a service, the definition of quality becomes:

> The quality of a service is the degree of conformance of all the relevant features and characteristics of the service to all of the aspects of the customer's need, limited by the price and delivery he or she will accept.

The only conceptual differences from product quality concern the meanings of the words, "features," "characteristics," and "delivery." For many services, it is hard to differentiate delivery from the activity so that it may be more appropriate to include it with the features and characteristics of the service, thereby reducing the last phrase to, "limited by the price he or she is willing to pay."

The product chain of conformance showed an alternation between specific concrete or abstract objects—the customer's need, the product requirement specification, the product's design, the purchased parts, and the manufactured product—and the marketing, design-development, purchasing, and manufacturing processes by which each object was changed into the next. The definition of the intermediate objects in a clear manner was essential for quality improvement. For many products it would be virtually impossible to correct an observed nonconformance between the two ends of the chain—the product and the customer's need—without first determining whether the nonconformance was between the product and the design, or between the product requirement specification and the customer's need, or between other adjacent objects in the chain. Quality improvement is also dependent upon the definition, analysis and improvement of the processes within the chain.

The service chain of conformance (Figure 15.1) shows the same alternation of abstract objects and processes. To make the concepts clearer, let us consider an example: the service I receive from my bank. Table 15.1 lists all of the aspects of my banking need. For satisfaction of that need I might expect to pay a price (though, in fact, I don't; the bank makes its profit by giving me noncompetitive interest rates rather than by charging me for its service), and I could judge the value-for-money of the service. Table 15.2 lists the features and characteristics of the service I actually receive from my bank.

Since I know nothing about the internal workings of a bank, I can only depict the two ends of the chain of conformance. Comparison of Tables 15.1 and 15.2 shows that my bank does not satisfy some aspects of my

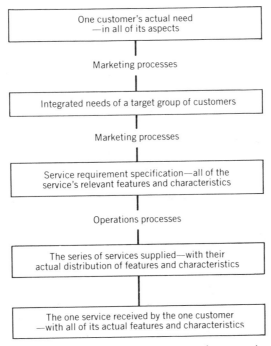

Figure 15.1.   Chain of conformance for a service.

need at all, and others only in ways that are troublesome to me. In one way, I have broken the rules of the game by including need aspects that no Ohio bank will currently satisfy. However, if an Ohio bank wanted to achieve quality improvement, one way it could do so would be to examine formally the needs of typical customers (except for the U.K. transfer, I guess my need is similar to that of many other customers) and compare it with the "service requirement specification" of the features and characteristics of the service they offer—and then see how they could reduce the degree of nonconformance between the two by cost effective actions. They could then examine the lower links of the chain of conformance in a similar way.

As commented, I have no knowledge of the internal workings of banks. I don't know if they even have a documented service requirement specification defining clearly the features and characteristics of the service they offer. However, whether defined or not, a chain of conformance must exist in practice. It is possible that quality improvement might best be achieved by explicitly defining the chain, and then, by establishing a priority list of improvement actions which address the objects and processes that constitute the chain.

TABLE 15.1. Aspects of the Writer's Banking Need

1. Keep cash balance safe
2. Receive credit up to the limit of my credit worthiness at a competitive interest rate
3. Receive competitive tax-free interest rate on the part of the cash balance, I assign as an IRA
4. Receive competitive interest rate on the rest of the cash balance
5. Enable employer to add salary to the cash/credit balance
6. Enable me to add cash and checks to cash/credit balance
7. Have regular bills paid out of cash/credit balance
8. Have irregular utility bills paid out of cash/credit balance
9. Have people paid to whom I write checks out of cash/credit balance
10. Have people paid to whom I give credit card slips out of cash/credit balance
11. Have money transferred to my U.K. bank out of cash/credit balance
12. Receive monthly statement of my credit/debit balance, IRA balance, transactions, interest paid and received, and interest rates

I believe that many of the other concepts and techniques of product quality improvement are likely to be applicable to services—management commitment and involvement, defect and failure definitions, inspection and test, quality auditing, process specification and control, defect measurement and Pareto analysis, multifunctional improvement teams, customer complaint analysis, quality circles, and so on—but I will leave it to managers of service businesses to search for and analyze the similarities between product and service quality.

EXTERNAL CUSTOMERS AND INTERNAL "CUSTOMERS"

Many of the parts of a business that are not directly within the product chain of conformance are like small service businesses. Examples are all of the work of the accounting department in paying wages and bills, receiving receivables, keeping books, and all of the logistical processes of the purchasing and sales departments. Just as many of the concepts and techniques of product quality improvement are applicable to actual service businesses, so they are likely to be applicable to such pseudo-service businesses. One helpful idea that is in vogue at the present time (though it was expressed by P. B. Crosby many years ago) is that every person or group providing such a service should explicitly decide who is the "customer" for that service. (Although this internal customer is in some ways

TABLE 15.2.   Features and Characteristics of the Service the Writer Receives from His Bank

1. Checking account:
     Keeps checking account cash balance safe
     Pays very low interest rate on balance
     Accepts direct deposits from employer
     Accepts cash or checks by personal visit to bank during banking hours, or through machine at other times
   Pays my checks presented to it
   Returns checks to me if account has no cash
   Gives monthly statement of balance and transactions by mail

2. Savings account:
     Keeps savings account cash balance safe
     Pays moderate interest rate
     Accepts transfers from checking account by personal visit during banking hours
     Accepts cash or checks by personal visit during banking hours, or through machine at other times
     Makes transfers to checking account by personal visit during banking hours, or through machine at other times, or by letter of instruction
     Gives monthly statement of balance and transactions by mail

3. Cash reserve account:
     Transfer money to checking account, if latter has insufficient cash to meet demands, up to agreed credit limit (thereby preventing return of checks)
     Charges high interest rate on balance
     Accepts checks to eliminate balance by personal visit during banking hours, or by mail
     Gives notification of every transaction, and monthly summary of transactions by mail

4. IRA account:
     Keeps IRA account balance safe
     Accepts check by personal visit and form filling during banking hours
     Processes withdrawals by personal visit during banking hours
     Pays competitive tax-free interest rate on balance
     Gives quarterly report, by mail, of transactions, interest and balance

5. Credit card accounts:
     Pays account of people to whom I give slips up to designated credit limit
     Accepts, by mail, checks against debit balance
     Charges high interest rate on balances not cleared by designated time
     Gives monthly statement of balance and transactions by mail

6. Special service:
     Transfers money to U.K. bank by personal visit during banking hours, form filling, and at special charge

analogous to a real customer, there are many important differences between the two, and the use of the same word for both can cause confusion. It is therefore clearer to use another word, e.g., receiver, for the internal receiver of a service.)

After having determined who the receiver of the service is, all of the aspects of their need can be determined (e.g., by asking) and then the features and characteristics of the service that will satisfy the need can be defined. The group providing the service can then establish its own measurements of the nonconformances between what is actually supplied and what was agreed should be supplied. Improvement actions can then be developed and applied. Because it costs less to give people what they really need, and to do so correctly the first time, programs addressing this issue should be very effective ways of improving business productivity.

Perhaps the most important difference between an external customer and an internal receiver concerns priority. Business success is largely determined by whether or not products sold to customers are best in quality compared to competing products (and I expect the same is true for services sold to customers though I know of no data to prove it). It is therefore vital that the priority accorded to product quality improvement is raised by management decision and action. It is not vital that the priority for applying quality improvement methods to all internal services be so raised. Each one will have a differing optimum priority level, taking account of the current total status of the unit and the resources available to it for improvement. If everything has priority, nothing has priority. Because a capability for quality improvement has wide applicability does not mean that priority for quality improvement should be widely spread. I confess to a neurotic suspicion that the Americans and British may always be looking for an excuse to divert their attention away from quality to the customer on to something more interesting, and that other nations, for example, the West Germans and the Japanese, may have such a tendency to a lesser extent. Improving the quality to every internal "customer" is a great idea provided that it does not delay improving the quality to the real customer.

CONCLUSION

I return now to a theme I introduced at the beginning: the theme of policy, honesty, priority, and capability. Business success is contingent on the superiority of the quality of the product or service sold—superiority compared to competing products or services. Such superiority can be achieved and maintained only by continuous, never ending quality improvement. To achieve quality improvement, the top management of the company must first establish improvement as a policy. The words of the policy are unimportant; it is the top management commitment and involvement that matter.

Parallel to the quality policy, the company must have a total business philosophy of honesty—not just a policy but a deeply ingrained climate of opinion throughout the company that accepts that there are legal and ethical constraints on all business activities. A company that is willing to lie to its customers cannot achieve superiority in quality if it has even a single honest competitor.

But policy and honesty are not enough. Left to reach its natural level, the priority accorded to quality improvement will never be high enough to achieve quality superiority (or even cost superiority). Sloppiness and boredom with detail are too much a part of human psychology. Superiority requires the unit's leader to elevate the priority accorded to quality improvement. A division manager who is a champion for quality improvement can raise its priority in that division. A chief executive who is a champion—assisted by the quality staff—can cause division managers, who would not of their own accord give quality improvement its necessary priority, to so do. The level of involvement, not just commitment, of some Japanese and American chief executives offers an example. Such priority can never be institutionalized. The moment the champion retires from the battle, the priority accorded to quality improvement starts to decay back toward its natural, inadequate level.

Even policy, honesty, and priority are not enough. There still has to be capability. I hope that this book has helped to increase the quality improvement capability of its readers. However, capability must be deeper than just quality concepts and techniques; it must embrace all of the activities of the functions whose processes make up the chain of conformance, marketing, design-development, purchasing, and manufacturing.

GLOSSARY

A dictionary lists all of the meanings of words. A glossary of technical terms is most useful if it defines terms within a particular field in a way that clarifies their logical relationships (this is practicable only if a limited number of terms is examined). The main unit of communication in a language is the sentence, and it is easiest to express terms and their logical relationships clearly if sentences are used for definitions. Dictionaries, for reasons of brevity, often use phrases, but brevity is not so important for a limited glossary. However, each definition should use no superfluous words, because extra words obscure the relationships between terms. Similarly, if parts of two terms express the same idea, they should use exactly the same words to define those parts. Definitions should not use synonyms in an attempt to express fine meanings; the same word should be used unless there is a clearly different idea to be expressed. Also, I feel that it is better to define activities like "inspect" and "test" as verbs than as nouns (as is usual in glossaries).

In this glossary, I give terms in only four fields: quality, quality costs, inspection, and defects.

QUALITY DEFINITIONS

The QUALITY OF A PRODUCT is the degree of conformance of all of the relevant features and characteristics of the product to all of the aspects of a customer's need, limited by the price and delivery he or she will accept.

The MARKETING QUALITY of a product is the degree of conformance of all of the features and characteristics defined in its product requirement specification to all of the aspects of a customer's need, limited by the price and delivery he or she will accept.

The DESIGN QUALITY of a product is the degree of conformance of all of the features and characteristics of a product made in conformance to the design to all of the features and characteristics defined in the product requirement specification.

The PURCHASING/MANUFACTURING QUALITY of a product is the degree of conformance of the product to the design of the product.

The DESIGN/PURCHASING/MANUFACTURING QUALITY of a product is the degree of conformance of all of the features and characteristics of the product to all of the features and characteristics defined in the product requirement specification.

QUALITY COST DEFINITIONS

The QUALITY COSTS of a division are the difference between the actual costs to the division of manufacturing and selling products and the costs to the division if there was no failure of the products during manufacturing or use, and no possibility of failure.

The APPRAISAL COSTS of a division are the costs of inspecting and testing purchased items and products during manufacturing because of the possibility of their failure.

The FAILURE COSTS of a division are the costs resulting from the actual failure of products during manufacture or use.

The PREVENTION COSTS of a division are the costs incurred in trying to reduce appraisal and failure costs.

INSPECTION DEFINITIONS

An ITEM is a concrete or abstract object. It is not an action or an activity. Typical examples are a material, component, subassembly, or product.

A PRODUCT is an item that is sold by a vendor to a customer.

A person INSPECTS an item by looking at it and comparing it with the specification of a required feature.

A person TESTS an item by applying a specified test equipment, and sometimes a specified stress, to the item, and comparing the response to the specification of a required characteristic.

A person MEASURES an item by applying a specified measuring equipment, and sometimes a stress, to the item and comparing the response to a measurement standard.

A customer USES a product and compares its features and characteristics to all of the aspects of his or her need.

FAILURE DEFINITIONS

An item FAILS, while being inspected, tested, or used, when it does not conform to a specified requirement or to an aspect of the customer's need.

A DEFECT is the part of an item that caused it to fail.

A DEFECTIVE is an item that contains one or more defects.

A person BLUNDERS when he or she makes a defect.

The difference between the actual and correct values of a measurement is the ERROR.

REFERENCES

1. P. B. Crosby, *Quality Is Free* (New York: McGraw-Hill, 1979).
2. "Looking for a Good Compact?," *Consumer Reports*, January 1984, 7–15.
3. Bradley T. Gale, *Quality as a Strategic Weapon* (Cambridge: The Strategic Planning Institute, 1985).
   Bradley T. Gale and Richard Klarans, "Formulating a Quality Improvement Strategy," *Journal of Business Strategy* (Winter 1985).
4. A. S. Grove, *High Output Management*, (New York: Random House, 1983), 28–33.
5. T. J. Peters and R. H. Waterman, Jr., *In Search of Excellence*, (New York: Harper and Row, 1982), 171–182.
6. C. E. Lauer, "Preferred Supplier Award," Private communication, Ford Motor Company, 1982.
7. F. James McDonald, *Community Financial Forum Series*, Ann Arbor, Michigan, September 21, 1982.
8. "Lessons of a Government Lawsuit," *New York Times*, 15 March, 1984.
9. K. G. Preston, "Liability for Falsified Quality Information," Private communication, TRW, May 2, 1984.
10. J. M. Juran, F. M. Gryna, Jr., and R. S. Bingham, Jr., *Quality Control Handbook, Third Edition* (New York: McGraw-Hill, 1974), 2–2.
11. *Glossary of Terms Used in Quality Control, Fourth Edition* (Berne: European Organization for Quality Control, 1976).
12. *Quality Systems Terminology*, ANSI/ASQC A3 (Milwaukee: American Society for Quality Control, 1978).
13. J. M. Groocock, "Conformance or Fitness for Use," *Quality, Journal of the EOQC* 2 (1980): 3–6.
14. J. M. Groocock, "Conformance or Fitness for Use? II," *Quality, Journal of the EOQC* 4 (1981): 3–6.
15. A. V. Feigenbaum, *Total Quality Control* (New York: McGraw-Hill, 1961), 85–106.

16. *Quality Costs: Ideas and Applications* (Milwaukee: American Society for Quality Control, 1984).
17. "Quality Progress," *Journal of the American Society for Quality Control* (April 1983): 16–58.
18. *Quality Costs—What and How, Second Edition* (Milwaukee: American Society for Quality Control, 1971).
19. J. M. Groocock, "Quality Costs and No-Failure Costs," *Quality, Journal of the EOQC* 1 (1977): 8–9.
20. J. M. Groocock, *The Cost of Quality* (London: Pitmans, 1974), 26.
21. D. M. Miller, "Profitability = Productivity + Price Recovery," *Harvard Business Review* (May-June, 1984): 145–153.
22. J. M. Groocock, "ITT Europe's 1975 Quality Cost Improvement Program," *Quality Assurance, Journal of the Institute of Quality Assurance* 2 (1976): 35–39.
23. A. R. Evans, "Customers Grade Quality," *Quality, Hitchcock Publishing,* (March 1984): 35–36.
24. W. A. Shewhart, *Economic Control of Quality of Manufactured Product* (New York: Van Nostrand, 1931).
25. E. Berne, *Games People Play* (New York: Grove Press, 1964).
26. R. Cogne, "Defects in an Electronic Switching System," Private communication, ITT Europe, 1980.
27. B. Lawson, "Component Functional Defective Rates," Private communication, ITT Europe, 1979.
28. J. M. Juran and F. M. Gryna, Jr., *Quality Planning and Analysis* (New York: McGraw-Hill, 1980), 26.
29. J. Campanella and F.J. Corcoran, "Principles of Quality Costs," *Quality Progress, Journal of the American Society for Quality Control* (April 1983): 16–22.
30. J. M. Groocock, "The Economics of Quality," *TRW Quality Communication,* (1983).
31. J. M. Groocock, "Silicon Planear Transistors and Diodes for Deep Water Submarine Cable Repeaters," *Microelectronics and Reliability* 8 (1969): 91–94.
32. J. M. Groocock, "The Recall of the Nova Fritex," *Quality Assurance, Journal of the Institute of Quality Assurance* 2 (1978): 9–11.
33. J. F. Halpin, *Zero Defects* (New York: McGraw-Hill, 1966).
34. I. Kusaba, "The QC Circle Activities in Japan," *Japanese Union of Scientists and Engineers* (1981).
35. R. A. Jones, *Total Quality Objective* (Cleveland: TRW's Automotive Worldwide Sector, 1985).
36. W. D. Hilt, *Management in Action* (Columbus: Battelle Press, 1985), 4.

INDEX